FAIRY TAIL
100 YEARS QUEST

1

HIRO MASHIMA   ATSUO UEDA

FAIRY TAIL 100 YEARS QUEST 1

CONTENTS!

CONTENTS

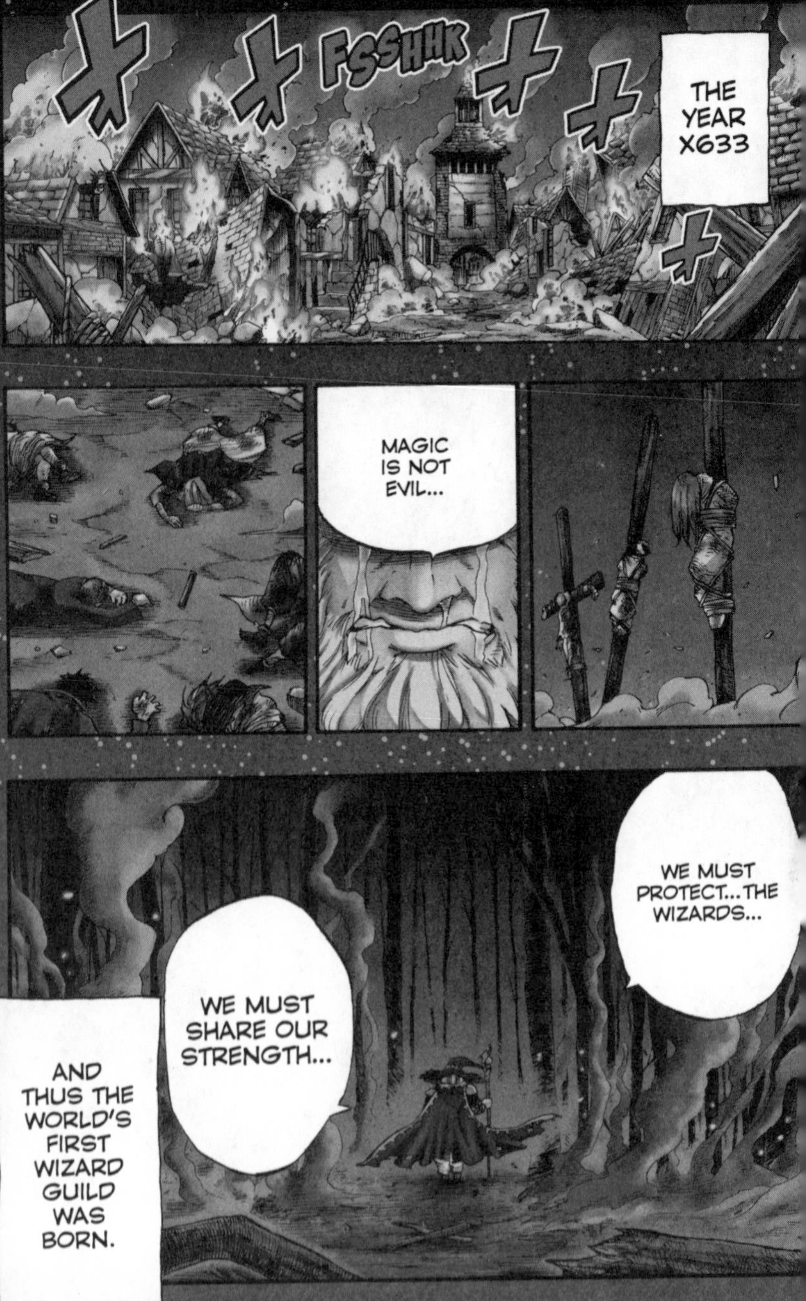
THE YEAR X633
FSSHHK
MAGIC IS NOT EVIL...
WE MUST PROTECT...THE WIZARDS...
WE MUST SHARE OUR STRENGTH...
AND THUS THE WORLD'S FIRST WIZARD GUILD WAS BORN.

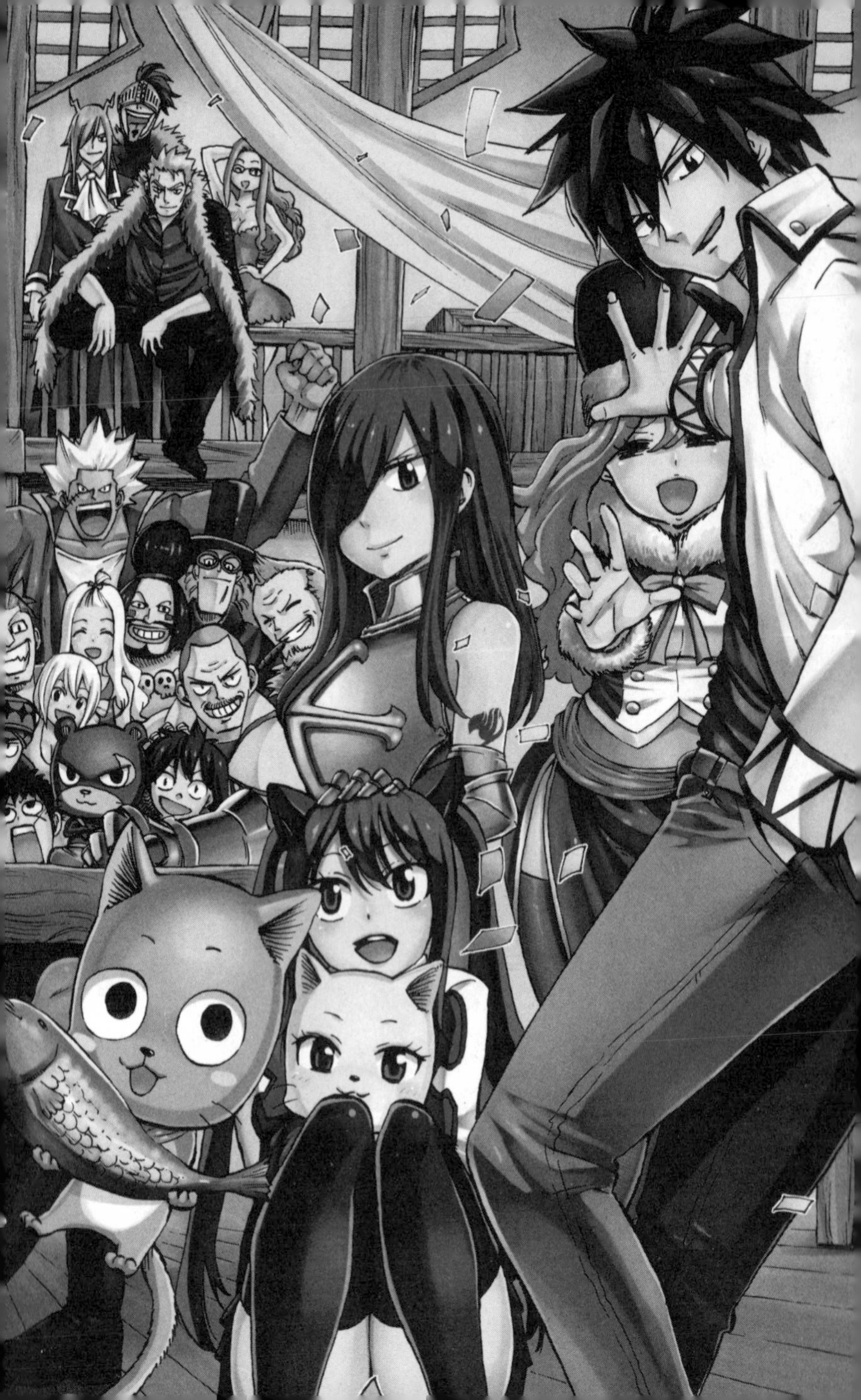

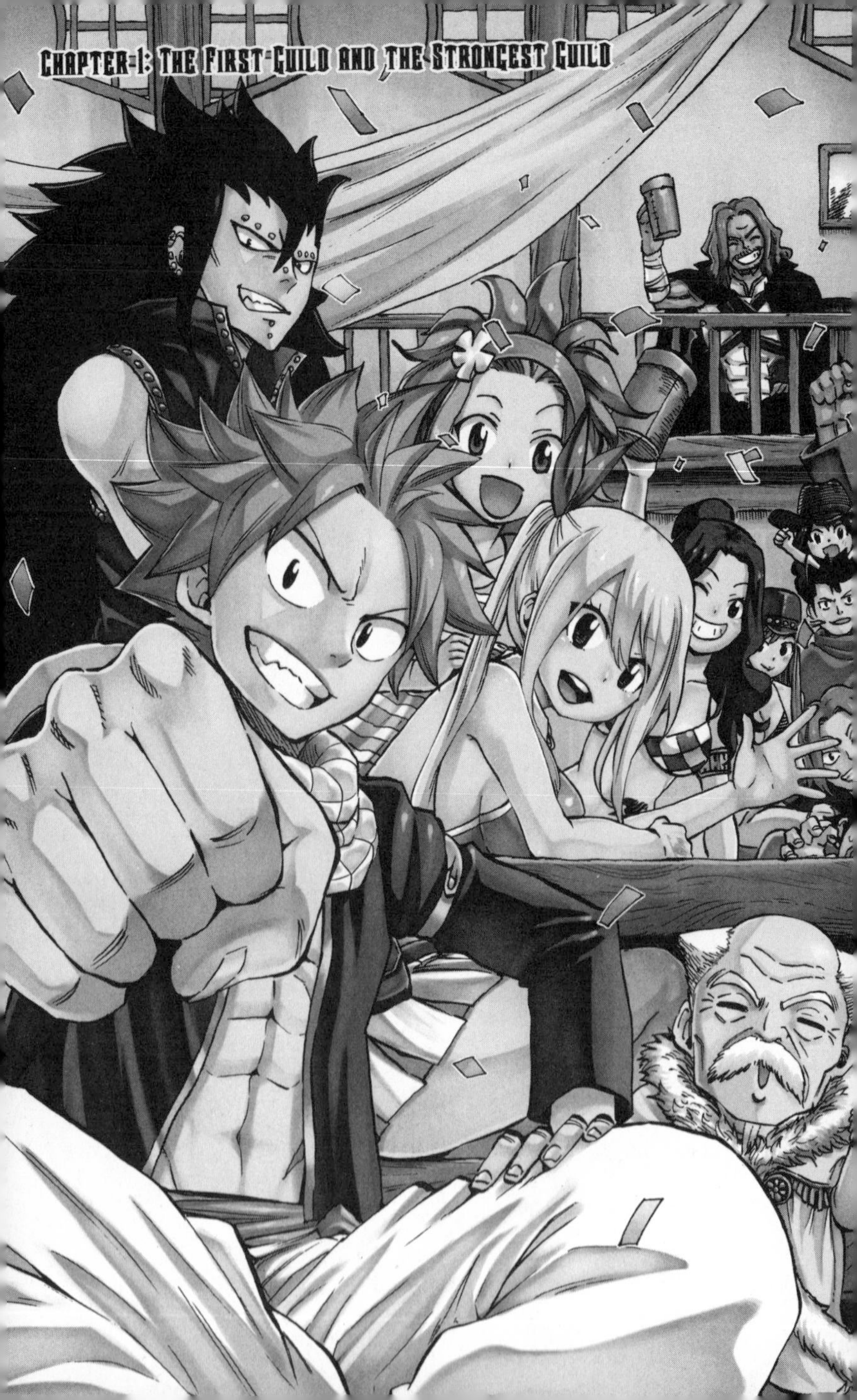
Chapter 1: The First Guild and the Strongest Guild

FAIRY TAIL
100 YEARS QUEST

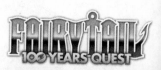

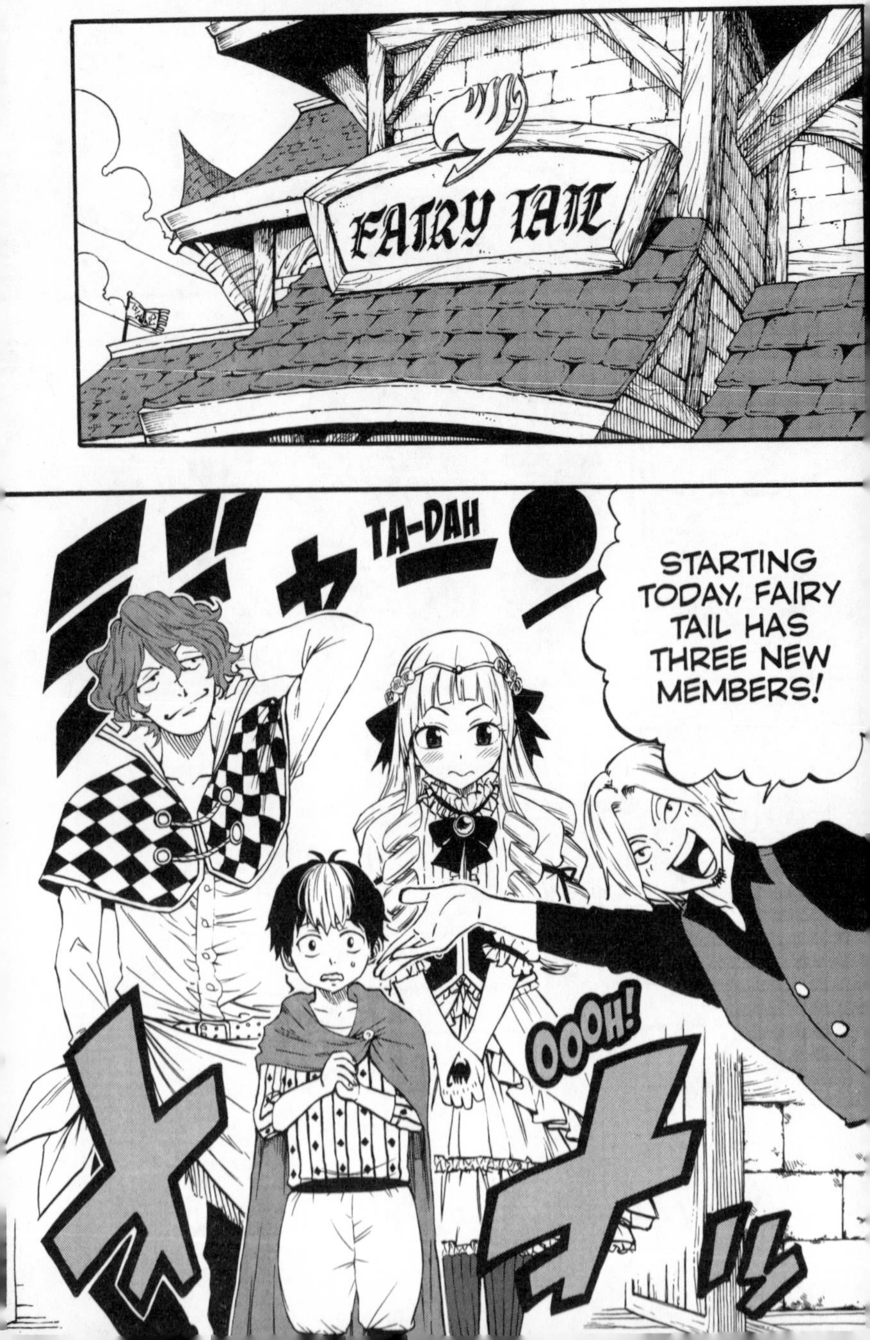
FAIRY TAIL
TA-DAH
STARTING TODAY, FAIRY TAIL HAS THREE NEW MEMBERS!
OOOH!

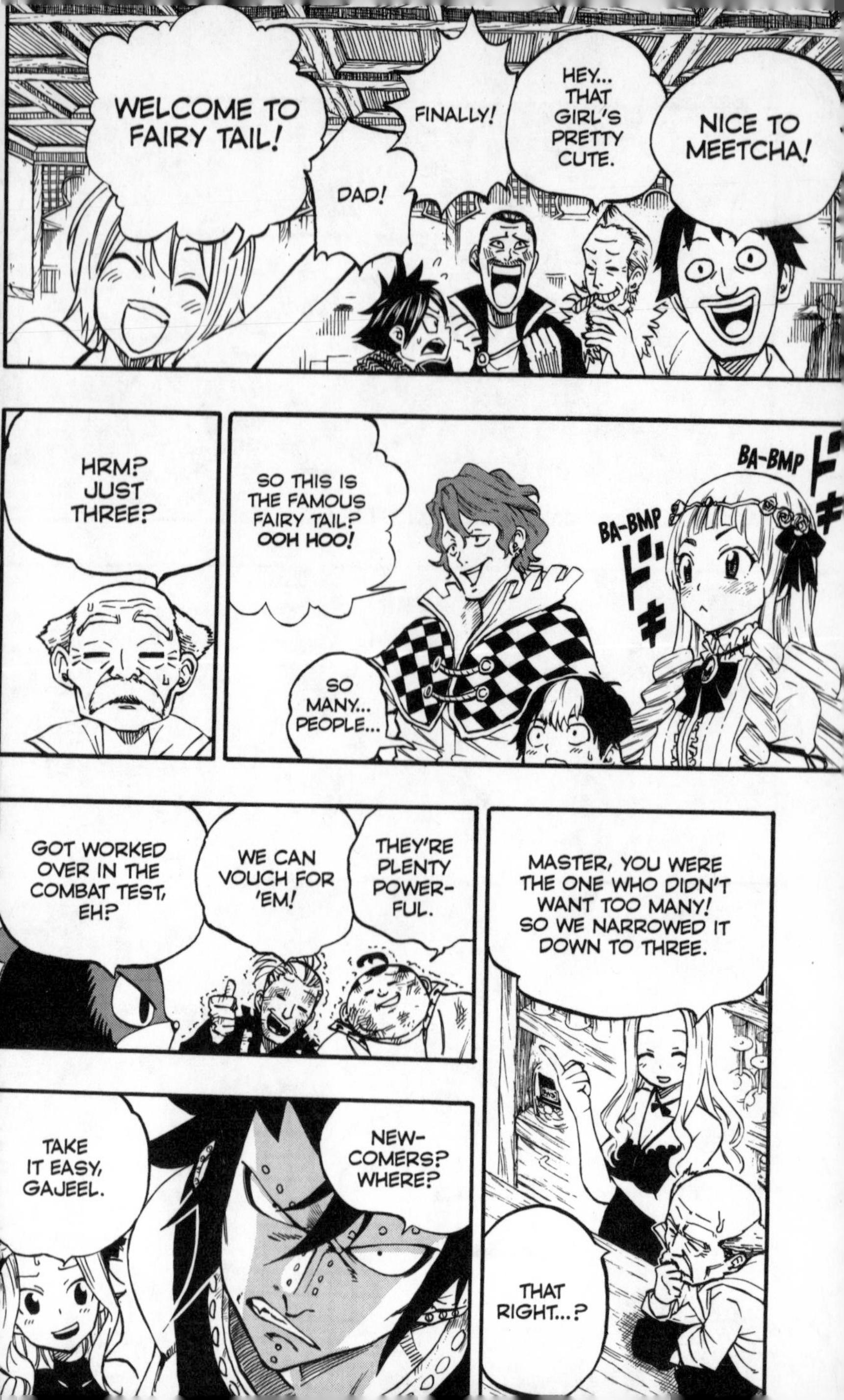
NICE TO MEETCHA!
HEY... THAT GIRL'S PRETTY CUTE.
FINALLY!
WELCOME TO FAIRY TAIL!
DAD!
BA-BMP
BA-BMP
SO THIS IS THE FAMOUS FAIRY TAIL? OOH HOO!
SO MANY... PEOPLE...
HRM? JUST THREE?
MASTER, YOU WERE THE ONE WHO DIDN'T WANT TOO MANY! SO WE NARROWED IT DOWN TO THREE.
THAT RIGHT...?
THEY'RE PLENTY POWER-FUL.
WE CAN VOUCH FOR 'EM!
GOT WORKED OVER IN THE COMBAT TEST, EH?
NEW-COMERS? WHERE?
TAKE IT EASY, GAJEEL.

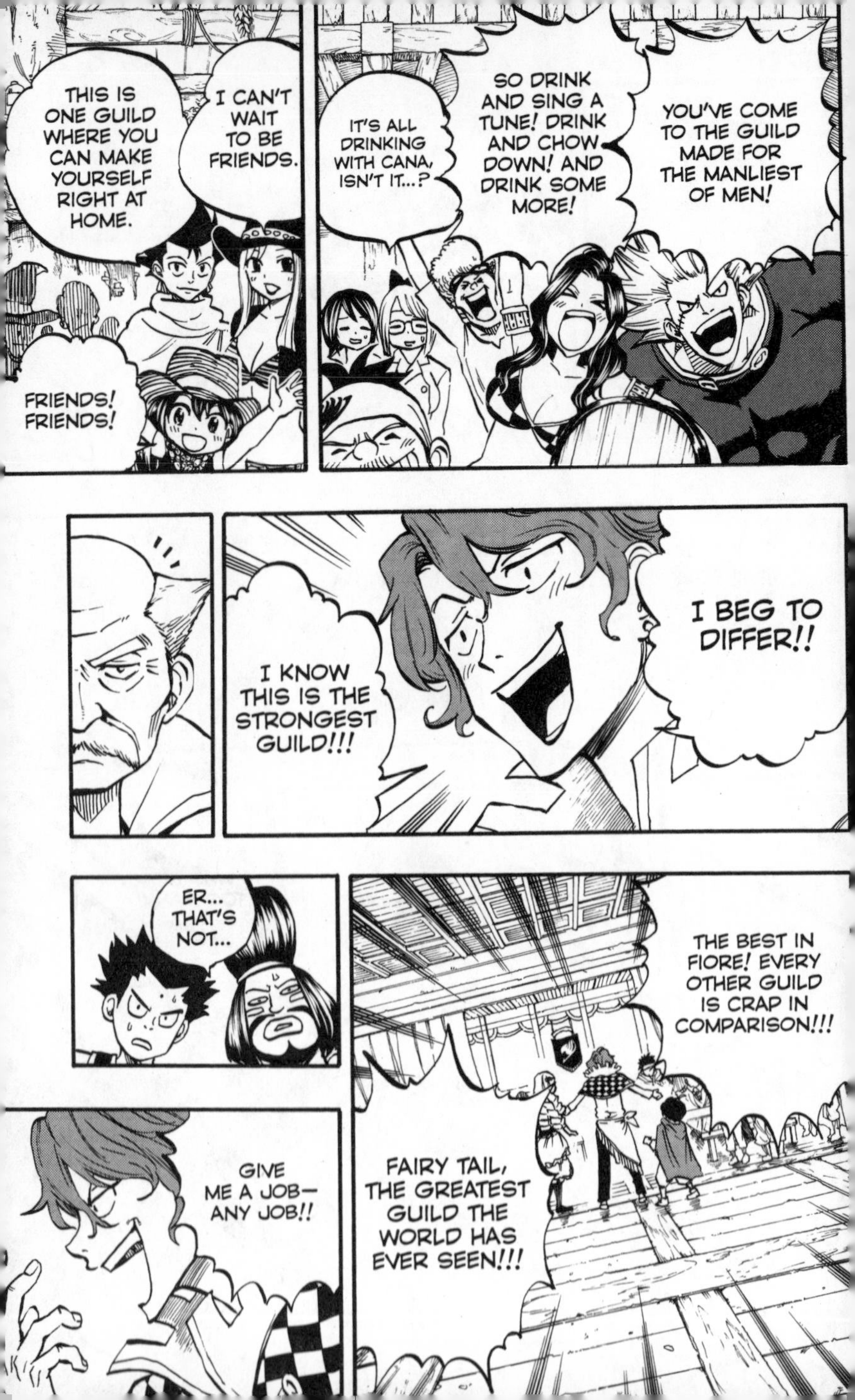
YOU'VE COME TO THE GUILD MADE FOR THE MANLIEST OF MEN!
SO DRINK AND SING A TUNE! DRINK AND CHOW DOWN! AND DRINK SOME MORE!
IT'S ALL DRINKING WITH CANA, ISN'T IT...?
I CAN'T WAIT TO BE FRIENDS.
THIS IS ONE GUILD WHERE YOU CAN MAKE YOURSELF RIGHT AT HOME.
FRIENDS! FRIENDS!
I BEG TO DIFFER!!
I KNOW THIS IS THE STRONGEST GUILD!!!
THE BEST IN FIORE! EVERY OTHER GUILD IS CRAP IN COMPARISON!!!
FAIRY TAIL, THE GREATEST GUILD THE WORLD HAS EVER SEEN!!!
ER... THAT'S NOT...
GIVE ME A JOB— ANY JOB!!

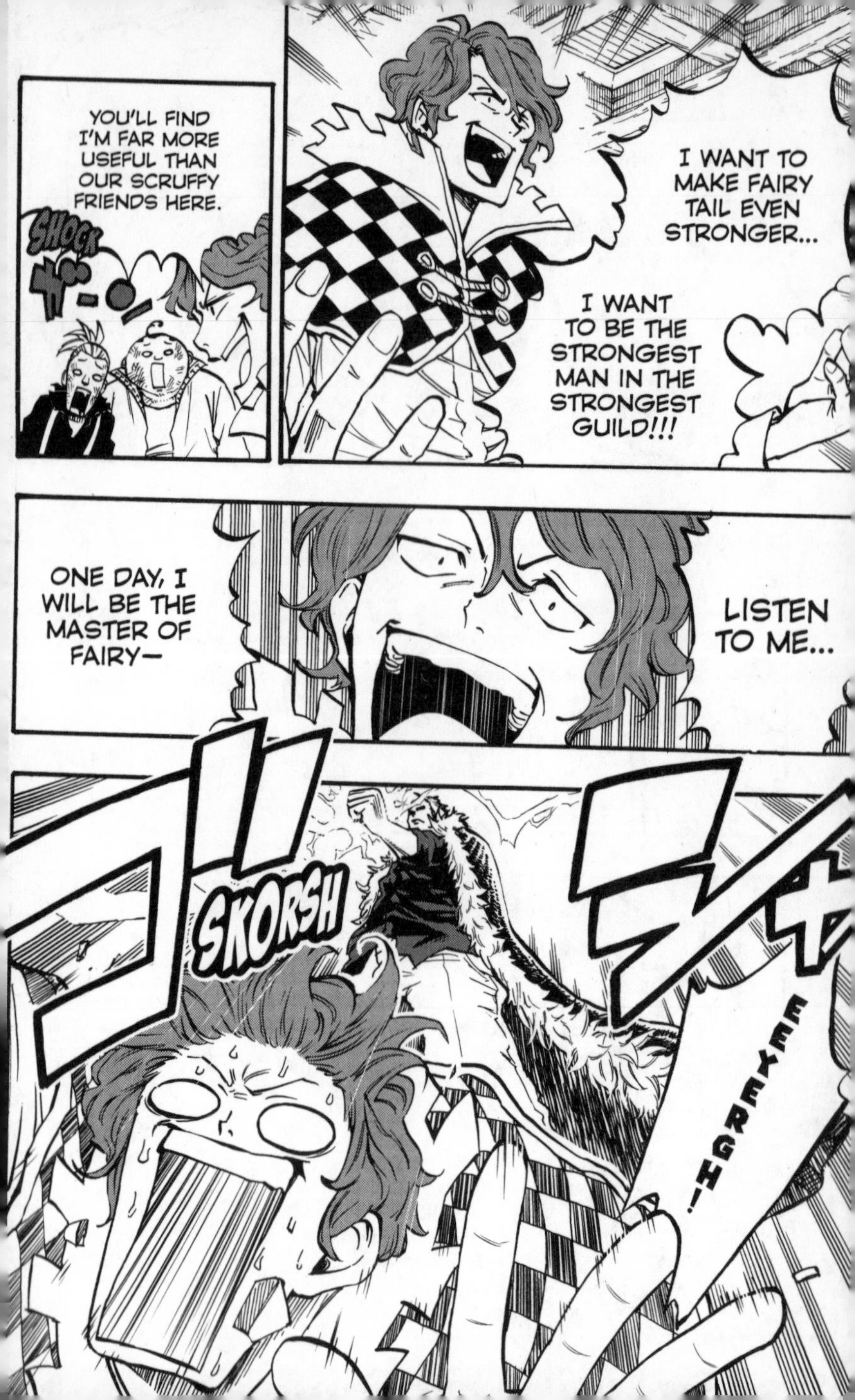
I WANT TO MAKE FAIRY TAIL EVEN STRONGER...
I WANT TO BE THE STRONGEST MAN IN THE STRONGEST GUILD!!!
YOU'LL FIND I'M FAR MORE USEFUL THAN OUR SCRUFFY FRIENDS HERE.
SHOCK
LISTEN TO ME...
ONE DAY, I WILL BE THE MASTER OF FAIRY—
SKORSH
EEEXERGH!!

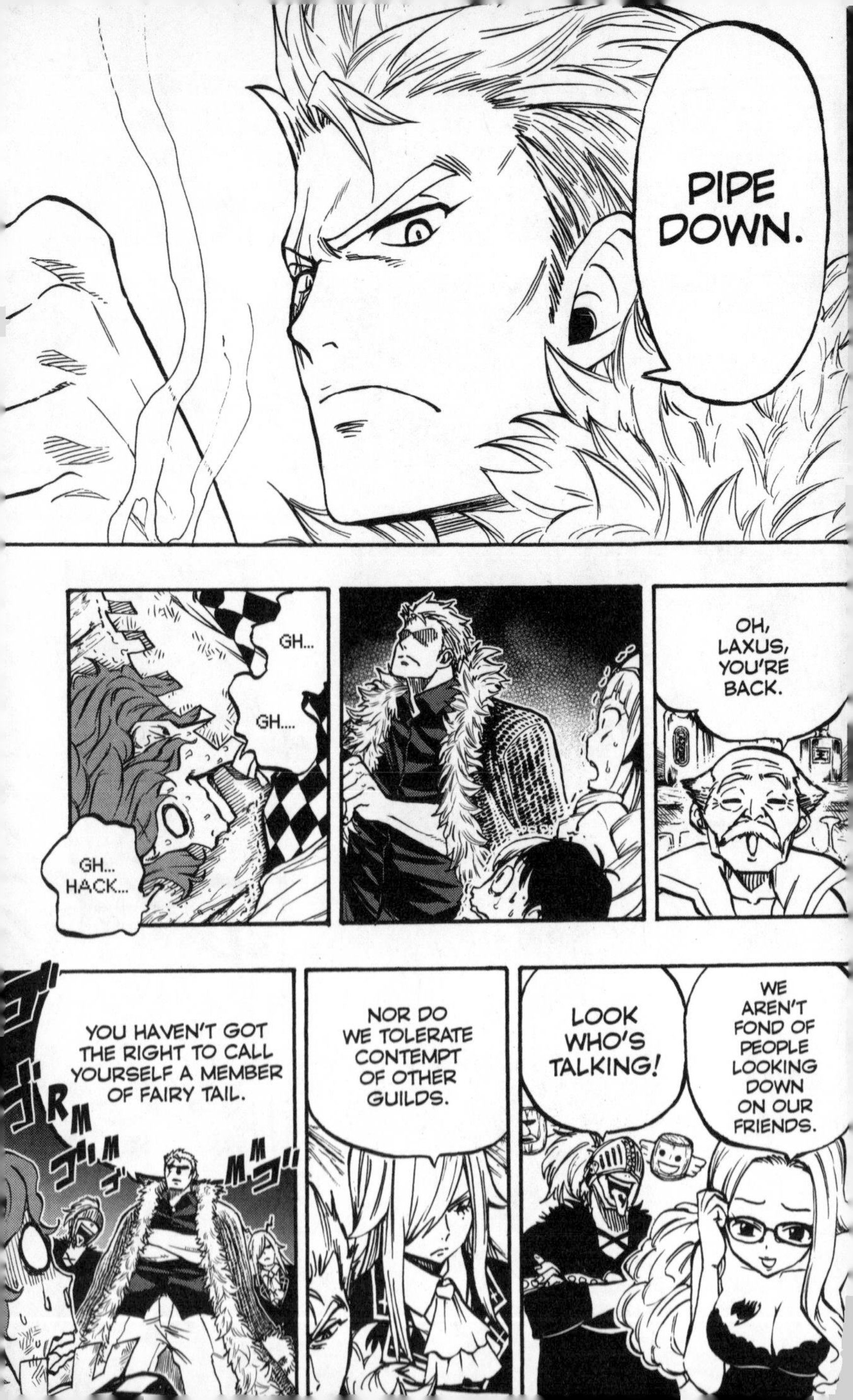
PIPE DOWN.
OH, LAXUS, YOU'RE BACK.
GH...
GH....
GH... HACK...
WE AREN'T FOND OF PEOPLE LOOKING DOWN ON OUR FRIENDS.
LOOK WHO'S TALKING!
NOR DO WE TOLERATE CONTEMPT OF OTHER GUILDS.
YOU HAVEN'T GOT THE RIGHT TO CALL YOURSELF A MEMBER OF FAIRY TAIL.

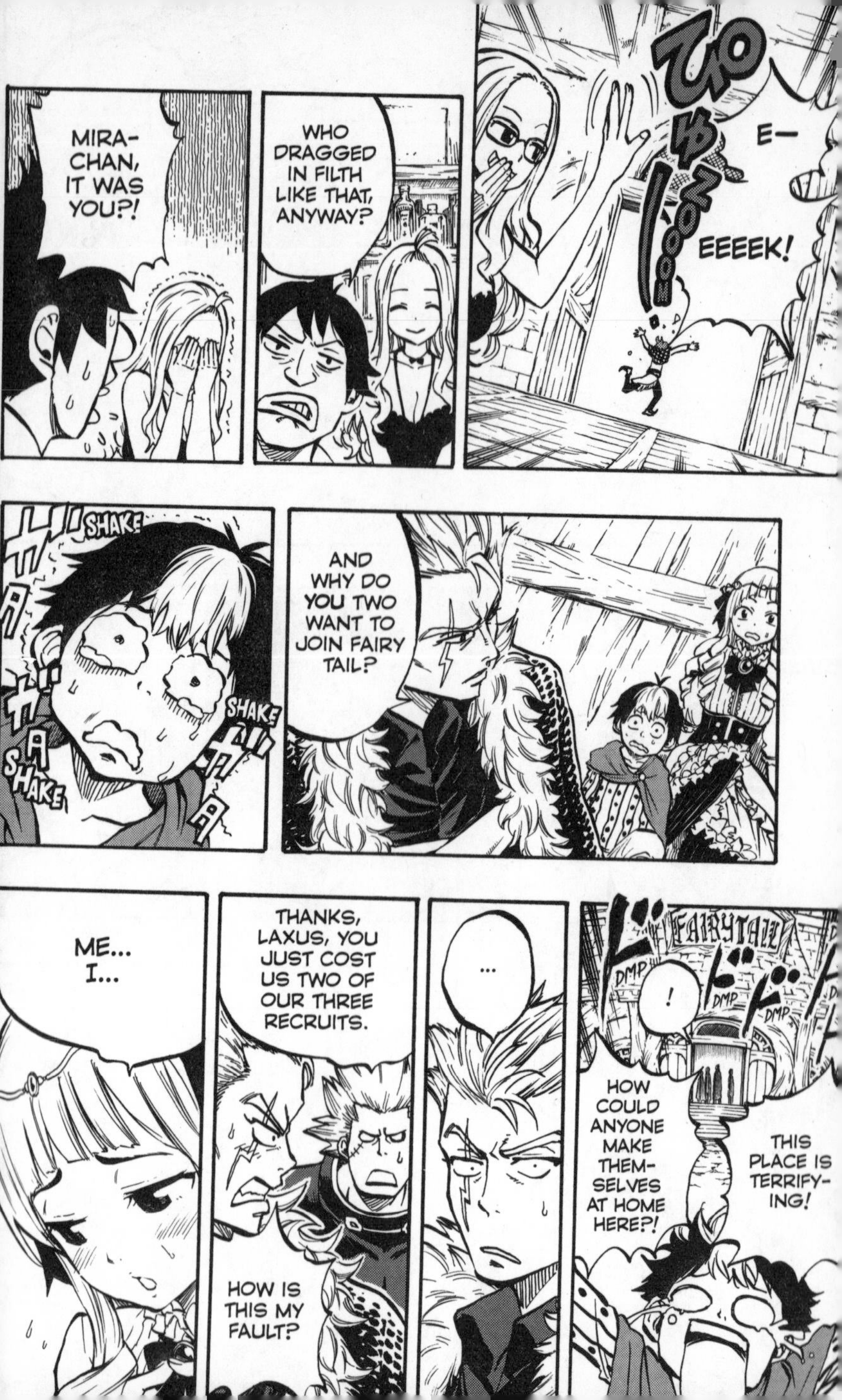
E—
EEEEK!
WHO DRAGGED IN FILTH LIKE THAT, ANYWAY?
MIRA-CHAN, IT WAS YOU?!
AND WHY DO YOU TWO WANT TO JOIN FAIRY TAIL?
SHAKE
SHAKE
SHAKE
FAIRYTAIL
DMP
DMP
DMP
!
THIS PLACE IS TERRIFY-ING!
HOW COULD ANYONE MAKE THEM-SELVES AT HOME HERE?!
...
THANKS, LAXUS, YOU JUST COST US TWO OF OUR THREE RECRUITS.
HOW IS THIS MY FAULT?
ME... I...

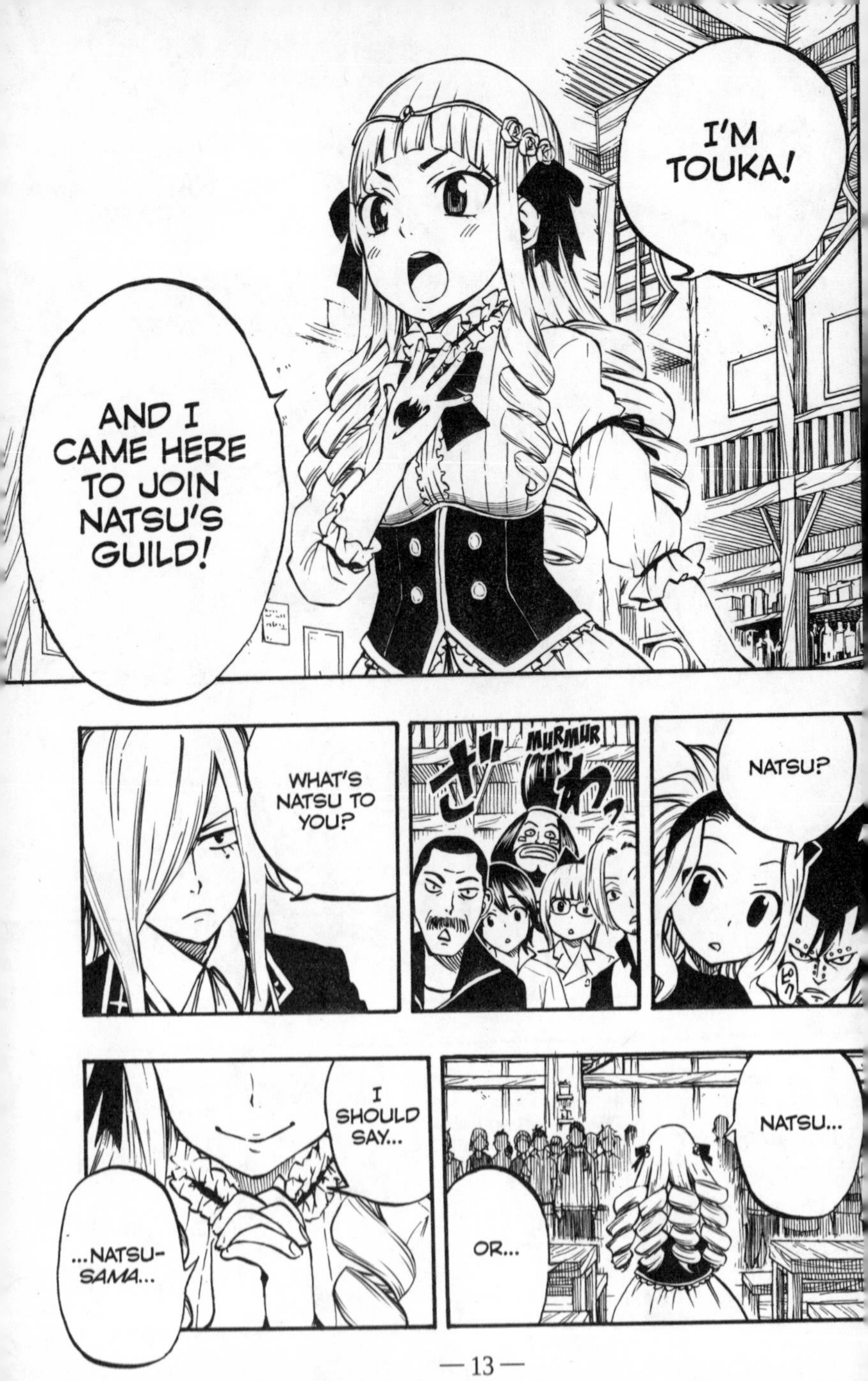
I'M TOUKA!
AND I CAME HERE TO JOIN NATSU'S GUILD!
NATSU?
MURMUR
WHAT'S NATSU TO YOU?
NATSU...
OR...
I SHOULD SAY...
...NATSU-SAMA...

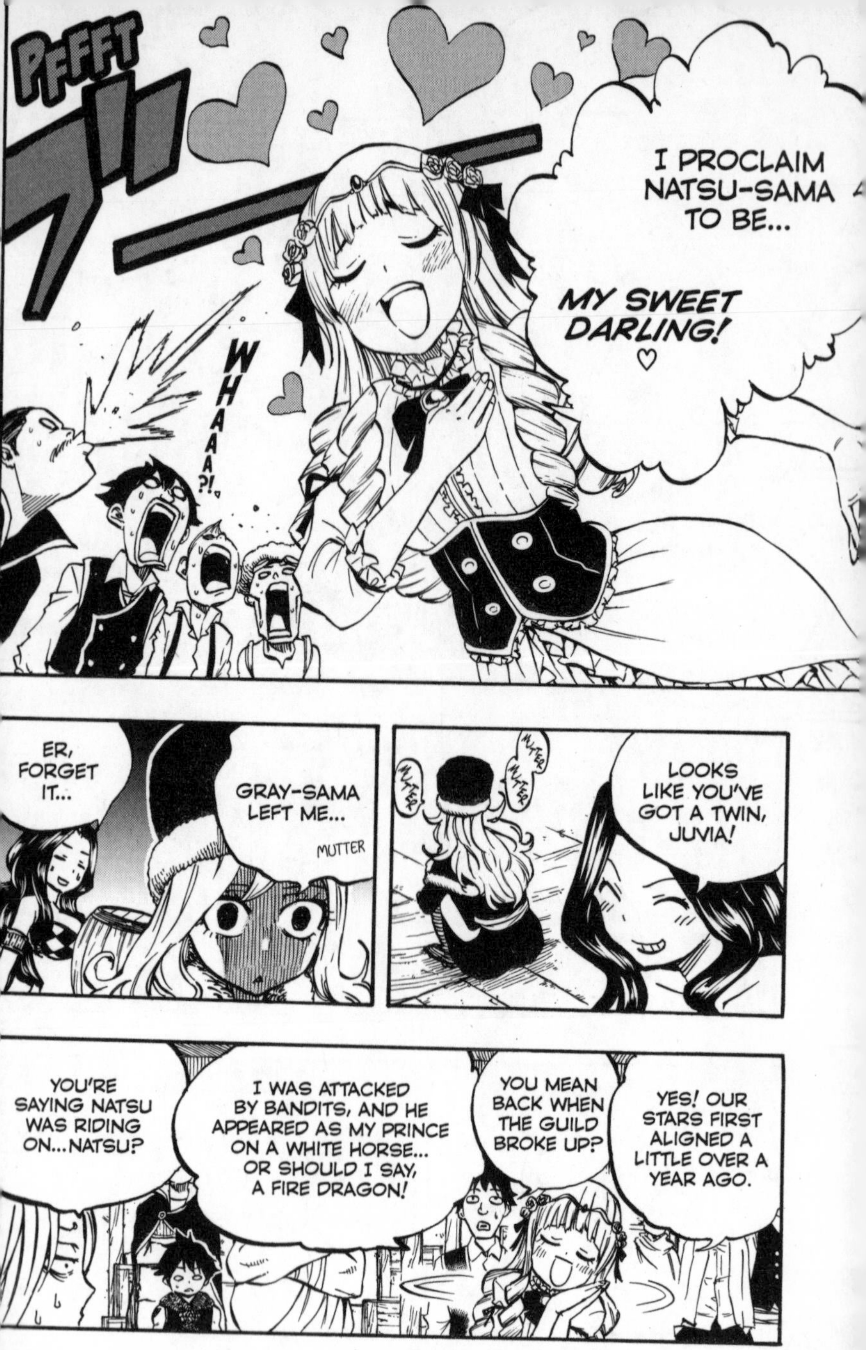
I PROCLAIM NATSU-SAMA TO BE...
MY SWEET DARLING! ♡
PFFFT
WHAAAA?!
LOOKS LIKE YOU'VE GOT A TWIN, JUVIA!
MUTTER MUTTER
MUTTER
GRAY-SAMA LEFT ME...
MUTTER
ER, FORGET IT...
YES! OUR STARS FIRST ALIGNED A LITTLE OVER A YEAR AGO.
YOU MEAN BACK WHEN THE GUILD BROKE UP?
I WAS ATTACKED BY BANDITS, AND HE APPEARED AS MY PRINCE ON A WHITE HORSE... OR SHOULD I SAY, A FIRE DRAGON!
YOU'RE SAYING NATSU WAS RIDING ON...NATSU?

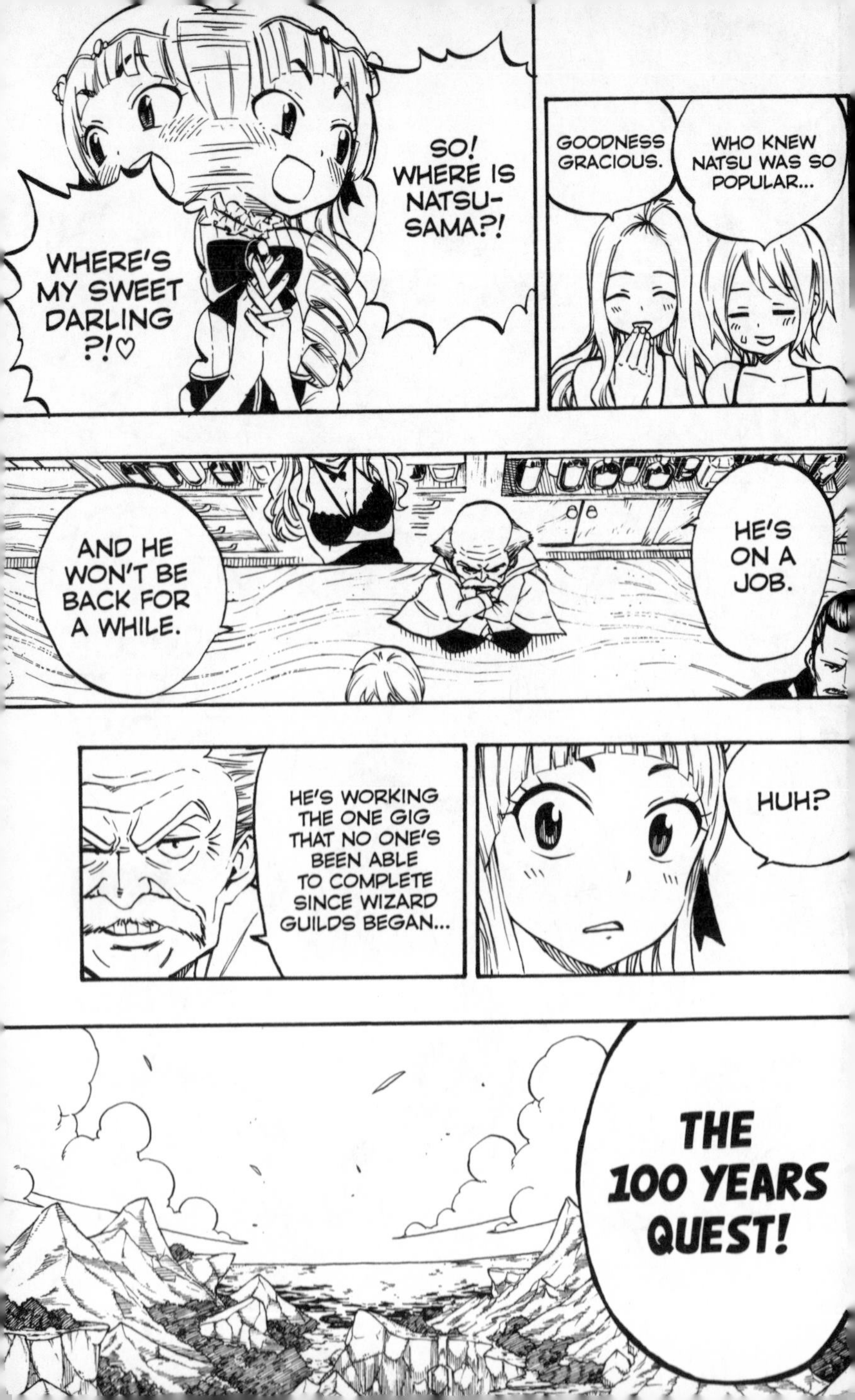
WHO KNEW NATSU WAS SO POPULAR...
GOODNESS GRACIOUS.
SO! WHERE IS NATSU-SAMA?!
WHERE'S MY SWEET DARLING ?!♡
HE'S ON A JOB.
AND HE WON'T BE BACK FOR A WHILE.
HUH?
HE'S WORKING THE ONE GIG THAT NO ONE'S BEEN ABLE TO COMPLETE SINCE WIZARD GUILDS BEGAN...
THE 100 YEARS QUEST!

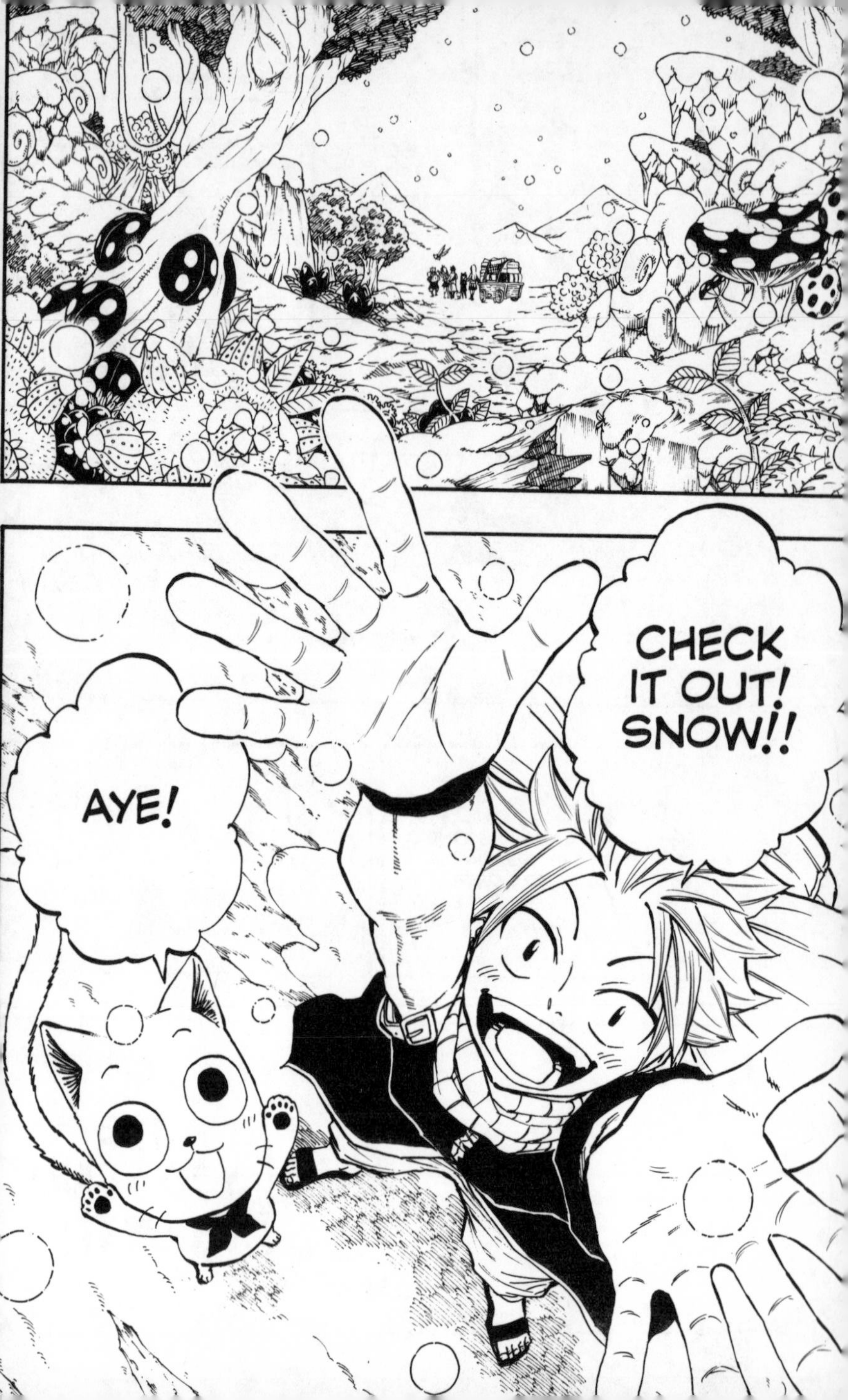
CHECK IT OUT! SNOW!!
AYE!

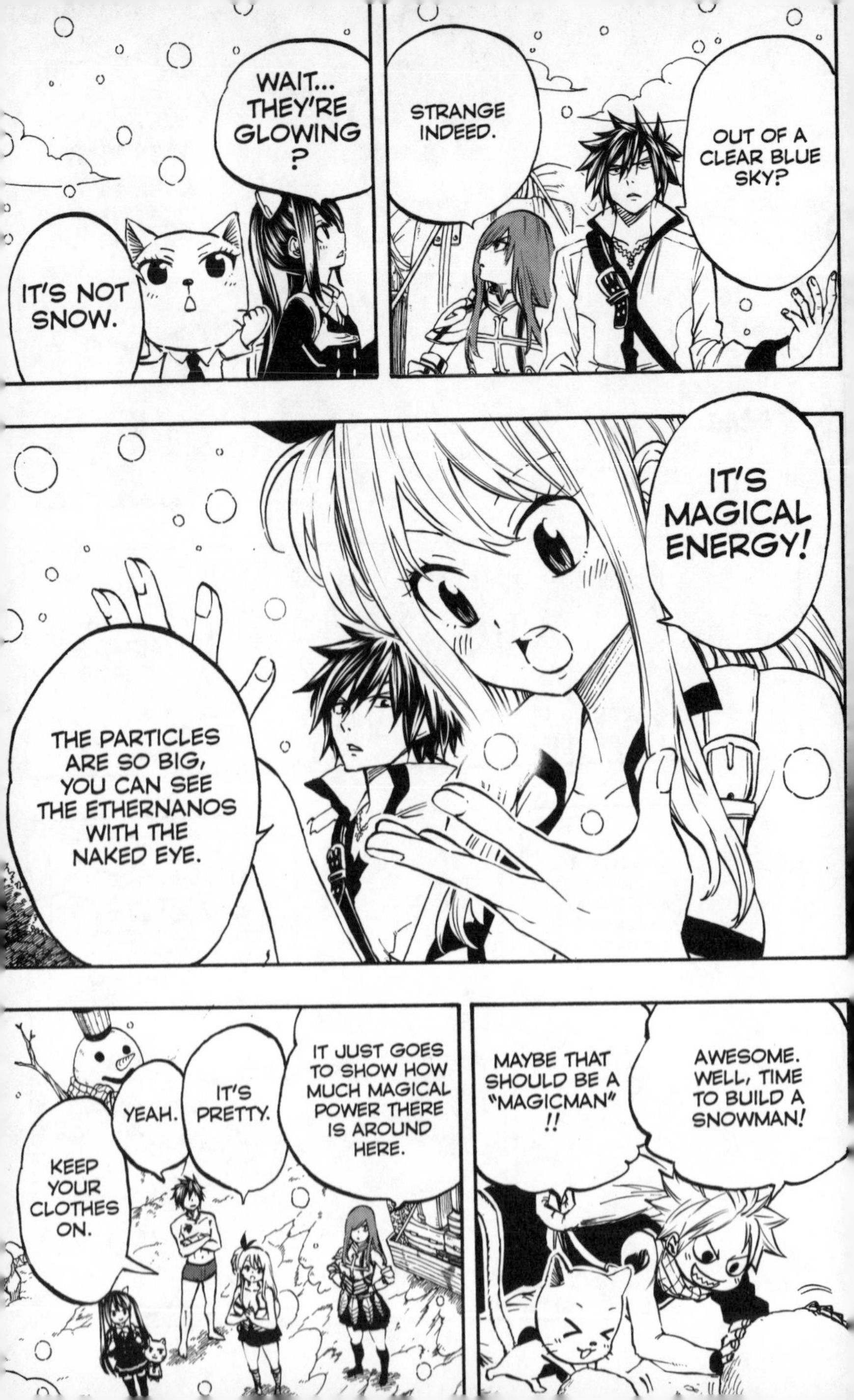
OUT OF A CLEAR BLUE SKY?
STRANGE INDEED.
WAIT... THEY'RE GLOWING?
IT'S NOT SNOW.
IT'S MAGICAL ENERGY!
THE PARTICLES ARE SO BIG, YOU CAN SEE THE ETHERNANOS WITH THE NAKED EYE.
AWESOME. WELL, TIME TO BUILD A SNOWMAN!
MAYBE THAT SHOULD BE A "MAGICMAN"!!
IT JUST GOES TO SHOW HOW MUCH MAGICAL POWER THERE IS AROUND HERE.
IT'S PRETTY.
YEAH.
KEEP YOUR CLOTHES ON.

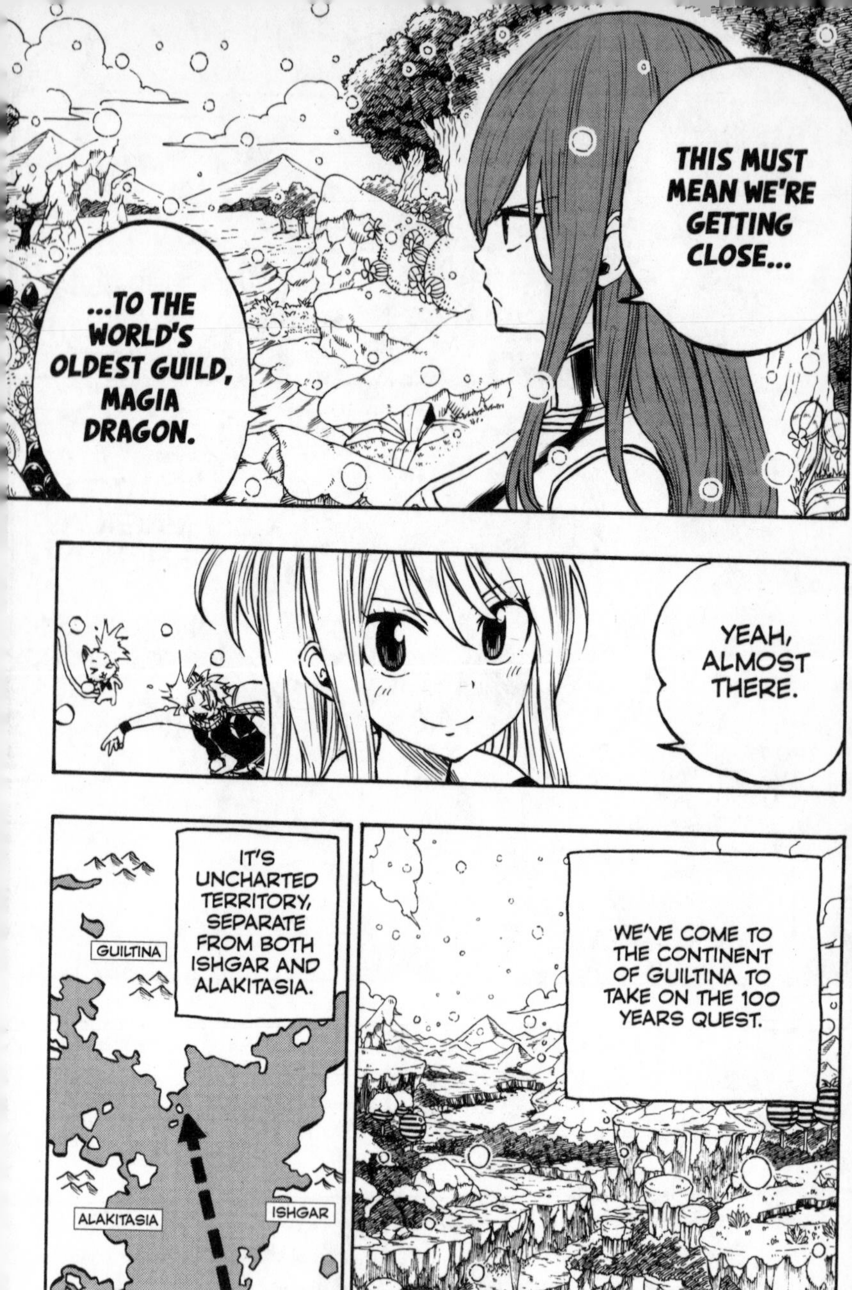
THIS MUST MEAN WE'RE GETTING CLOSE...
...TO THE WORLD'S OLDEST GUILD, MAGIA DRAGON.
YEAH, ALMOST THERE.
WE'VE COME TO THE CONTINENT OF GUILTINA TO TAKE ON THE 100 YEARS QUEST.
IT'S UNCHARTED TERRITORY, SEPARATE FROM BOTH ISHGAR AND ALAKITASIA.
GUILTINA
ALAKITASIA
ISHGAR

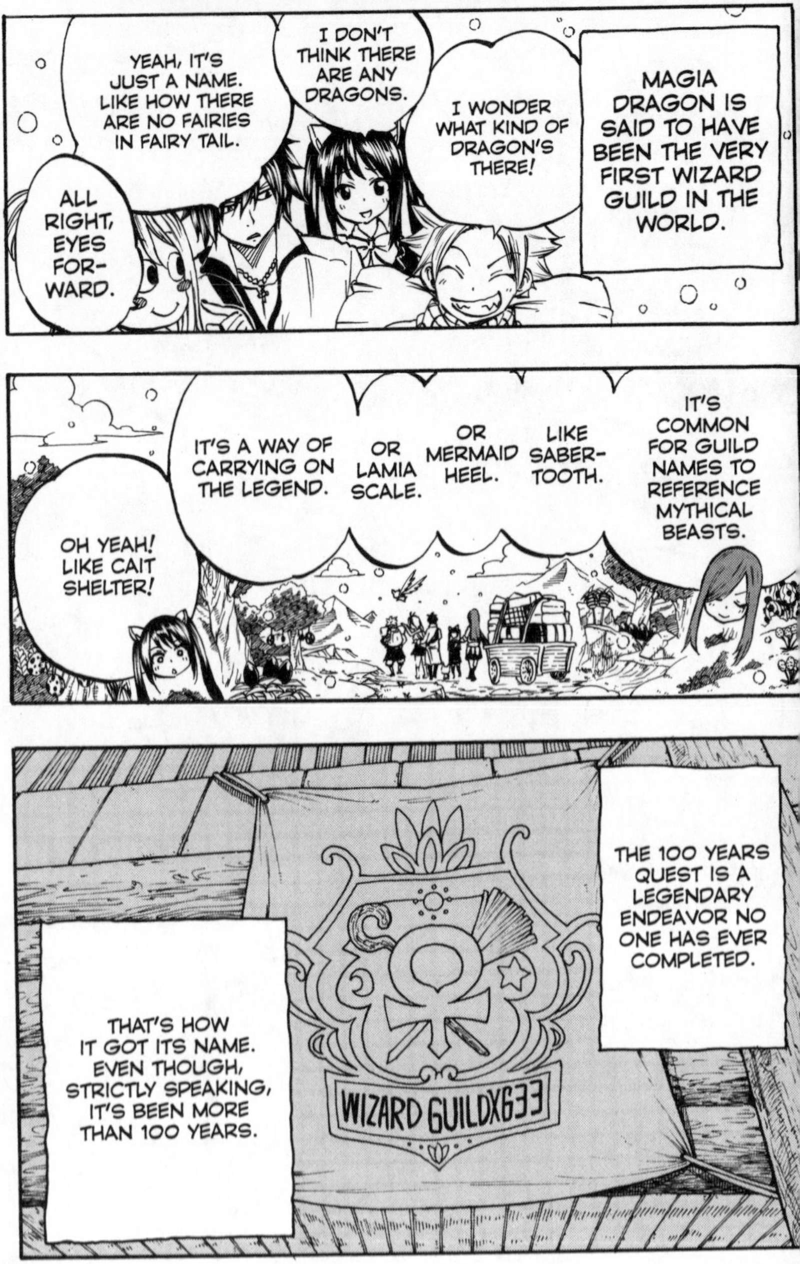
MAGIA DRAGON IS SAID TO HAVE BEEN THE VERY FIRST WIZARD GUILD IN THE WORLD.
I WONDER WHAT KIND OF DRAGON'S THERE!
I DON'T THINK THERE ARE ANY DRAGONS.
YEAH, IT'S JUST A NAME. LIKE HOW THERE ARE NO FAIRIES IN FAIRY TAIL.
ALL RIGHT, EYES FOR-WARD.
IT'S COMMON FOR GUILD NAMES TO REFERENCE MYTHICAL BEASTS.
LIKE SABER-TOOTH.
OR MERMAID HEEL.
OR LAMIA SCALE.
IT'S A WAY OF CARRYING ON THE LEGEND.
OH YEAH! LIKE CAIT SHELTER!
THE 100 YEARS QUEST IS A LEGENDARY ENDEAVOR NO ONE HAS EVER COMPLETED.
WIZARD GUILDX633
THAT'S HOW IT GOT ITS NAME. EVEN THOUGH, STRICTLY SPEAKING, IT'S BEEN MORE THAN 100 YEARS.

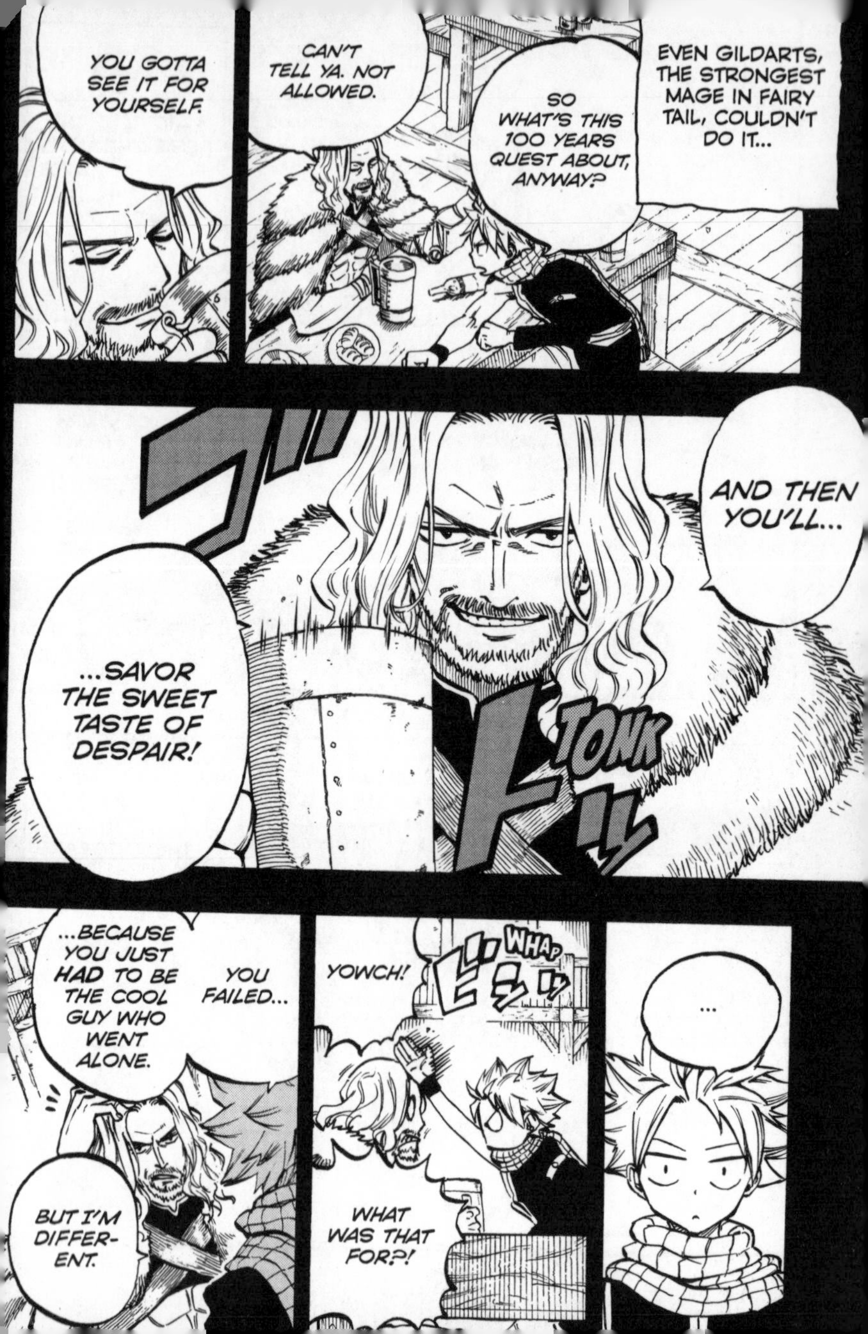
EVEN GILDARTS, THE STRONGEST MAGE IN FAIRY TAIL, COULDN'T DO IT...
SO WHAT'S THIS 100 YEARS QUEST ABOUT, ANYWAY?
CAN'T TELL YA. NOT ALLOWED.
YOU GOTTA SEE IT FOR YOURSELF.
AND THEN YOU'LL...
...SAVOR THE SWEET TASTE OF DESPAIR!
TONK
...
WHAP
YOWCH!
WHAT WAS THAT FOR?!
YOU FAILED...
...BECAUSE YOU JUST **HAD** TO BE THE COOL GUY WHO WENT ALONE.
BUT I'M DIFFERENT.

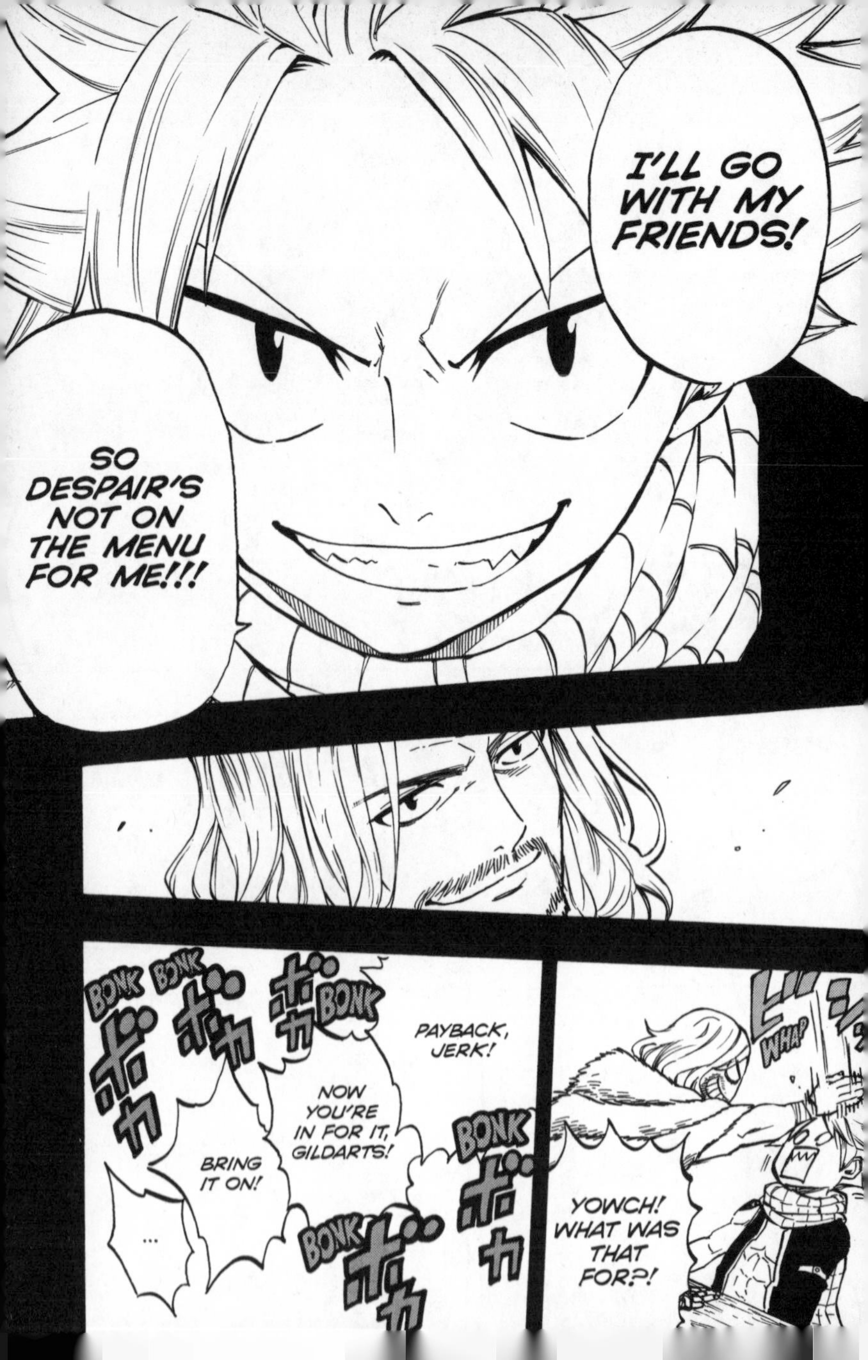
I'LL GO WITH MY FRIENDS!
SO DESPAIR'S NOT ON THE MENU FOR ME!!!
WHAP
YOWCH! WHAT WAS THAT FOR?!
BONK
PAYBACK, JERK!
NOW YOU'RE IN FOR IT, GILDARTS!
BONK BONK
BONK
BRING IT ON!
BONK
...

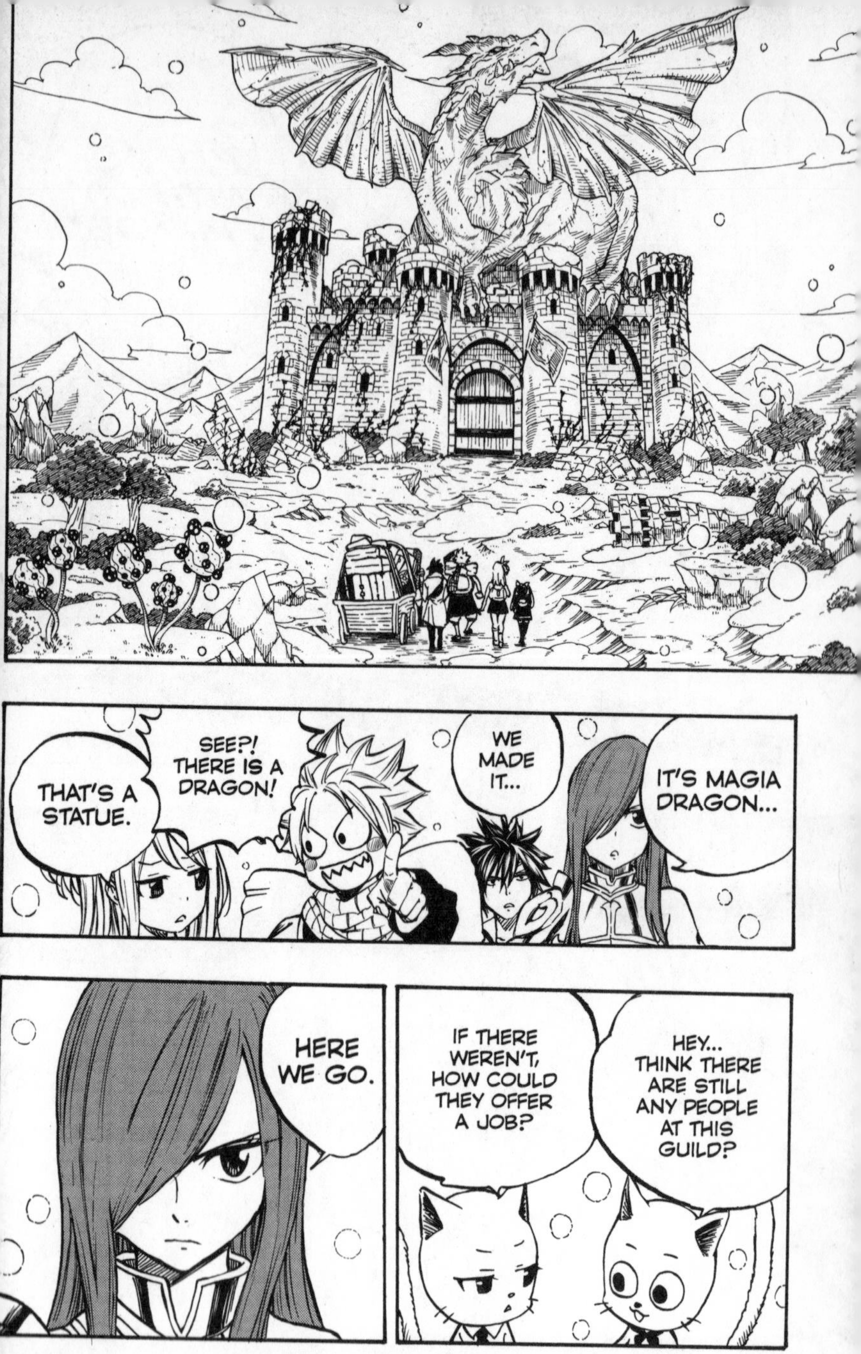
IT'S MAGIA DRAGON...
WE MADE IT...
SEE?! THERE IS A DRAGON!
THAT'S A STATUE.
HEY... THINK THERE ARE STILL ANY PEOPLE AT THIS GUILD?
IF THERE WEREN'T, HOW COULD THEY OFFER A JOB?
HERE WE GO.

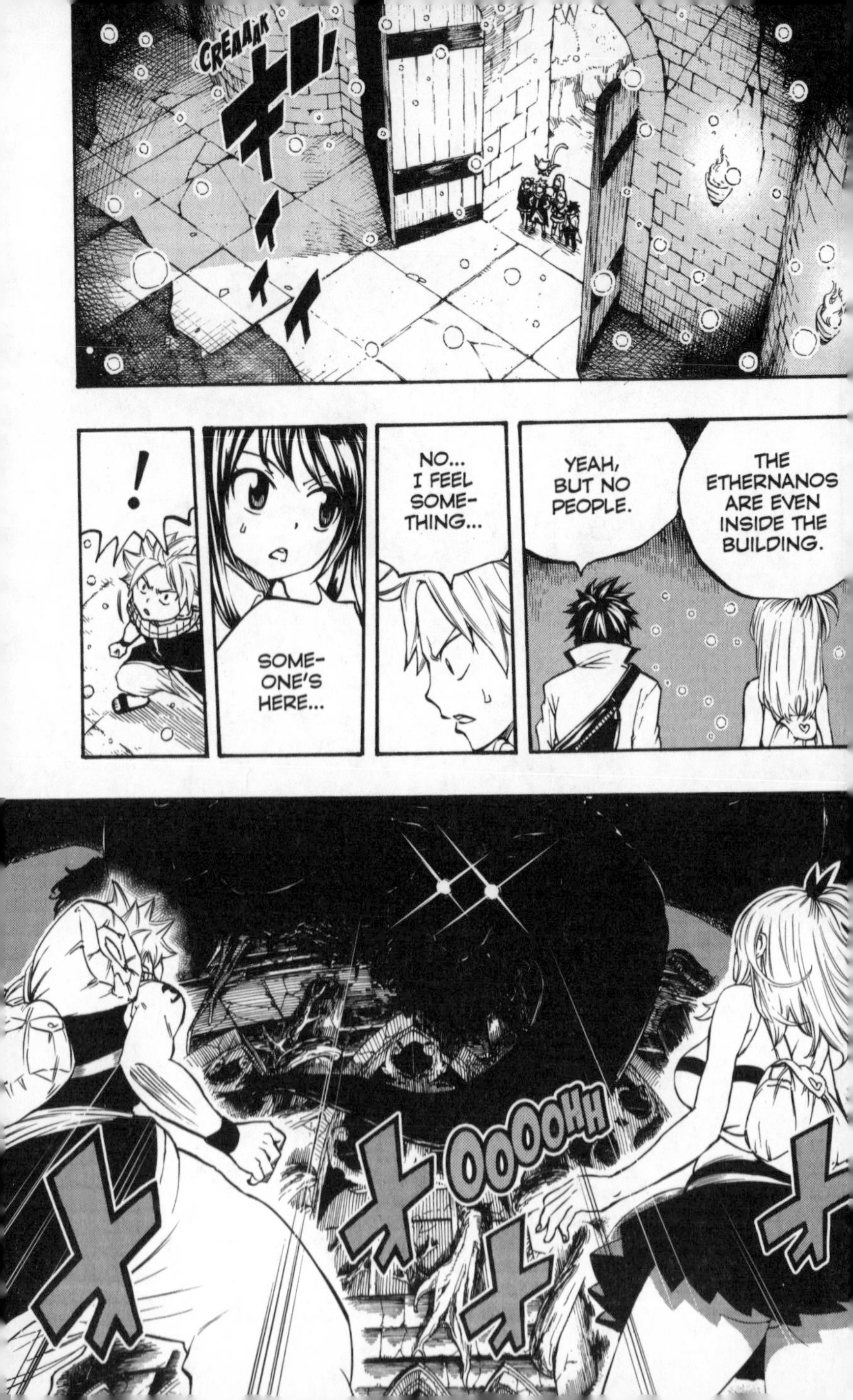
CREAAAK
THE ETHERNANOS ARE EVEN INSIDE THE BUILDING.
YEAH, BUT NO PEOPLE.
NO... I FEEL SOMETHING...
SOMEONE'S HERE...
!
OOOOHH

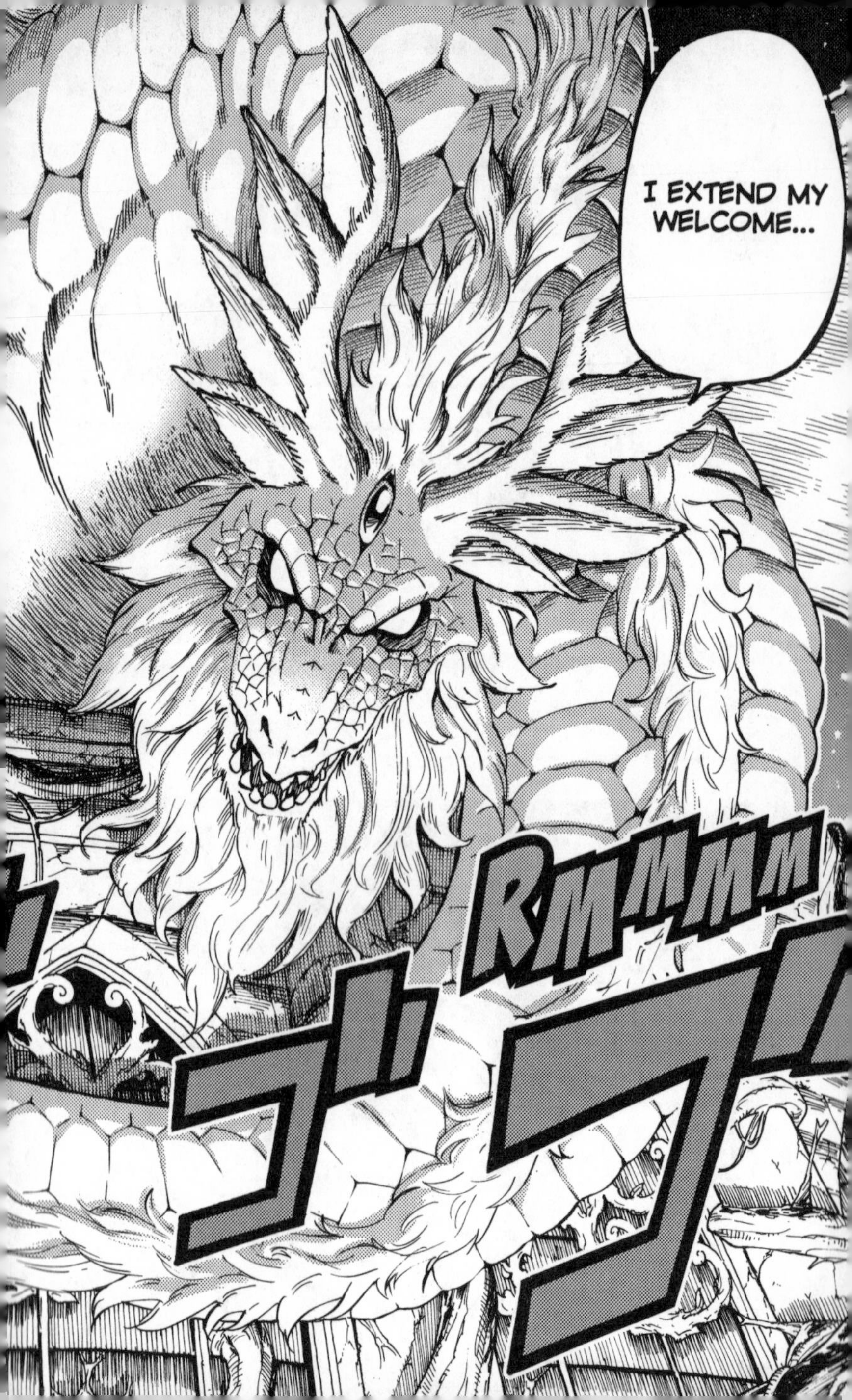
I EXTEND MY WELCOME...
RMMMMM

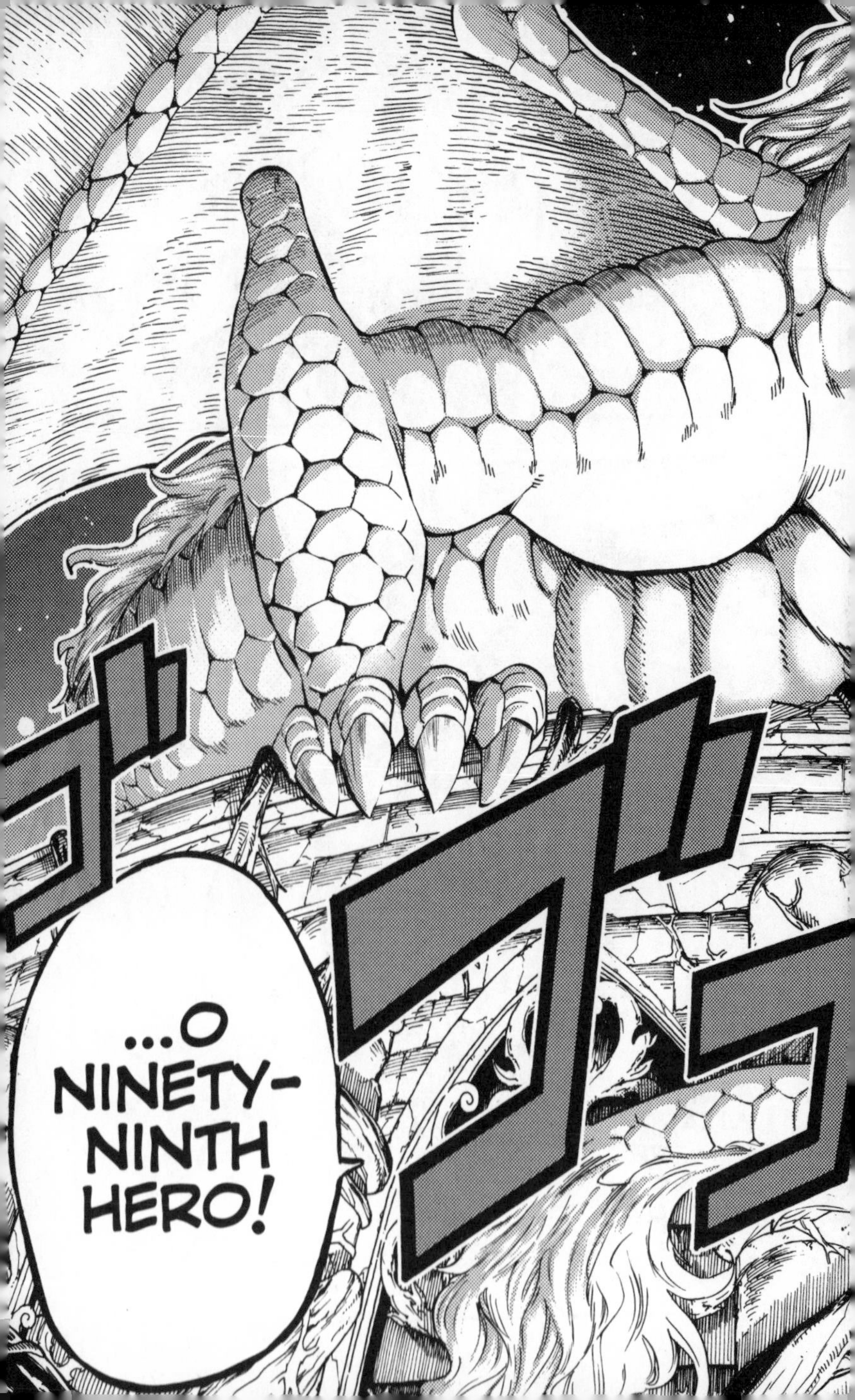
...O NINETY-NINTH HERO!

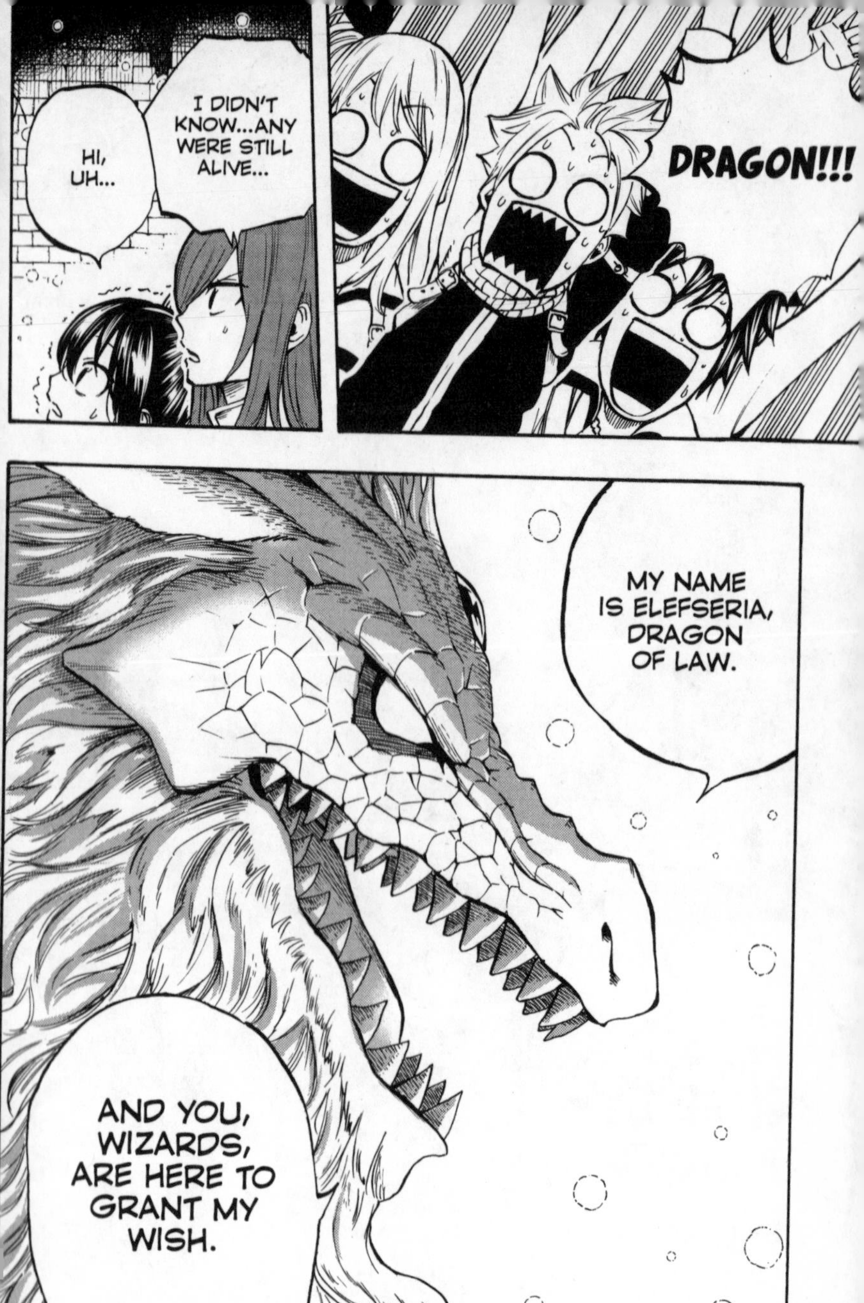
DRAGON!!!
I DIDN'T KNOW...ANY WERE STILL ALIVE...
HI, UH...
MY NAME IS ELEFSERIA, DRAGON OF LAW.
AND YOU, WIZARDS, ARE HERE TO GRANT MY WISH.

FAIRY TAIL 100 YEARS QUEST

CHAPTER 2: THE DRAGON SLAYERS' LINEAGE

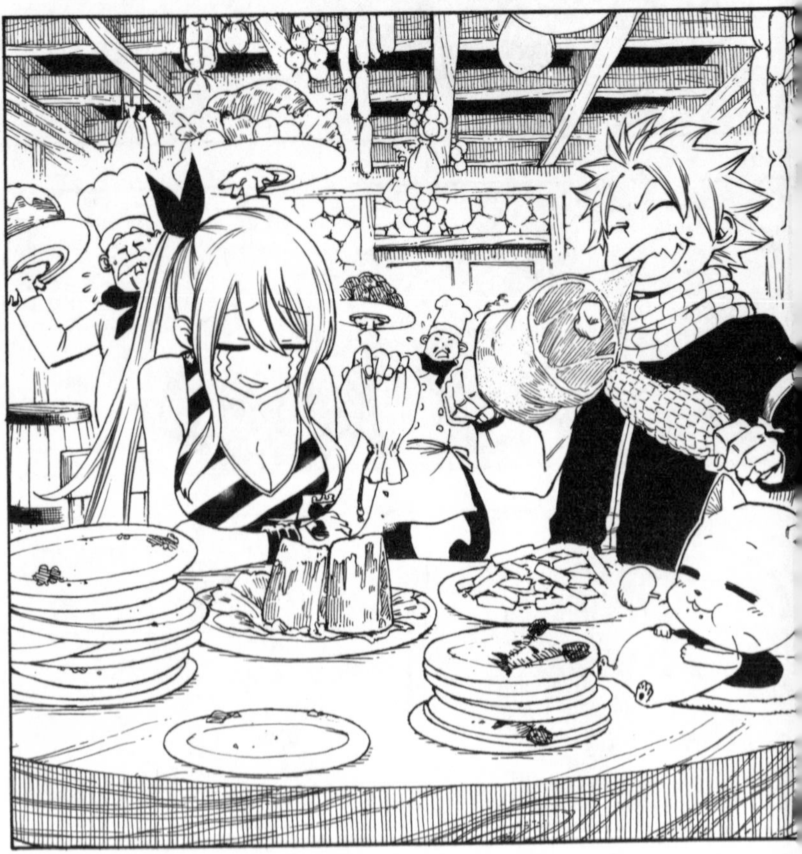

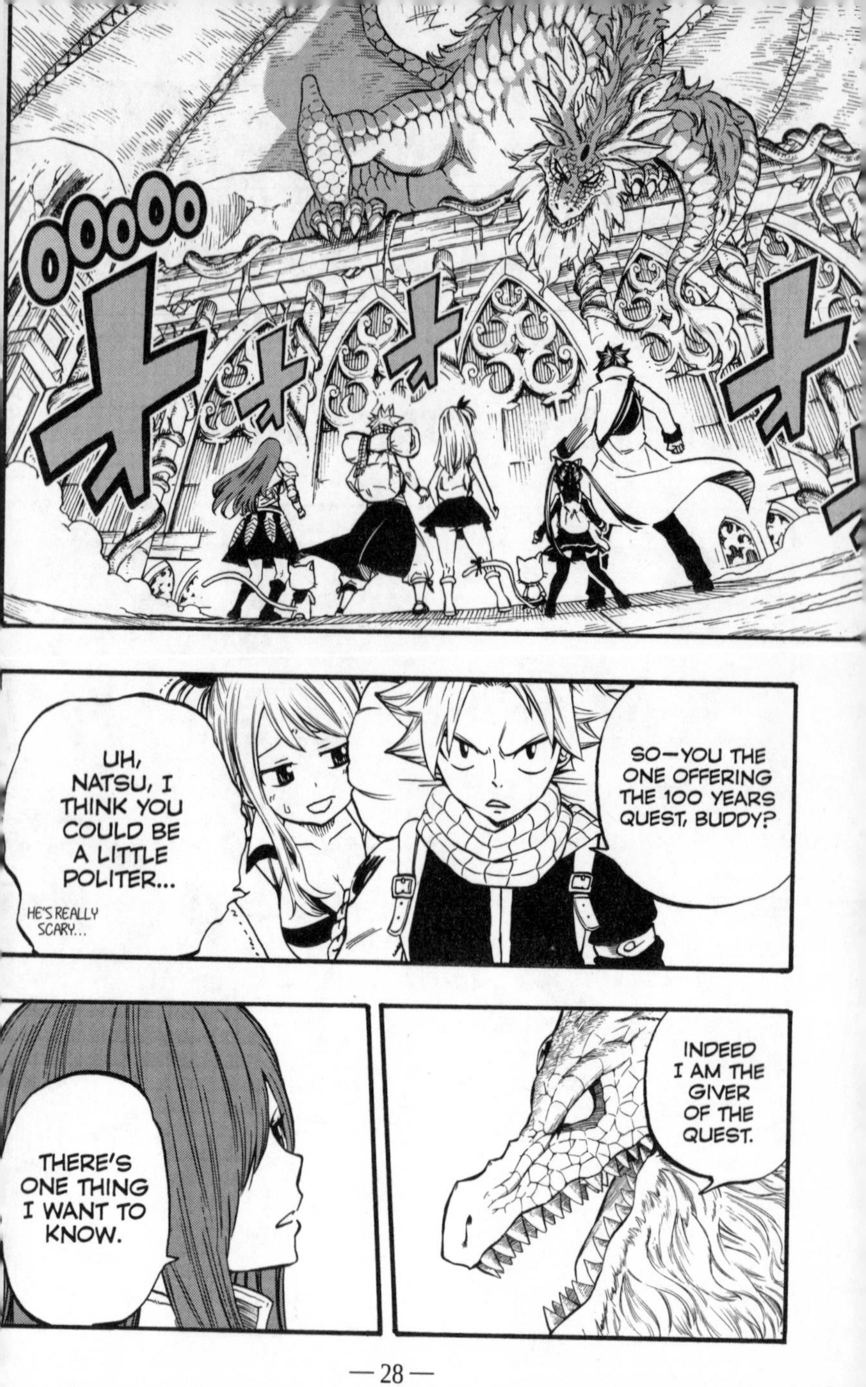
OOOOO
SO—YOU THE ONE OFFERING THE 100 YEARS QUEST, BUDDY?
UH, NATSU, I THINK YOU COULD BE A LITTLE POLITER...
HE'S REALLY SCARY...
INDEED I AM THE GIVER OF THE QUEST.
THERE'S ONE THING I WANT TO KNOW.

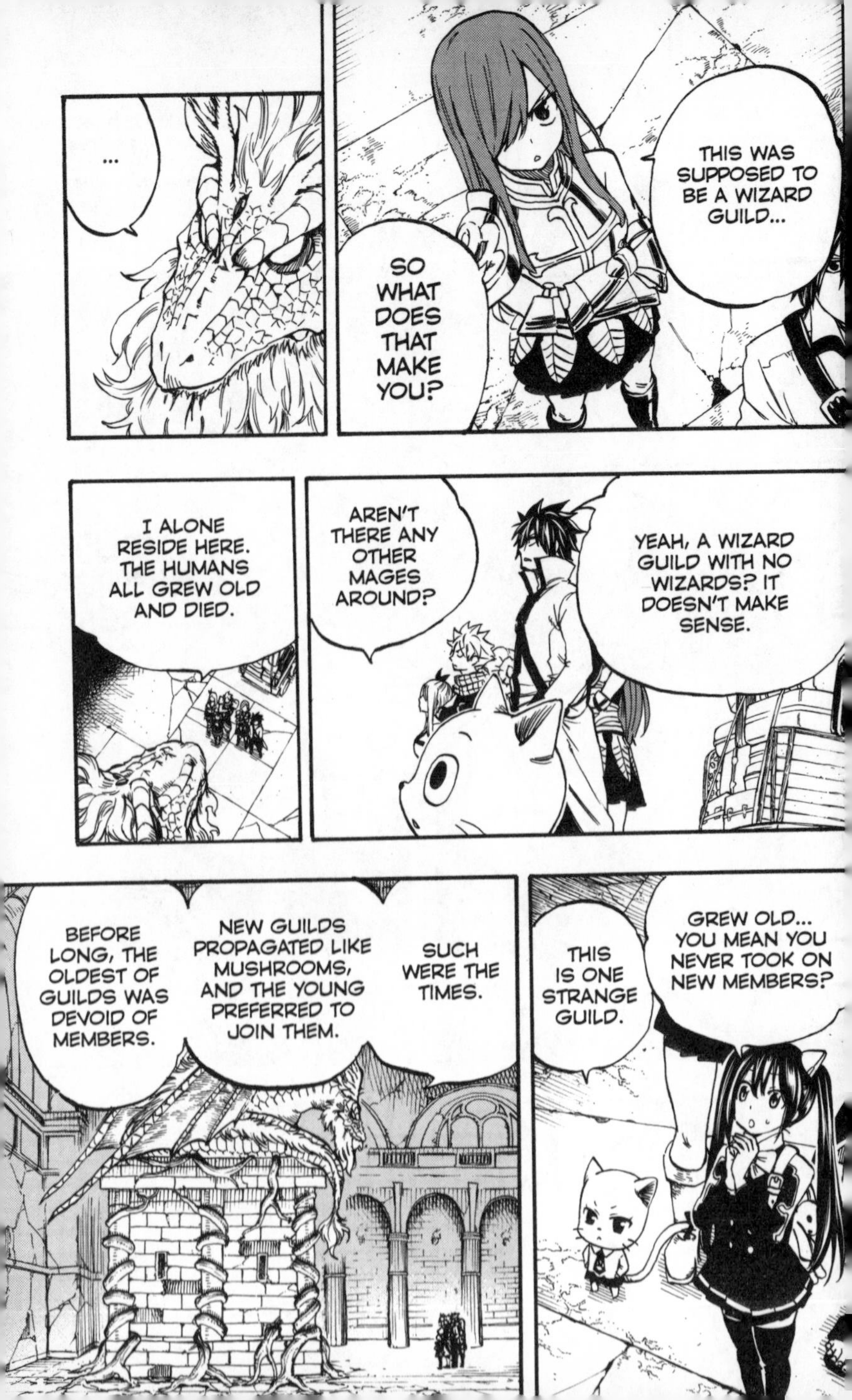
THIS WAS SUPPOSED TO BE A WIZARD GUILD...
SO WHAT DOES THAT MAKE YOU?
...
YEAH, A WIZARD GUILD WITH NO WIZARDS? IT DOESN'T MAKE SENSE.
AREN'T THERE ANY OTHER MAGES AROUND?
I ALONE RESIDE HERE. THE HUMANS ALL GREW OLD AND DIED.
GREW OLD... YOU MEAN YOU NEVER TOOK ON NEW MEMBERS?
THIS IS ONE STRANGE GUILD.
SUCH WERE THE TIMES.
NEW GUILDS PROPAGATED LIKE MUSHROOMS, AND THE YOUNG PREFERRED TO JOIN THEM.
BEFORE LONG, THE OLDEST OF GUILDS WAS DEVOID OF MEMBERS.

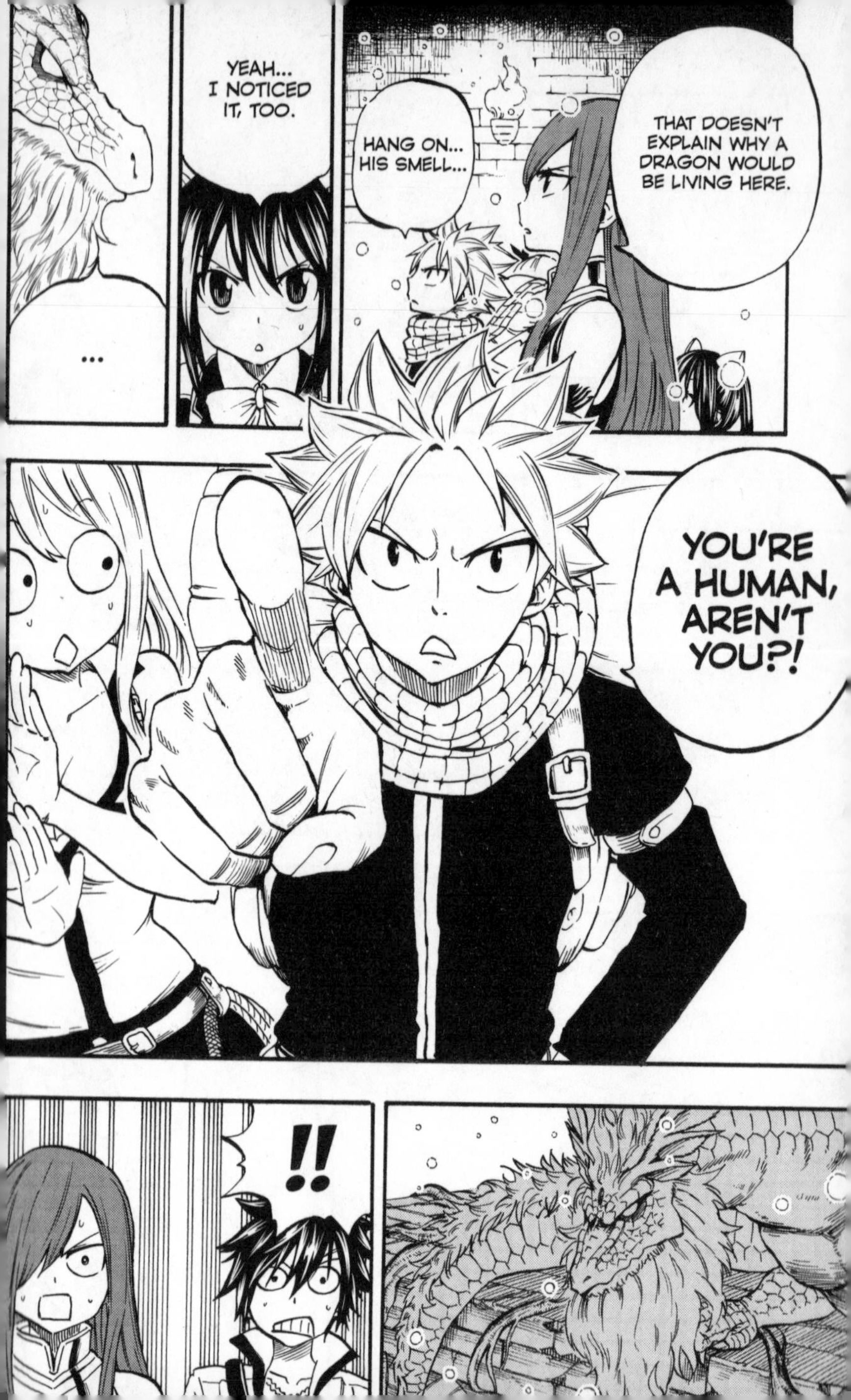
THAT DOESN'T EXPLAIN WHY A DRAGON WOULD BE LIVING HERE.
HANG ON... HIS SMELL...
YEAH... I NOTICED IT, TOO.
...
YOU'RE A HUMAN, AREN'T YOU?!
!!

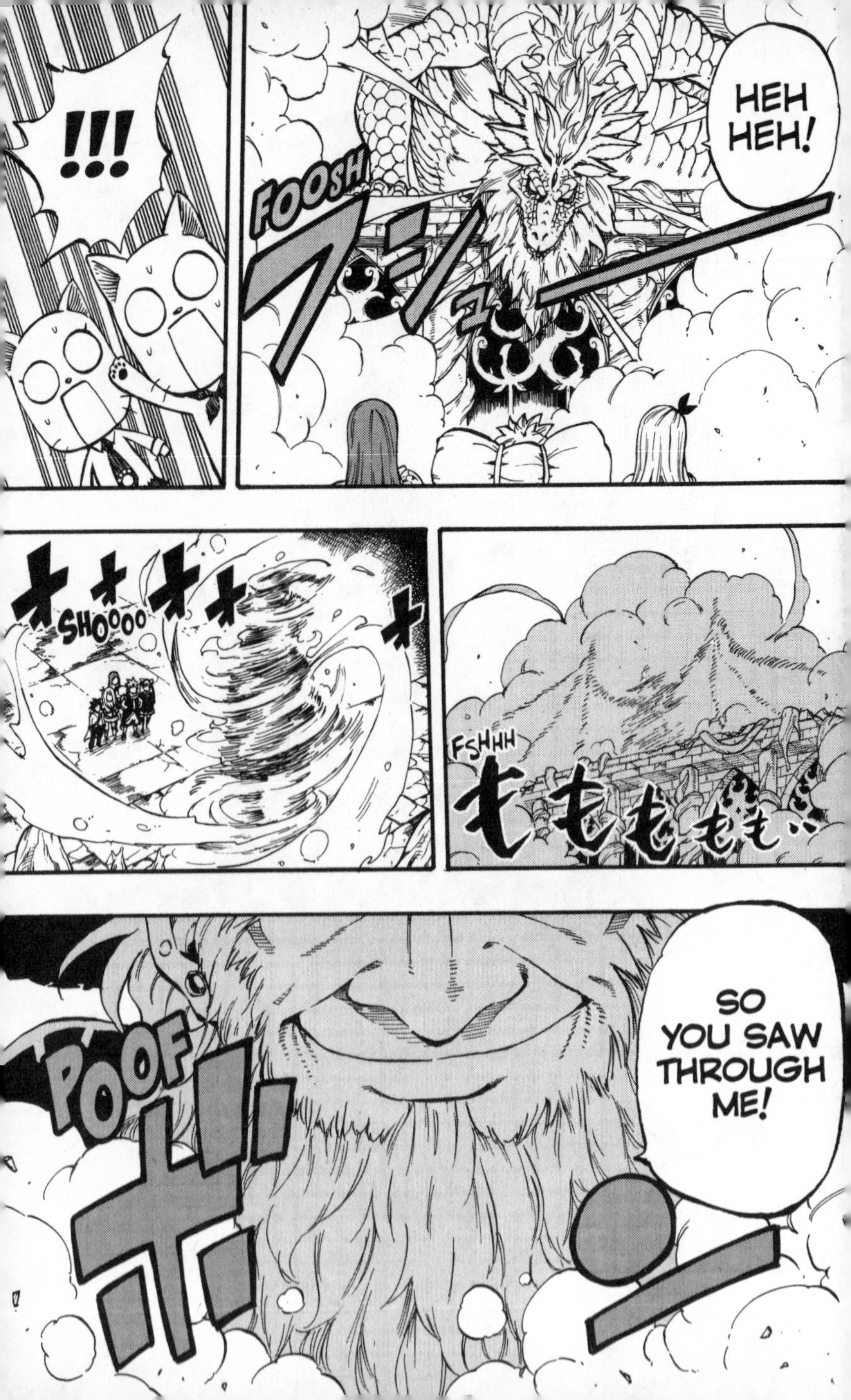
HEH HEH!
FOOSH
!!!
FSHHH
SHOOOO
SO YOU SAW THROUGH ME!
POOF

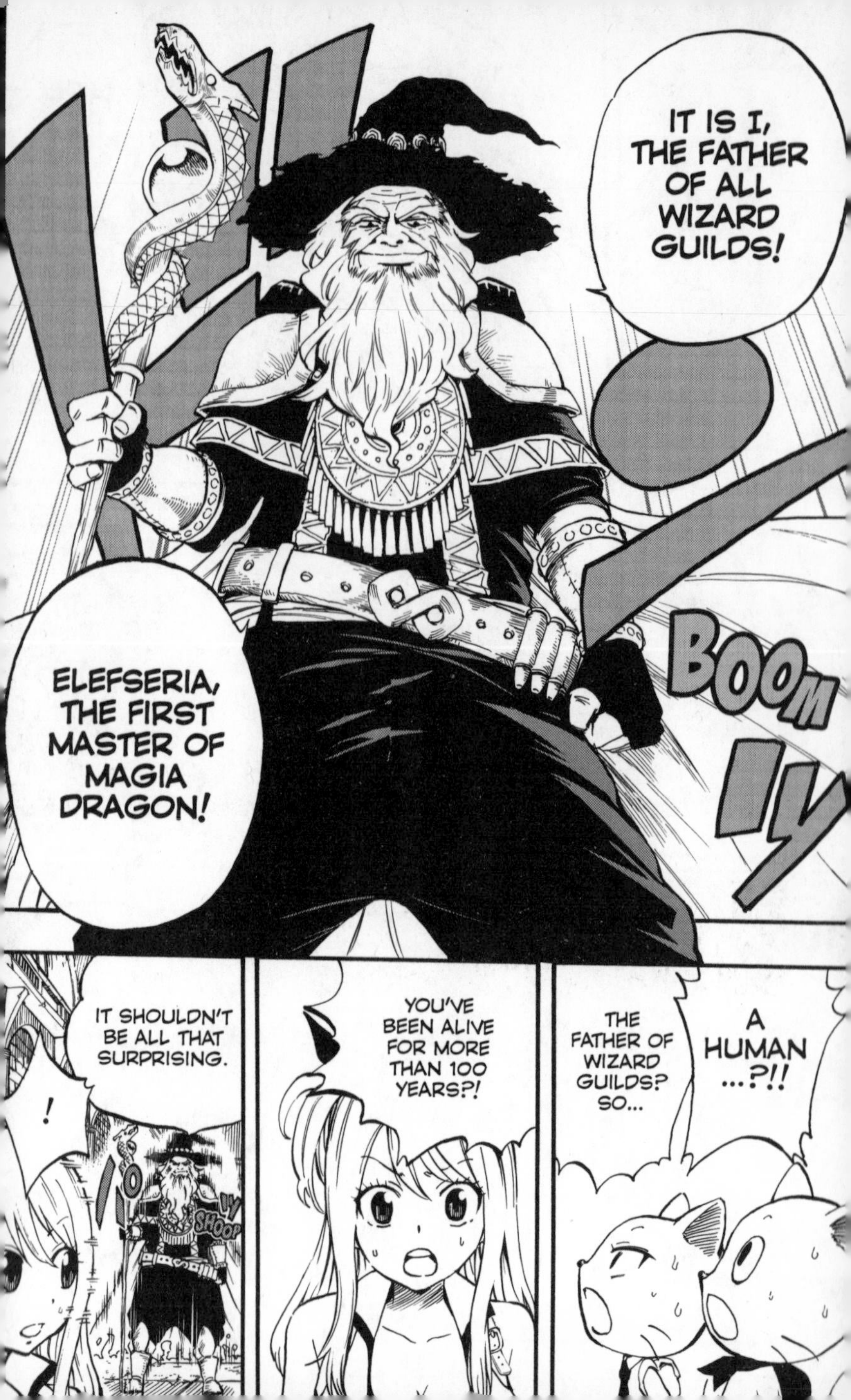
IT IS I, THE FATHER OF ALL WIZARD GUILDS!
BOOM
ELEFSERIA, THE FIRST MASTER OF MAGIA DRAGON!
THE FATHER OF WIZARD GUILDS? SO...
A HUMAN ...?!!
YOU'VE BEEN ALIVE FOR MORE THAN 100 YEARS?!
IT SHOULDN'T BE ALL THAT SURPRISING.
!
SHOOP

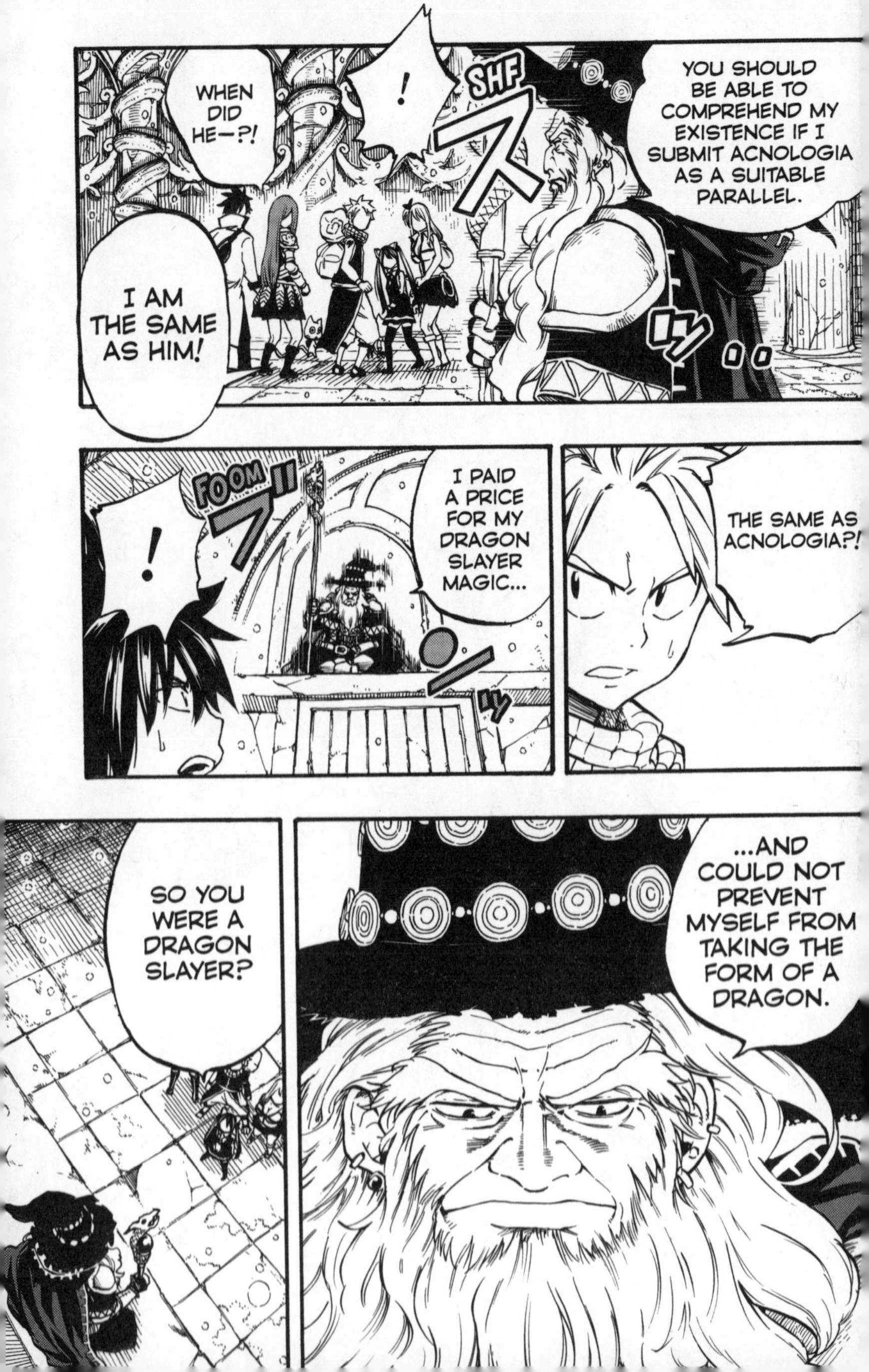
YOU SHOULD BE ABLE TO COMPREHEND MY EXISTENCE IF I SUBMIT ACNOLOGIA AS A SUITABLE PARALLEL.
SHF
!
WHEN DID HE—?!
I AM THE SAME AS HIM!
THE SAME AS ACNOLOGIA?!
I PAID A PRICE FOR MY DRAGON SLAYER MAGIC...
FOOM
!
...AND COULD NOT PREVENT MYSELF FROM TAKING THE FORM OF A DRAGON.
SO YOU WERE A DRAGON SLAYER?

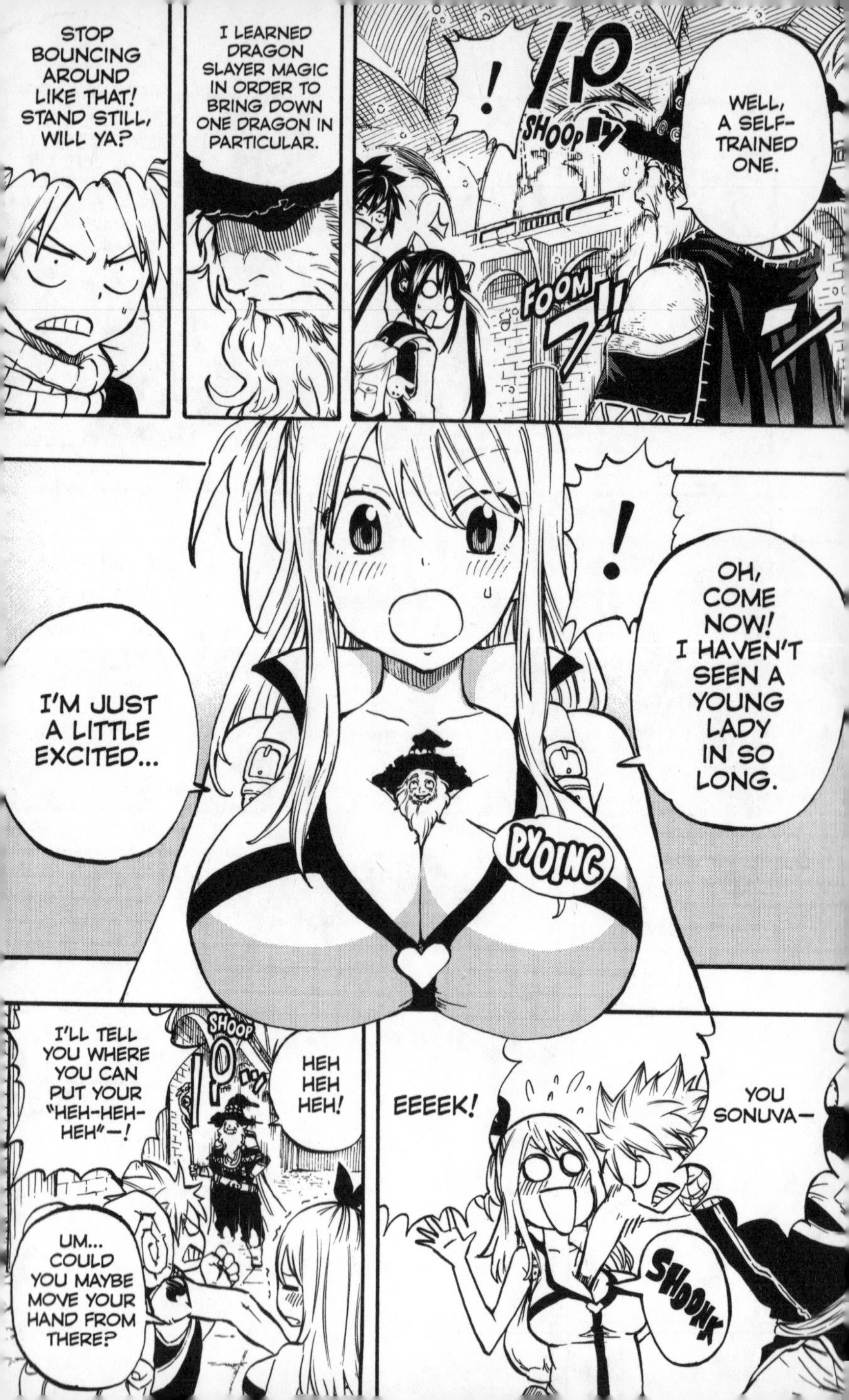
WELL, A SELF-TRAINED ONE.
!
SHOOP
FOOM
I LEARNED DRAGON SLAYER MAGIC IN ORDER TO BRING DOWN ONE DRAGON IN PARTICULAR.
STOP BOUNCING AROUND LIKE THAT! STAND STILL, WILL YA?
!
OH, COME NOW! I HAVEN'T SEEN A YOUNG LADY IN SO LONG.
PYOING
I'M JUST A LITTLE EXCITED...
YOU SONUVA—
EEEEK!
SHOOK
HEH HEH HEH!
I'LL TELL YOU WHERE YOU CAN PUT YOUR "HEH-HEH-HEH"—!
SHOOP
UM... COULD YOU MAYBE MOVE YOUR HAND FROM THERE?

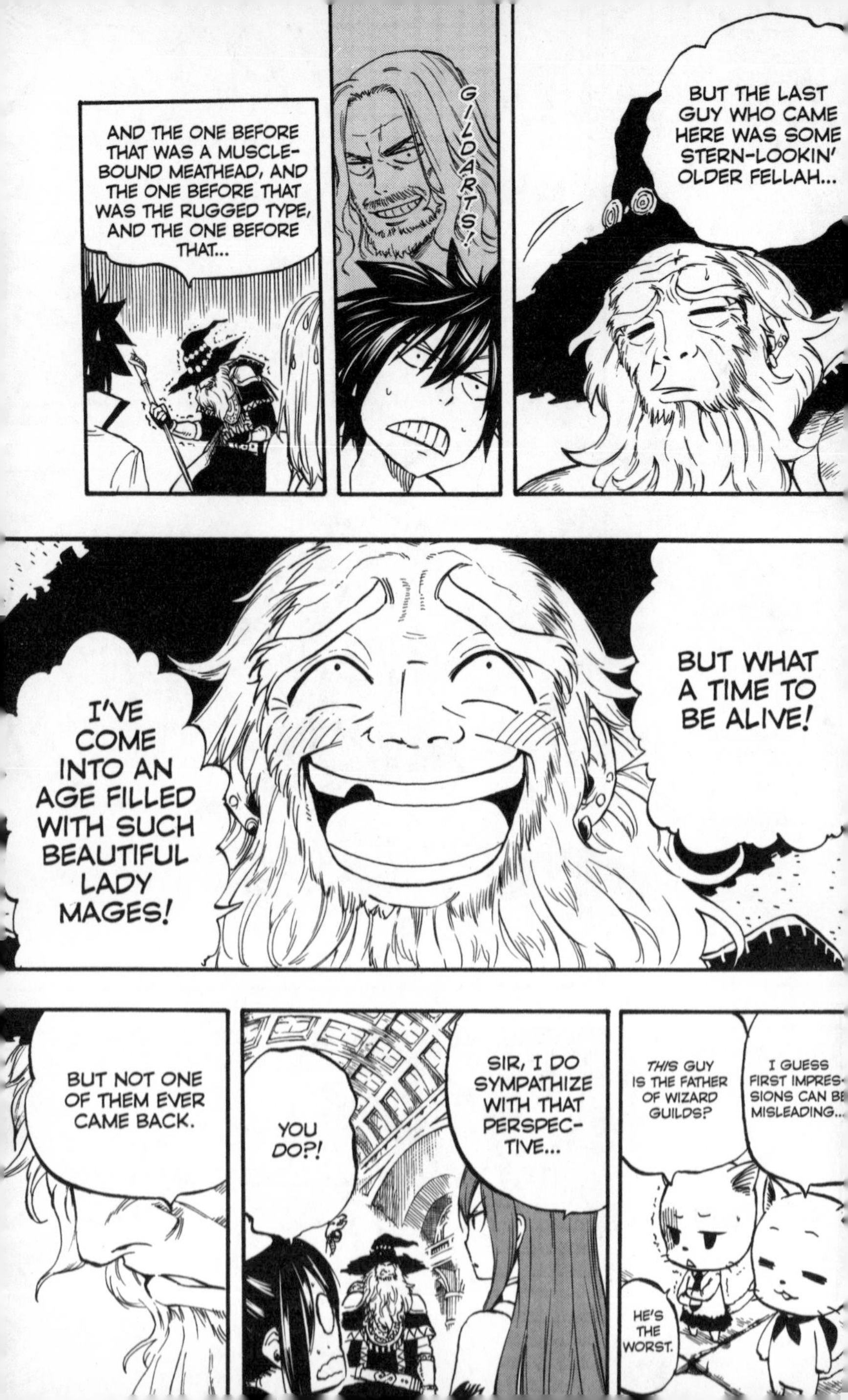
BUT THE LAST GUY WHO CAME HERE WAS SOME STERN-LOOKIN' OLDER FELLAH...
GILDARTS!
AND THE ONE BEFORE THAT WAS A MUSCLE-BOUND MEATHEAD, AND THE ONE BEFORE THAT WAS THE RUGGED TYPE, AND THE ONE BEFORE THAT...
BUT WHAT A TIME TO BE ALIVE!
I'VE COME INTO AN AGE FILLED WITH SUCH BEAUTIFUL LADY MAGES!
I GUESS FIRST IMPRES-SIONS CAN BE MISLEADING...
THIS GUY IS THE FATHER OF WIZARD GUILDS?
HE'S THE WORST.
SIR, I DO SYMPATHIZE WITH THAT PERSPEC-TIVE...
YOU *DO*?!
BUT NOT ONE OF THEM EVER CAME BACK.

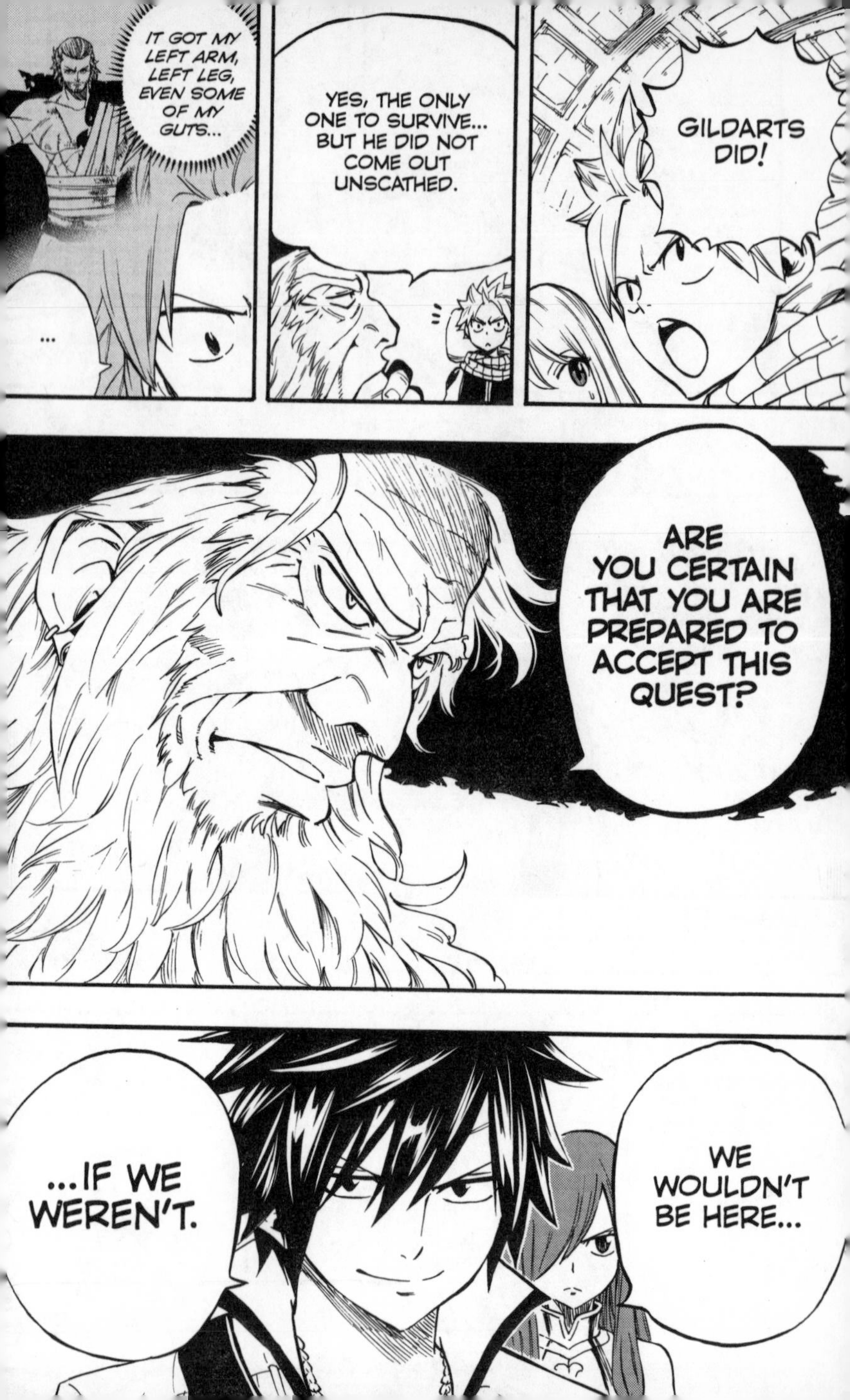
GILDARTS DID!
YES, THE ONLY ONE TO SURVIVE... BUT HE DID NOT COME OUT UNSCATHED.
IT GOT MY LEFT ARM, LEFT LEG, EVEN SOME OF MY GUTS...
...
ARE YOU CERTAIN THAT YOU ARE PREPARED TO ACCEPT THIS QUEST?
WE WOULDN'T BE HERE...
...IF WE WEREN'T.

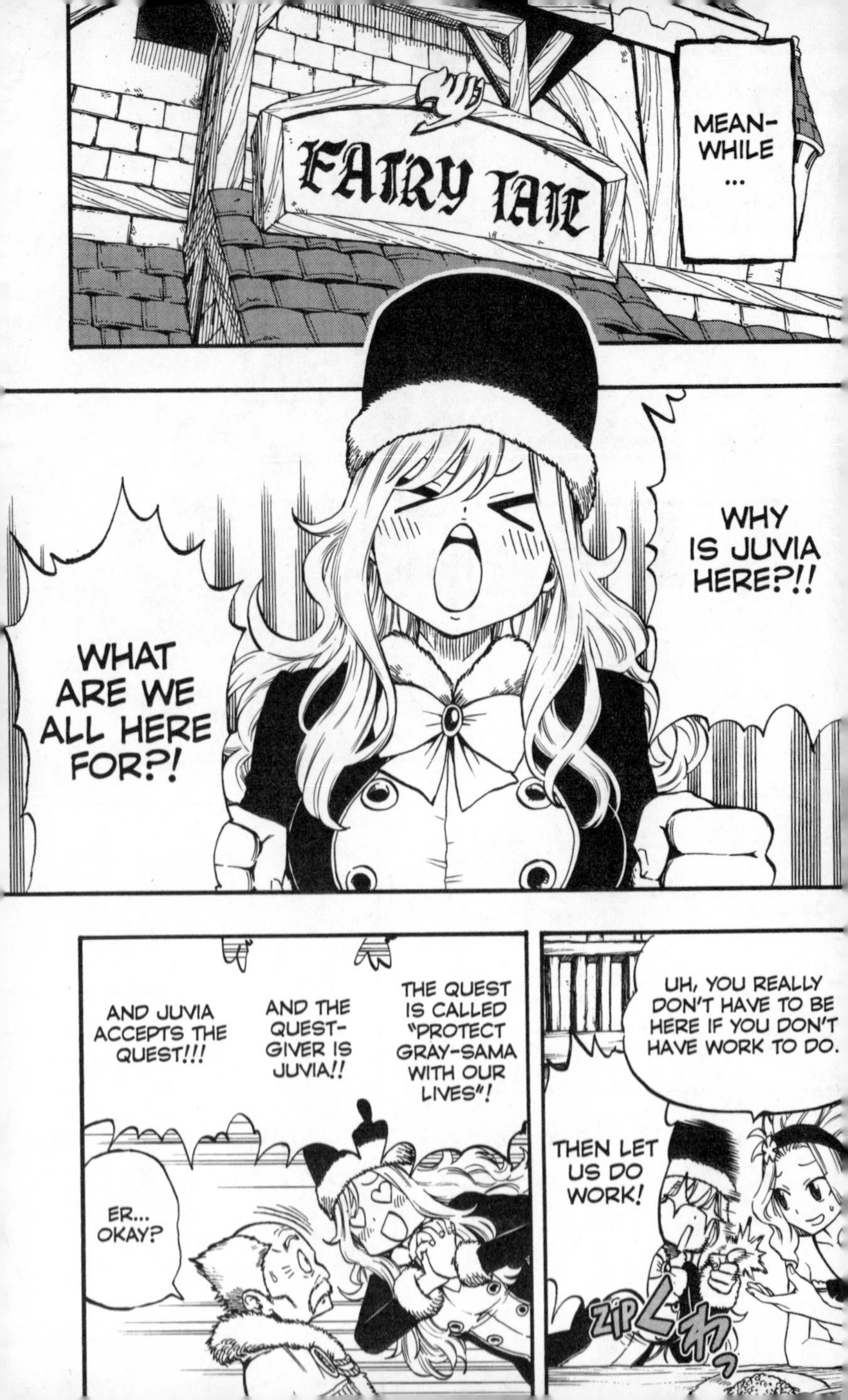
FAIRY TAIL
MEAN-WHILE ...
WHY IS JUVIA HERE?!!
WHAT ARE WE ALL HERE FOR?!
UH, YOU REALLY DON'T HAVE TO BE HERE IF YOU DON'T HAVE WORK TO DO.
THEN LET US DO WORK!
ZIP
くわっ
THE QUEST IS CALLED "PROTECT GRAY-SAMA WITH OUR LIVES"!
AND THE QUEST-GIVER IS JUVIA!!
AND JUVIA ACCEPTS THE QUEST!!!
ER... OKAY?

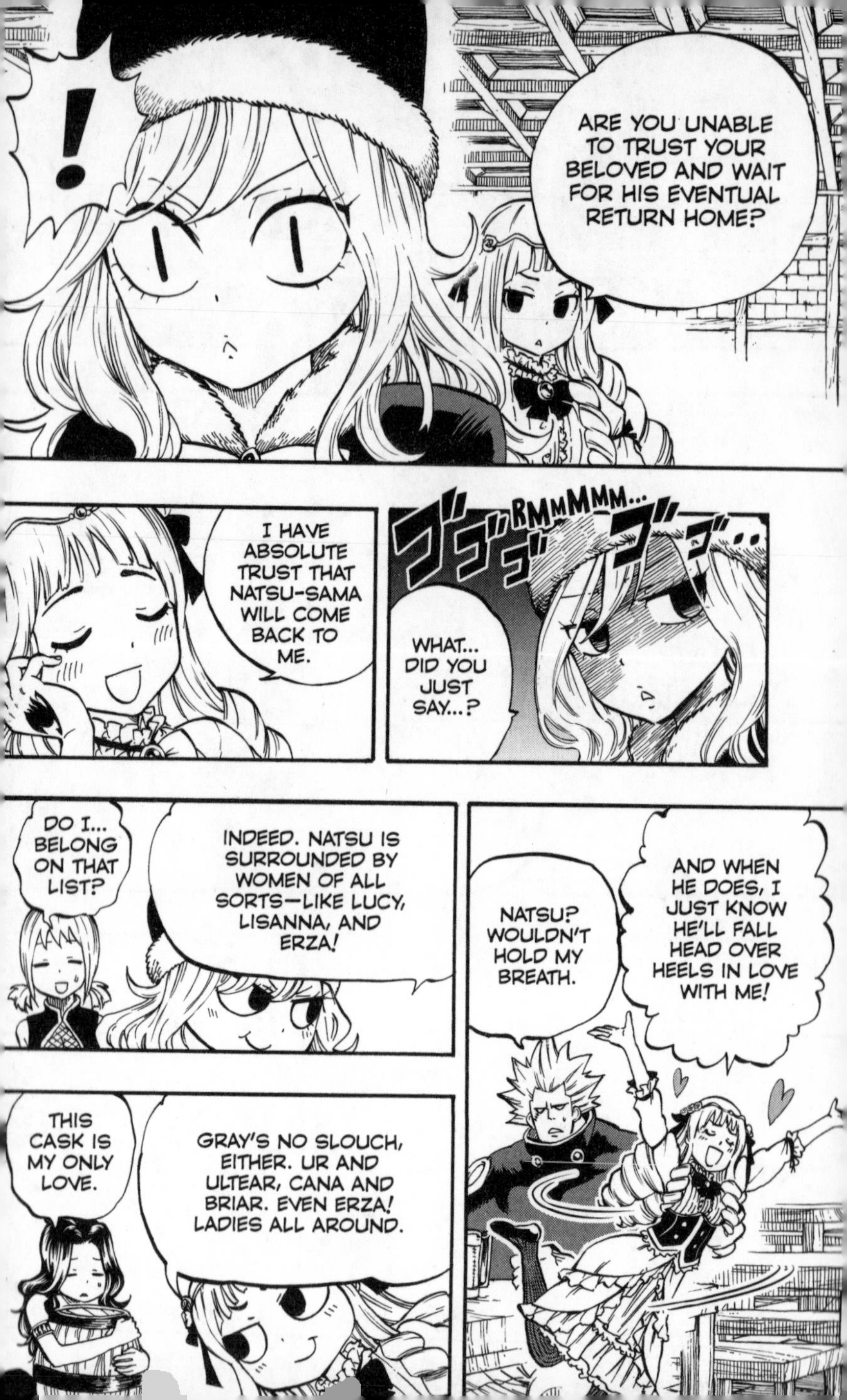
ARE YOU UNABLE TO TRUST YOUR BELOVED AND WAIT FOR HIS EVENTUAL RETURN HOME?
!
RMMMMM...
WHAT... DID YOU JUST SAY...?
I HAVE ABSOLUTE TRUST THAT NATSU-SAMA WILL COME BACK TO ME.
AND WHEN HE DOES, I JUST KNOW HE'LL FALL HEAD OVER HEELS IN LOVE WITH ME!
NATSU? WOULDN'T HOLD MY BREATH.
INDEED. NATSU IS SURROUNDED BY WOMEN OF ALL SORTS—LIKE LUCY, LISANNA, AND ERZA!
DO I... BELONG ON THAT LIST?
GRAY'S NO SLOUCH, EITHER. UR AND ULTEAR, CANA AND BRIAR. EVEN ERZA! LADIES ALL AROUND.
THIS CASK IS MY ONLY LOVE.

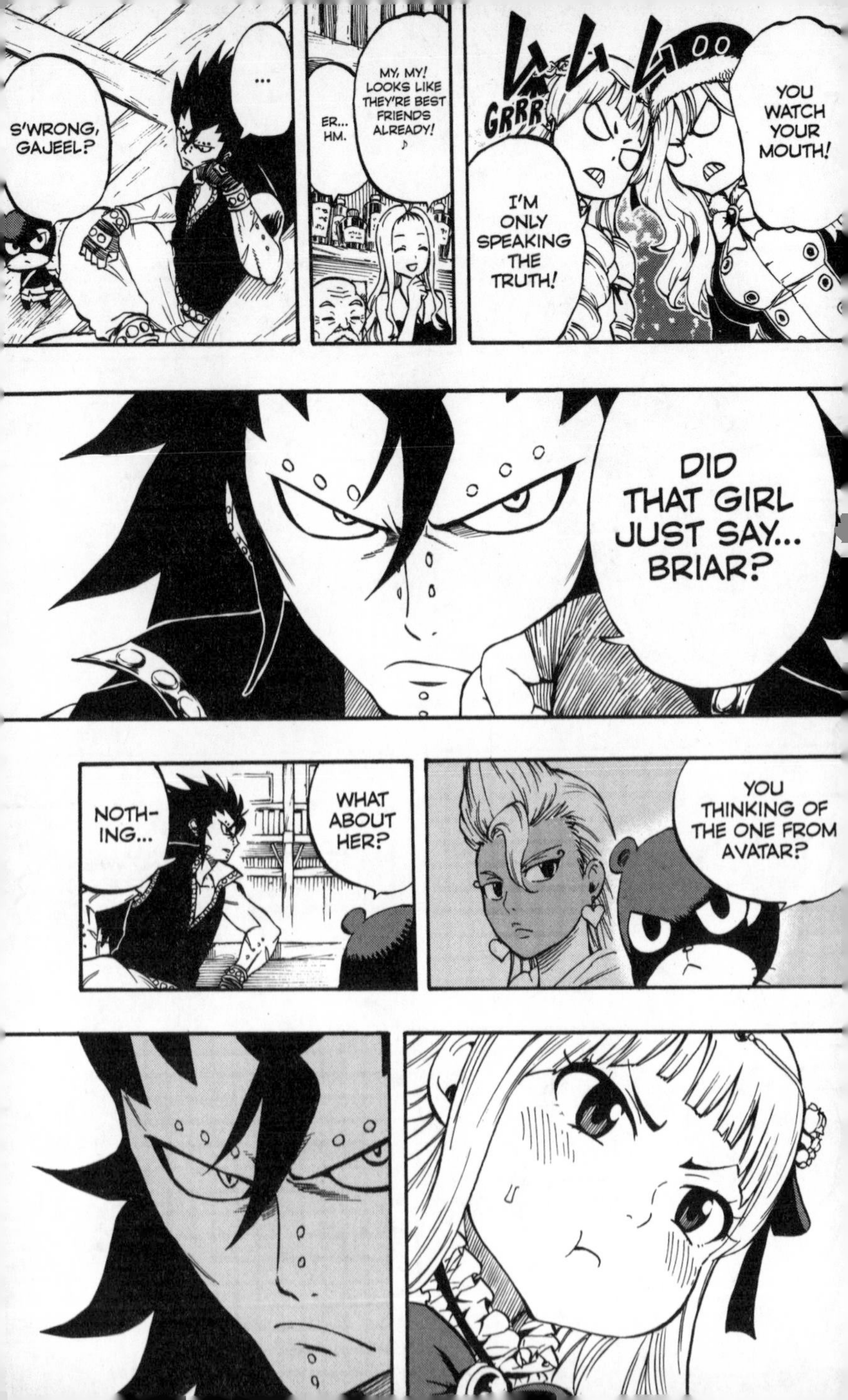
ムムム
GRRR
YOU WATCH YOUR MOUTH!
I'M ONLY SPEAKING THE TRUTH!
MY, MY! LOOKS LIKE THEY'RE BEST FRIENDS ALREADY! ♪
ER... HM.
...
S'WRONG, GAJEEL?
DID THAT GIRL JUST SAY... BRIAR?
YOU THINKING OF THE ONE FROM AVATAR?
WHAT ABOUT HER?
NOTHING...

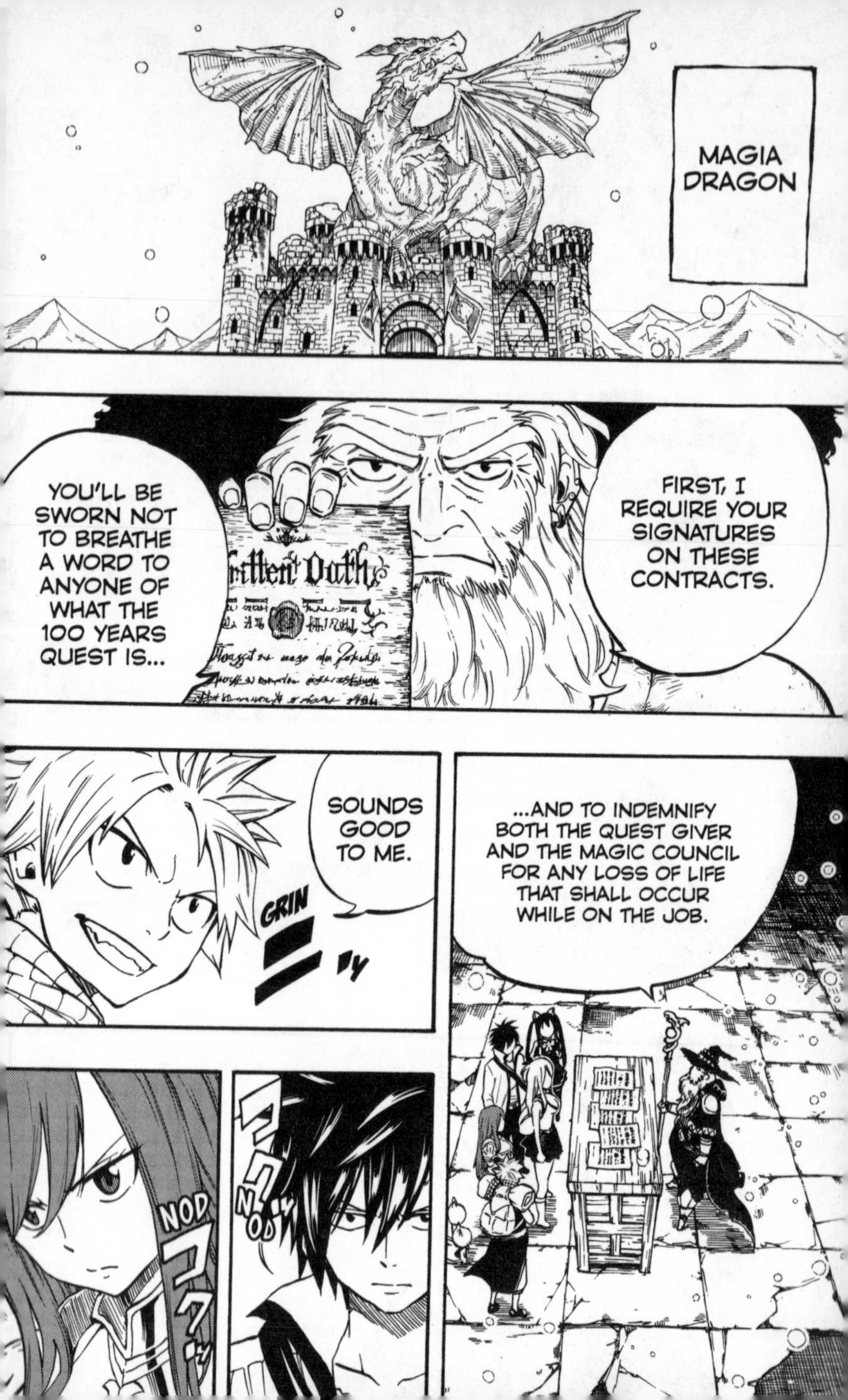
MAGIA DRAGON
FIRST, I REQUIRE YOUR SIGNATURES ON THESE CONTRACTS.
YOU'LL BE SWORN NOT TO BREATHE A WORD TO ANYONE OF WHAT THE 100 YEARS QUEST IS...
...AND TO INDEMNIFY BOTH THE QUEST GIVER AND THE MAGIC COUNCIL FOR ANY LOSS OF LIFE THAT SHALL OCCUR WHILE ON THE JOB.
SOUNDS GOOD TO ME.
GRIN
NOD
NOD

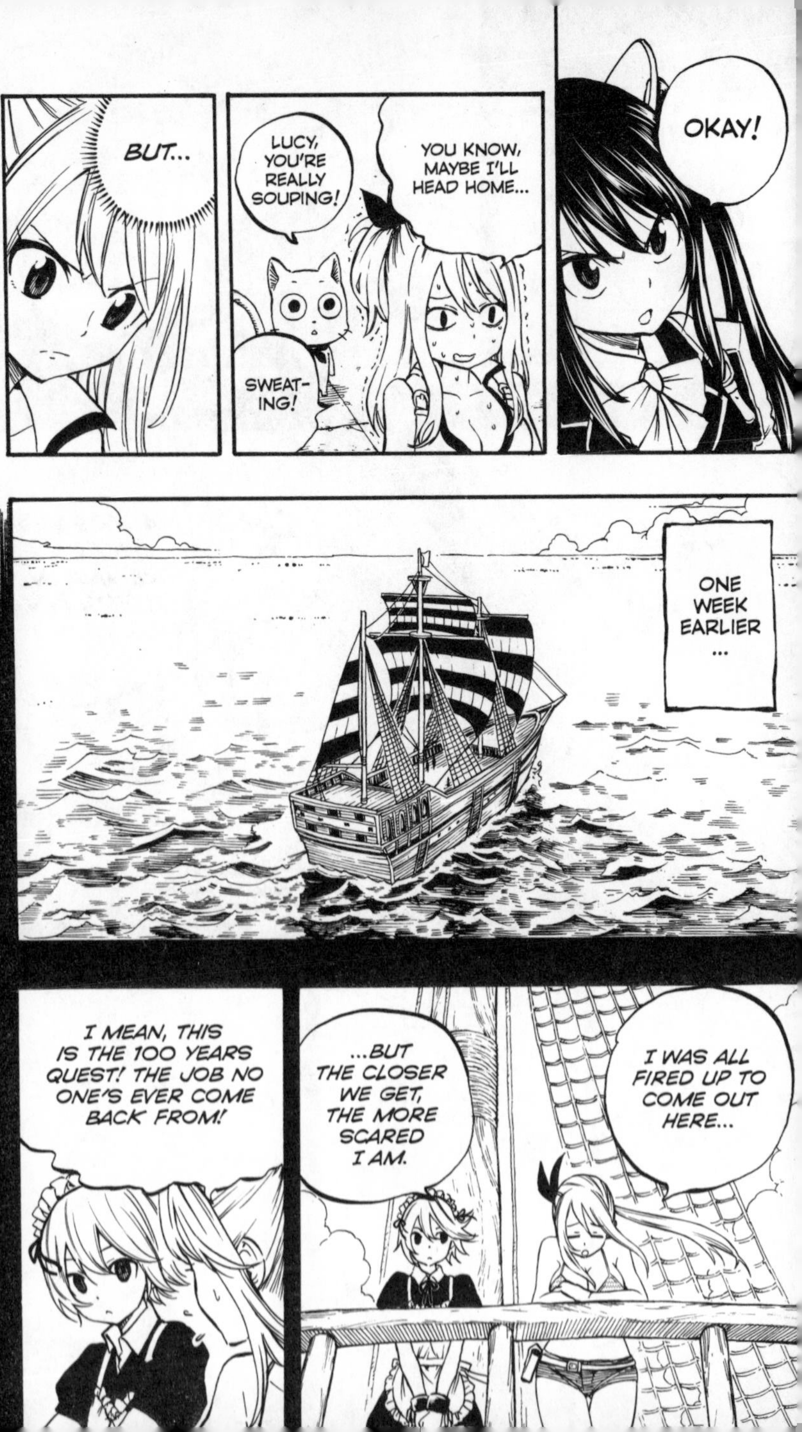
OKAY!
YOU KNOW, MAYBE I'LL HEAD HOME...
LUCY, YOU'RE REALLY SOUPING!
SWEAT-ING!
BUT...
ONE WEEK EARLIER ...
I WAS ALL FIRED UP TO COME OUT HERE...
...BUT THE CLOSER WE GET, THE MORE SCARED I AM.
I MEAN, THIS IS THE 100 YEARS QUEST! THE JOB NO ONE'S EVER COME BACK FROM!

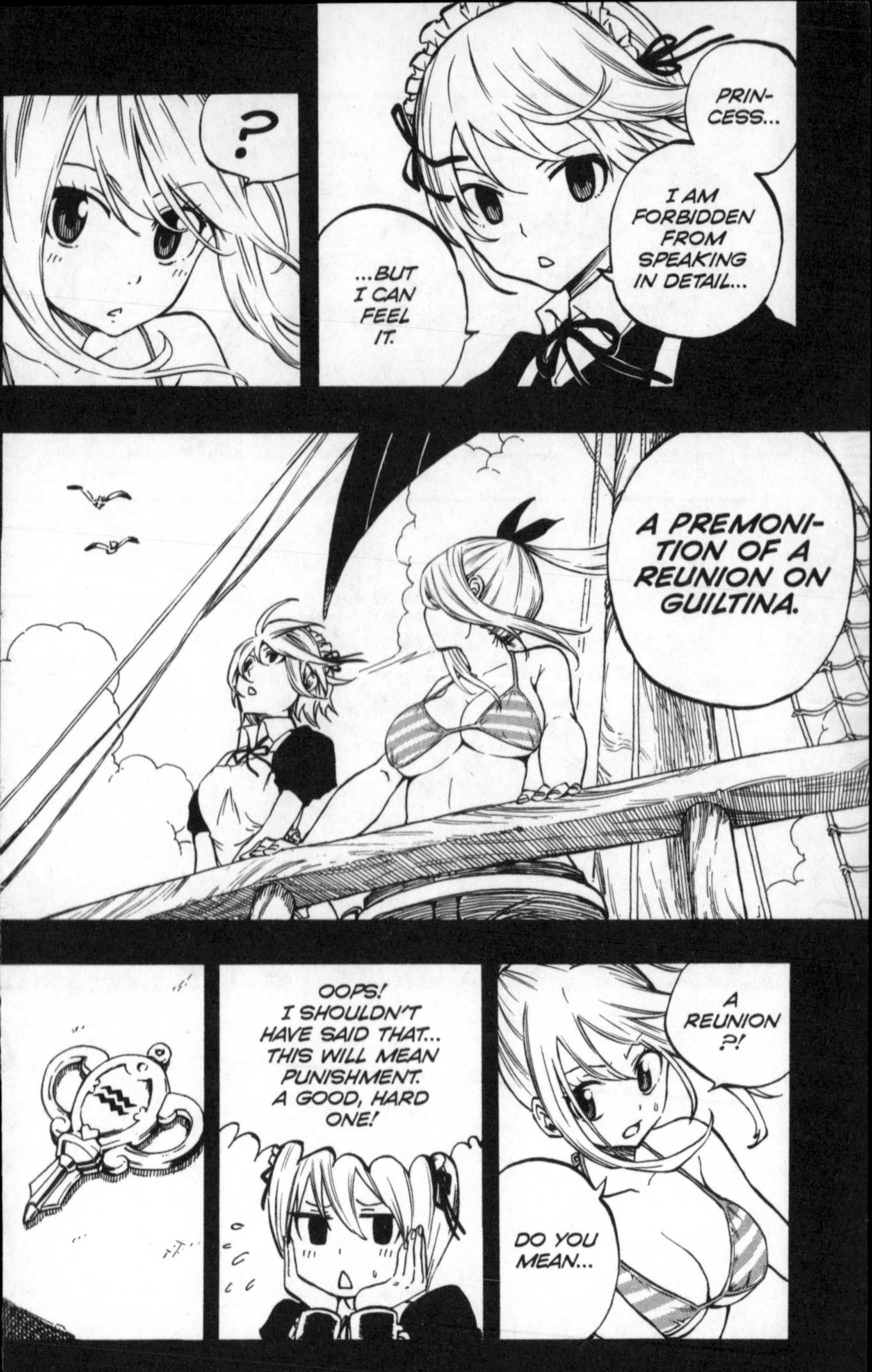
PRIN-CESS...
I AM FORBIDDEN FROM SPEAKING IN DETAIL...
...BUT I CAN FEEL IT.
?
A PREMONI-TION OF A REUNION ON GUILTINA.
A REUNION ?!
DO YOU MEAN...
OOPS! I SHOULDN'T HAVE SAID THAT... THIS WILL MEAN PUNISHMENT. A GOOD, HARD ONE!

SKRITCH

I'M GOING FOR IT!

AFTER ALL, MY FRIENDS WILL BE WITH ME!!

NAME *Lucy Heartfilia*

NOW, SPILL IT!

TELL US ALL ABOUT THE 100 YEARS QUEST!

PING

Written Oaths

Lucy Heartfilia

VERY WELL.

SHFF

IT'S PATENTLY SIMPLE.

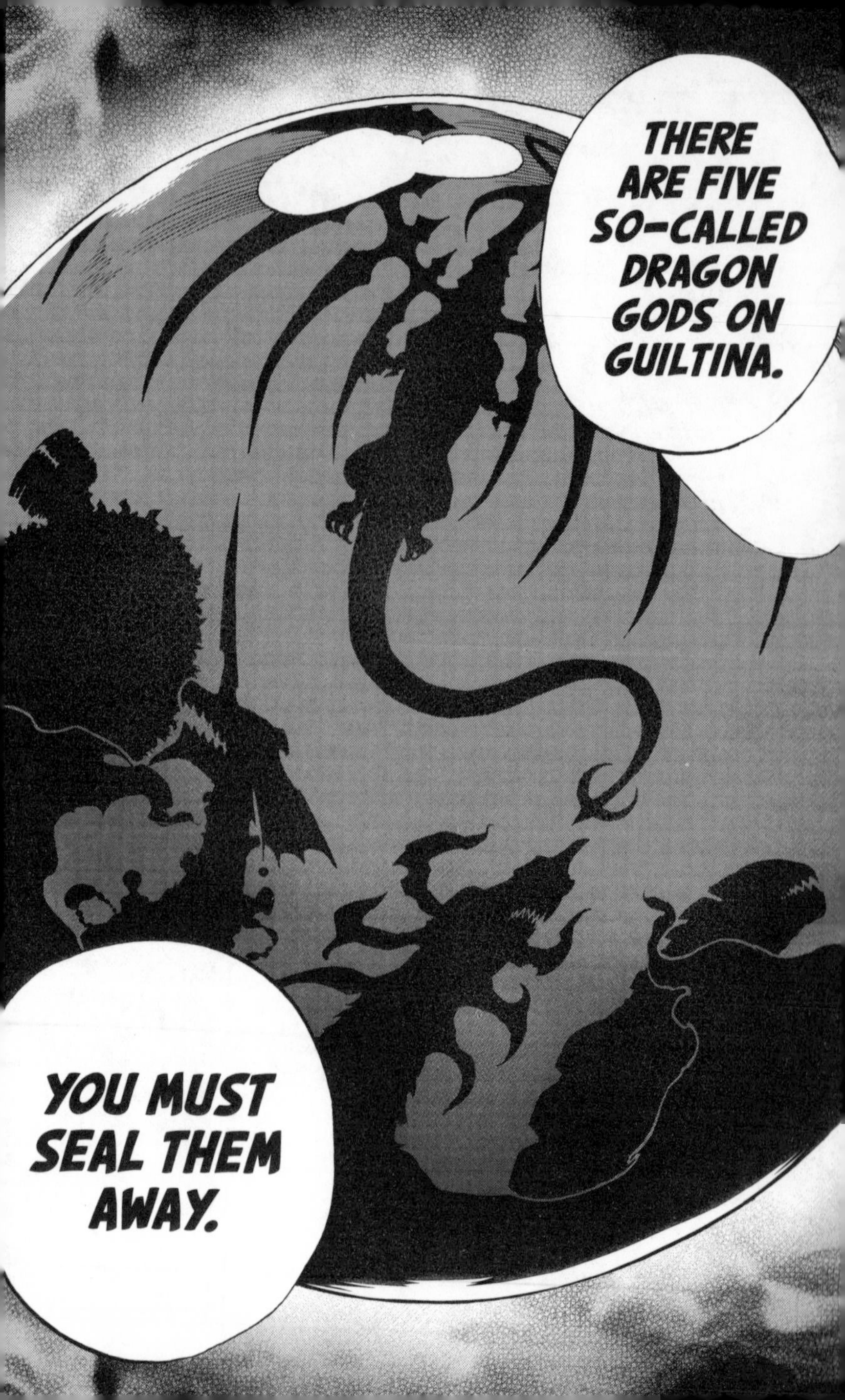
THERE ARE FIVE SO-CALLED DRAGON GODS ON GUILTINA.
YOU MUST SEAL THEM AWAY.

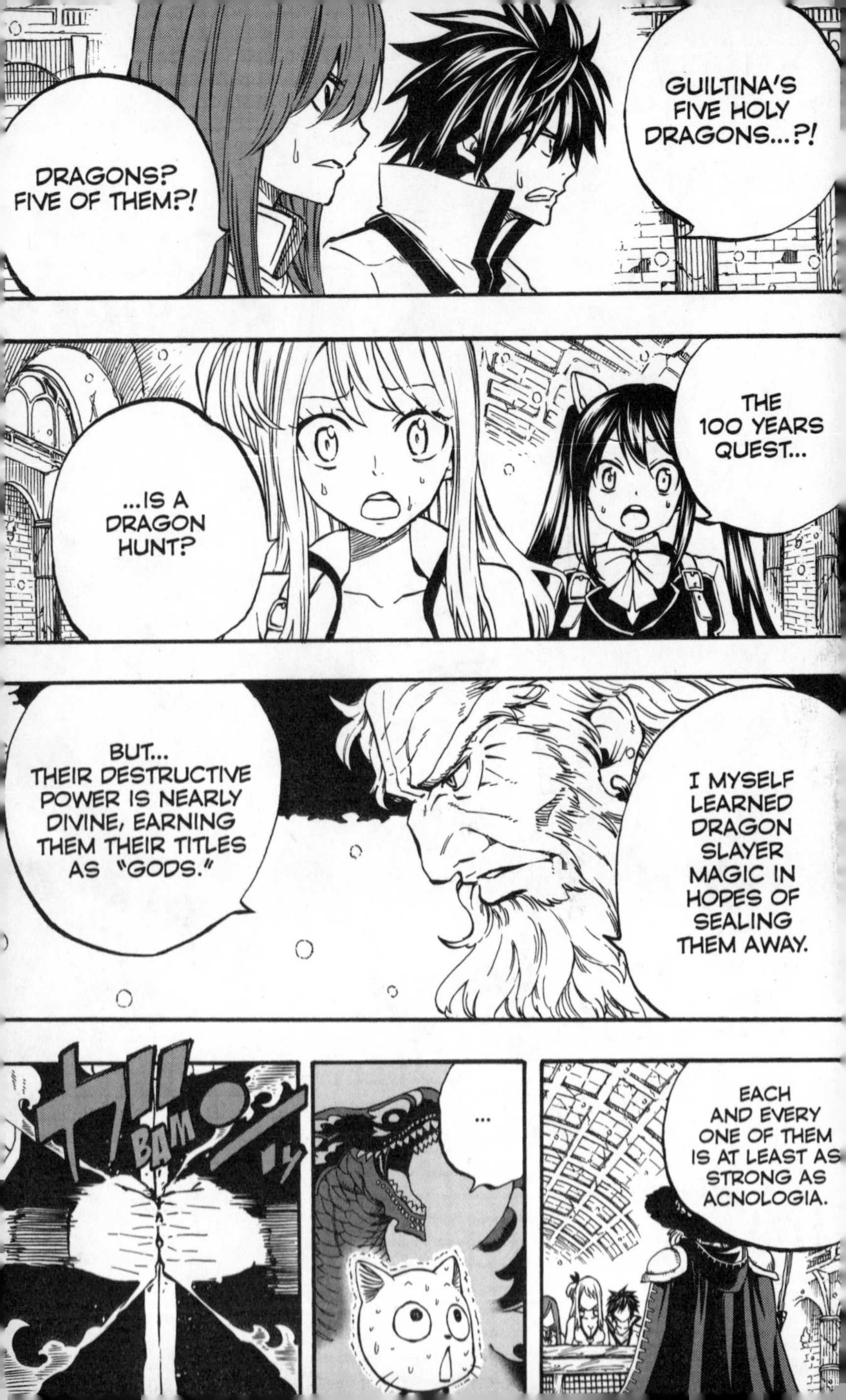
GUILTINA'S FIVE HOLY DRAGONS...?!
DRAGONS? FIVE OF THEM?!
THE 100 YEARS QUEST...
...IS A DRAGON HUNT?
I MYSELF LEARNED DRAGON SLAYER MAGIC IN HOPES OF SEALING THEM AWAY.
BUT... THEIR DESTRUCTIVE POWER IS NEARLY DIVINE, EARNING THEM THEIR TITLES AS "GODS."
EACH AND EVERY ONE OF THEM IS AT LEAST AS STRONG AS ACNOLOGIA.
...
BAM

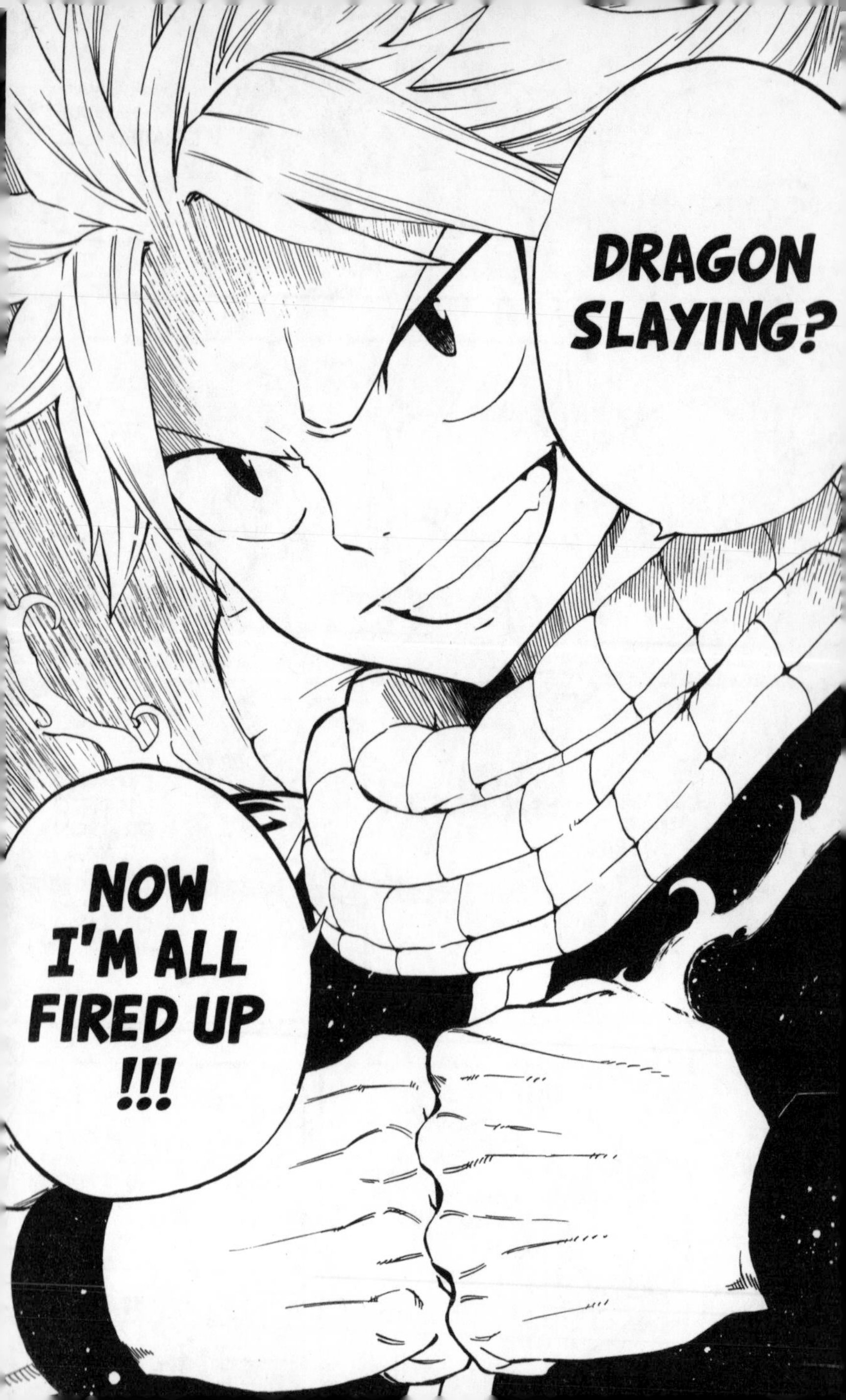
DRAGON SLAYING?
NOW I'M ALL FIRED UP !!!

FAIRY TAIL 100 YEARS QUEST

Chapter 3: The Last Hope

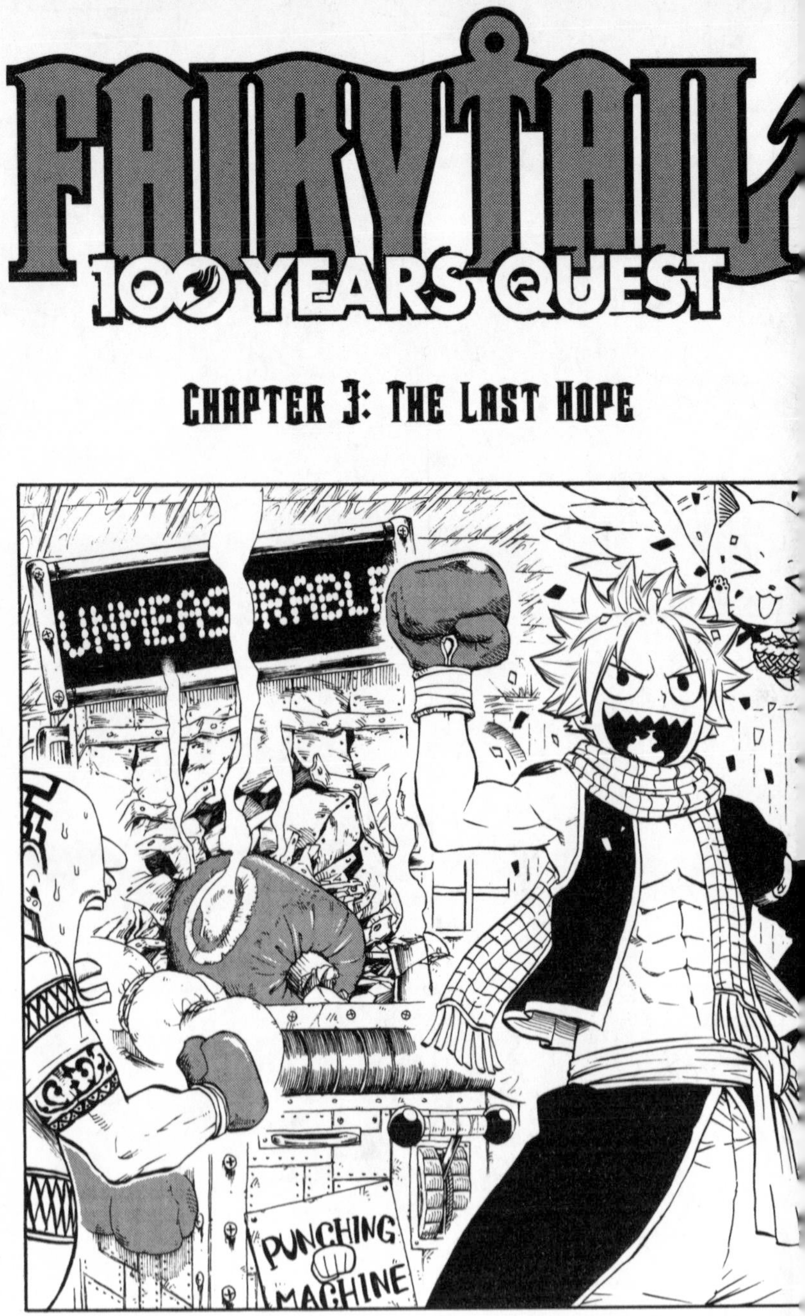
UNMEASURABLE
PUNCHING MACHINE

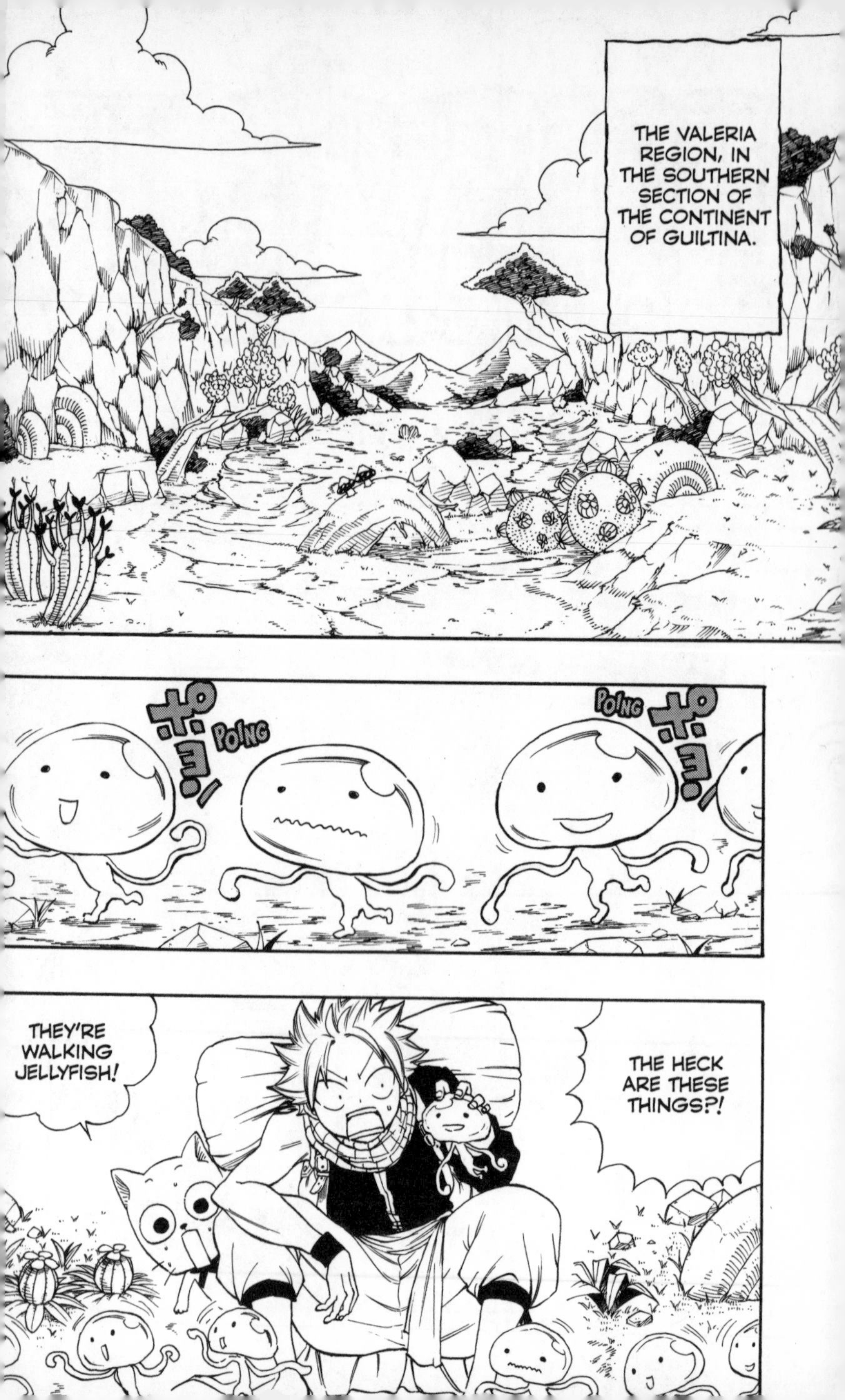
THE VALERIA REGION, IN THE SOUTHERN SECTION OF THE CONTINENT OF GUILTINA.
POING
POING
THE HECK ARE THESE THINGS?!
THEY'RE WALKING JELLYFISH!

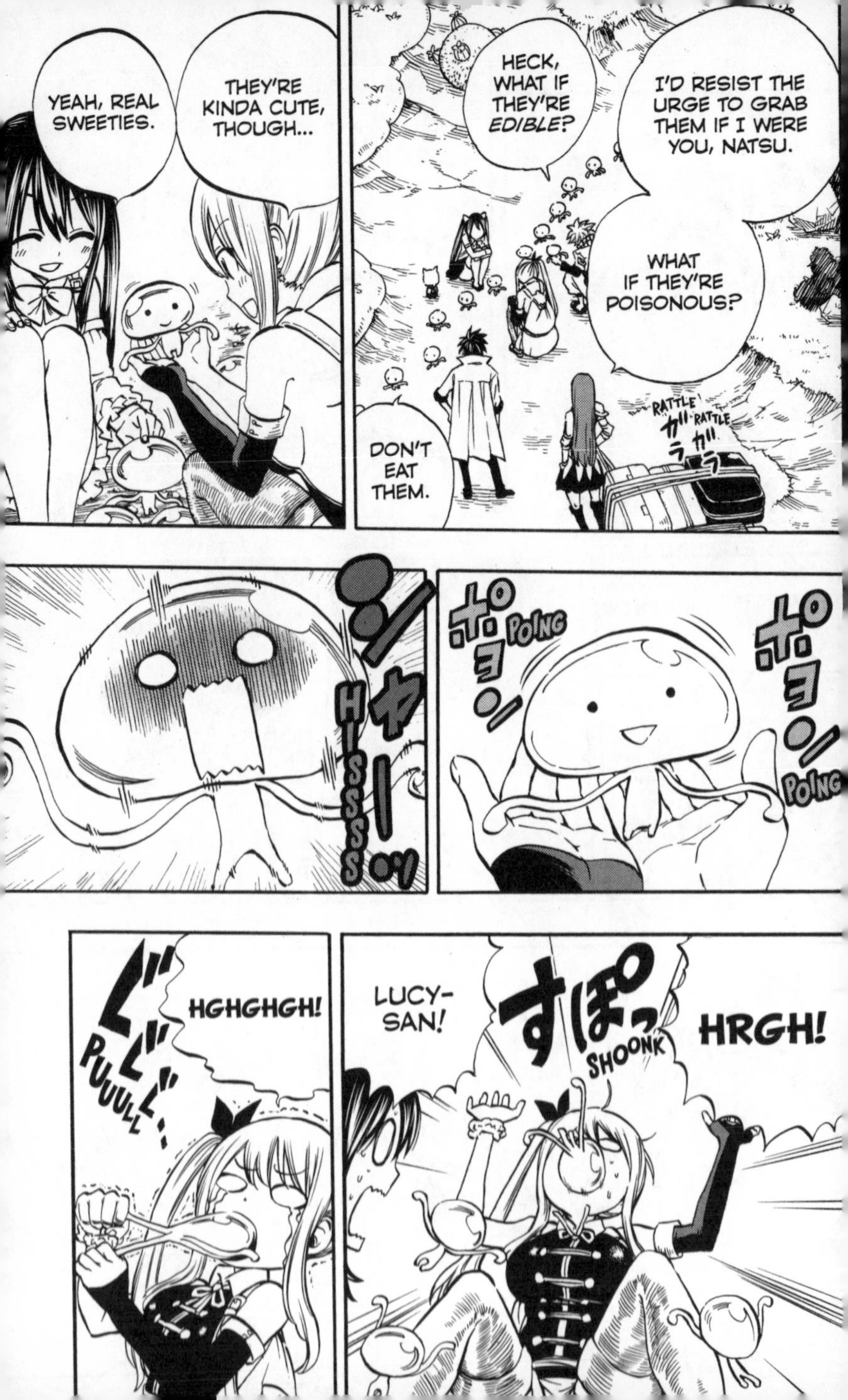
I'D RESIST THE URGE TO GRAB THEM IF I WERE YOU, NATSU.
HECK, WHAT IF THEY'RE *EDIBLE*?
WHAT IF THEY'RE POISONOUS?
ガラ RATTLE ガラ RATTLE
DON'T EAT THEM.
THEY'RE KINDA CUTE, THOUGH...
YEAH, REAL SWEETIES.
ポヨン POING
ポヨン POING
シャー!! HISSS
HRGH!
すぽっ SHOONK
LUCY-SAN!
HGHGHGH!
PUUULL

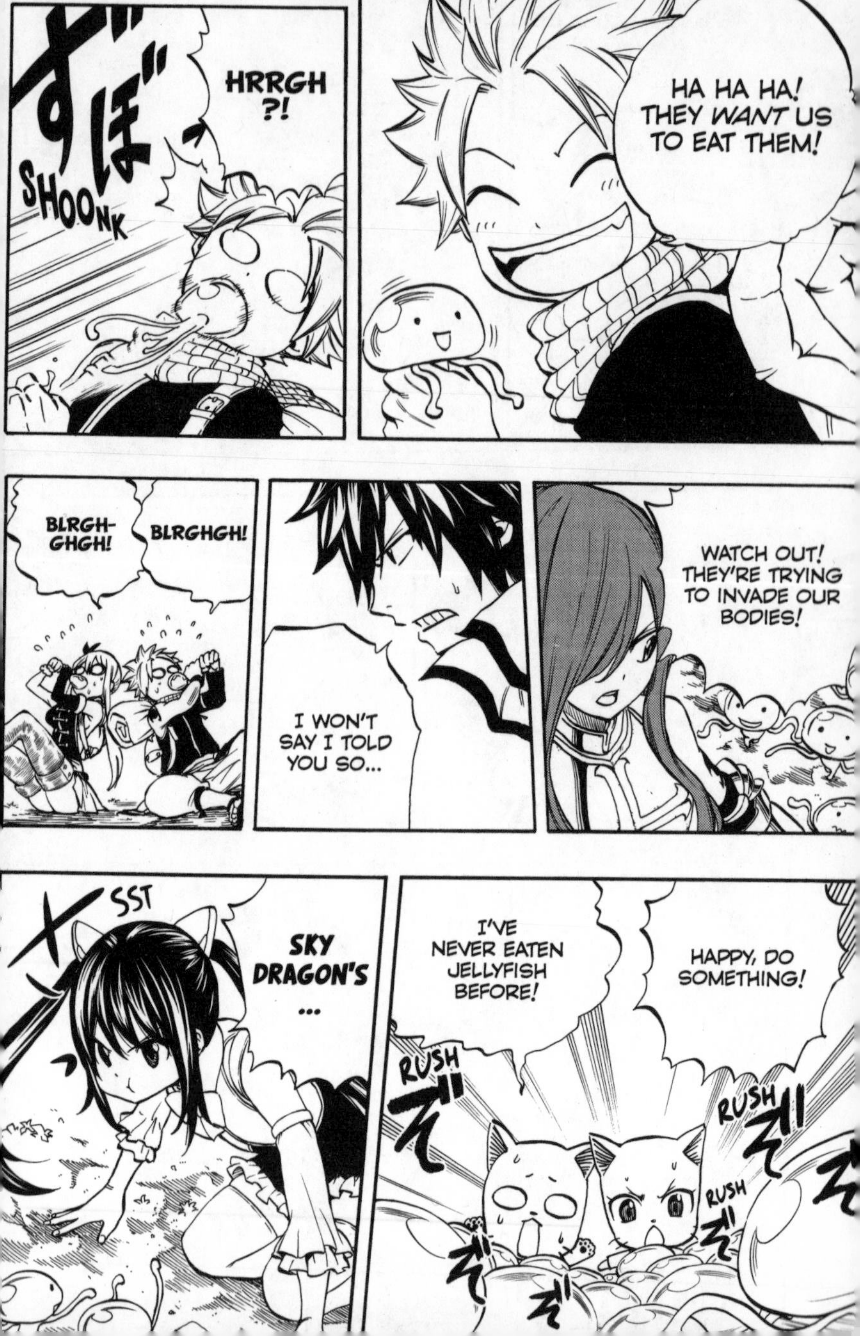
HA HA HA! THEY WANT US TO EAT THEM!
ずぼ
SHOONK
HRRGH ?!
WATCH OUT! THEY'RE TRYING TO INVADE OUR BODIES!
I WON'T SAY I TOLD YOU SO...
BLRGHGH!
BLRGH-GHGH!
HAPPY, DO SOMETHING!
I'VE NEVER EATEN JELLYFISH BEFORE!
RUSH
RUSH
RUSH
SST
SKY DRAGON'S ...

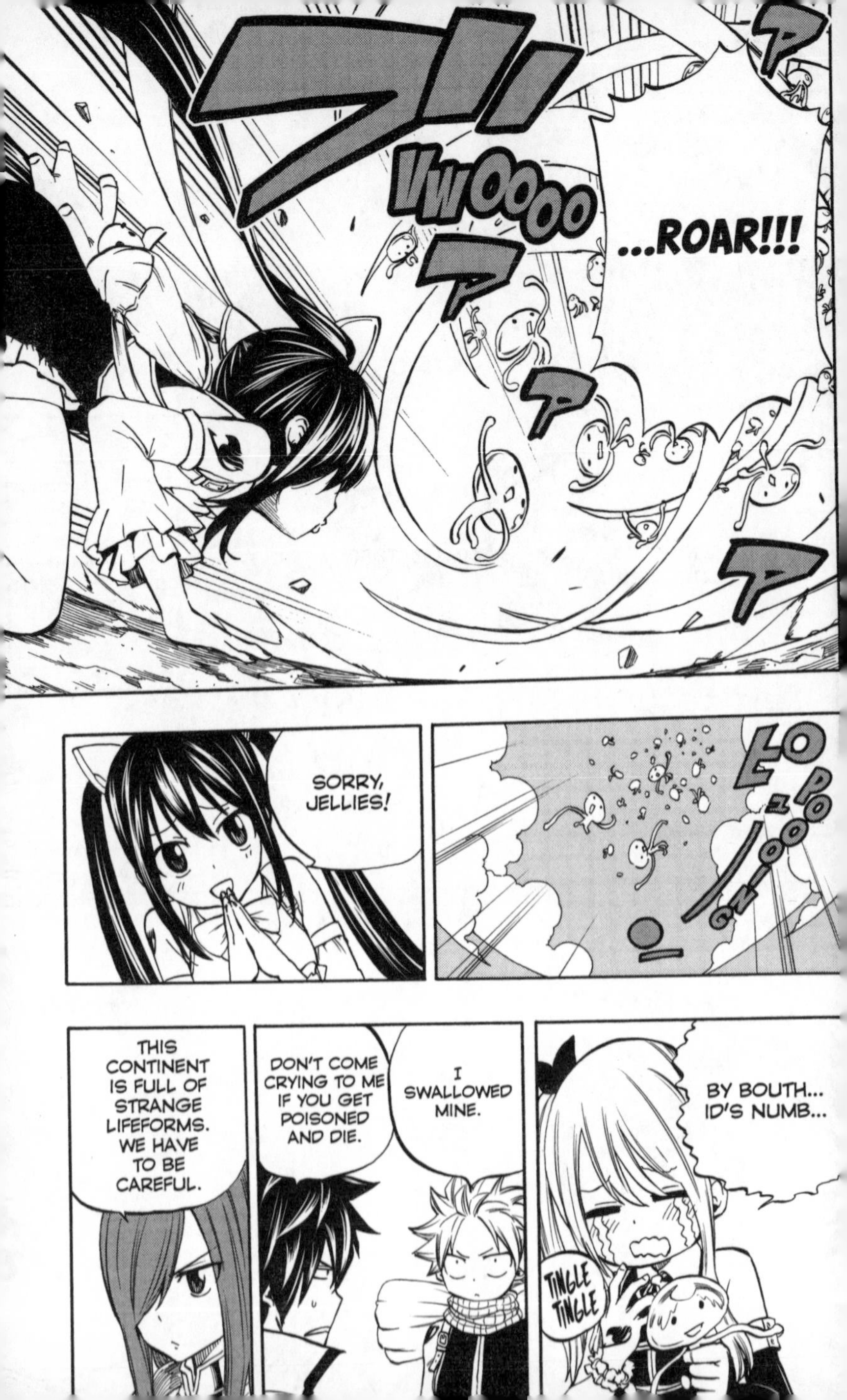
...ROAR!!!
VWOOOO
POOONG
SORRY, JELLIES!
BY BOUTH... ID'S NUMB...
TINGLE TINGLE
I SWALLOWED MINE.
DON'T COME CRYING TO ME IF YOU GET POISONED AND DIE.
THIS CONTINENT IS FULL OF STRANGE LIFEFORMS. WE HAVE TO BE CAREFUL.

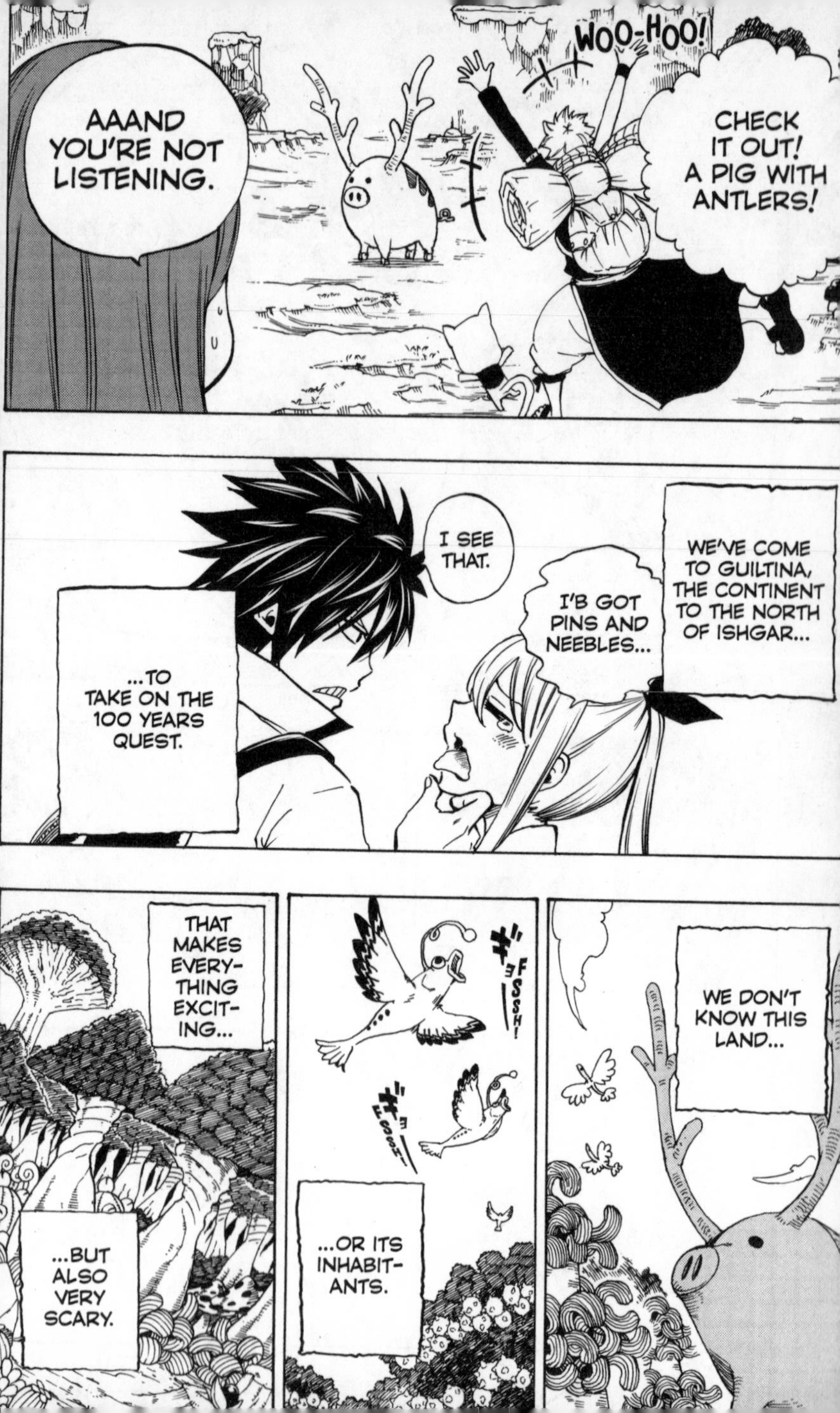
WOO-HOO!
CHECK IT OUT! A PIG WITH ANTLERS!
AAAND YOU'RE NOT LISTENING.
WE'VE COME TO GUILTINA, THE CONTINENT TO THE NORTH OF ISHGAR...
I'B GOT PINS AND NEEBLES...
I SEE THAT.
...TO TAKE ON THE 100 YEARS QUEST.
WE DON'T KNOW THIS LAND...
FSSSH!
...OR ITS INHABIT-ANTS.
THAT MAKES EVERY-THING EXCIT-ING...
...BUT ALSO VERY SCARY.

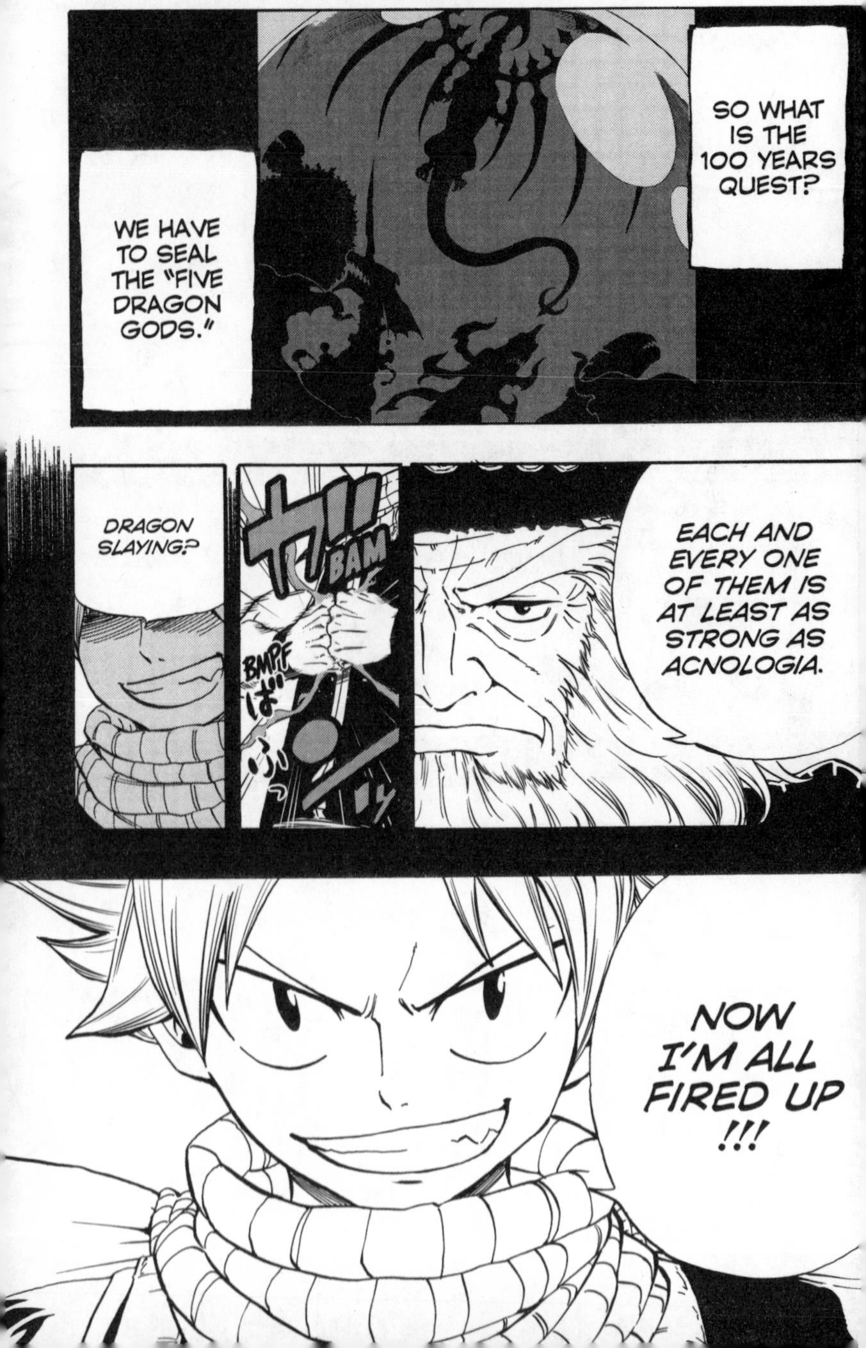
SO WHAT IS THE 100 YEARS QUEST?
WE HAVE TO SEAL THE "FIVE DRAGON GODS."
EACH AND EVERY ONE OF THEM IS AT LEAST AS STRONG AS ACNOLOGIA.
BAM
BMPF
DRAGON SLAYING?
NOW I'M ALL FIRED UP !!!

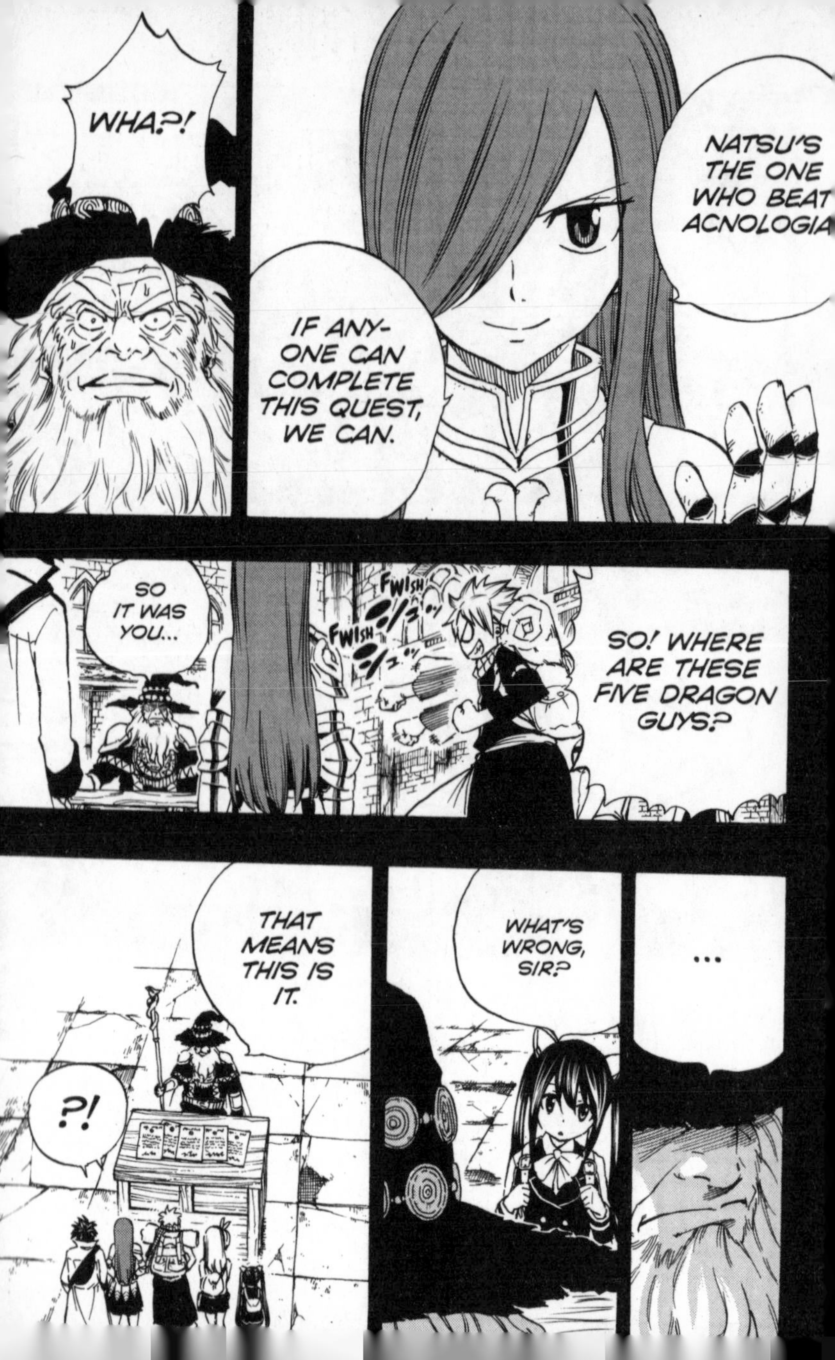
NATSU'S THE ONE WHO BEAT ACNOLOGIA
IF ANY-ONE CAN COMPLETE THIS QUEST, WE CAN.
WHA?!
SO! WHERE ARE THESE FIVE DRAGON GUYS?
FWISH
FWISH
SO IT WAS YOU...
...
WHAT'S WRONG, SIR?
THAT MEANS THIS IS IT.
?!

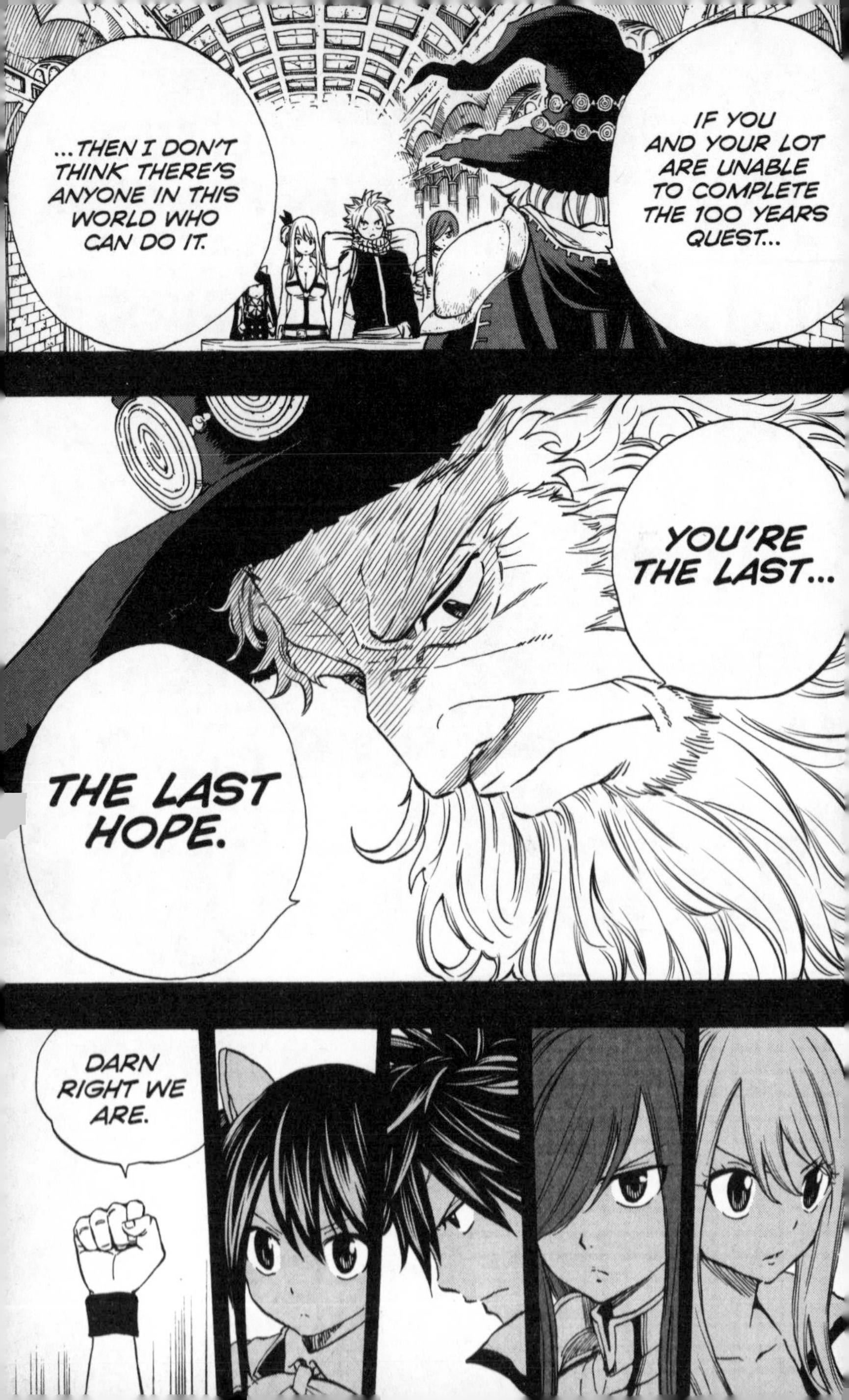
IF YOU AND YOUR LOT ARE UNABLE TO COMPLETE THE 100 YEARS QUEST...
...THEN I DON'T THINK THERE'S ANYONE IN THIS WORLD WHO CAN DO IT.
YOU'RE THE LAST...
THE LAST HOPE.
DARN RIGHT WE ARE.

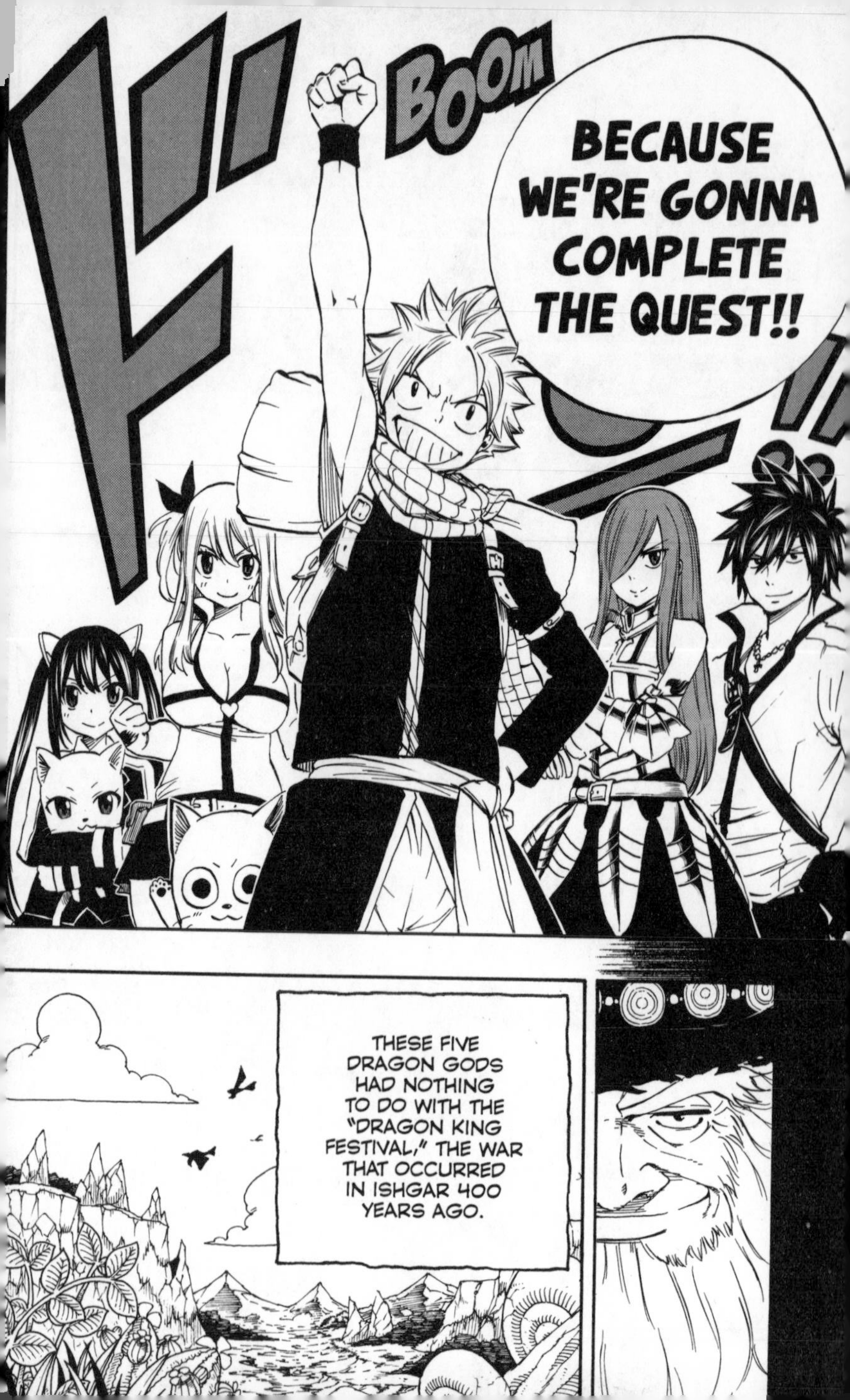
BOOM
BECAUSE WE'RE GONNA COMPLETE THE QUEST!!
THESE FIVE DRAGON GODS HAD NOTHING TO DO WITH THE "DRAGON KING FESTIVAL," THE WAR THAT OCCURRED IN ISHGAR 400 YEARS AGO.

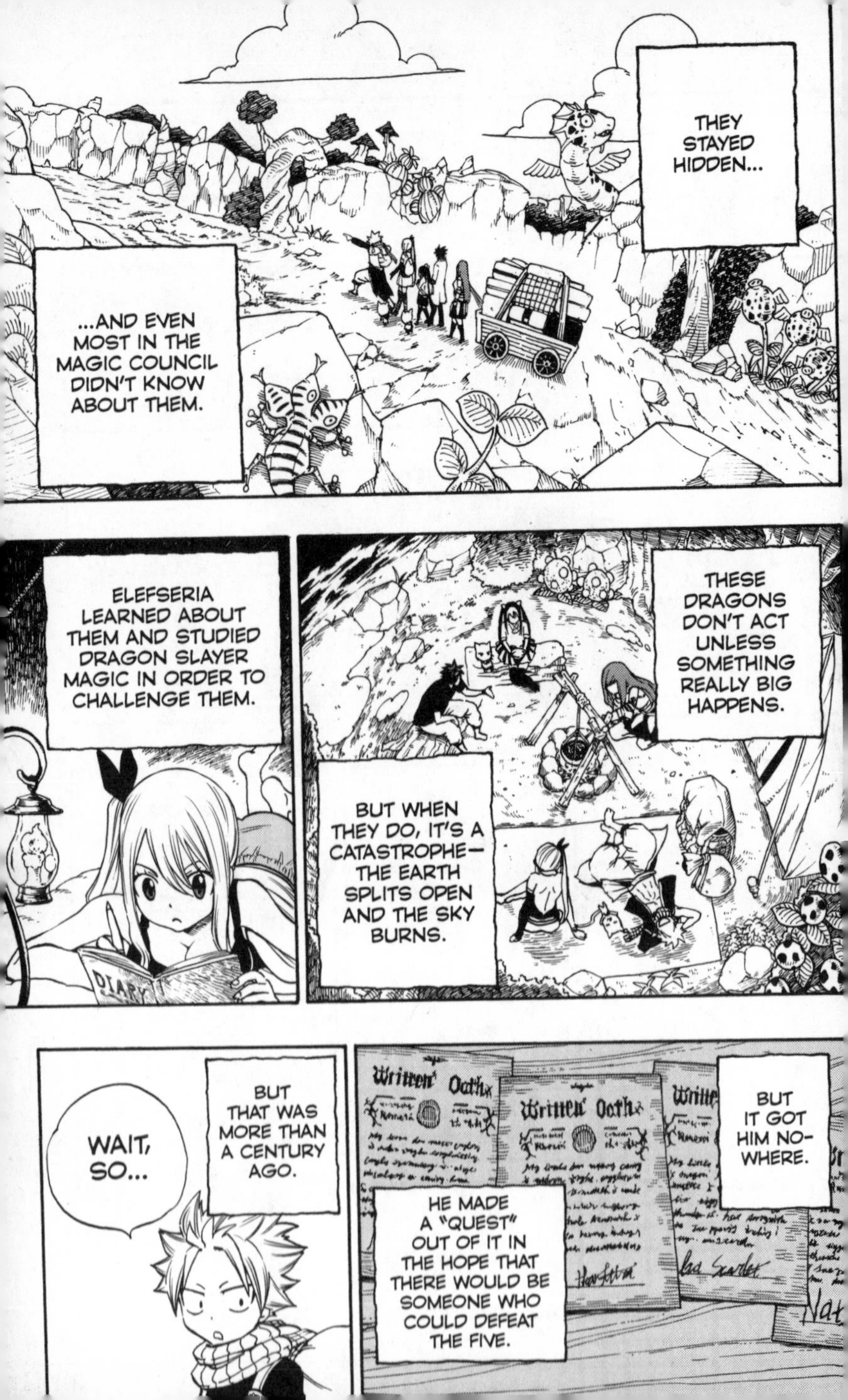

THEY STAYED HIDDEN...
...AND EVEN MOST IN THE MAGIC COUNCIL DIDN'T KNOW ABOUT THEM.
THESE DRAGONS DON'T ACT UNLESS SOMETHING REALLY BIG HAPPENS.
BUT WHEN THEY DO, IT'S A CATASTROPHE— THE EARTH SPLITS OPEN AND THE SKY BURNS.
ELEFSERIA LEARNED ABOUT THEM AND STUDIED DRAGON SLAYER MAGIC IN ORDER TO CHALLENGE THEM.
DIARY
BUT IT GOT HIM NO-WHERE.
HE MADE A "QUEST" OUT OF IT IN THE HOPE THAT THERE WOULD BE SOMEONE WHO COULD DEFEAT THE FIVE.
BUT THAT WAS MORE THAN A CENTURY AGO.
WAIT, SO...

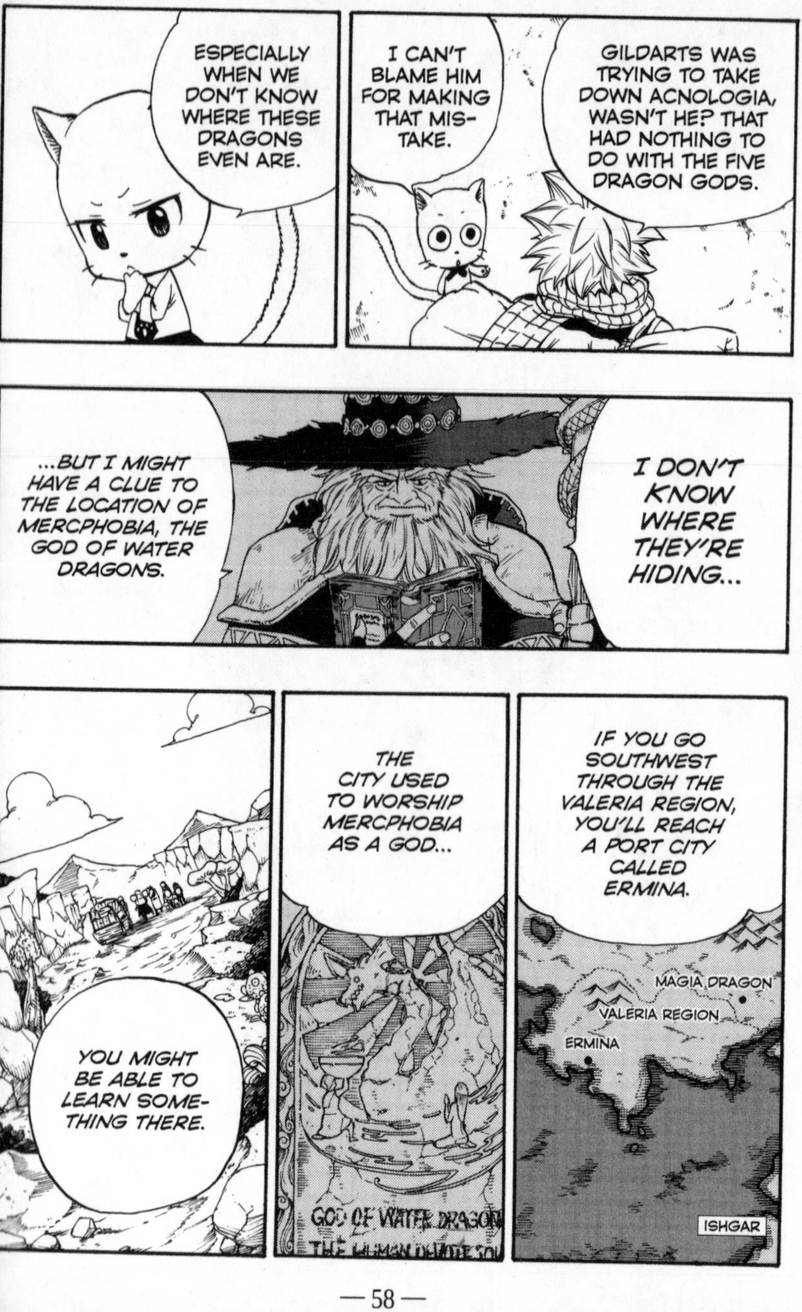
GILDARTS WAS TRYING TO TAKE DOWN ACNOLOGIA, WASN'T HE? THAT HAD NOTHING TO DO WITH THE FIVE DRAGON GODS.
I CAN'T BLAME HIM FOR MAKING THAT MIS-TAKE.
ESPECIALLY WHEN WE DON'T KNOW WHERE THESE DRAGONS EVEN ARE.
I DON'T KNOW WHERE THEY'RE HIDING...
...BUT I MIGHT HAVE A CLUE TO THE LOCATION OF MERCPHOBIA, THE GOD OF WATER DRAGONS.
IF YOU GO SOUTHWEST THROUGH THE VALERIA REGION, YOU'LL REACH A PORT CITY CALLED ERMINA.
MAGIA DRAGON
VALERIA REGION
ERMINA
ISHGAR
THE CITY USED TO WORSHIP MERCPHOBIA AS A GOD...
YOU MIGHT BE ABLE TO LEARN SOME-THING THERE.

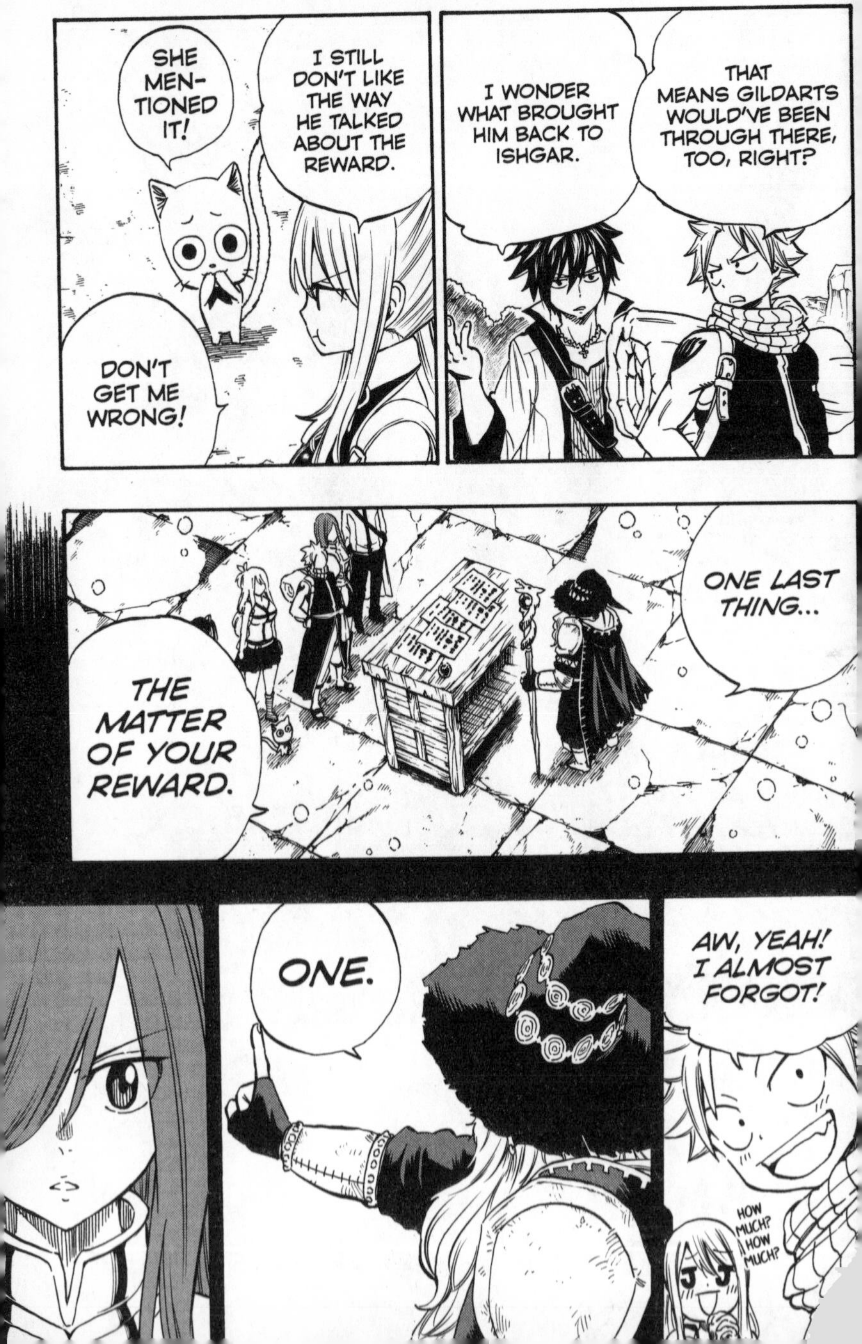
THAT MEANS GILDARTS WOULD'VE BEEN THROUGH THERE, TOO, RIGHT?
I WONDER WHAT BROUGHT HIM BACK TO ISHGAR.
I STILL DON'T LIKE THE WAY HE TALKED ABOUT THE REWARD.
SHE MENTIONED IT!
DON'T GET ME WRONG!
ONE LAST THING...
THE MATTER OF YOUR REWARD.
AW, YEAH! I ALMOST FORGOT!
HOW MUCH? HOW MUCH?
ONE.

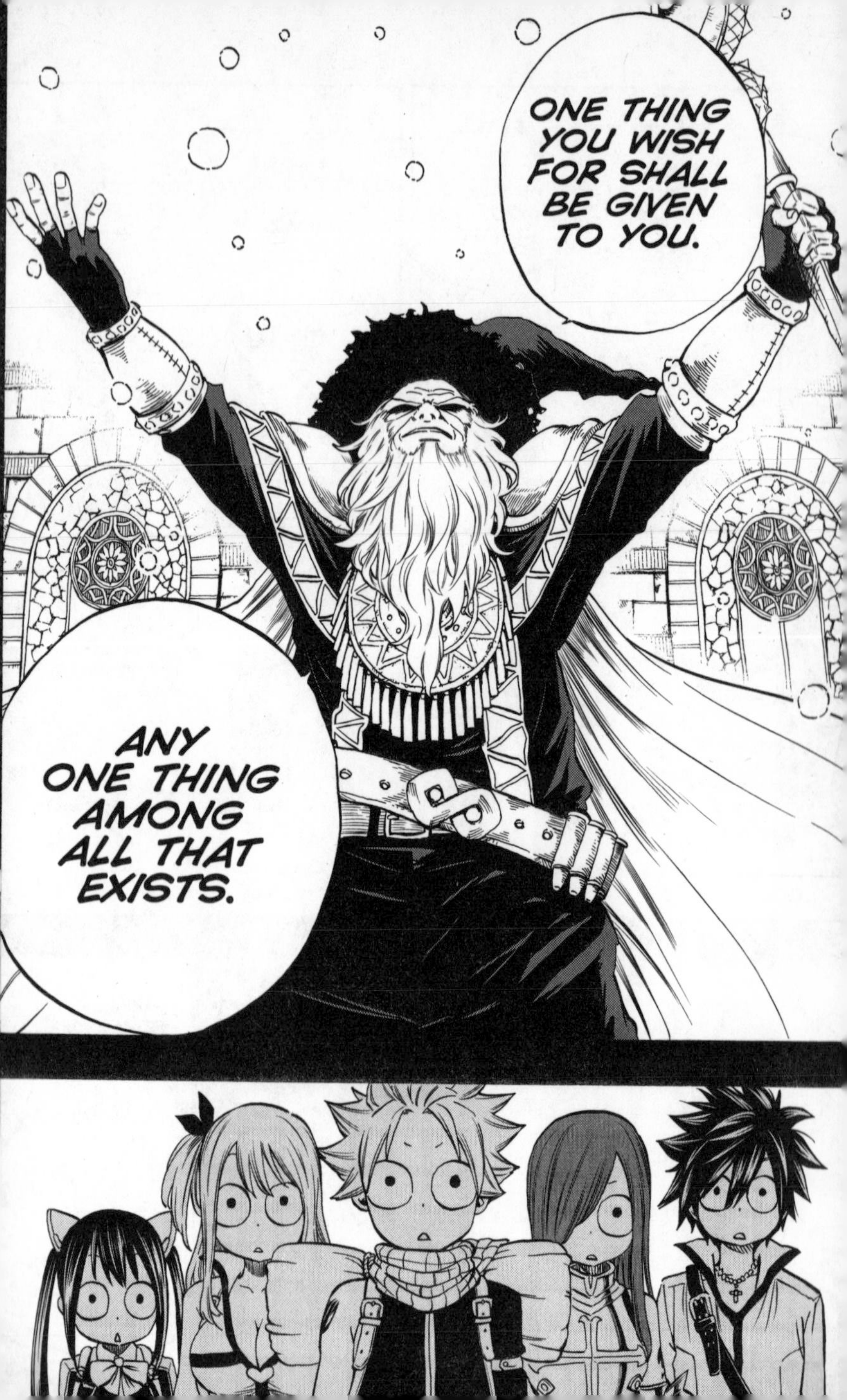
ONE THING YOU WISH FOR SHALL BE GIVEN TO YOU.
ANY ONE THING AMONG ALL THAT EXISTS.

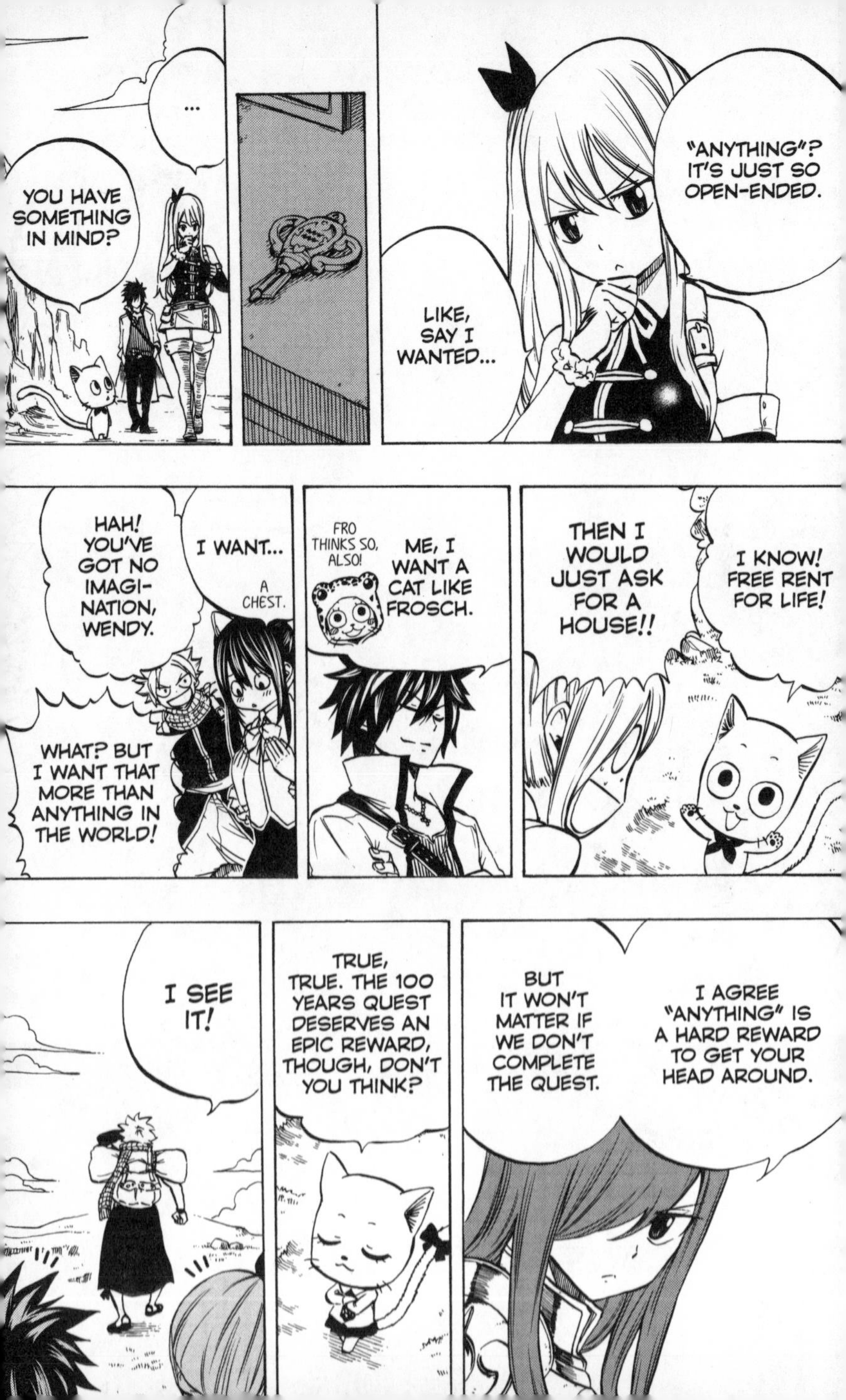
"ANYTHING"? IT'S JUST SO OPEN-ENDED.
LIKE, SAY I WANTED...
...
YOU HAVE SOMETHING IN MIND?
I KNOW! FREE RENT FOR LIFE!
THEN I WOULD JUST ASK FOR A HOUSE!!
ME, I WANT A CAT LIKE FROSCH.
FRO THINKS SO, ALSO!
I WANT...
A CHEST.
HAH! YOU'VE GOT NO IMAGI-NATION, WENDY.
WHAT? BUT I WANT THAT MORE THAN ANYTHING IN THE WORLD!
I AGREE "ANYTHING" IS A HARD REWARD TO GET YOUR HEAD AROUND.
BUT IT WON'T MATTER IF WE DON'T COMPLETE THE QUEST.
TRUE, TRUE. THE 100 YEARS QUEST DESERVES AN EPIC REWARD, THOUGH, DON'T YOU THINK?
I SEE IT!

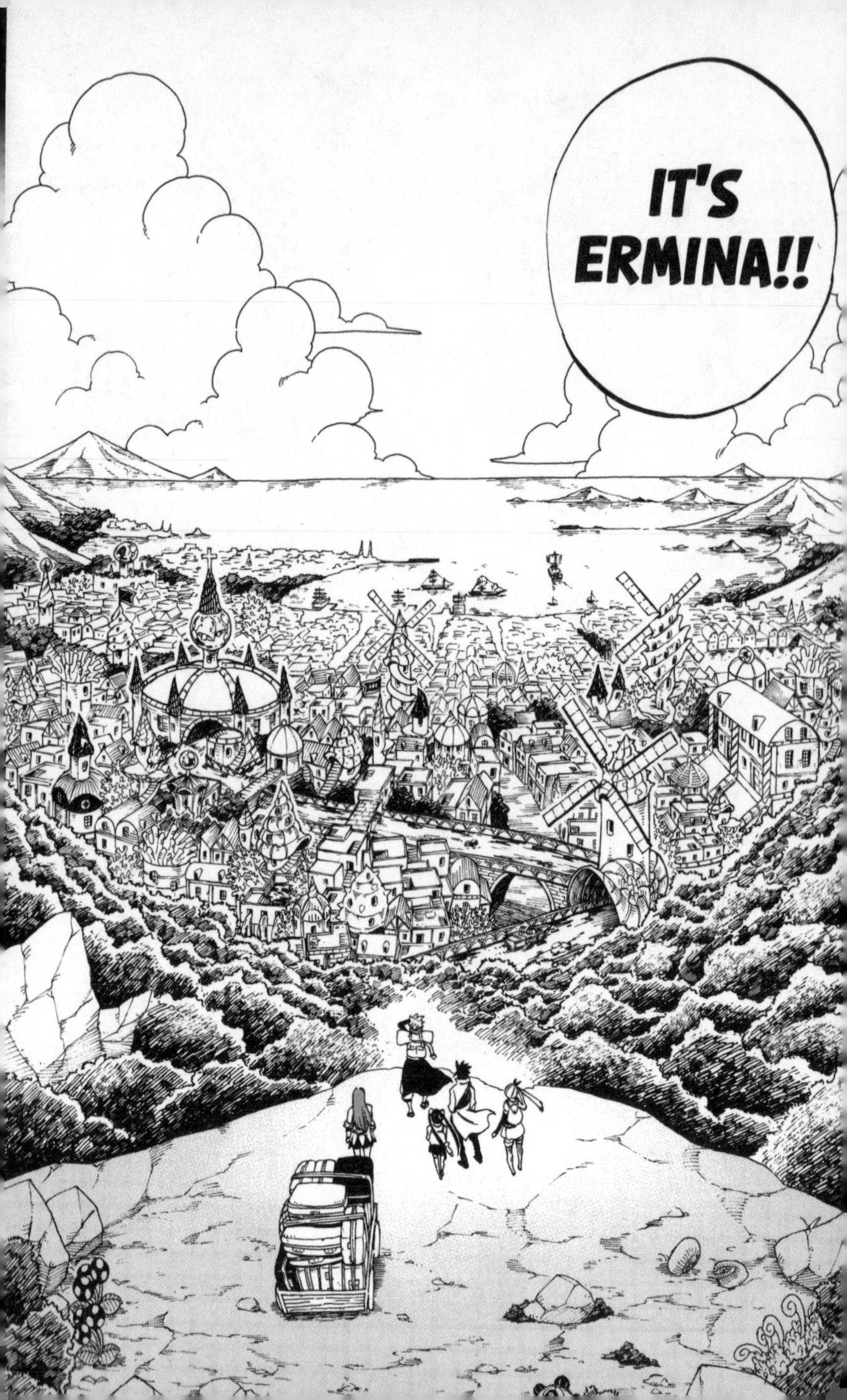
IT'S ERMINA!!

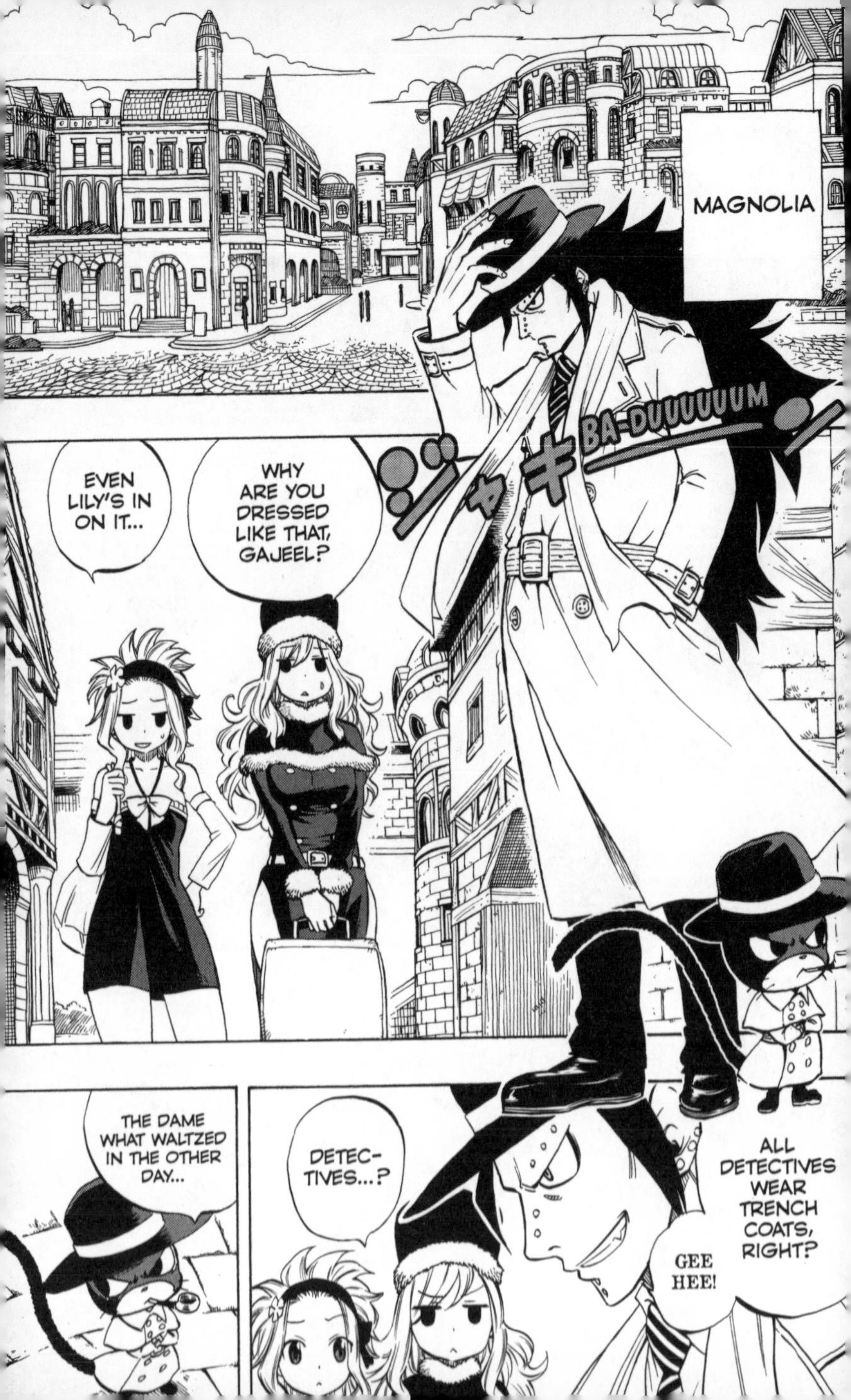
MAGNOLIA
BA-DUUUUUUM
WHY ARE YOU DRESSED LIKE THAT, GAJEEL?
EVEN LILY'S IN ON IT...
ALL DETECTIVES WEAR TRENCH COATS, RIGHT?
GEE HEE!
DETEC-TIVES...?
THE DAME WHAT WALTZED IN THE OTHER DAY...

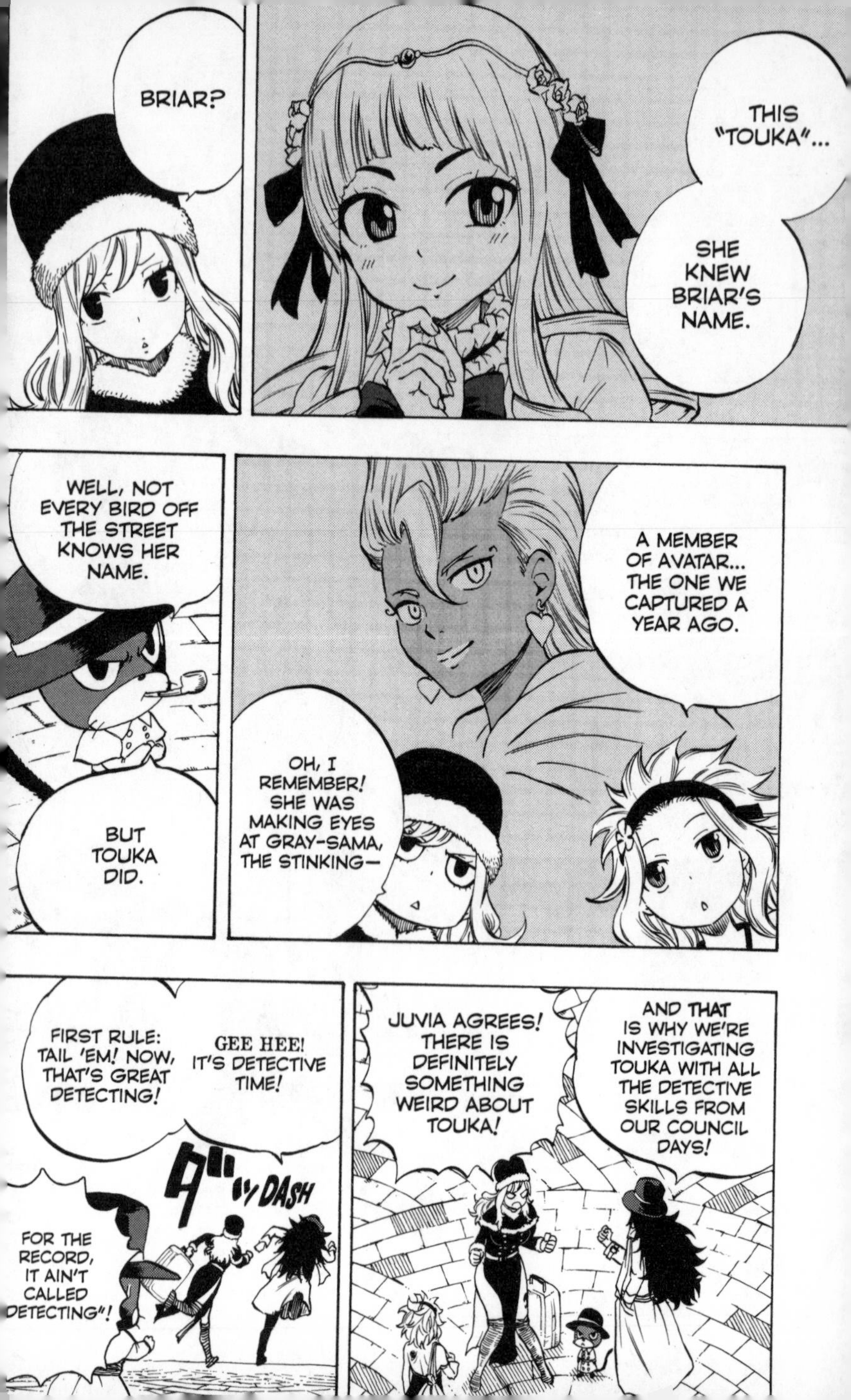
THIS "TOUKA"...
SHE KNEW BRIAR'S NAME.
BRIAR?
A MEMBER OF AVATAR... THE ONE WE CAPTURED A YEAR AGO.
OH, I REMEMBER! SHE WAS MAKING EYES AT GRAY-SAMA, THE STINKING—
WELL, NOT EVERY BIRD OFF THE STREET KNOWS HER NAME.
BUT TOUKA DID.
AND THAT IS WHY WE'RE INVESTIGATING TOUKA WITH ALL THE DETECTIVE SKILLS FROM OUR COUNCIL DAYS!
JUVIA AGREES! THERE IS DEFINITELY SOMETHING WEIRD ABOUT TOUKA!
GEE HEE! IT'S DETECTIVE TIME!
FIRST RULE: TAIL 'EM! NOW, THAT'S GREAT DETECTING!
DASH
FOR THE RECORD, IT AIN'T CALLED DETECTING"!

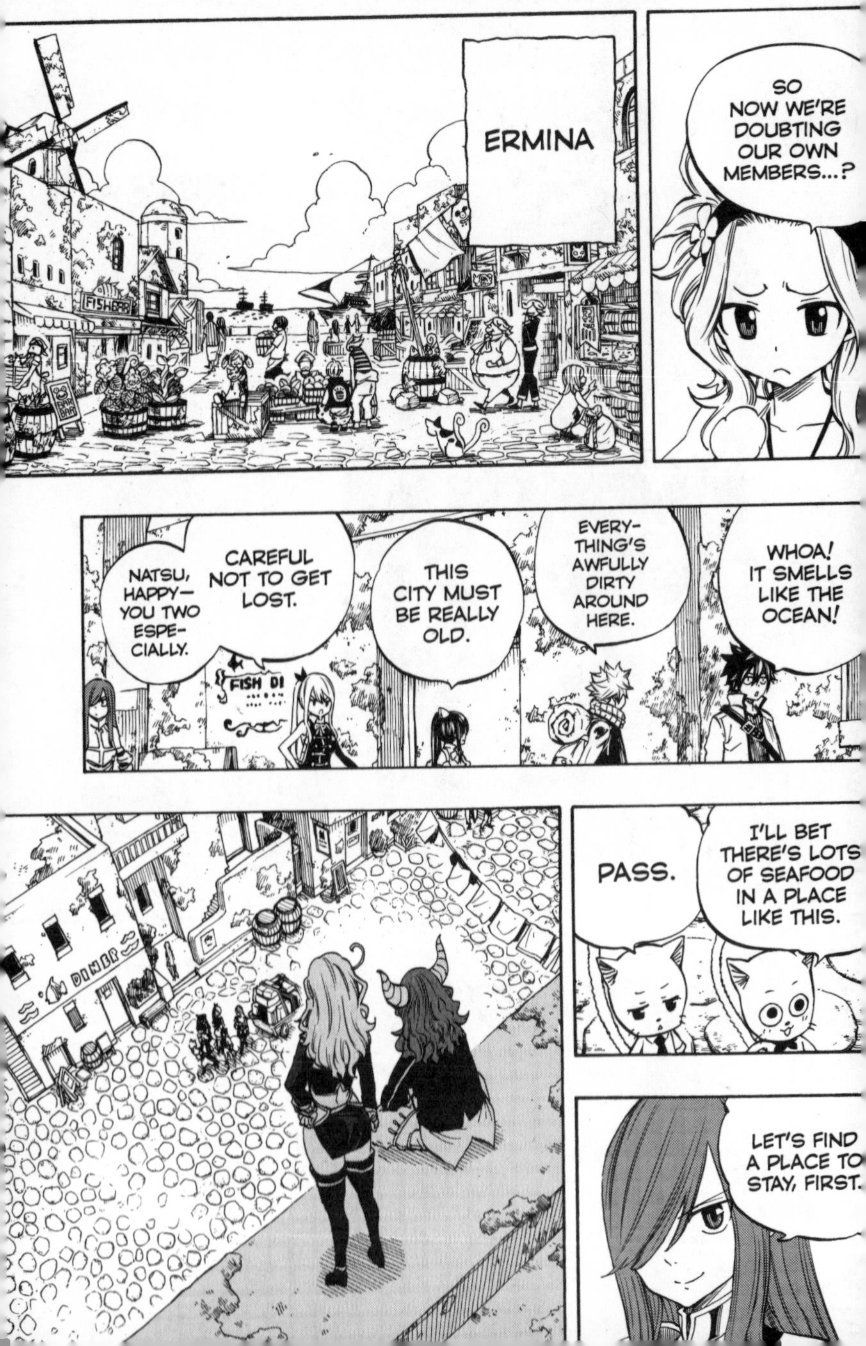
SO NOW WE'RE DOUBTING OUR OWN MEMBERS...?
ERMINA
WHOA! IT SMELLS LIKE THE OCEAN!
EVERY-THING'S AWFULLY DIRTY AROUND HERE.
THIS CITY MUST BE REALLY OLD.
CAREFUL NOT TO GET LOST.
NATSU, HAPPY— YOU TWO ESPE-CIALLY.
FISH DI
I'LL BET THERE'S LOTS OF SEAFOOD IN A PLACE LIKE THIS.
PASS.
LET'S FIND A PLACE TO STAY, FIRST.

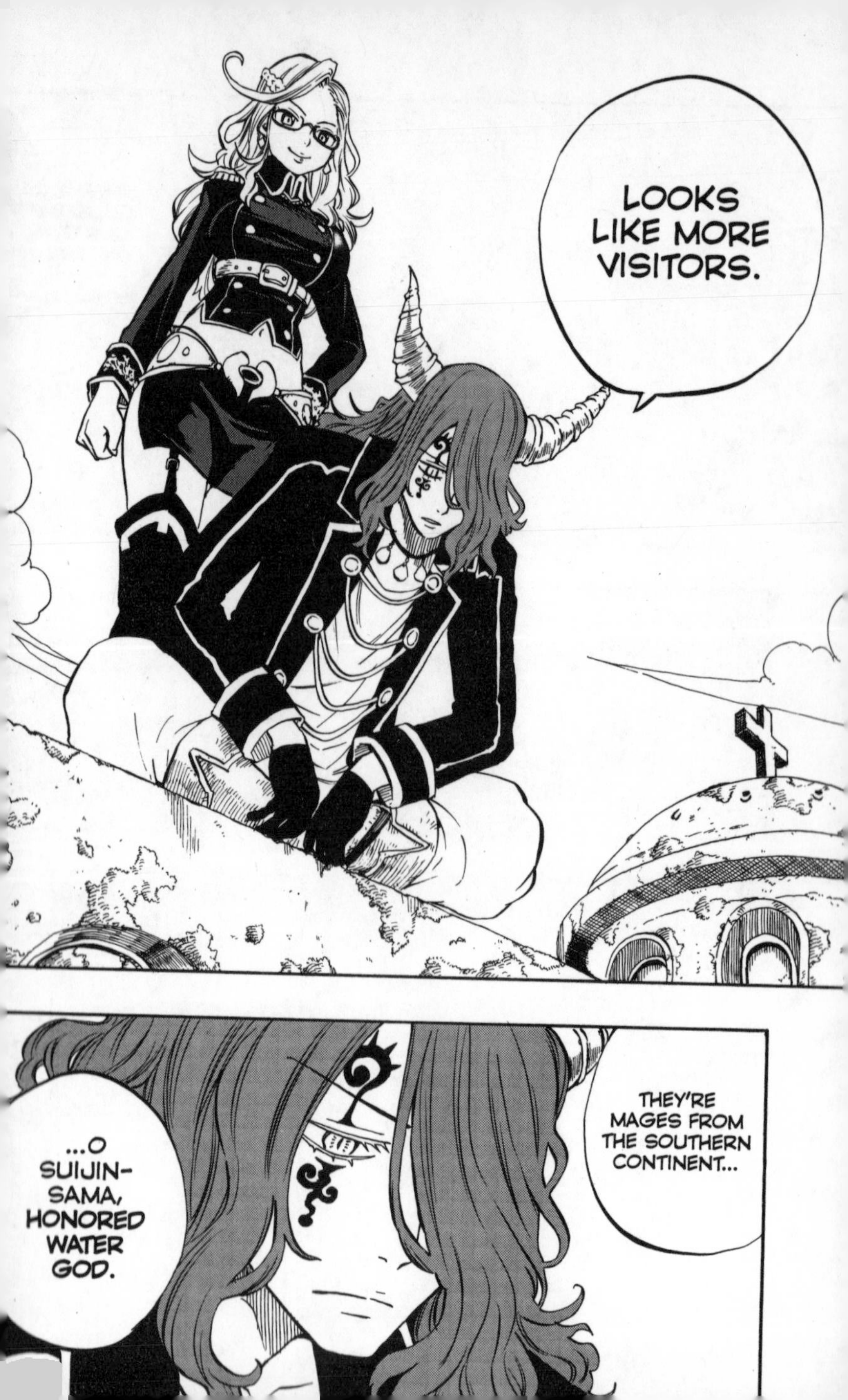
LOOKS LIKE MORE VISITORS.
THEY'RE MAGES FROM THE SOUTHERN CONTINENT...
...O SUIJIN-SAMA, HONORED WATER GOD.

FAIRY TAIL 100 YEARS QUEST

Chapter 4: Amazing Ermina

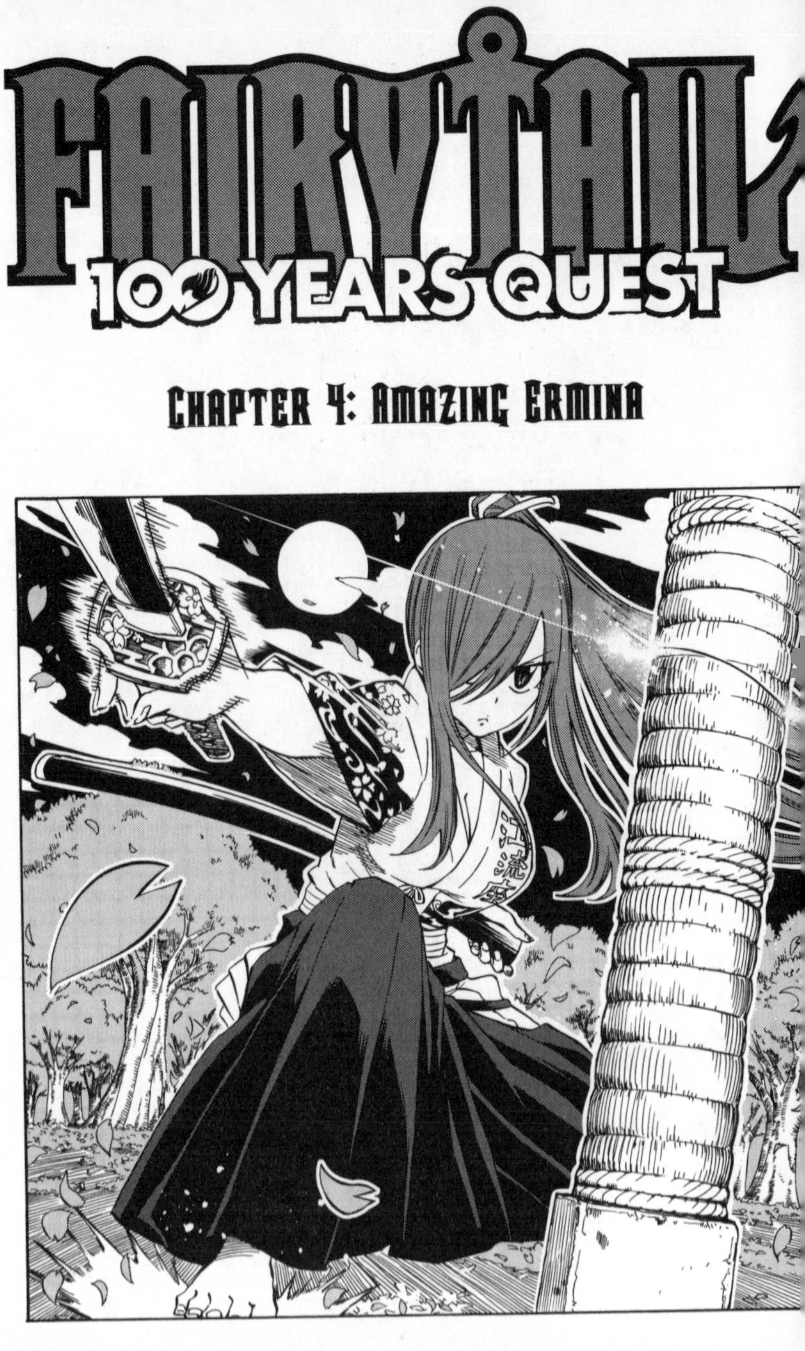

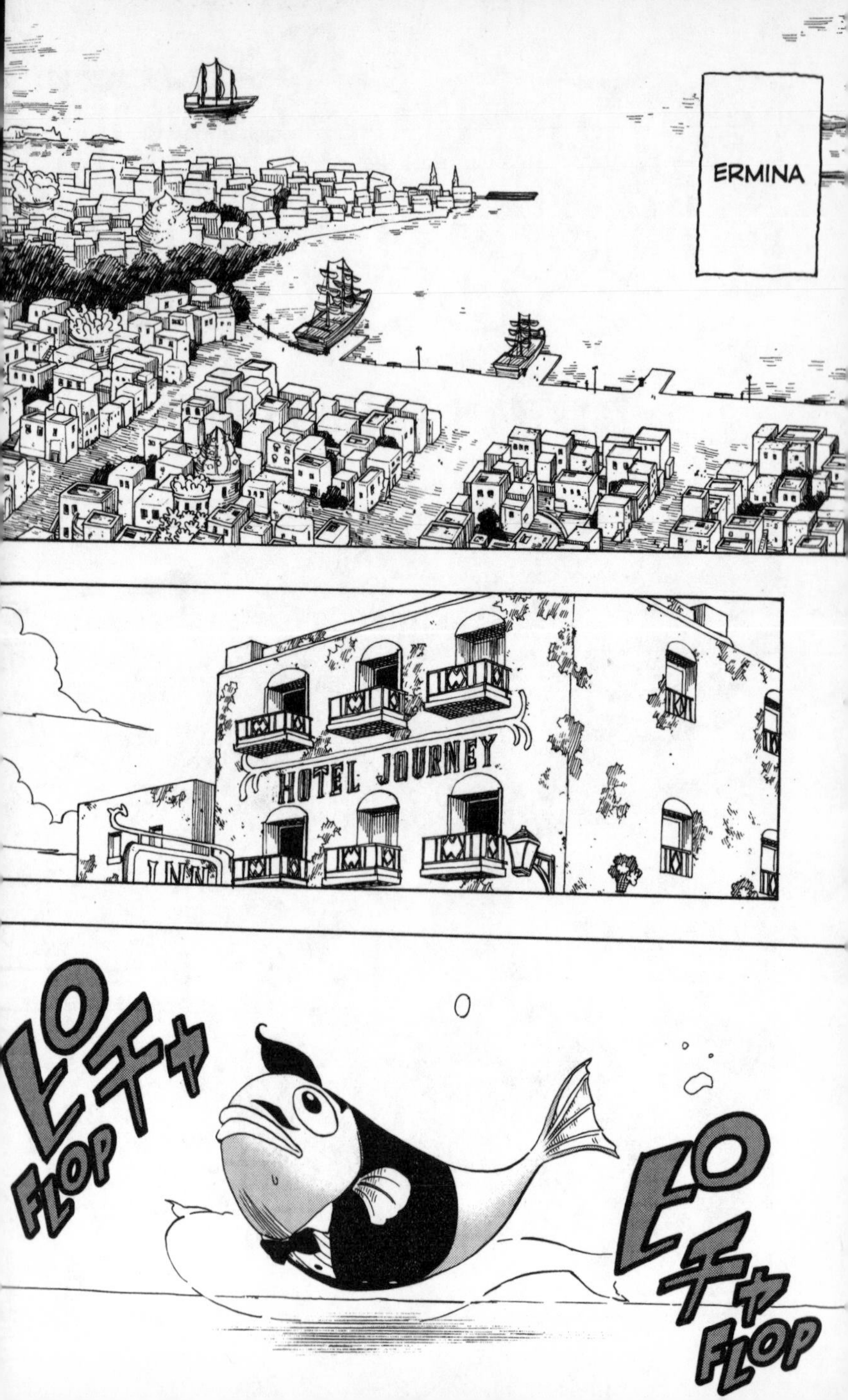
ERMINA
HOTEL JOURNEY
INN
ピチャ FLOP
ピチャ FLOP

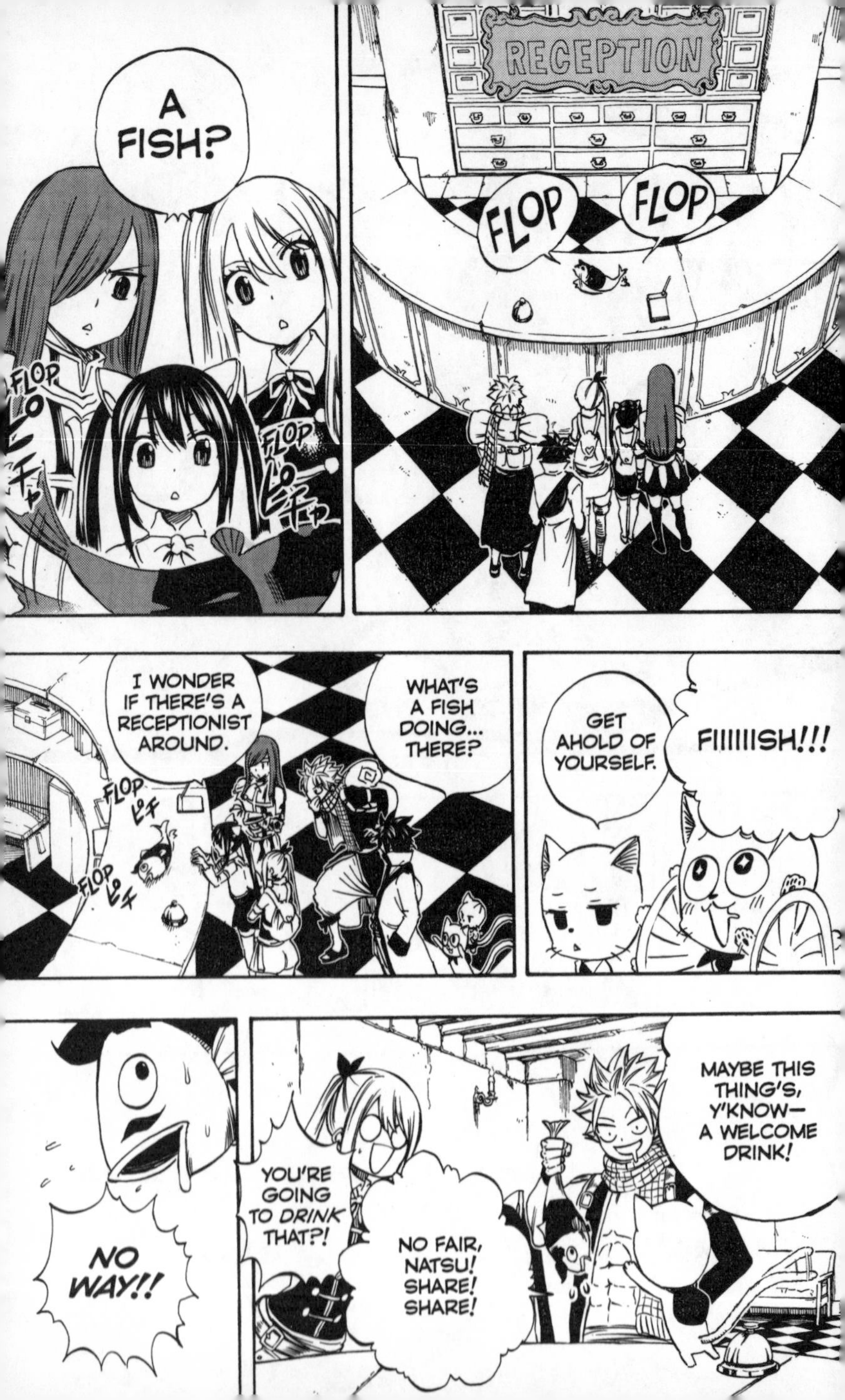
RECEPTION
FLOP
FLOP
A FISH?
FLOP ピチャ
FLOP ピチャ
FIIIIIISH!!!
GET AHOLD OF YOURSELF.
WHAT'S A FISH DOING... THERE?
I WONDER IF THERE'S A RECEPTIONIST AROUND.
FLOP ピチ
FLOP ピチ
MAYBE THIS THING'S, Y'KNOW— A WELCOME DRINK!
YOU'RE GOING TO *DRINK* THAT?!
NO FAIR, NATSU! SHARE! SHARE!
NO WAY!!

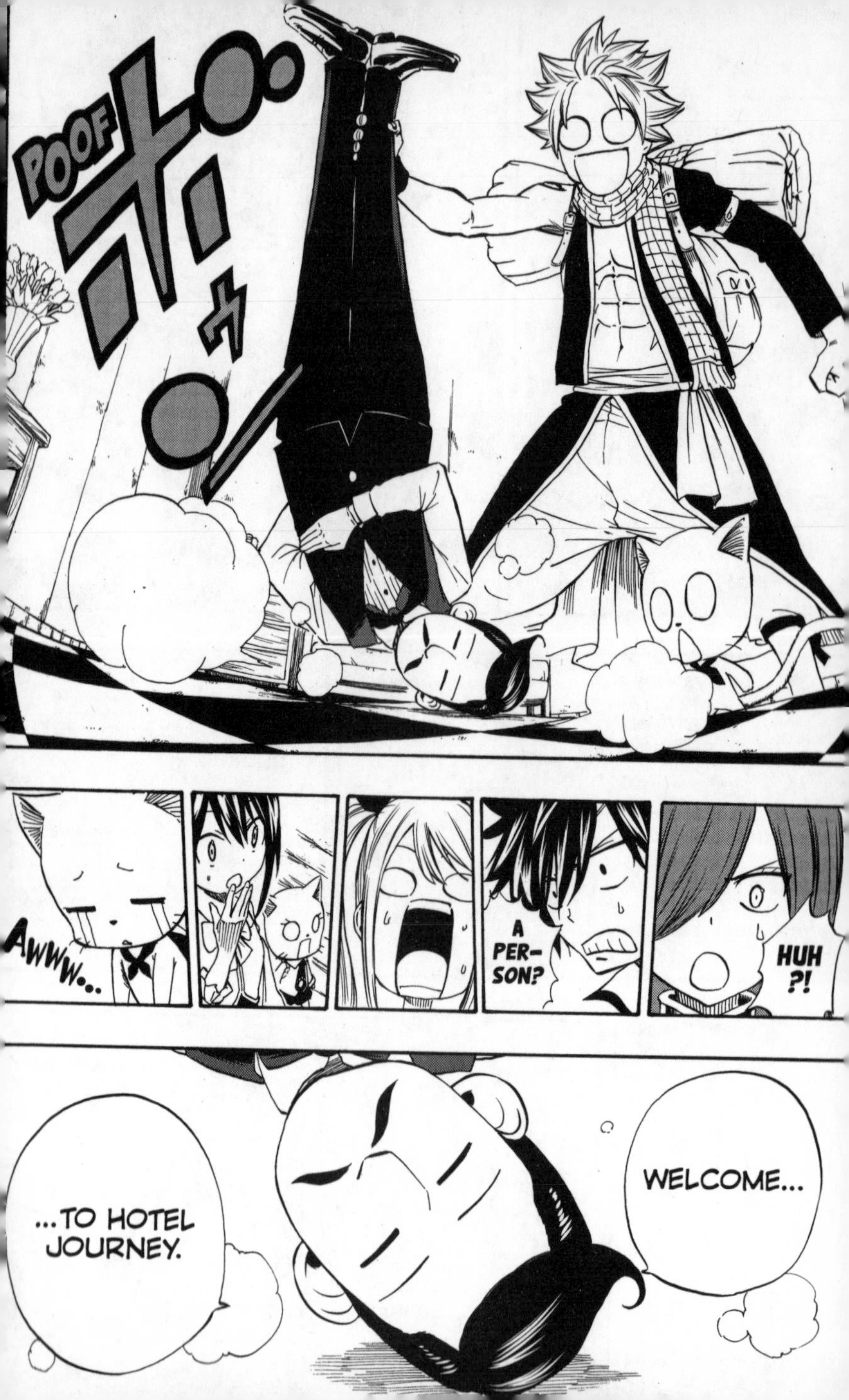
POOF
HUH ?!
A PER- SON?
AWWW...
WELCOME...
...TO HOTEL JOURNEY.

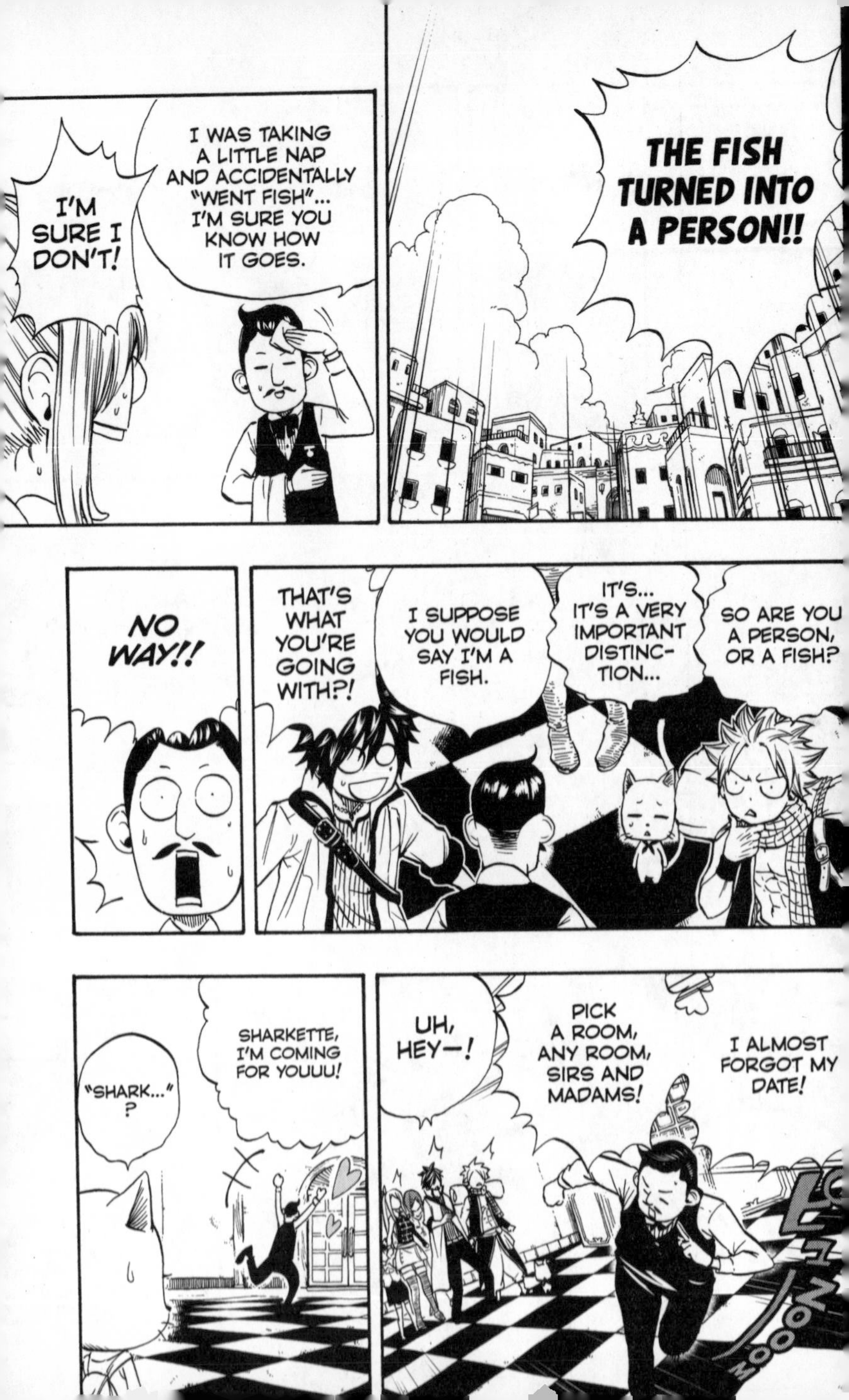
THE FISH TURNED INTO A PERSON!!
I WAS TAKING A LITTLE NAP AND ACCIDENTALLY "WENT FISH"... I'M SURE YOU KNOW HOW IT GOES.
I'M SURE I DON'T!
SO ARE YOU A PERSON, OR A FISH?
IT'S... IT'S A VERY IMPORTANT DISTINCTION...
I SUPPOSE YOU WOULD SAY I'M A FISH.
THAT'S WHAT YOU'RE GOING WITH?!
NO WAY!!
I ALMOST FORGOT MY DATE!
PICK A ROOM, ANY ROOM, SIRS AND MADAMS!
UH, HEY—!
ZOOOM
SHARKETTE, I'M COMING FOR YOUUU!
"SHARK..." ?

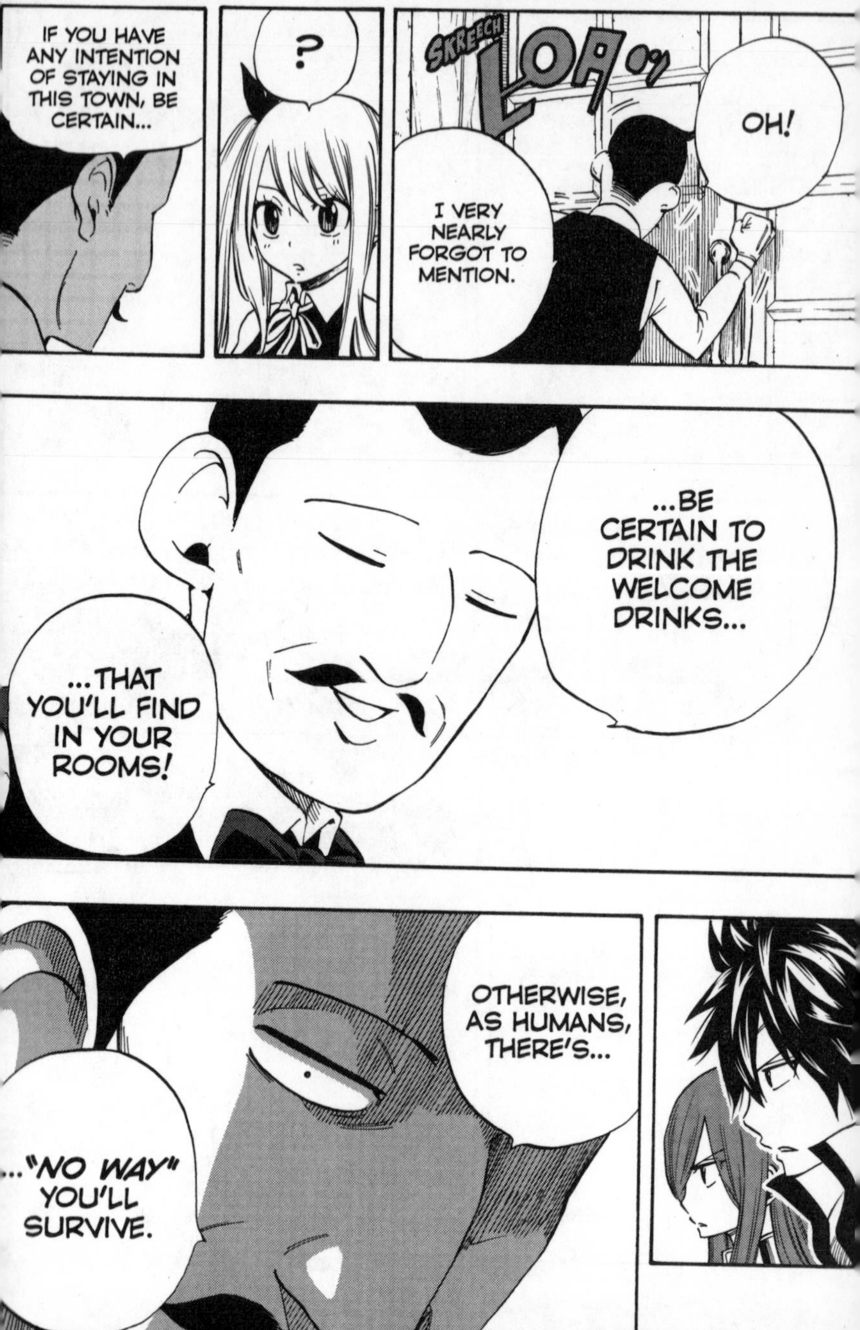
SKREECH
OH!
I VERY NEARLY FORGOT TO MENTION.
?
IF YOU HAVE ANY INTENTION OF STAYING IN THIS TOWN, BE CERTAIN...
...BE CERTAIN TO DRINK THE WELCOME DRINKS...
...THAT YOU'LL FIND IN YOUR ROOMS!
OTHERWISE, AS HUMANS, THERE'S...
..."NO WAY" YOU'LL SURVIVE.

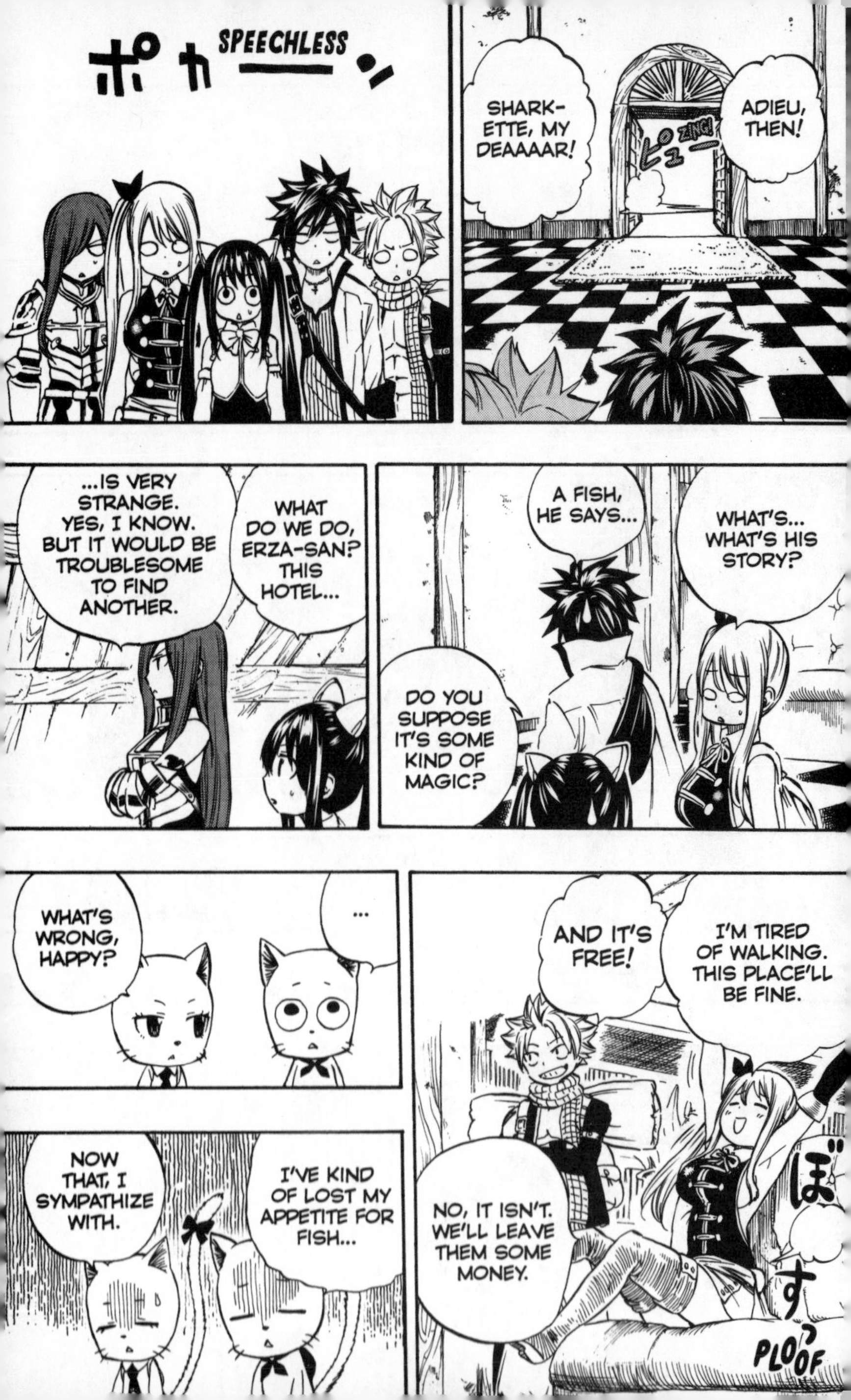
ADIEU, THEN!
ZING!
SHARK-ETTE, MY DEAAAAR!
SPEECHLESS
WHAT'S... WHAT'S HIS STORY?
A FISH, HE SAYS...
DO YOU SUPPOSE IT'S SOME KIND OF MAGIC?
WHAT DO WE DO, ERZA-SAN? THIS HOTEL...
...IS VERY STRANGE. YES, I KNOW. BUT IT WOULD BE TROUBLESOME TO FIND ANOTHER.
I'M TIRED OF WALKING. THIS PLACE'LL BE FINE.
AND IT'S FREE!
NO, IT ISN'T. WE'LL LEAVE THEM SOME MONEY.
PLOOF
...
WHAT'S WRONG, HAPPY?
I'VE KIND OF LOST MY APPETITE FOR FISH...
NOW THAT, I SYMPATHIZE WITH.

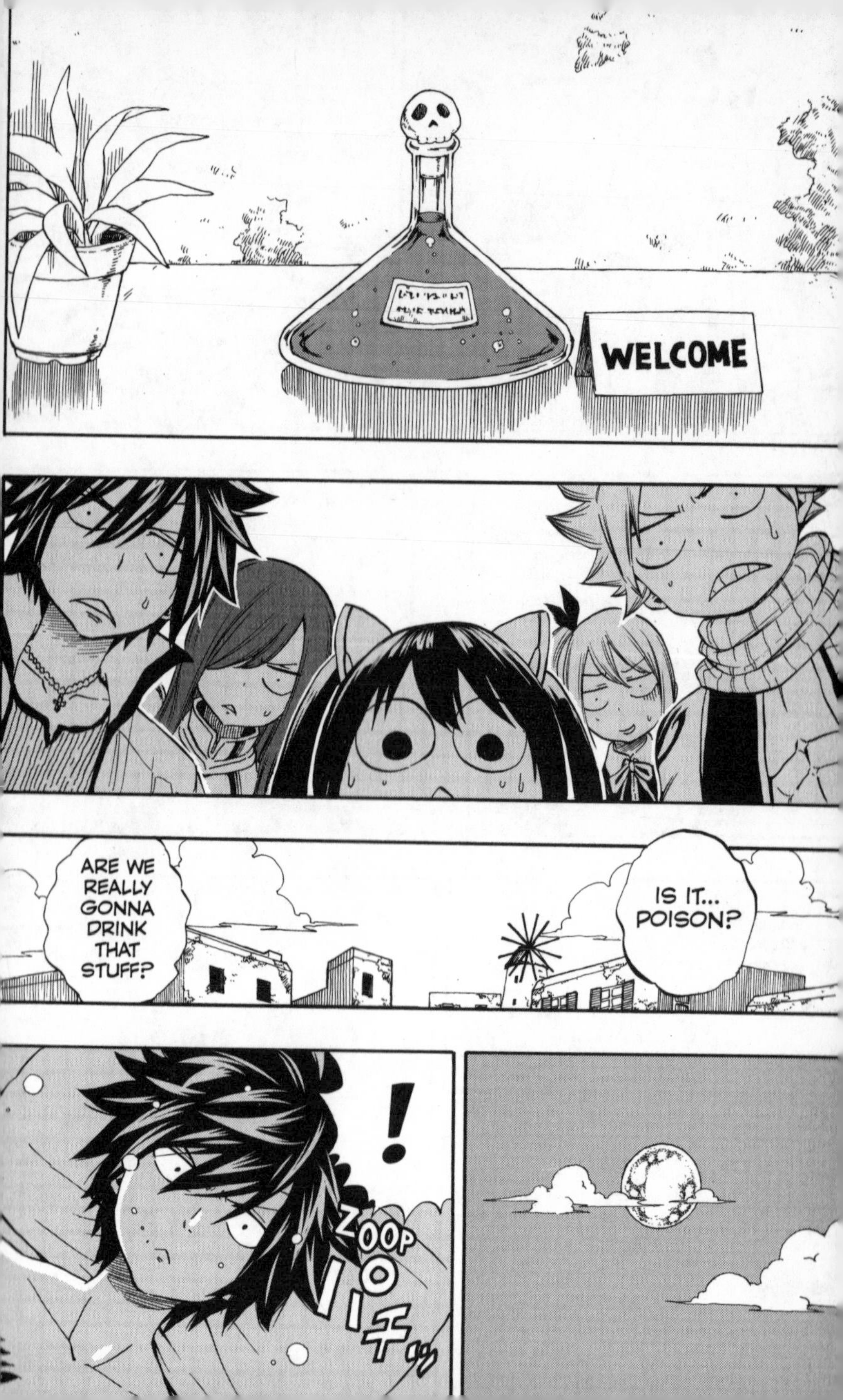
WELCOME
IS IT... POISON?
ARE WE REALLY GONNA DRINK THAT STUFF?
!
ZOOP

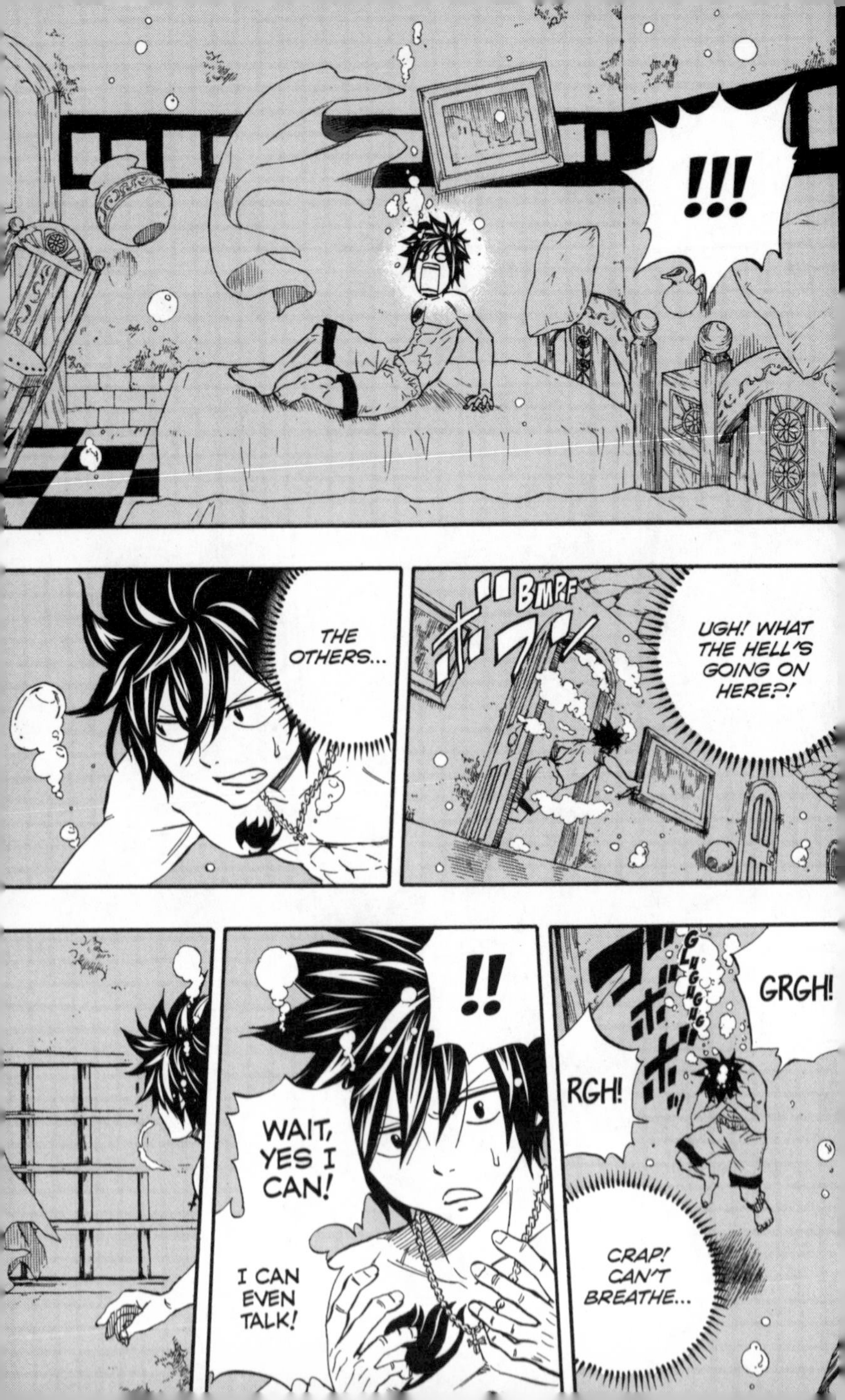
!!!
BMPF
UGH! WHAT THE HELL'S GOING ON HERE?!
THE OTHERS...
GRGH!
RGH!
CRAP! CAN'T BREATHE...
!!
WAIT, YES I CAN!
I CAN EVEN TALK!

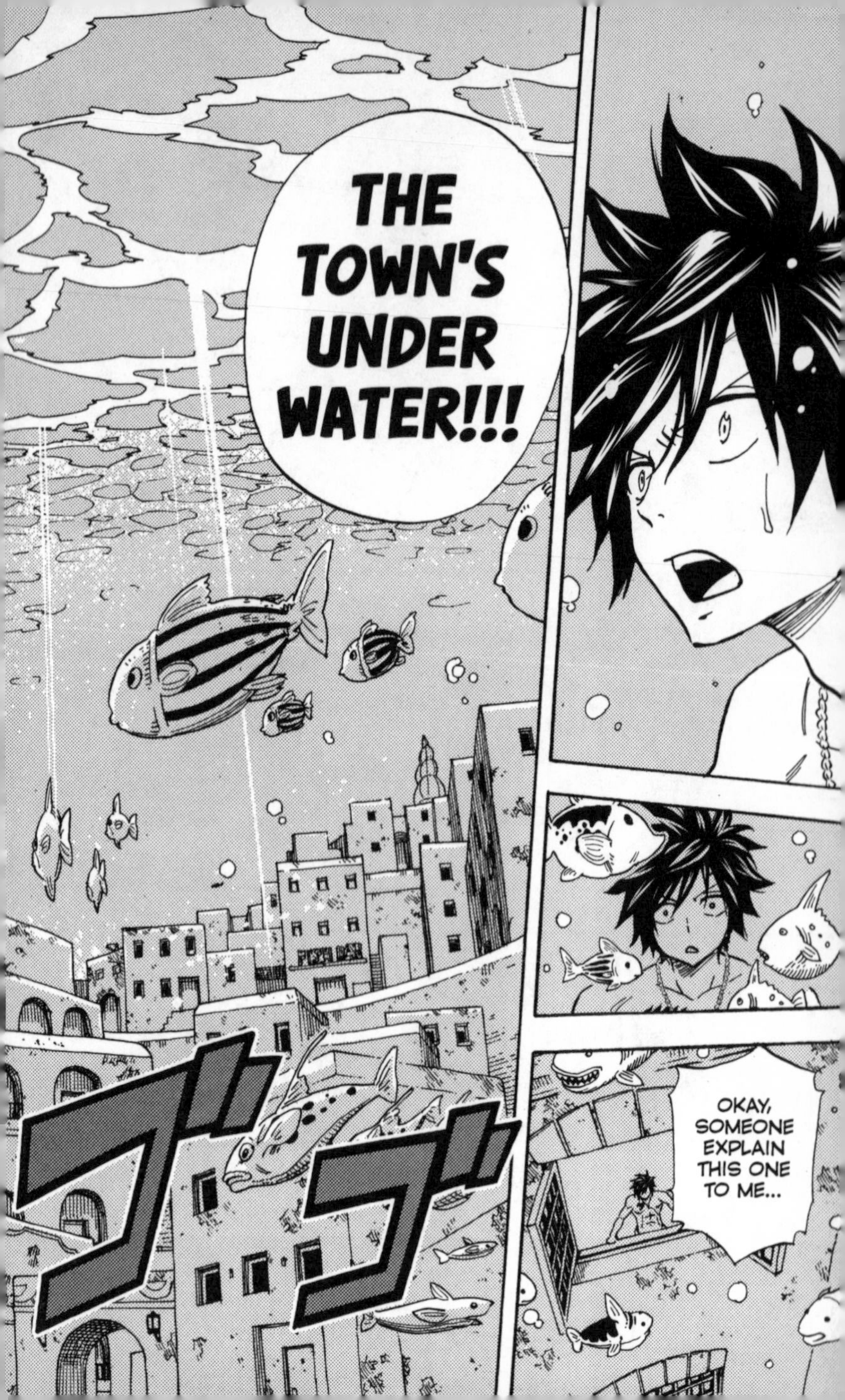
OKAY, SOMEONE EXPLAIN THIS ONE TO ME...
THE TOWN'S UNDER WATER!!!
ゴゴ

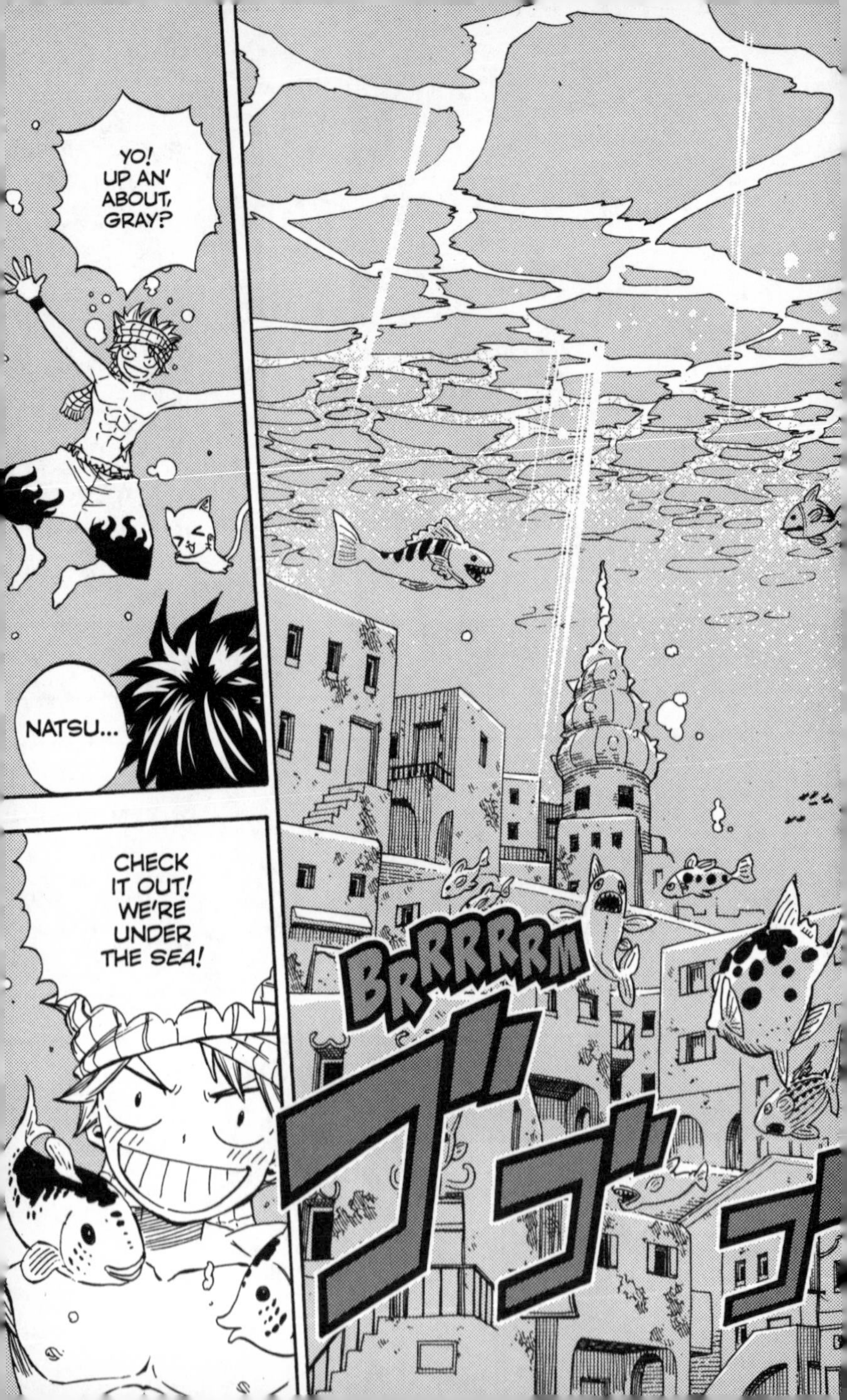
BRRRRRM
ゴゴゴ
YO! UP AN' ABOUT, GRAY?
NATSU...
CHECK IT OUT! WE'RE UNDER THE SEA!

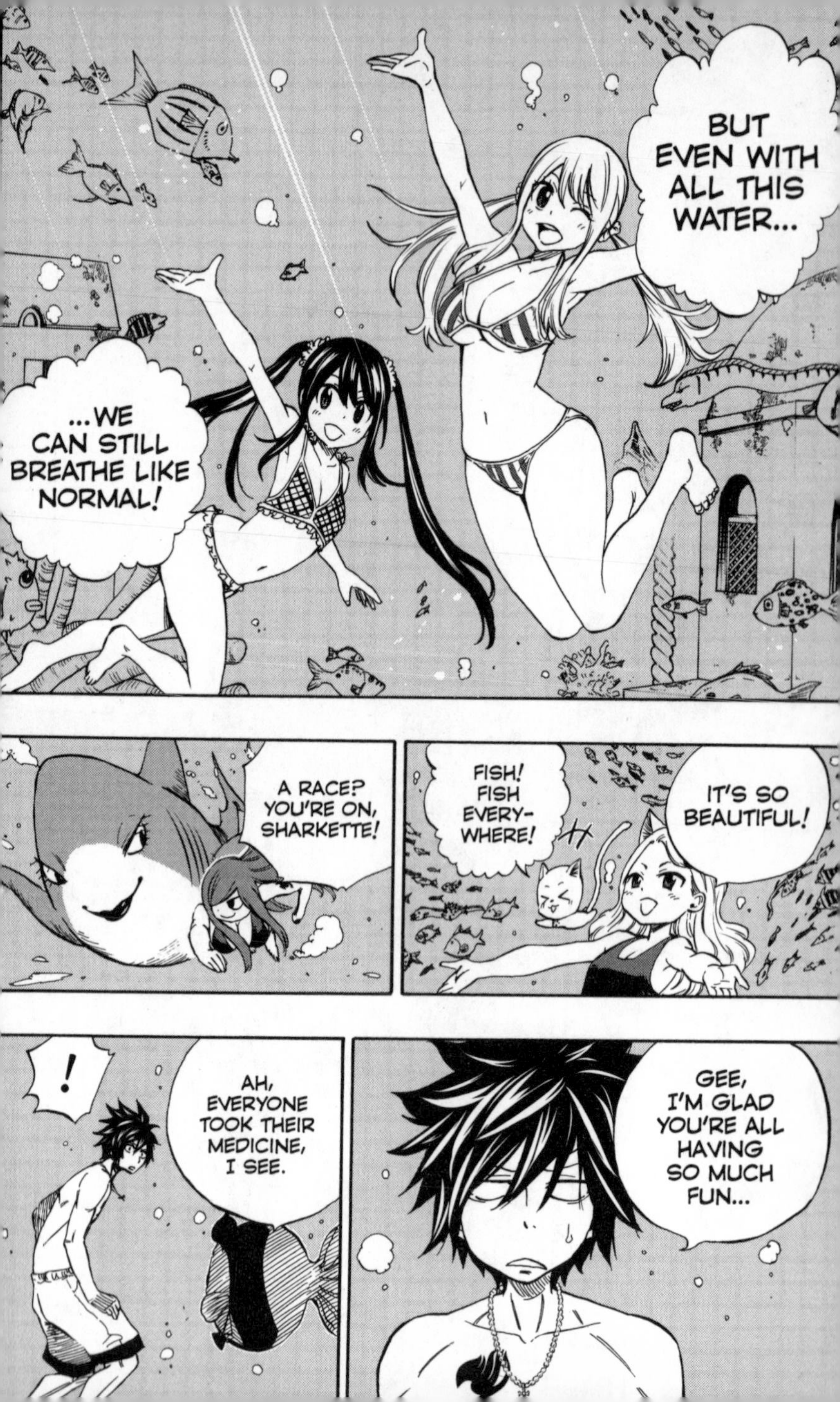
BUT EVEN WITH ALL THIS WATER...
...WE CAN STILL BREATHE LIKE NORMAL!
IT'S SO BEAUTIFUL!
FISH! FISH EVERY-WHERE!
A RACE? YOU'RE ON, SHARKETTE!
GEE, I'M GLAD YOU'RE ALL HAVING SO MUCH FUN...
AH, EVERYONE TOOK THEIR MEDICINE, I SEE.
!

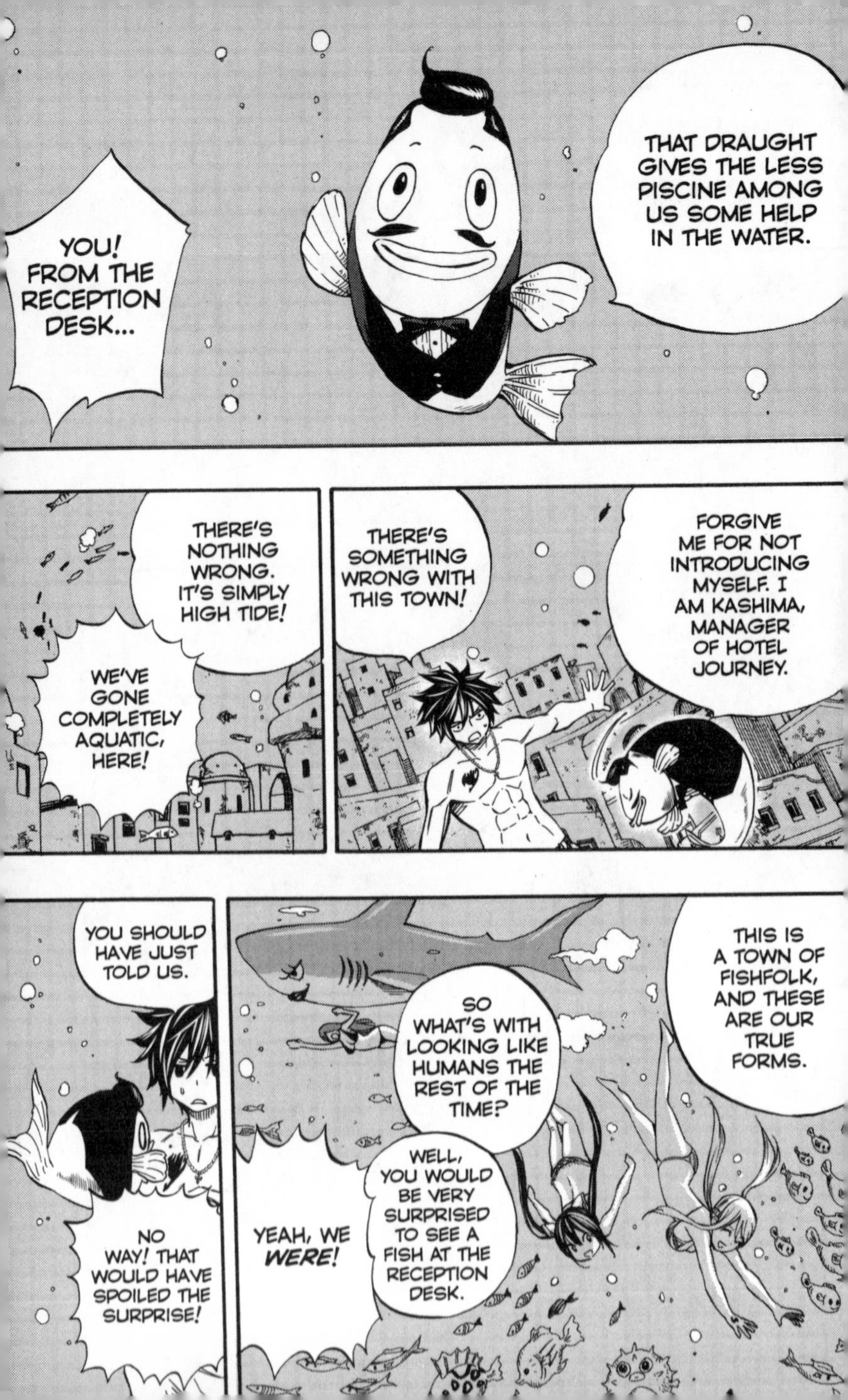
THAT DRAUGHT GIVES THE LESS PISCINE AMONG US SOME HELP IN THE WATER.
YOU! FROM THE RECEPTION DESK...
FORGIVE ME FOR NOT INTRODUCING MYSELF. I AM KASHIMA, MANAGER OF HOTEL JOURNEY.
THERE'S SOMETHING WRONG WITH THIS TOWN!
THERE'S NOTHING WRONG. IT'S SIMPLY HIGH TIDE!
WE'VE GONE COMPLETELY AQUATIC, HERE!
THIS IS A TOWN OF FISHFOLK, AND THESE ARE OUR TRUE FORMS.
SO WHAT'S WITH LOOKING LIKE HUMANS THE REST OF THE TIME?
WELL, YOU WOULD BE VERY SURPRISED TO SEE A FISH AT THE RECEPTION DESK.
YEAH, WE *WERE*!
YOU SHOULD HAVE JUST TOLD US.
NO WAY! THAT WOULD HAVE SPOILED THE SURPRISE!

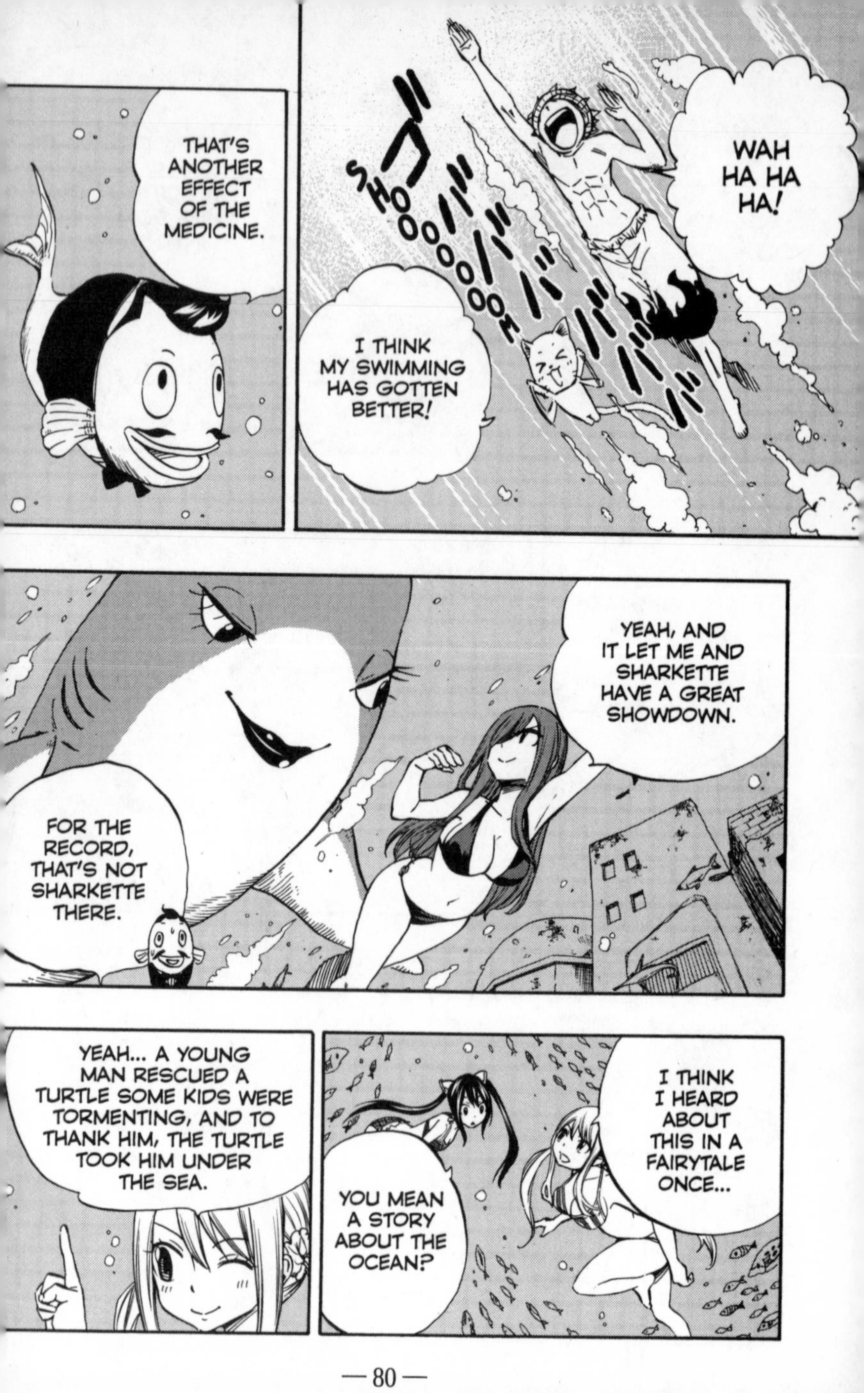
WAH HA HA HA!
SHOOOOOOOM
I THINK MY SWIMMING HAS GOTTEN BETTER!
THAT'S ANOTHER EFFECT OF THE MEDICINE.
YEAH, AND IT LET ME AND SHARKETTE HAVE A GREAT SHOWDOWN.
FOR THE RECORD, THAT'S NOT SHARKETTE THERE.
I THINK I HEARD ABOUT THIS IN A FAIRYTALE ONCE...
YOU MEAN A STORY ABOUT THE OCEAN?
YEAH... A YOUNG MAN RESCUED A TURTLE SOME KIDS WERE TORMENTING, AND TO THANK HIM, THE TURTLE TOOK HIM UNDER THE SEA.

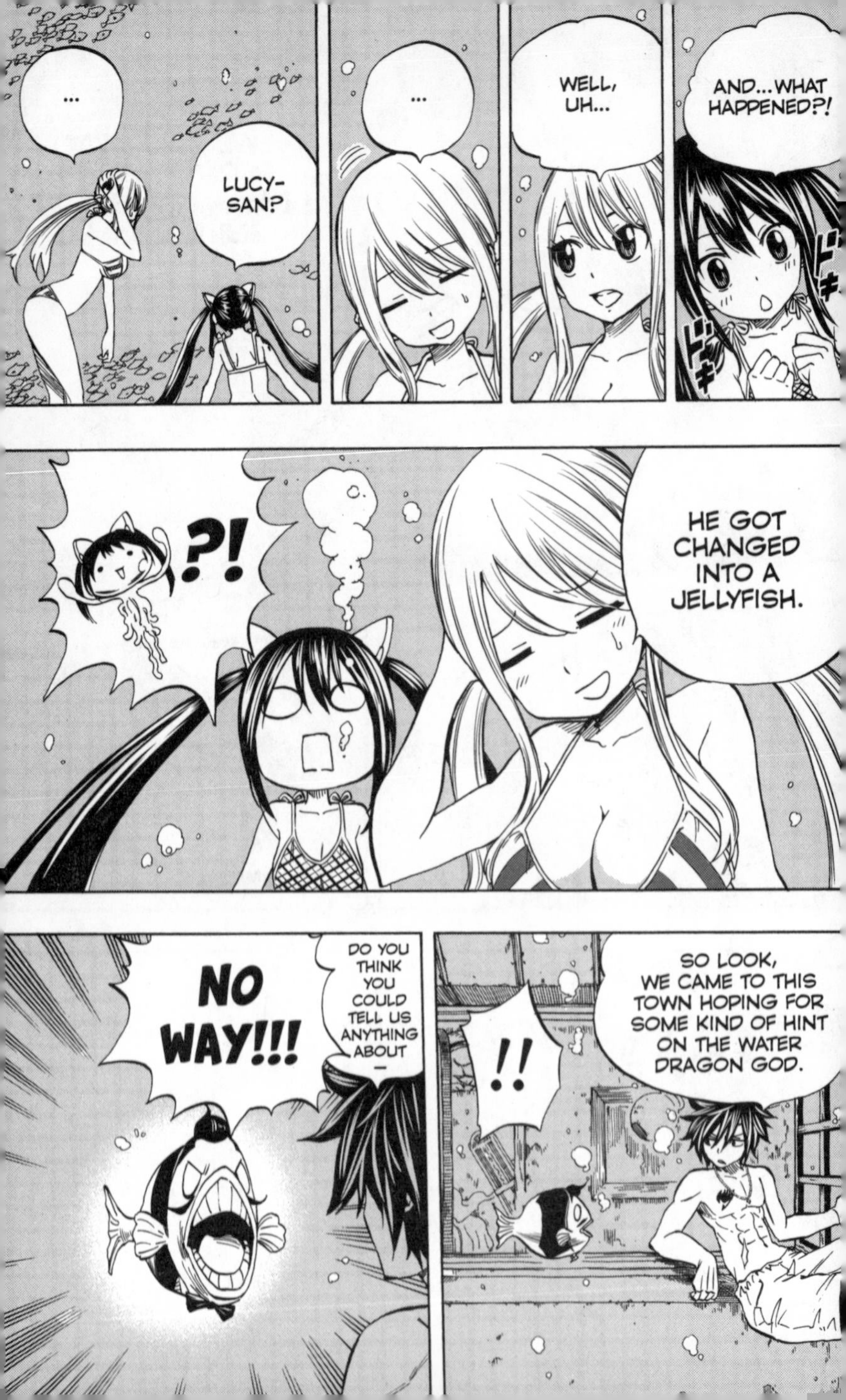
AND...WHAT HAPPENED?!
WELL, UH...
...
LUCY-SAN?
...
HE GOT CHANGED INTO A JELLYFISH.
?!
SO LOOK, WE CAME TO THIS TOWN HOPING FOR SOME KIND OF HINT ON THE WATER DRAGON GOD.
!!
DO YOU THINK YOU COULD TELL US ANYTHING ABOUT —
NO WAY!!!

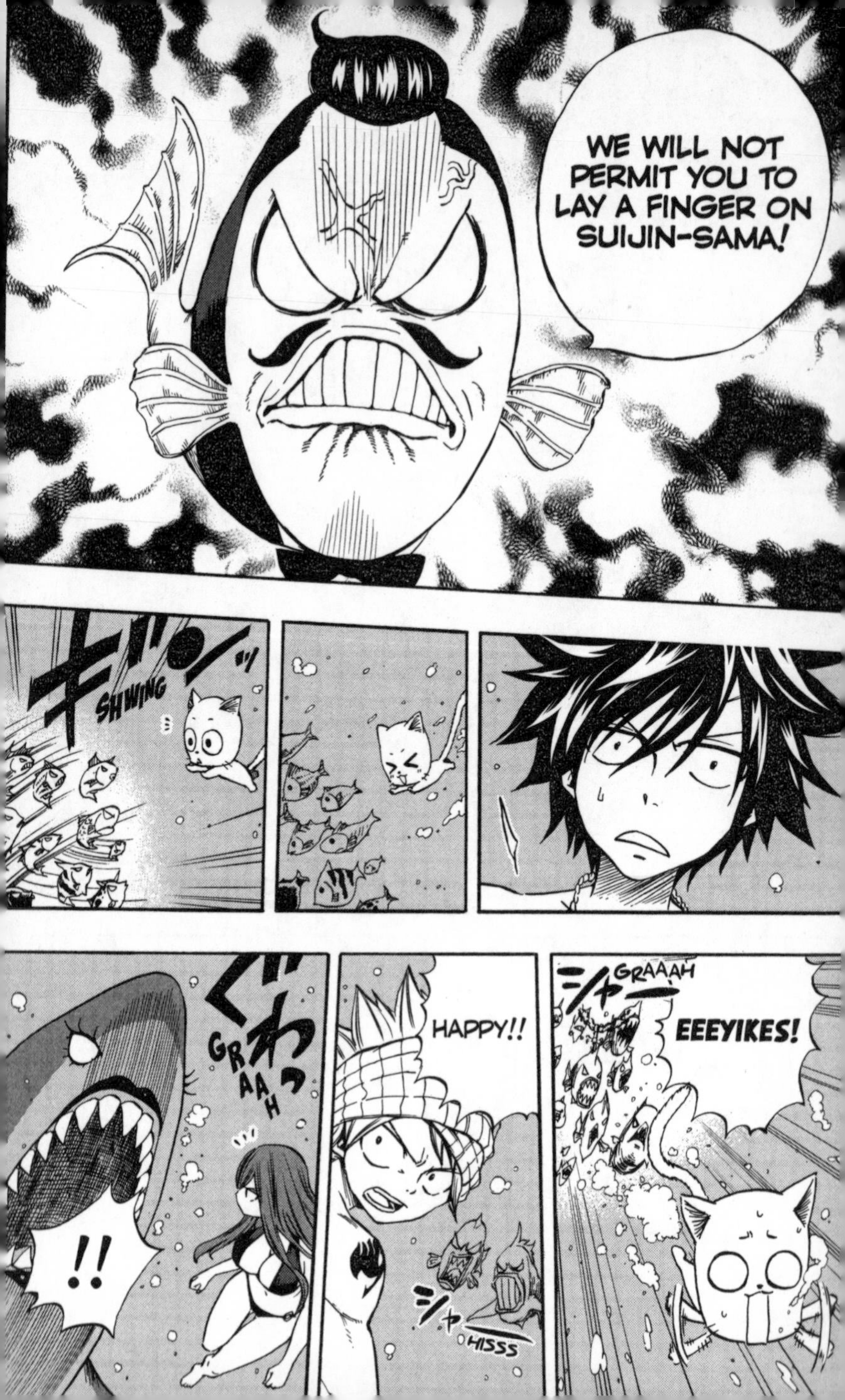
WE WILL NOT PERMIT YOU TO LAY A FINGER ON SUIJIN-SAMA!
SHWING
GRAAAH
EEEYIKES!
HAPPY!!
HISSS
GRAAH
!!

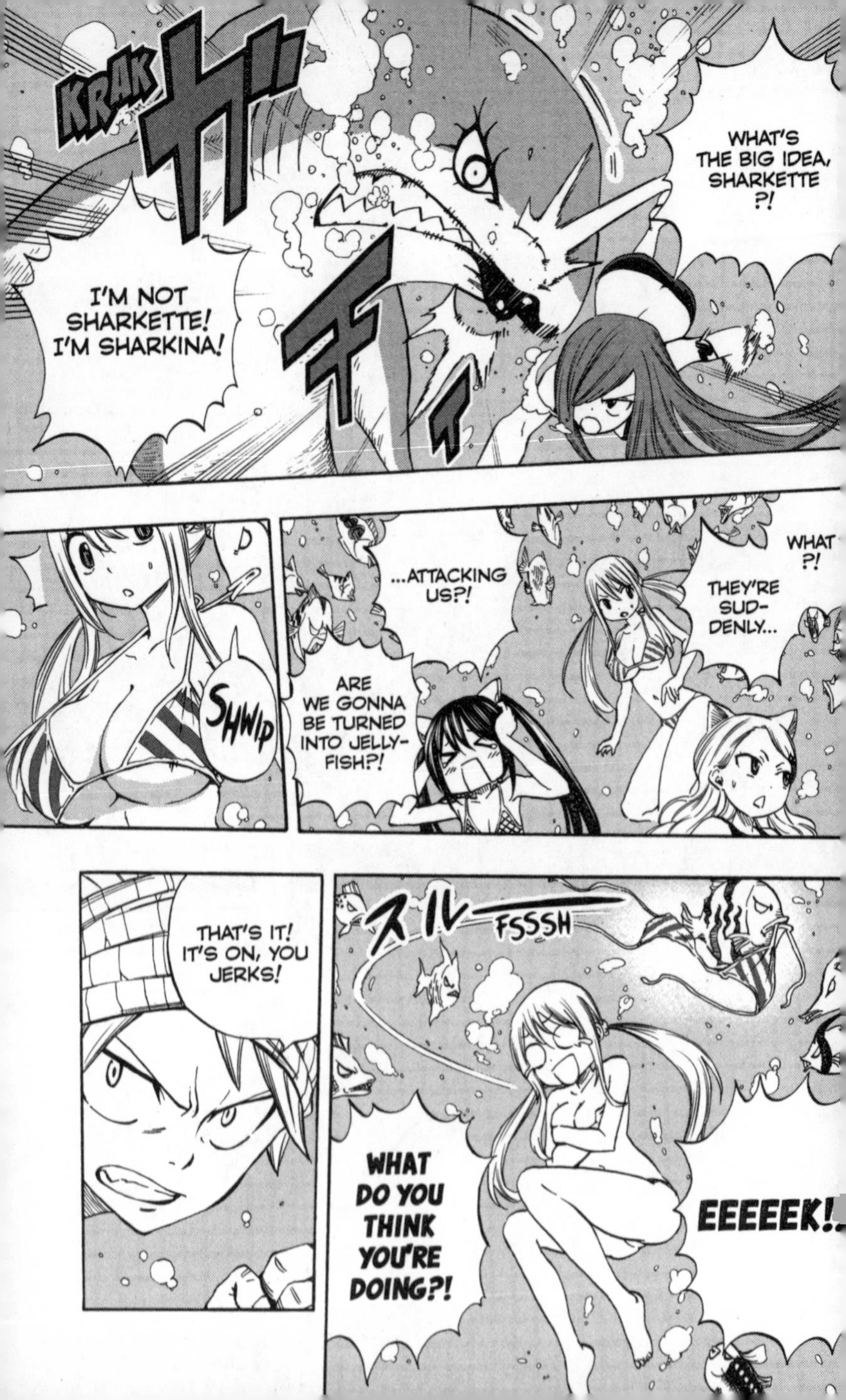
KRAK
WHAT'S THE BIG IDEA, SHARKETTE ?!
I'M NOT SHARKETTE! I'M SHARKINA!
WHAT ?!
THEY'RE SUD- DENLY...
...ATTACKING US?!
ARE WE GONNA BE TURNED INTO JELLY- FISH?!
SHWIP
FSSSH
EEEEEK!
WHAT DO YOU THINK YOU'RE DOING?!
THAT'S IT! IT'S ON, YOU JERKS!

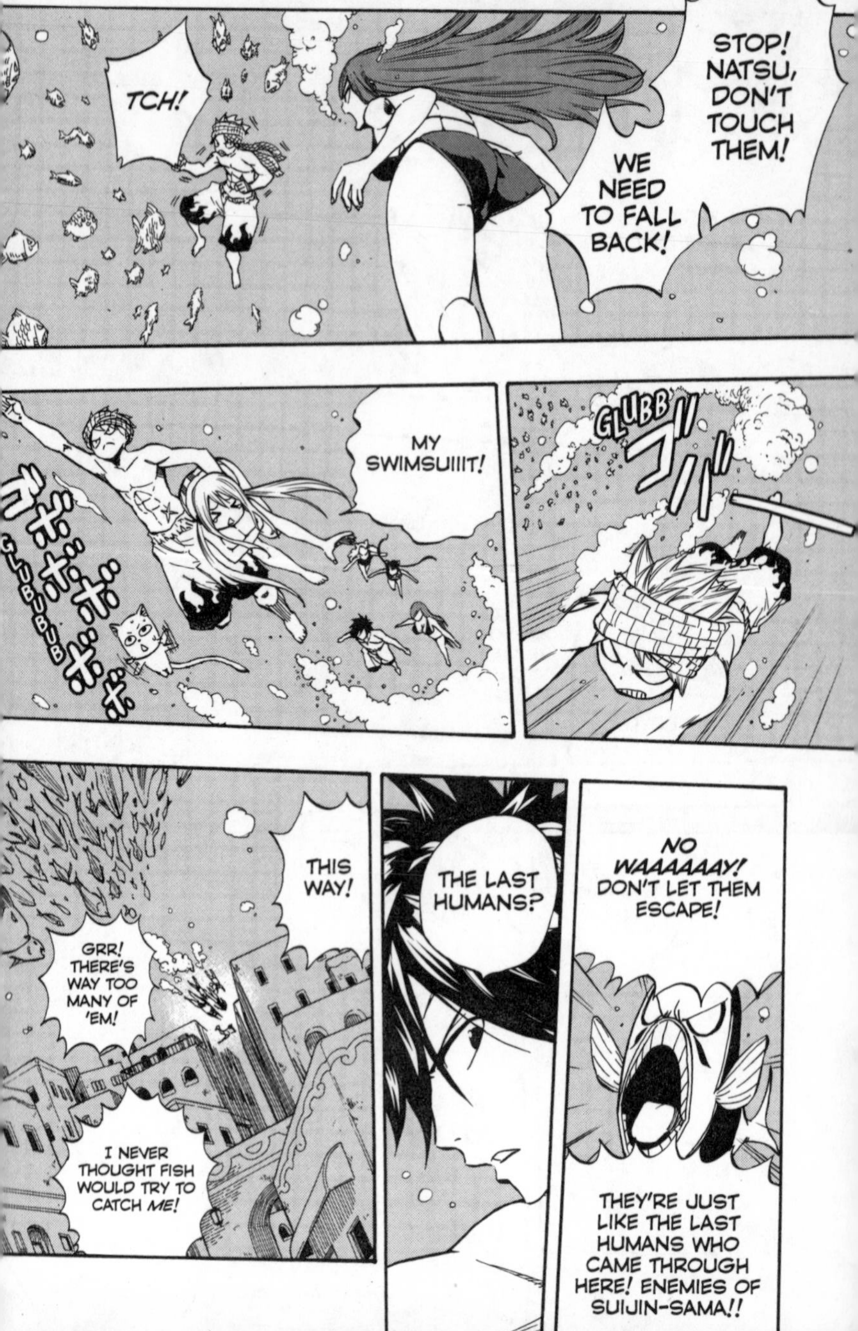
STOP! NATSU, DON'T TOUCH THEM!
WE NEED TO FALL BACK!
TCH!
GLUBB
MY SWIMSUIIIT!
GLUBUBUB
NO *WAAAAAAY!* DON'T LET THEM ESCAPE!
THEY'RE JUST LIKE THE LAST HUMANS WHO CAME THROUGH HERE! ENEMIES OF SUIJIN-SAMA!!
THE LAST HUMANS?
THIS WAY!
GRR! THERE'S WAY TOO MANY OF 'EM!
I NEVER THOUGHT FISH WOULD TRY TO CATCH *ME!*

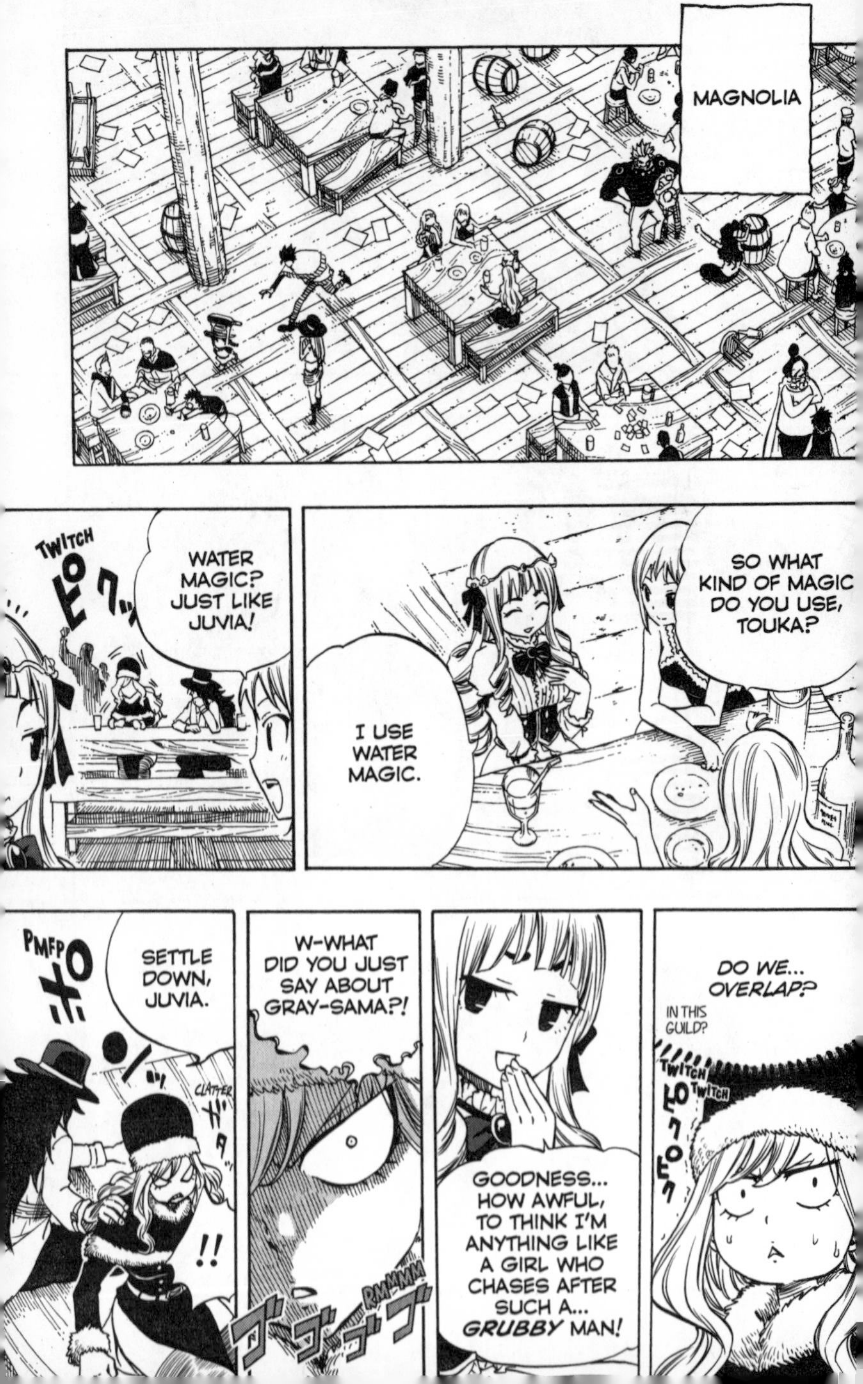
MAGNOLIA
SO WHAT KIND OF MAGIC DO YOU USE, TOUKA?
I USE WATER MAGIC.
TWITCH
WATER MAGIC? JUST LIKE JUVIA!
DO WE... OVERLAP?
IN THIS GUILD?
TWITCH TWITCH
GOODNESS... HOW AWFUL, TO THINK I'M ANYTHING LIKE A GIRL WHO CHASES AFTER SUCH A... *GRUBBY* MAN!
W-WHAT DID YOU JUST SAY ABOUT GRAY-SAMA?!
RMMMM
PMFP
SETTLE DOWN, JUVIA.
CLATTER
!!

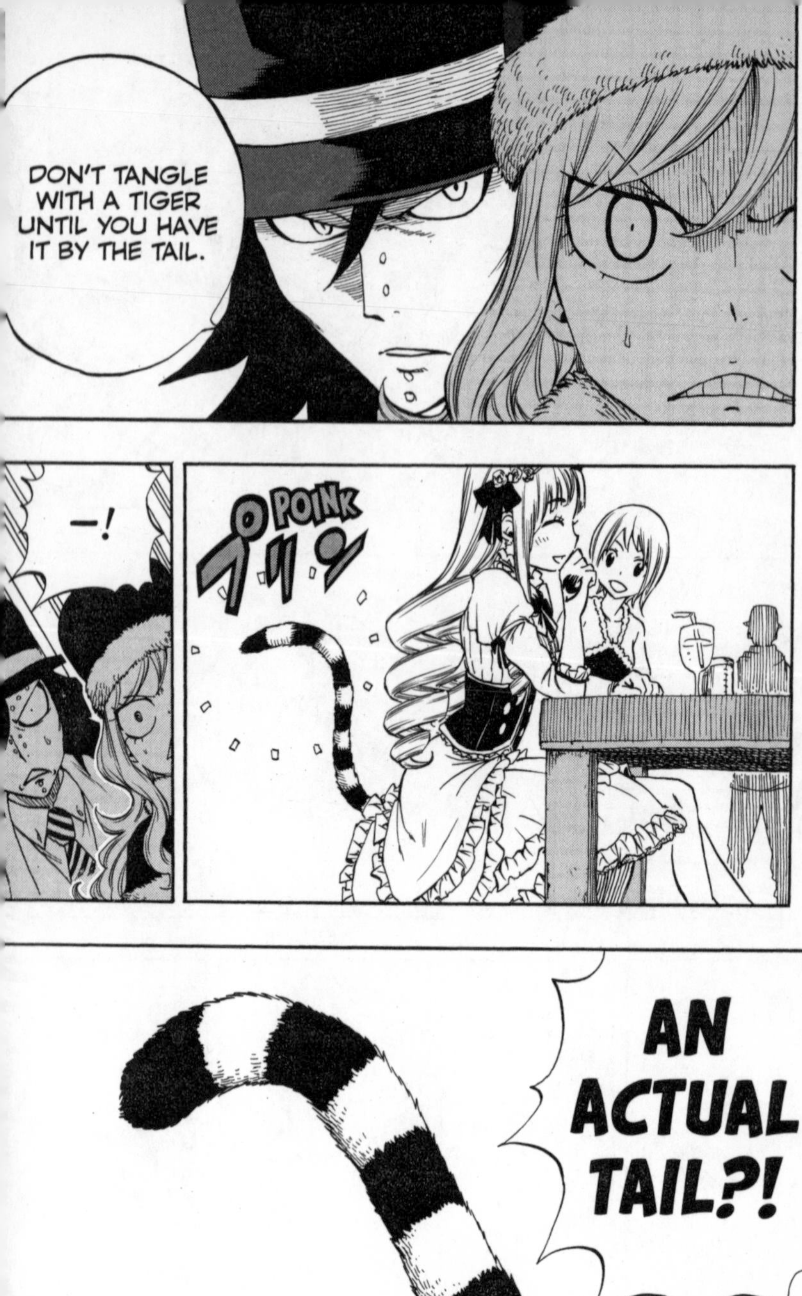
DON'T TANGLE WITH A TIGER UNTIL YOU HAVE IT BY THE TAIL.
POINK
—!
AN ACTUAL TAIL?!

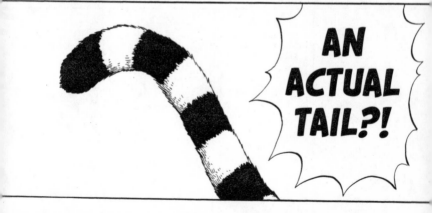

FAIRY TAIL
100 YEARS QUEST

Chapter 5: The Sealing of the Five Dragon Gods

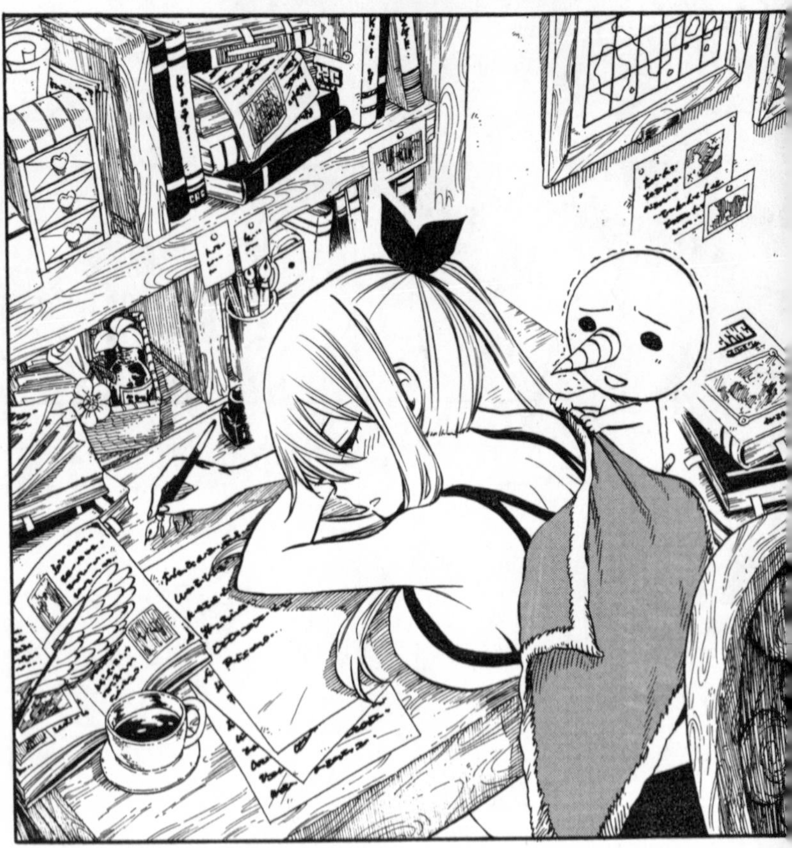

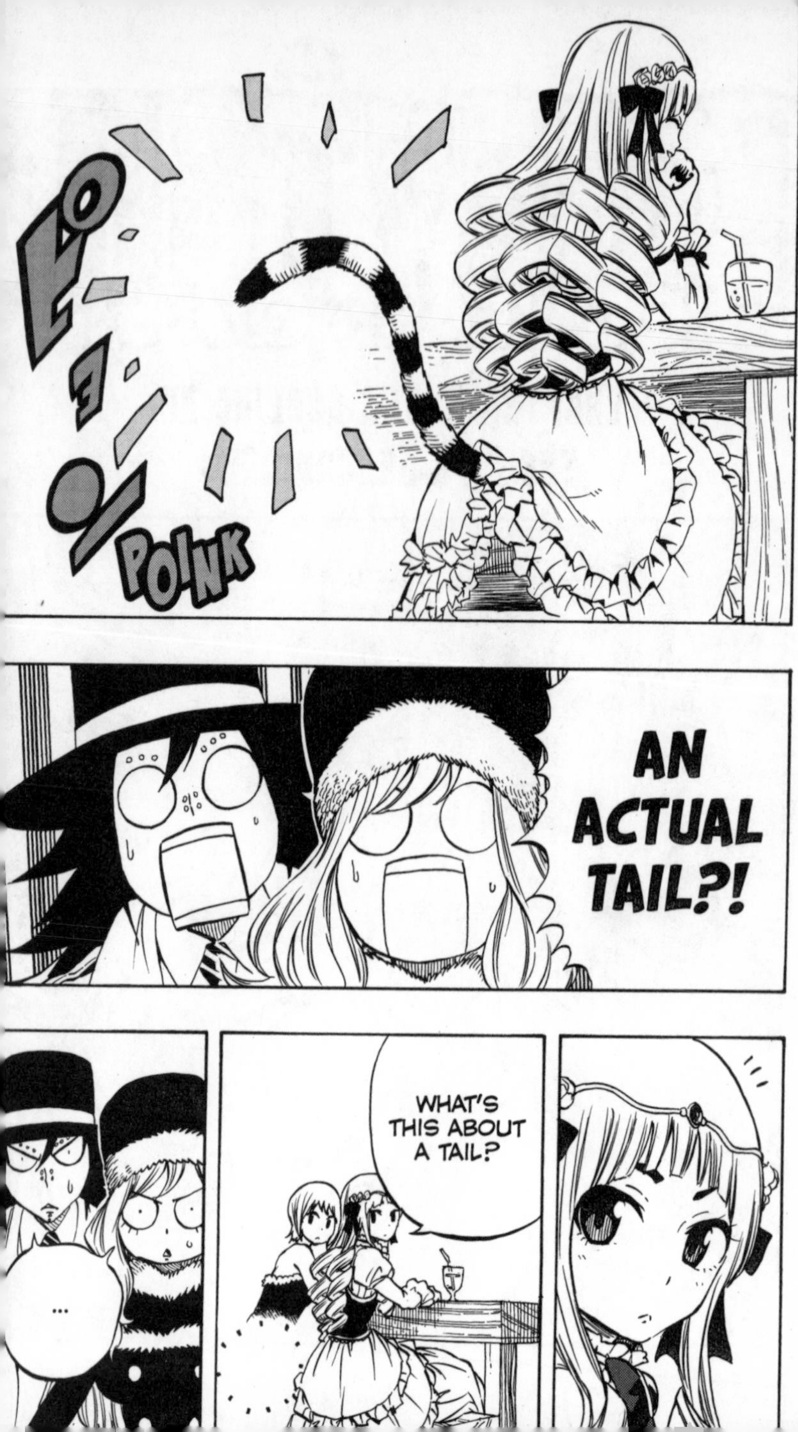
POINK
AN ACTUAL TAIL?!
WHAT'S THIS ABOUT A TAIL?
...

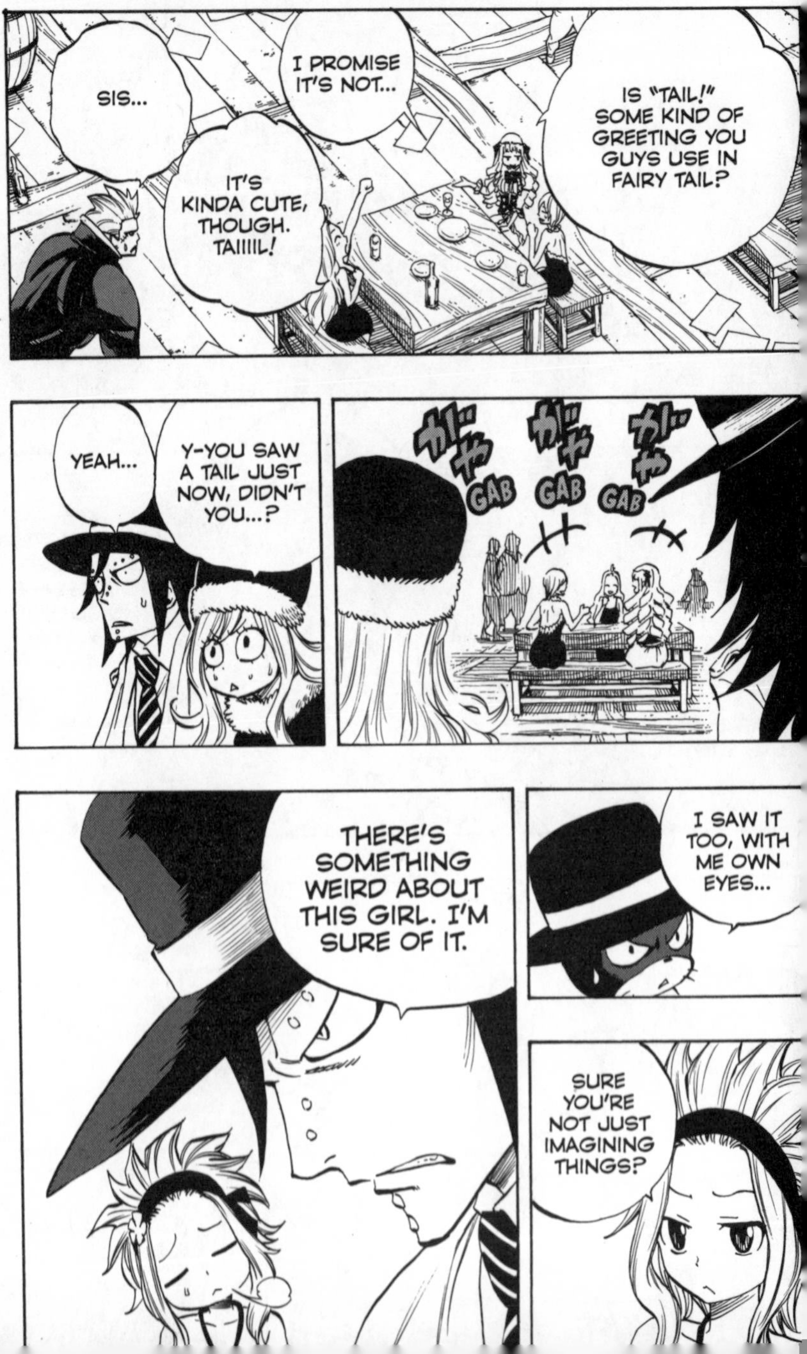
IS "TAIL!" SOME KIND OF GREETING YOU GUYS USE IN FAIRY TAIL?
I PROMISE IT'S NOT...
IT'S KINDA CUTE, THOUGH. TAIIIIL!
SIS...
GAB GAB GAB
Y-YOU SAW A TAIL JUST NOW, DIDN'T YOU...?
YEAH...
I SAW IT TOO, WITH ME OWN EYES...
SURE YOU'RE NOT JUST IMAGINING THINGS?
THERE'S SOMETHING WEIRD ABOUT THIS GIRL. I'M SURE OF IT.

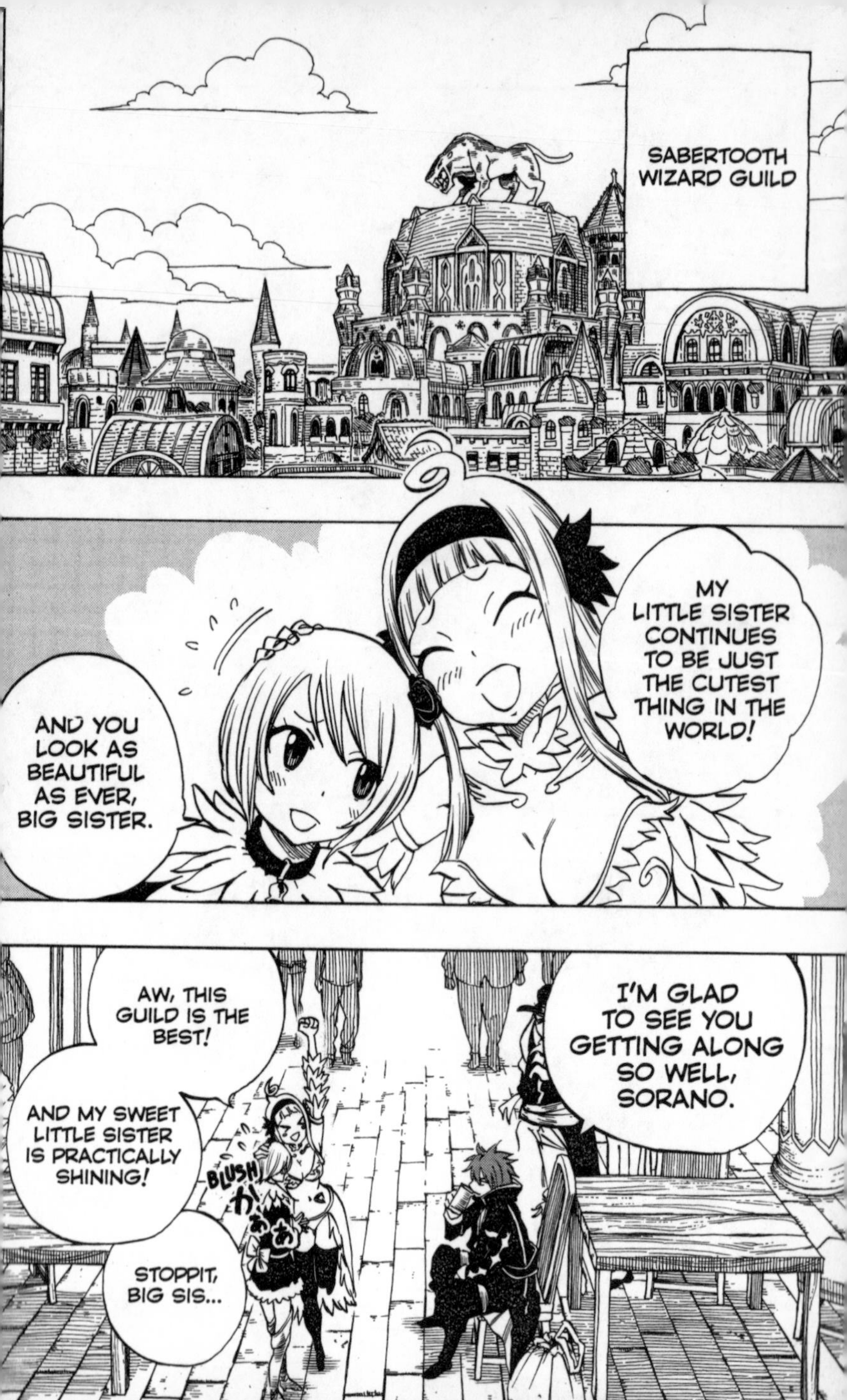
SABERTOOTH WIZARD GUILD
MY LITTLE SISTER CONTINUES TO BE JUST THE CUTEST THING IN THE WORLD!
AND YOU LOOK AS BEAUTIFUL AS EVER, BIG SISTER.
I'M GLAD TO SEE YOU GETTING ALONG SO WELL, SORANO.
AW, THIS GUILD IS THE BEST!
AND MY SWEET LITTLE SISTER IS PRACTICALLY SHINING!
BLUSH!
STOPPIT, BIG SIS...

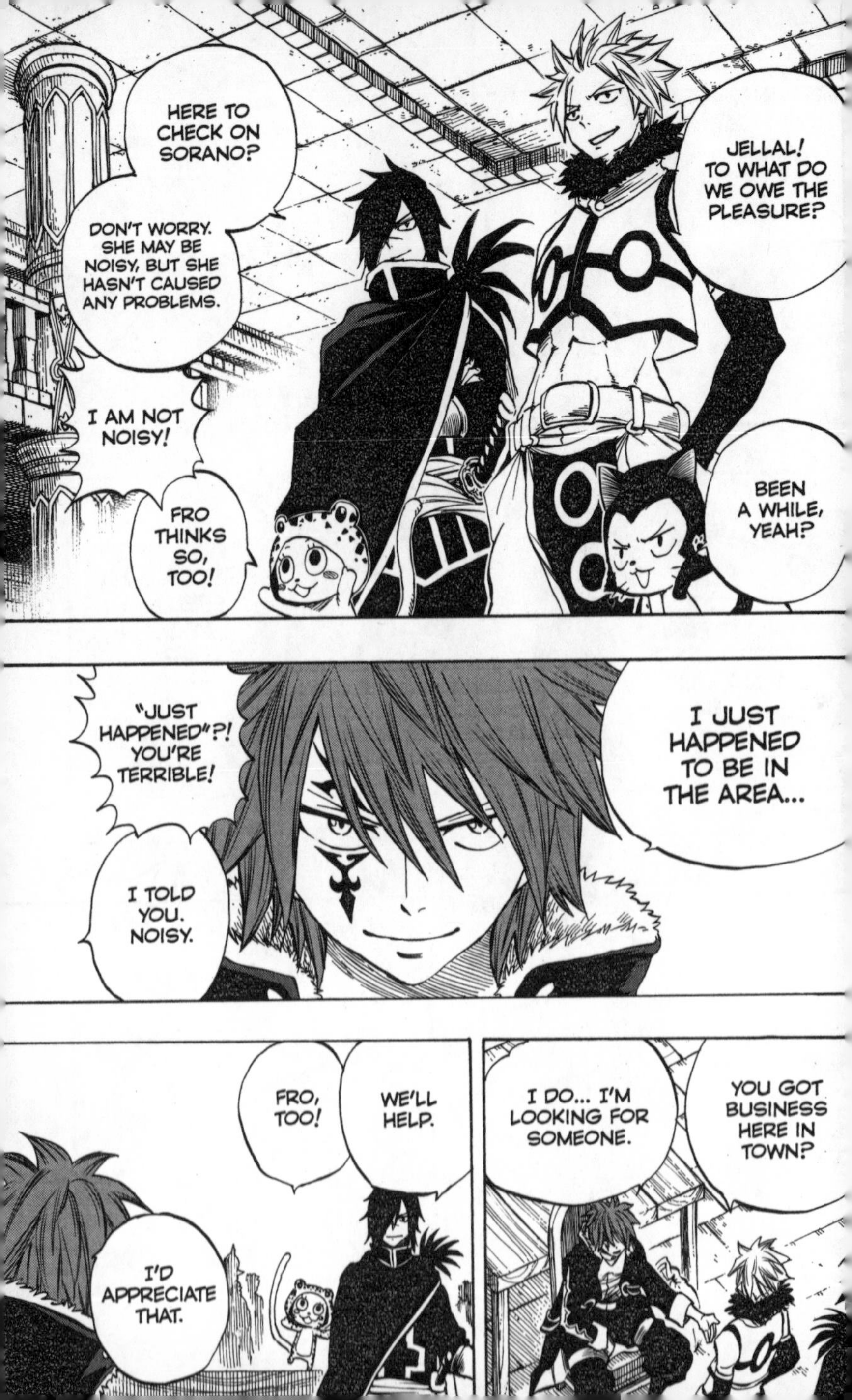
JELLAL! TO WHAT DO WE OWE THE PLEASURE?
BEEN A WHILE, YEAH?
HERE TO CHECK ON SORANO?
DON'T WORRY. SHE MAY BE NOISY, BUT SHE HASN'T CAUSED ANY PROBLEMS.
I AM NOT NOISY!
FRO THINKS SO, TOO!
I JUST HAPPENED TO BE IN THE AREA...
"JUST HAPPENED"?! YOU'RE TERRIBLE!
I TOLD YOU. NOISY.
YOU GOT BUSINESS HERE IN TOWN?
I DO... I'M LOOKING FOR SOMEONE.
WE'LL HELP.
FRO, TOO!
I'D APPRECIATE THAT.

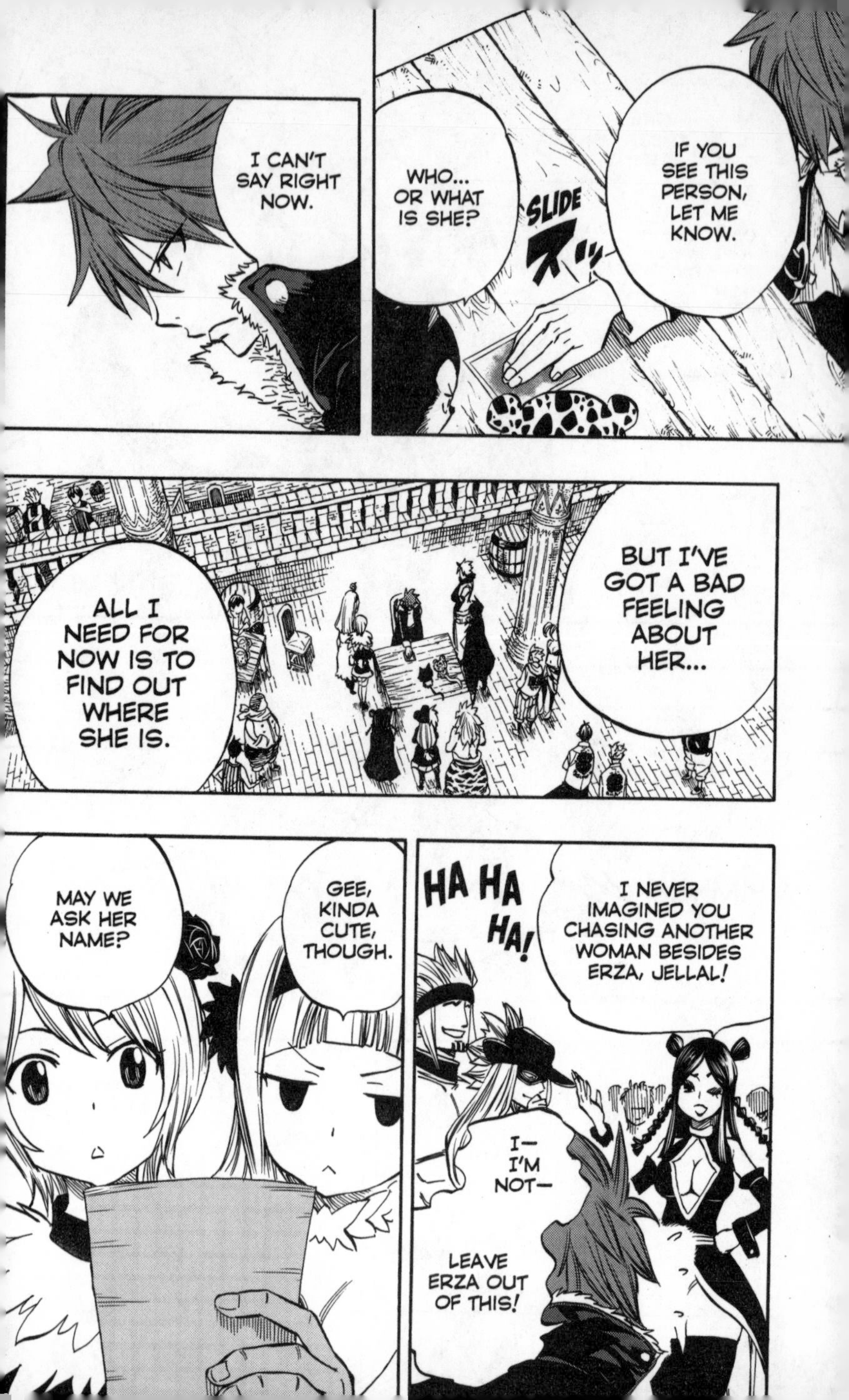
IF YOU SEE THIS PERSON, LET ME KNOW.
SLIDE
WHO... OR WHAT IS SHE?
I CAN'T SAY RIGHT NOW.
BUT I'VE GOT A BAD FEELING ABOUT HER...
ALL I NEED FOR NOW IS TO FIND OUT WHERE SHE IS.
I NEVER IMAGINED YOU CHASING ANOTHER WOMAN BESIDES ERZA, JELLAL!
HA HA HA!
I— I'M NOT—
LEAVE ERZA OUT OF THIS!
GEE, KINDA CUTE, THOUGH.
MAY WE ASK HER NAME?

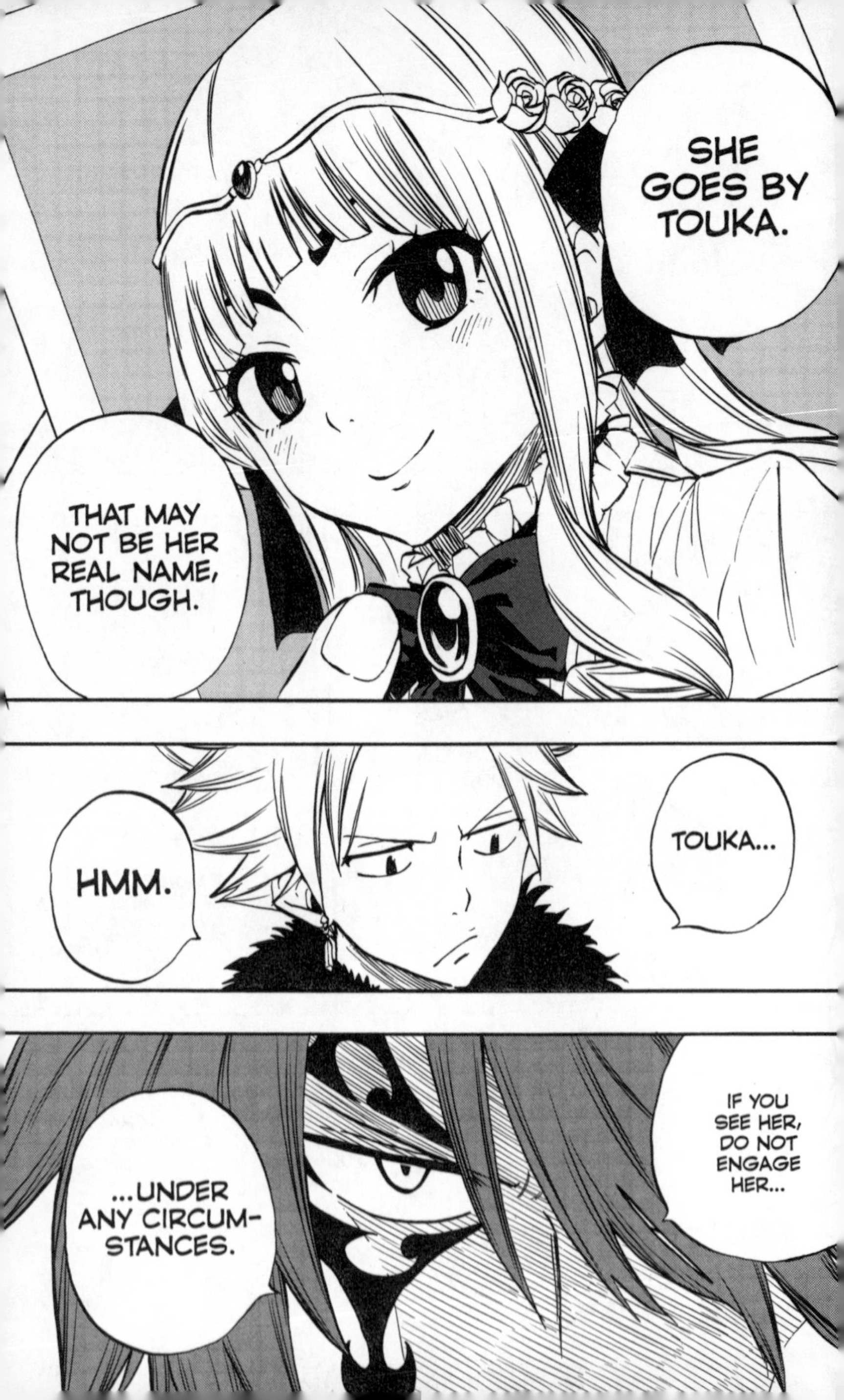
SHE GOES BY TOUKA.
THAT MAY NOT BE HER REAL NAME, THOUGH.
TOUKA...
HMM.
IF YOU SEE HER, DO NOT ENGAGE HER...
...UNDER ANY CIRCUM-STANCES.

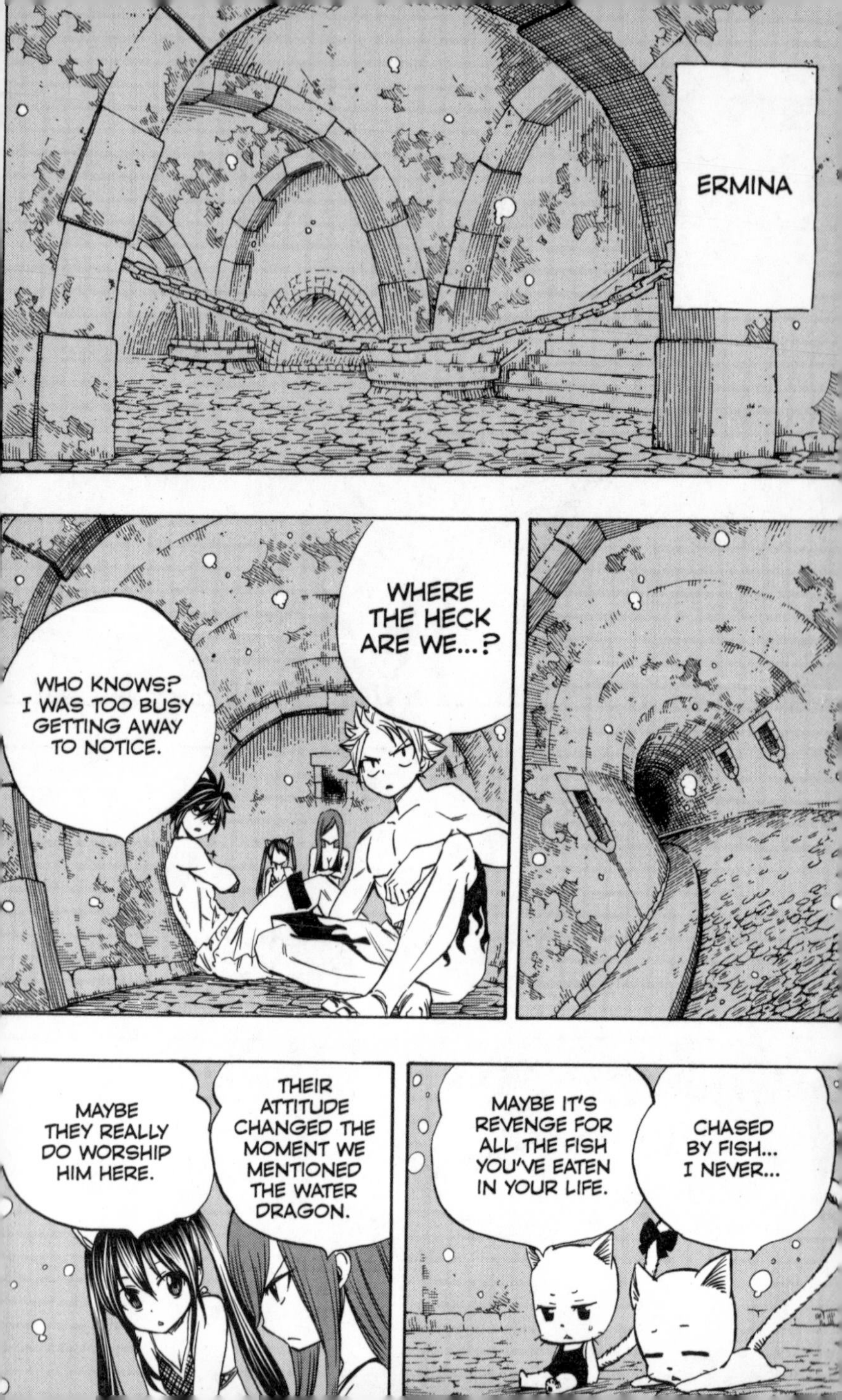
ERMINA
WHERE THE HECK ARE WE...?
WHO KNOWS? I WAS TOO BUSY GETTING AWAY TO NOTICE.
CHASED BY FISH... I NEVER...
MAYBE IT'S REVENGE FOR ALL THE FISH YOU'VE EATEN IN YOUR LIFE.
THEIR ATTITUDE CHANGED THE MOMENT WE MENTIONED THE WATER DRAGON.
MAYBE THEY REALLY DO WORSHIP HIM HERE.

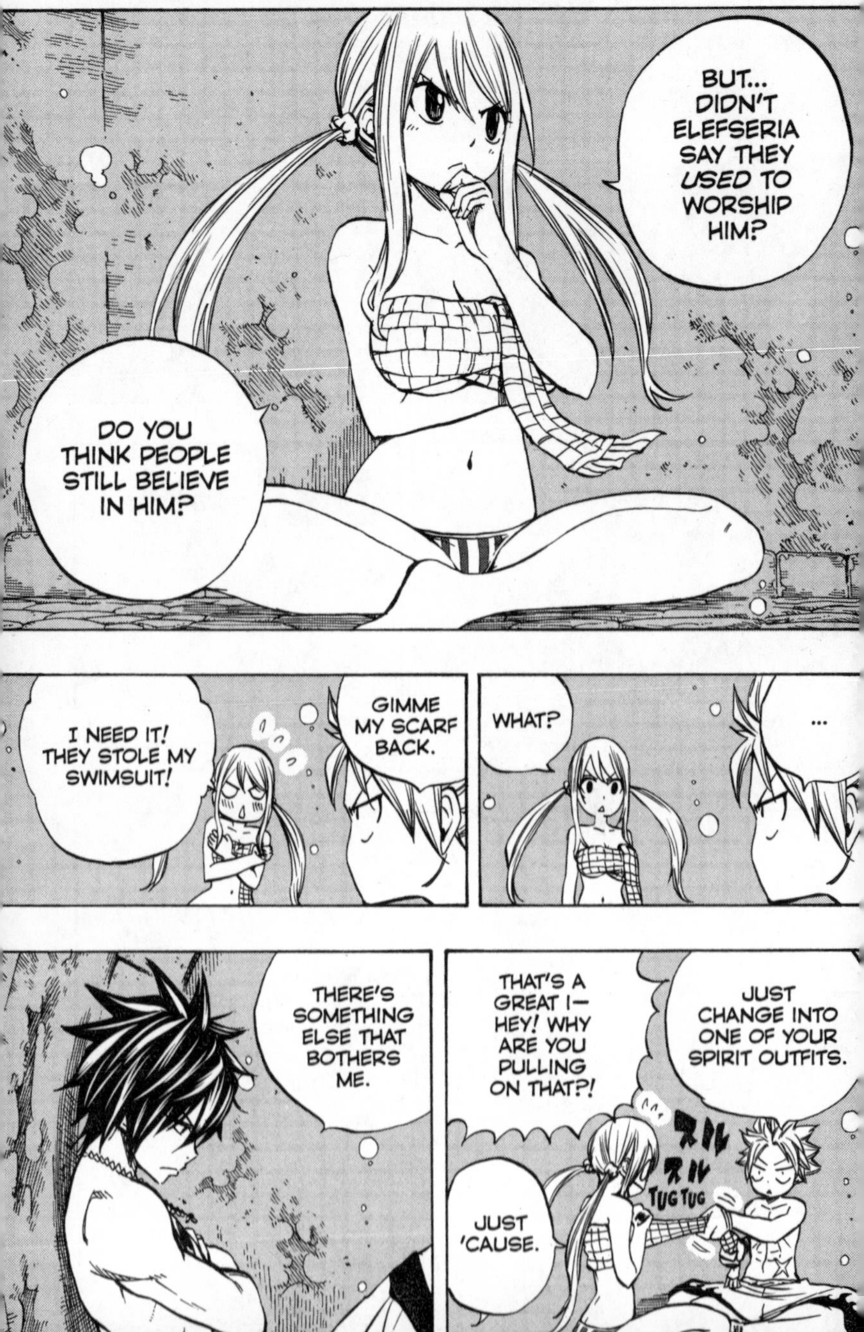
BUT... DIDN'T ELEFSERIA SAY THEY *USED* TO WORSHIP HIM?
DO YOU THINK PEOPLE STILL BELIEVE IN HIM?
...
WHAT?
GIMME MY SCARF BACK.
I NEED IT! THEY STOLE MY SWIMSUIT!
JUST CHANGE INTO ONE OF YOUR SPIRIT OUTFITS.
THAT'S A GREAT I— HEY! WHY ARE YOU PULLING ON THAT?!
スルスル
TUG TUG
JUST 'CAUSE.
THERE'S SOMETHING ELSE THAT BOTHERS ME.

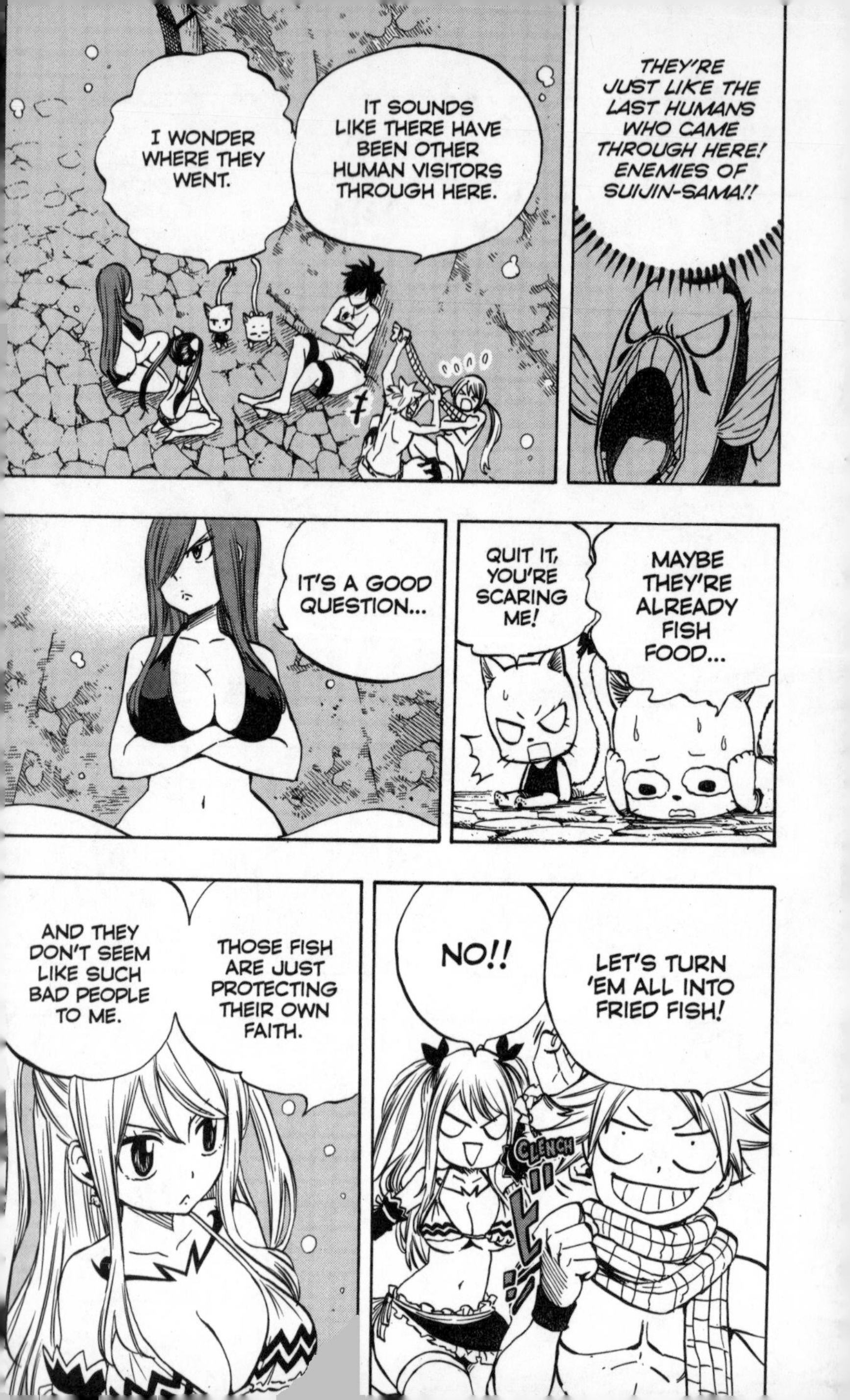
THEY'RE JUST LIKE THE LAST HUMANS WHO CAME THROUGH HERE! ENEMIES OF SUIJIN-SAMA!!
IT SOUNDS LIKE THERE HAVE BEEN OTHER HUMAN VISITORS THROUGH HERE.
I WONDER WHERE THEY WENT.
MAYBE THEY'RE ALREADY FISH FOOD...
QUIT IT, YOU'RE SCARING ME!
IT'S A GOOD QUESTION...
LET'S TURN 'EM ALL INTO FRIED FISH!
NO!!
CLENCH
THOSE FISH ARE JUST PROTECTING THEIR OWN FAITH.
AND THEY DON'T SEEM LIKE SUCH BAD PEOPLE TO ME.

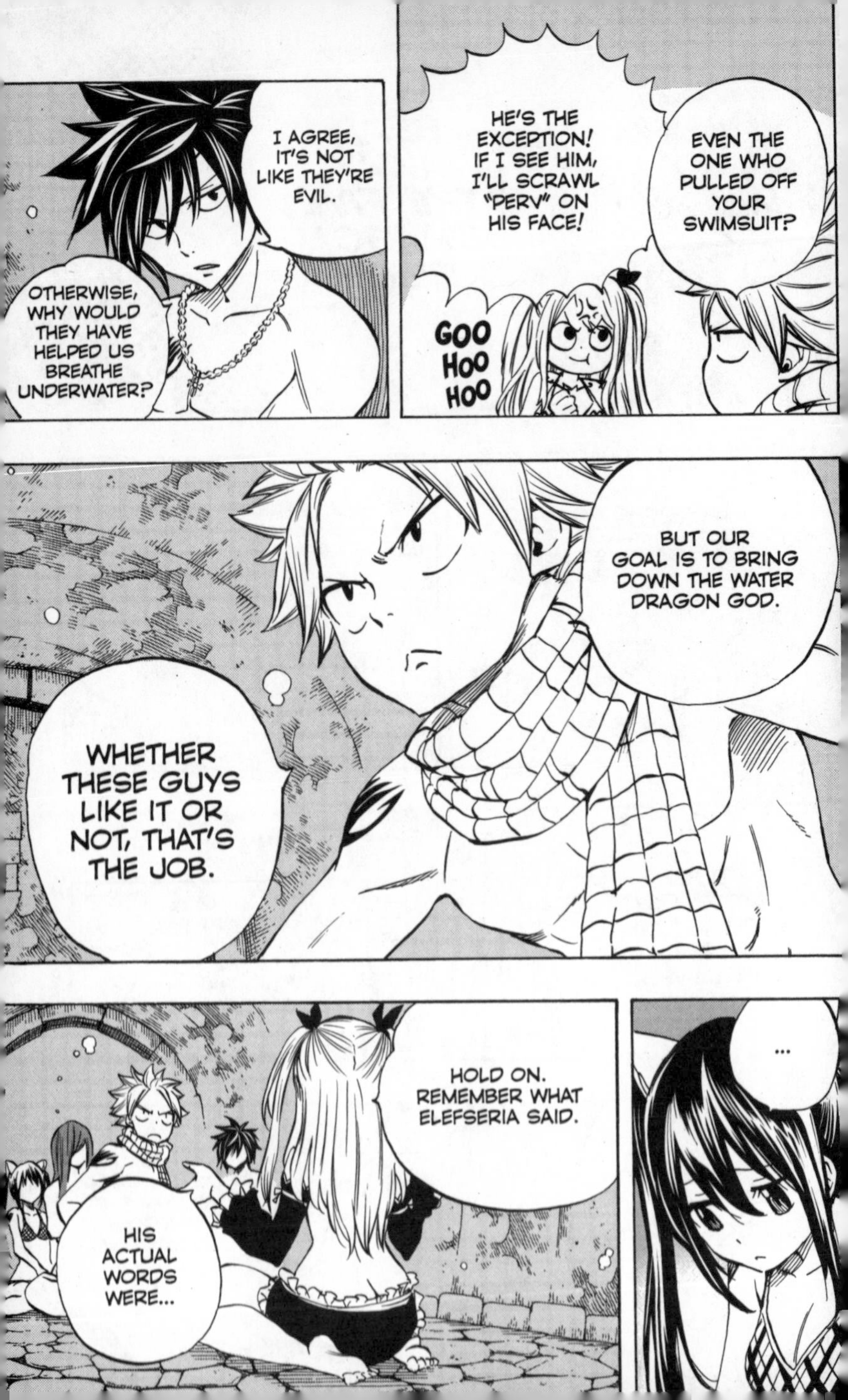
EVEN THE ONE WHO PULLED OFF YOUR SWIMSUIT?
HE'S THE EXCEPTION! IF I SEE HIM, I'LL SCRAWL "PERV" ON HIS FACE!
GOO HOO HOO
I AGREE, IT'S NOT LIKE THEY'RE EVIL.
OTHERWISE, WHY WOULD THEY HAVE HELPED US BREATHE UNDERWATER?
BUT OUR GOAL IS TO BRING DOWN THE WATER DRAGON GOD.
WHETHER THESE GUYS LIKE IT OR NOT, THAT'S THE JOB.
...
HOLD ON. REMEMBER WHAT ELEFSERIA SAID.
HIS ACTUAL WORDS WERE...

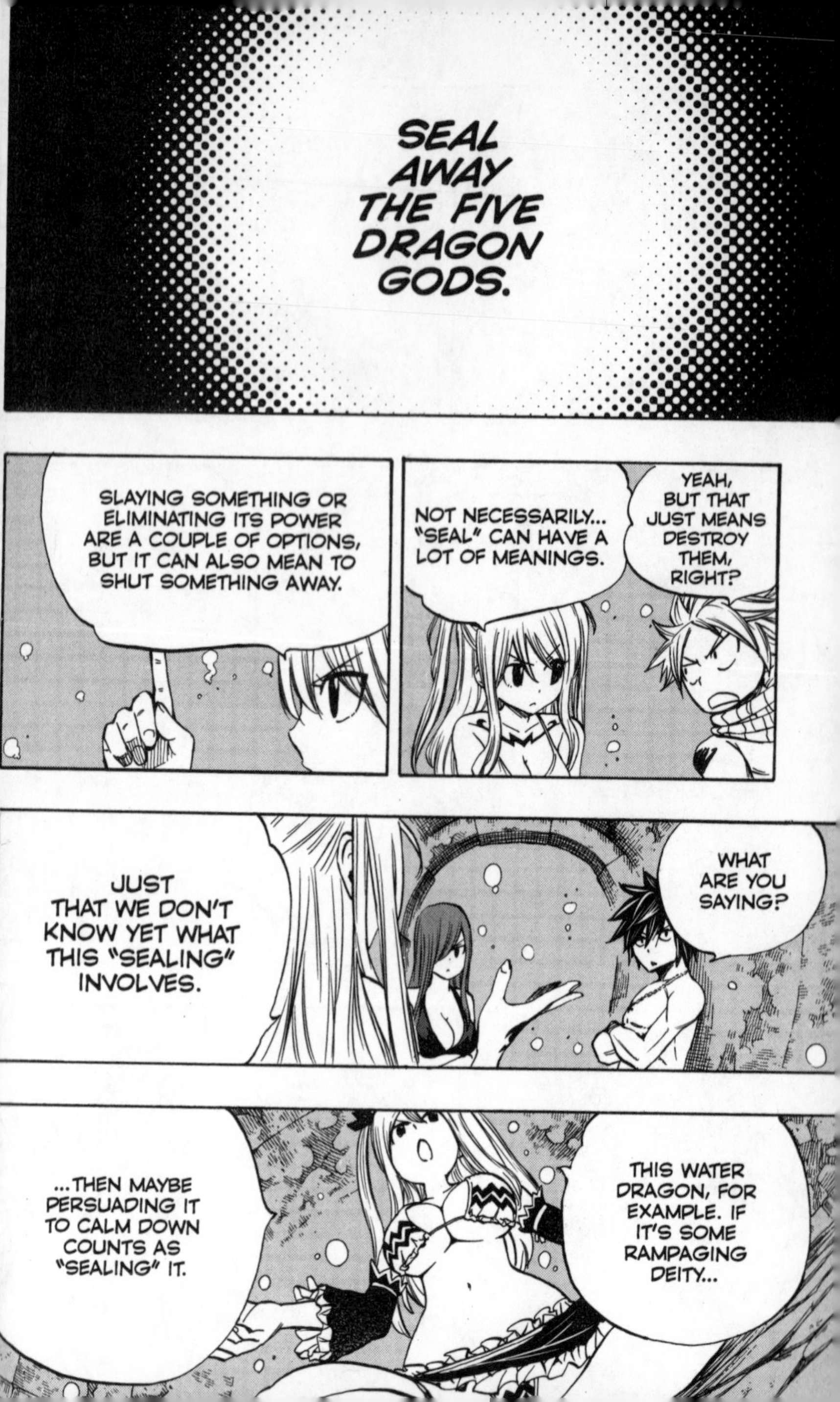

SEAL AWAY THE FIVE DRAGON GODS.
YEAH, BUT THAT JUST MEANS DESTROY THEM, RIGHT?
NOT NECESSARILY... "SEAL" CAN HAVE A LOT OF MEANINGS.
SLAYING SOMETHING OR ELIMINATING ITS POWER ARE A COUPLE OF OPTIONS, BUT IT CAN ALSO MEAN TO SHUT SOMETHING AWAY.
WHAT ARE YOU SAYING?
JUST THAT WE DON'T KNOW YET WHAT THIS "SEALING" INVOLVES.
THIS WATER DRAGON, FOR EXAMPLE. IF IT'S SOME RAMPAGING DEITY...
...THEN MAYBE PERSUADING IT TO CALM DOWN COUNTS AS "SEALING" IT.

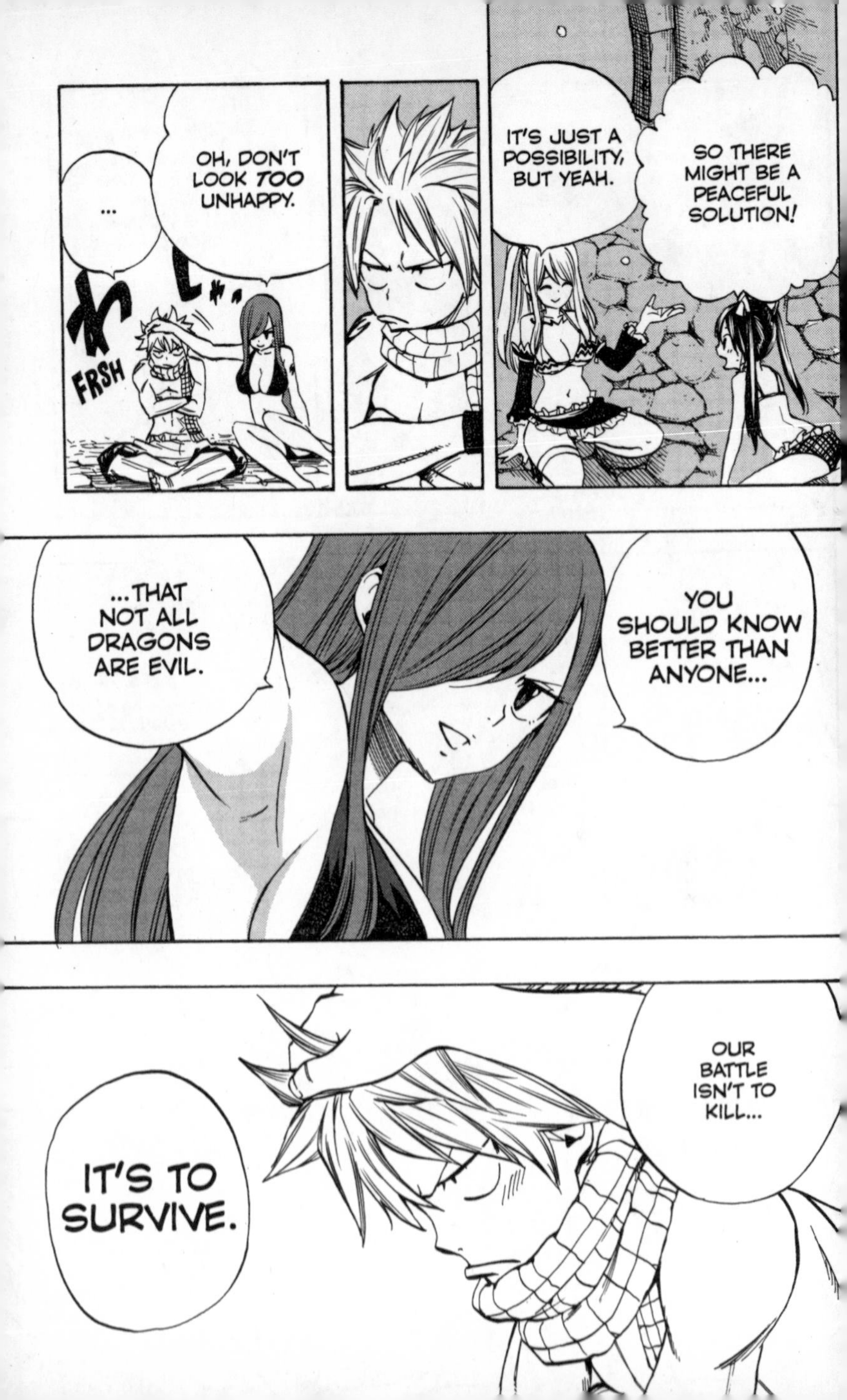
SO THERE MIGHT BE A PEACEFUL SOLUTION!
IT'S JUST A POSSIBILITY, BUT YEAH.
OH, DON'T LOOK *TOO* UNHAPPY.
...
FRSH
YOU SHOULD KNOW BETTER THAN ANYONE...
...THAT NOT ALL DRAGONS ARE EVIL.
OUR BATTLE ISN'T TO KILL...
IT'S TO SURVIVE.

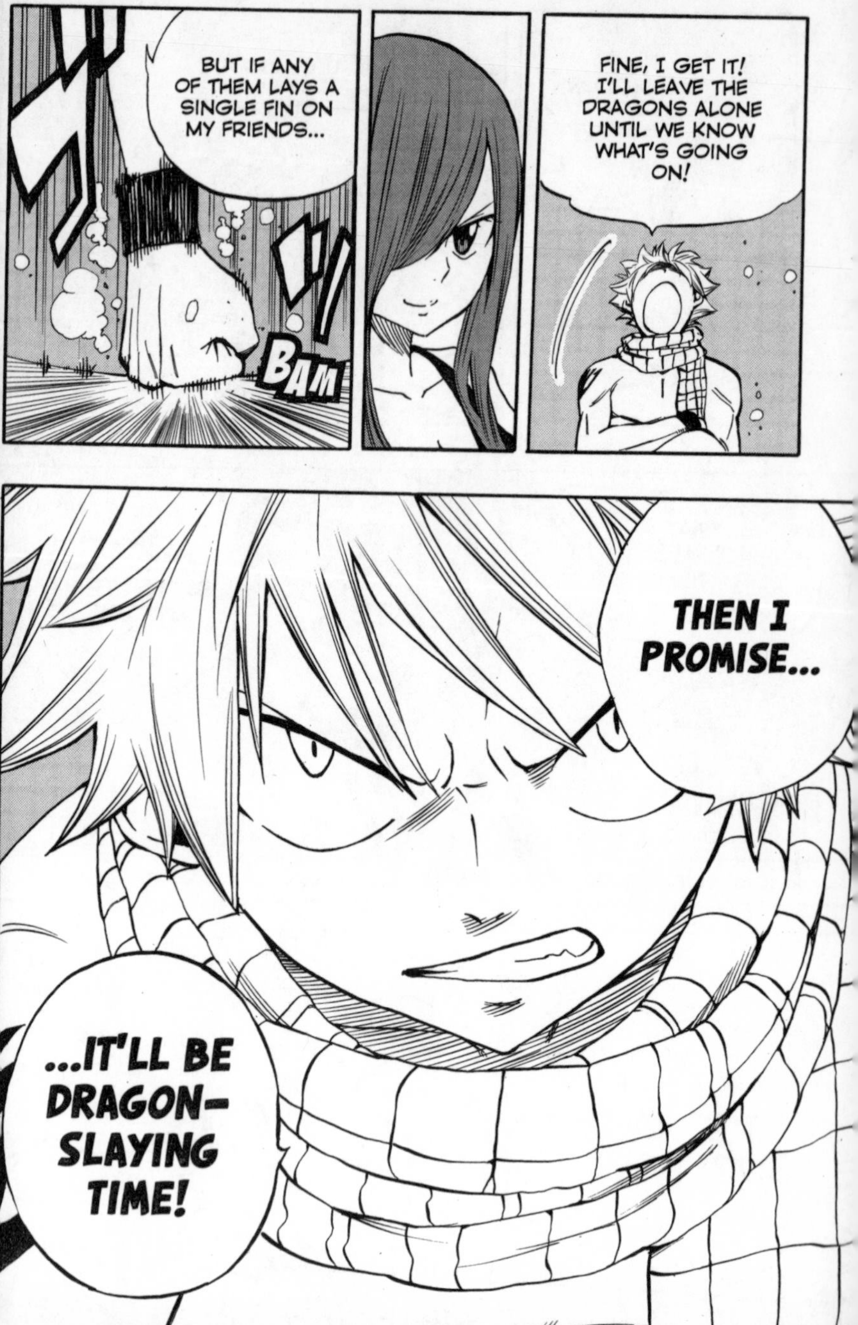
FINE, I GET IT! I'LL LEAVE THE DRAGONS ALONE UNTIL WE KNOW WHAT'S GOING ON!
BUT IF ANY OF THEM LAYS A SINGLE FIN ON MY FRIENDS...
BAM
THEN I PROMISE...
...IT'LL BE DRAGON-SLAYING TIME!

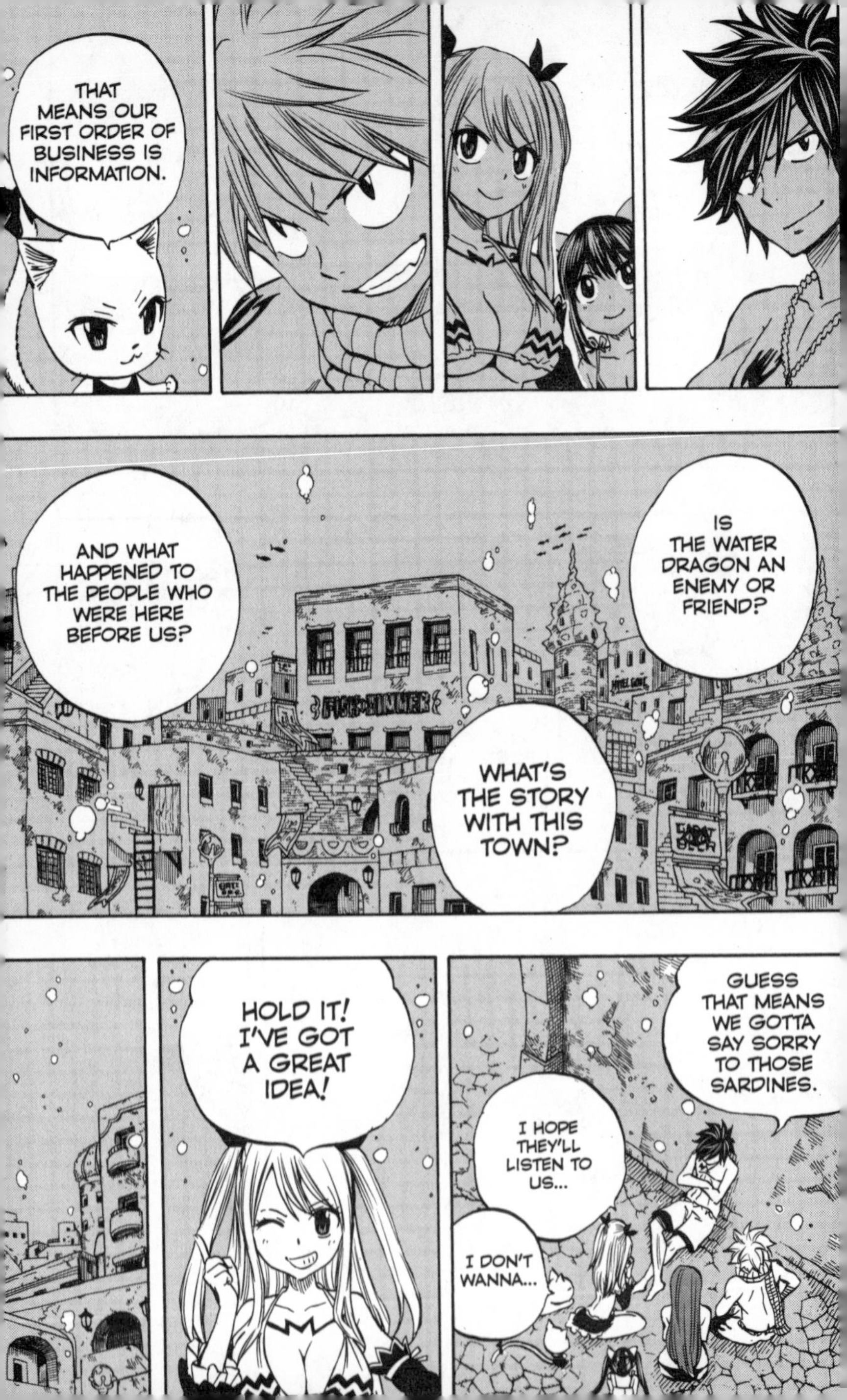
THAT MEANS OUR FIRST ORDER OF BUSINESS IS INFORMATION.
IS THE WATER DRAGON AN ENEMY OR FRIEND?
WHAT'S THE STORY WITH THIS TOWN?
AND WHAT HAPPENED TO THE PEOPLE WHO WERE HERE BEFORE US?
GUESS THAT MEANS WE GOTTA SAY SORRY TO THOSE SARDINES.
I HOPE THEY'LL LISTEN TO US...
I DON'T WANNA...
HOLD IT! I'VE GOT A GREAT IDEA!

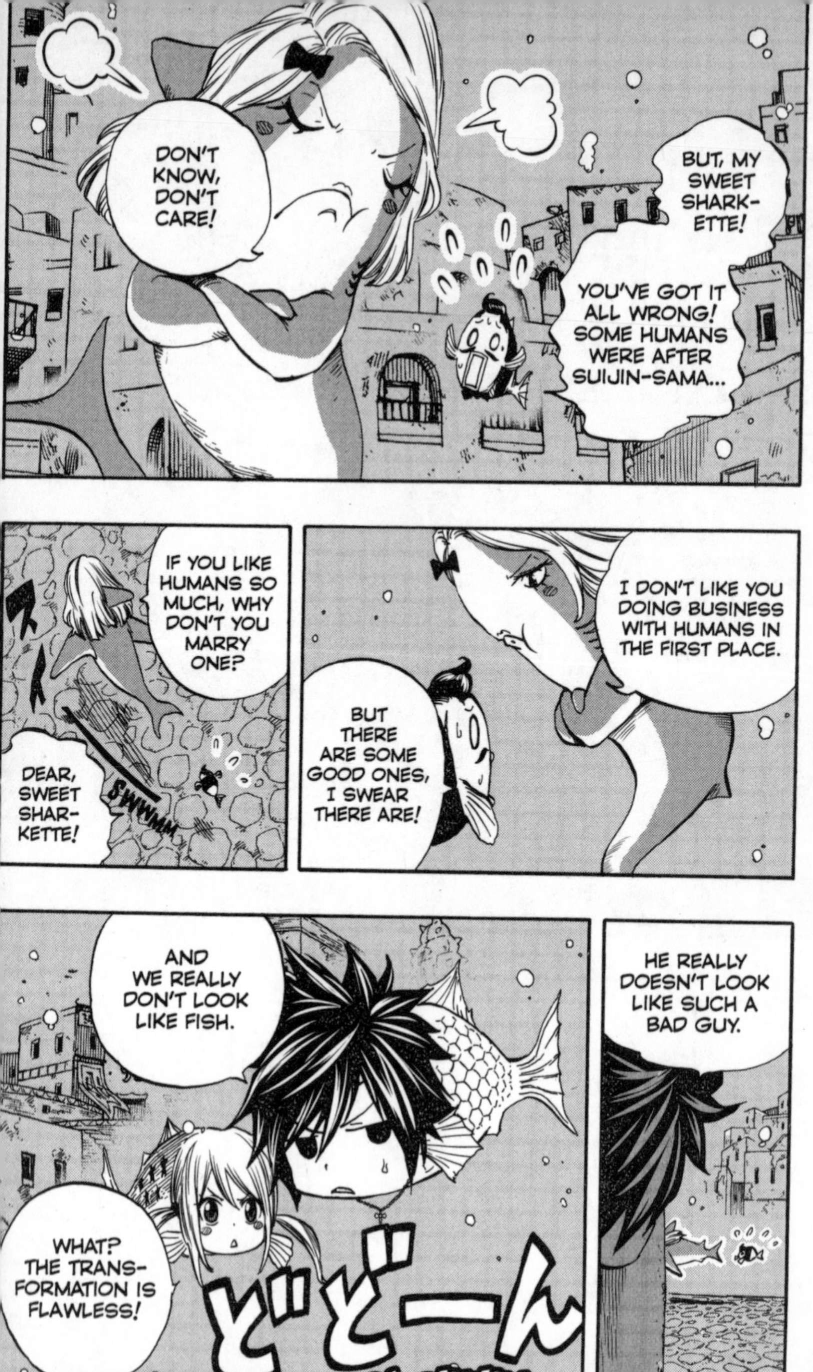
BUT, MY SWEET SHARK-ETTE!
YOU'VE GOT IT ALL WRONG! SOME HUMANS WERE AFTER SUIJIN-SAMA...
DON'T KNOW, DON'T CARE!
I DON'T LIKE YOU DOING BUSINESS WITH HUMANS IN THE FIRST PLACE.
BUT THERE ARE SOME GOOD ONES, I SWEAR THERE ARE!
IF YOU LIKE HUMANS SO MUCH, WHY DON'T YOU MARRY ONE?
SWWMM
DEAR, SWEET SHAR-KETTE!
HE REALLY DOESN'T LOOK LIKE SUCH A BAD GUY.
AND WE REALLY DON'T LOOK LIKE FISH.
WHAT? THE TRANS-FORMATION IS FLAWLESS!
どどーん
BA-BUUUM

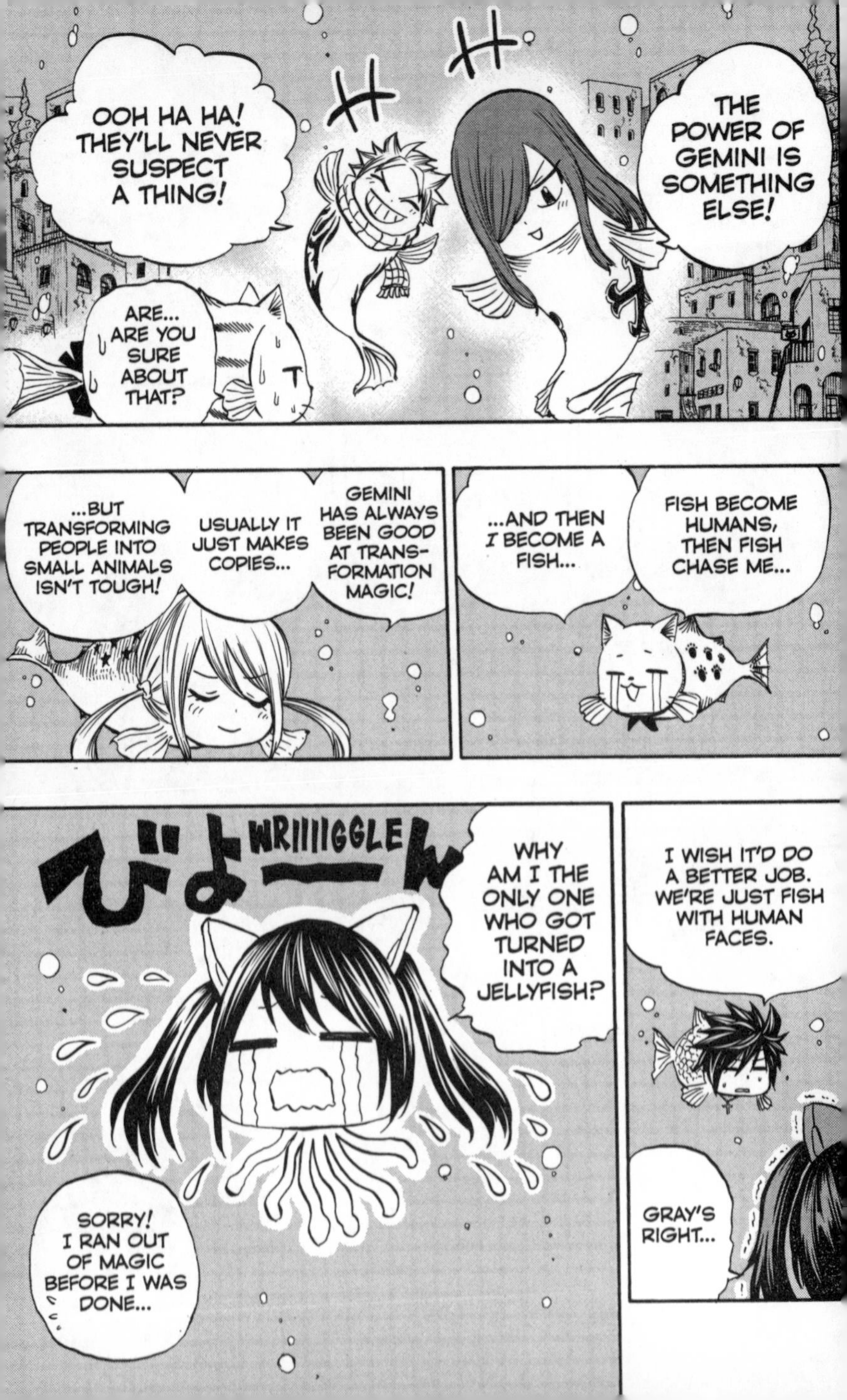
THE POWER OF GEMINI IS SOMETHING ELSE!
OOH HA HA! THEY'LL NEVER SUSPECT A THING!
ARE... ARE YOU SURE ABOUT THAT?
FISH BECOME HUMANS, THEN FISH CHASE ME...
...AND THEN *I* BECOME A FISH...
GEMINI HAS ALWAYS BEEN GOOD AT TRANS-FORMATION MAGIC!
USUALLY IT JUST MAKES COPIES...
...BUT TRANSFORMING PEOPLE INTO SMALL ANIMALS ISN'T TOUGH!
I WISH IT'D DO A BETTER JOB. WE'RE JUST FISH WITH HUMAN FACES.
GRAY'S RIGHT...
WHY AM I THE ONLY ONE WHO GOT TURNED INTO A JELLYFISH?
びよーーん WRIIIIGGLE
SORRY! I RAN OUT OF MAGIC BEFORE I WAS DONE...

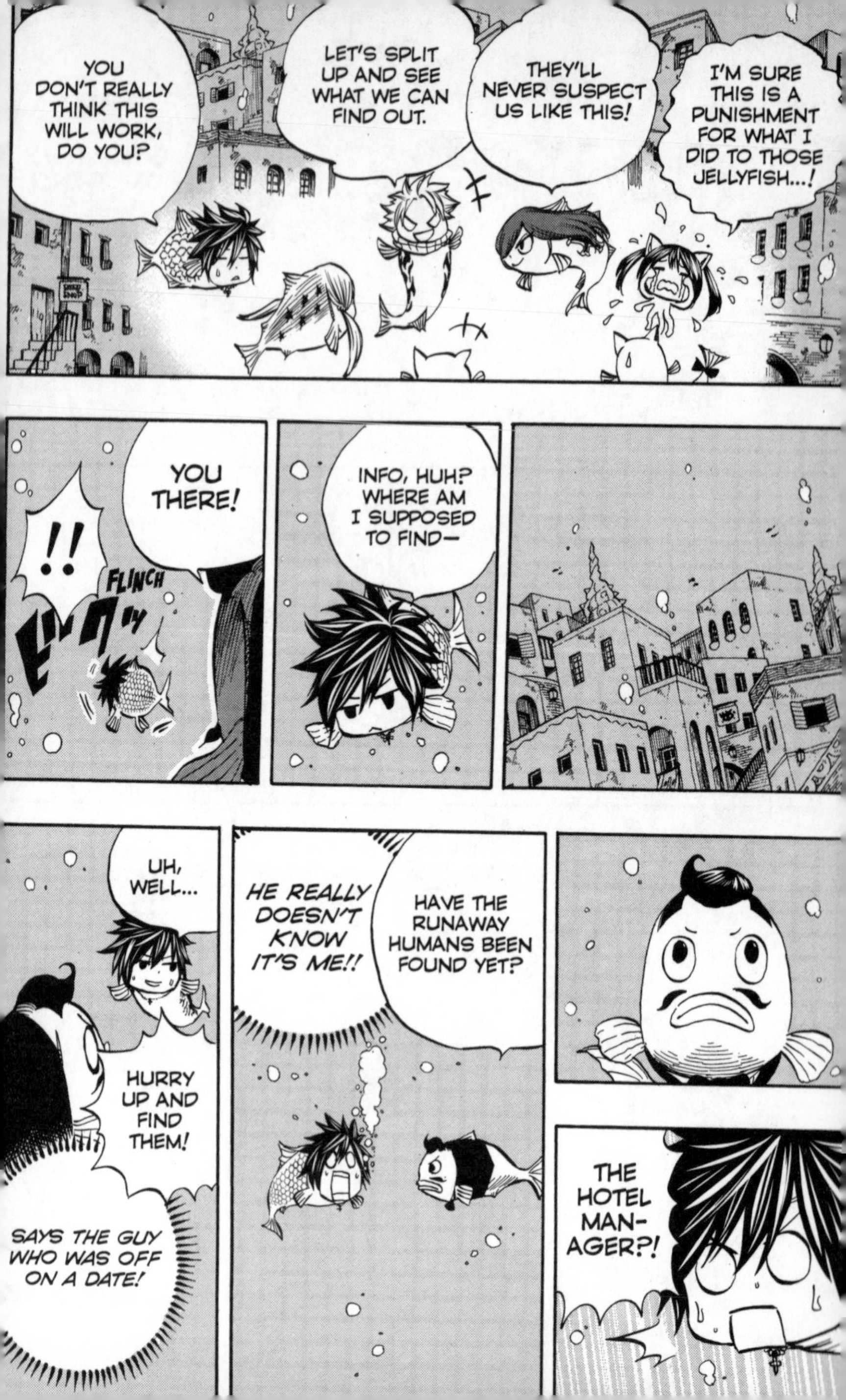
I'M SURE THIS IS A PUNISHMENT FOR WHAT I DID TO THOSE JELLYFISH...!
THEY'LL NEVER SUSPECT US LIKE THIS!
LET'S SPLIT UP AND SEE WHAT WE CAN FIND OUT.
YOU DON'T REALLY THINK THIS WILL WORK, DO YOU?
INFO, HUH? WHERE AM I SUPPOSED TO FIND—
YOU THERE!
!!
FLINCH
THE HOTEL MAN-AGER?!
HAVE THE RUNAWAY HUMANS BEEN FOUND YET?
HE REALLY DOESN'T KNOW IT'S ME!!
UH, WELL...
HURRY UP AND FIND THEM!
SAYS THE GUY WHO WAS OFF ON A DATE!

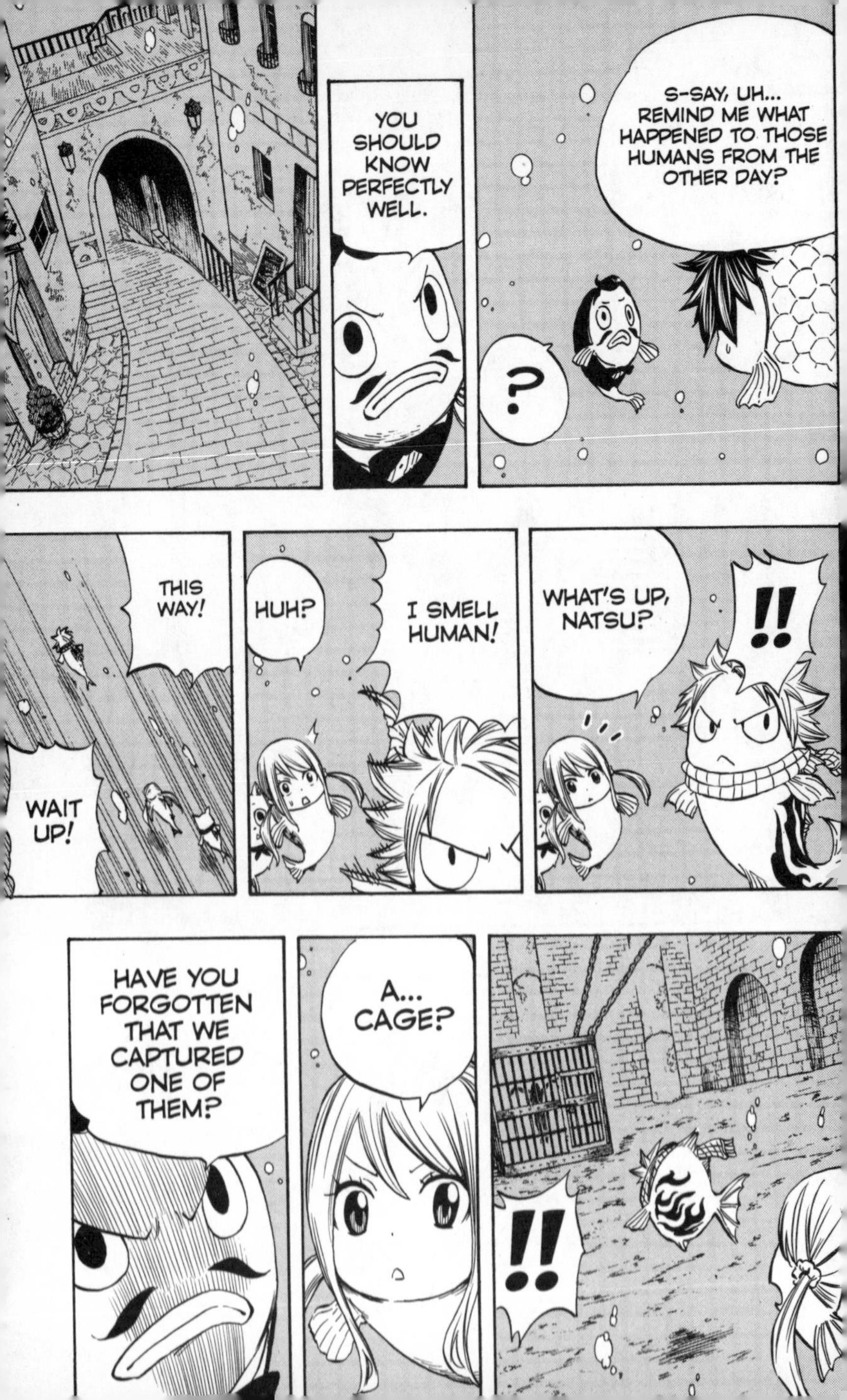
S-SAY, UH... REMIND ME WHAT HAPPENED TO THOSE HUMANS FROM THE OTHER DAY?
?
YOU SHOULD KNOW PERFECTLY WELL.
!!
WHAT'S UP, NATSU?
I SMELL HUMAN!
HUH?
THIS WAY!
WAIT UP!
!!
A... CAGE?
HAVE YOU FORGOTTEN THAT WE CAPTURED ONE OF THEM?

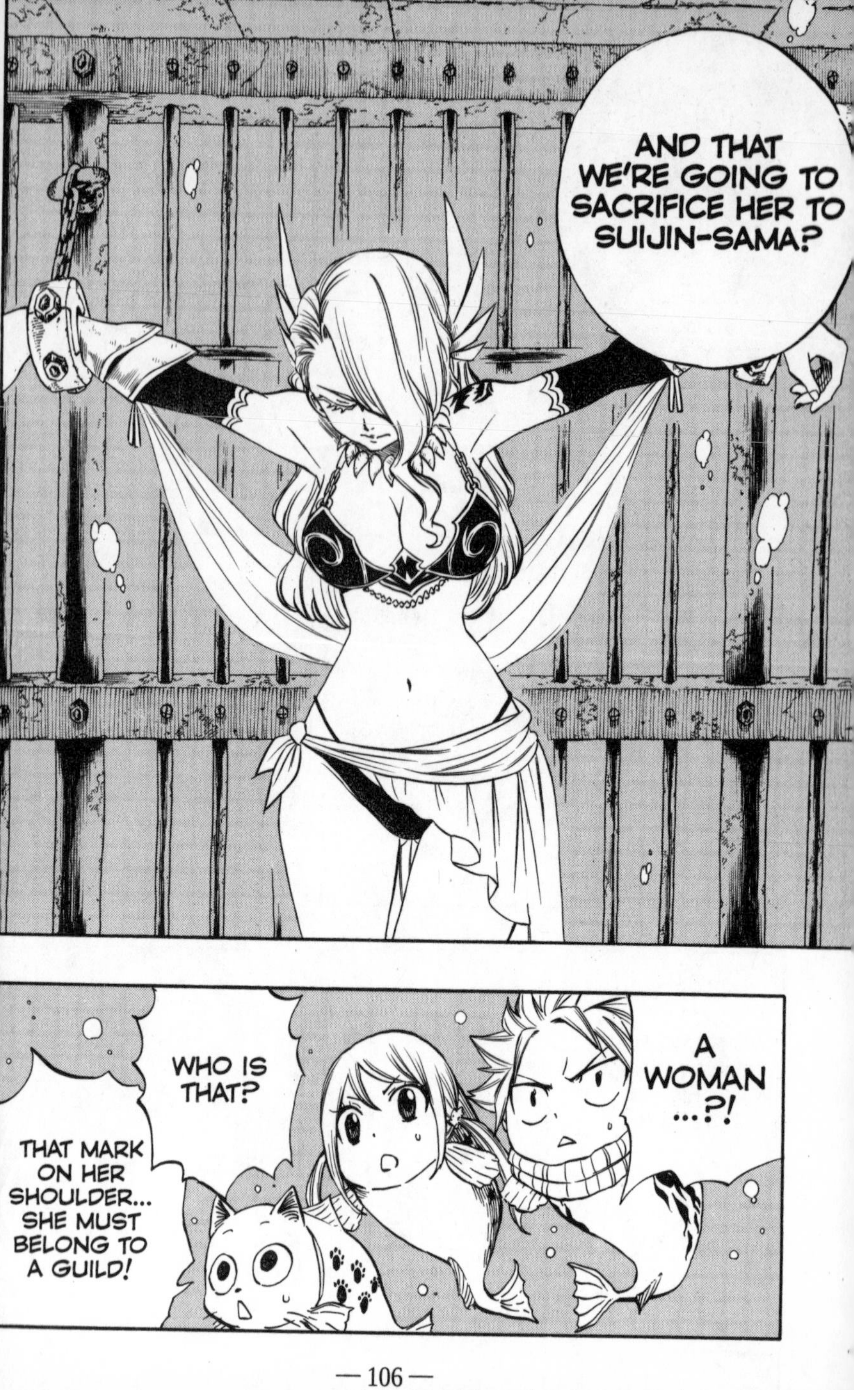
AND THAT WE'RE GOING TO SACRIFICE HER TO SUIJIN-SAMA?
A WOMAN ...?!
WHO IS THAT?
THAT MARK ON HER SHOULDER... SHE MUST BELONG TO A GUILD!

FAIRY TAIL 100 YEARS QUEST

Chapter 6: The Slaying Blade

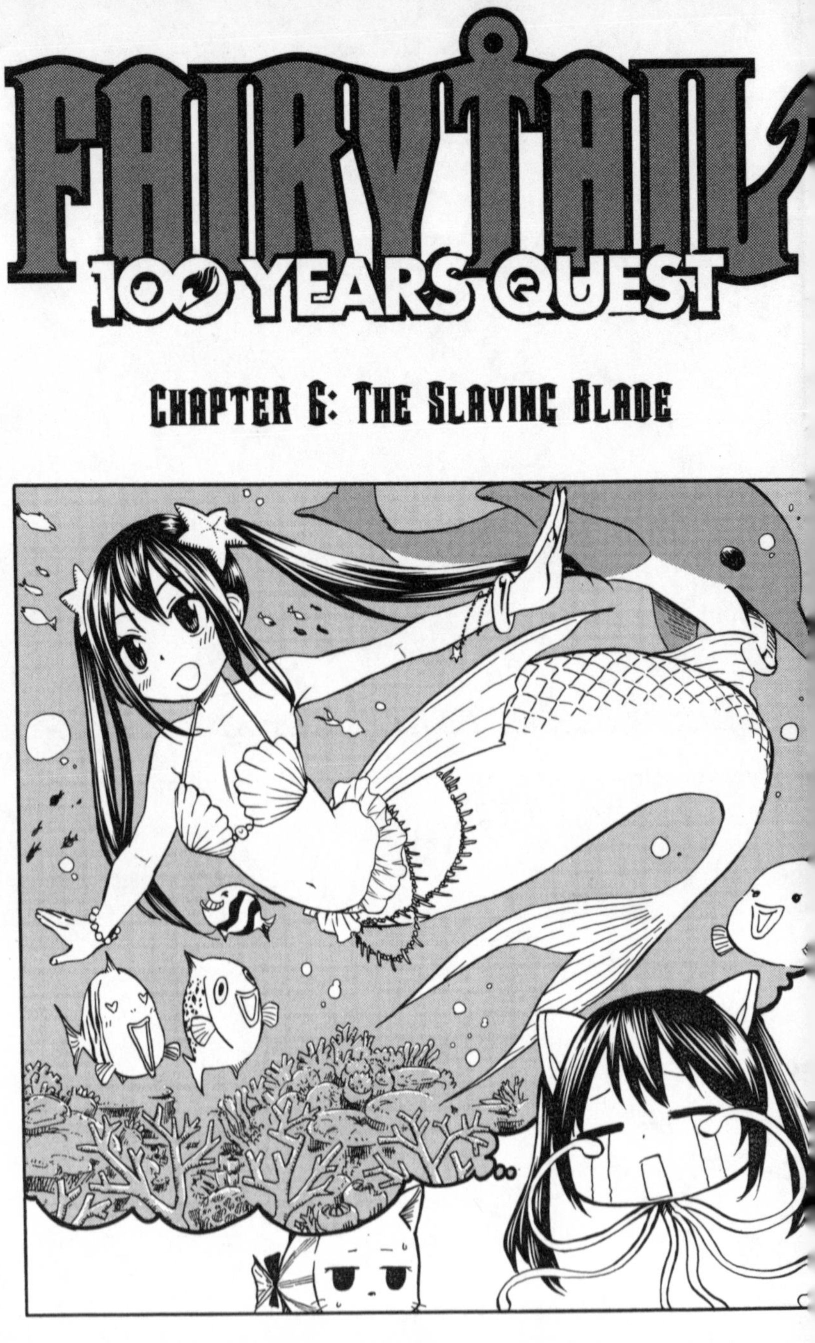

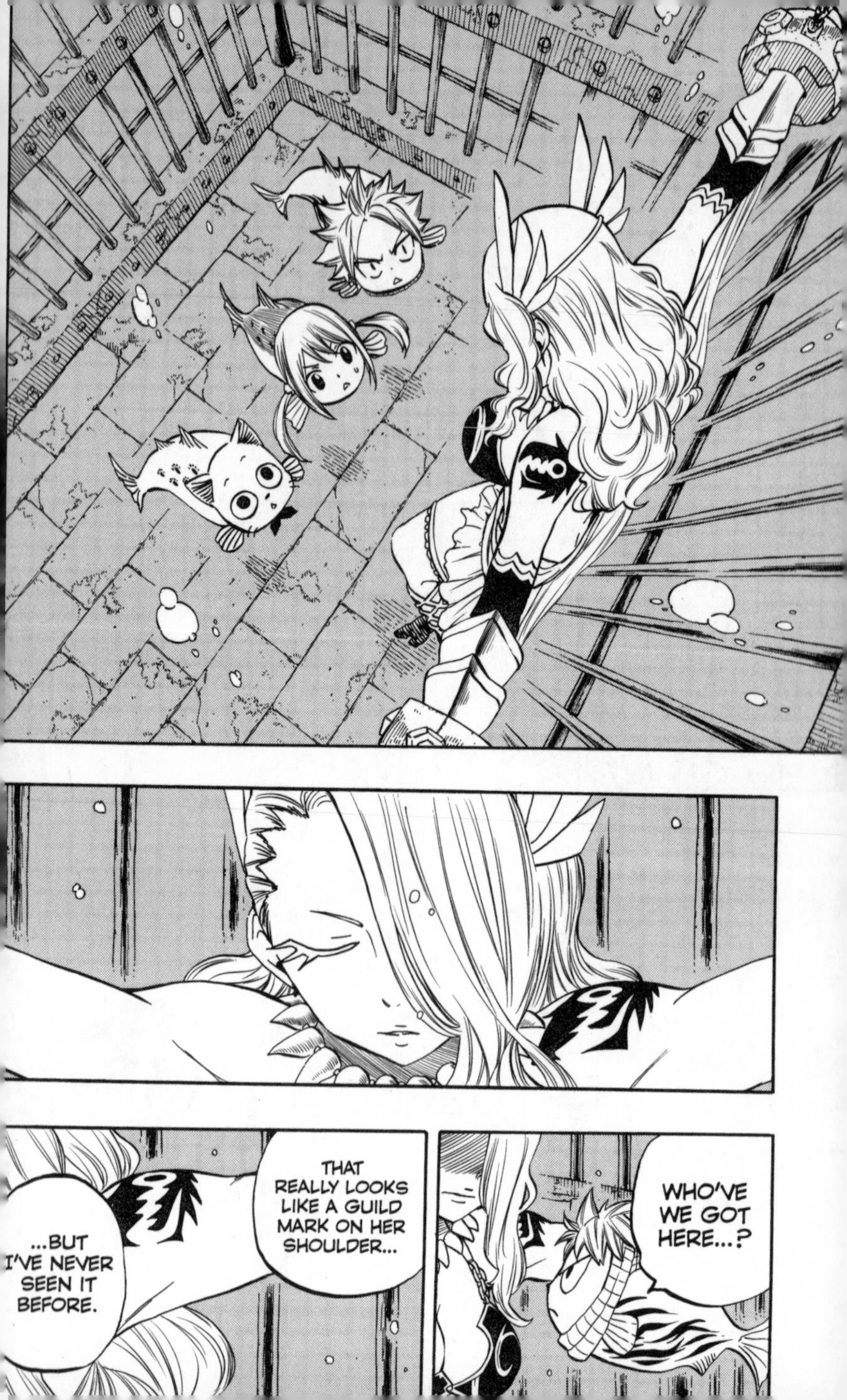
WHO'VE WE GOT HERE...?
THAT REALLY LOOKS LIKE A GUILD MARK ON HER SHOULDER...
...BUT I'VE NEVER SEEN IT BEFORE.

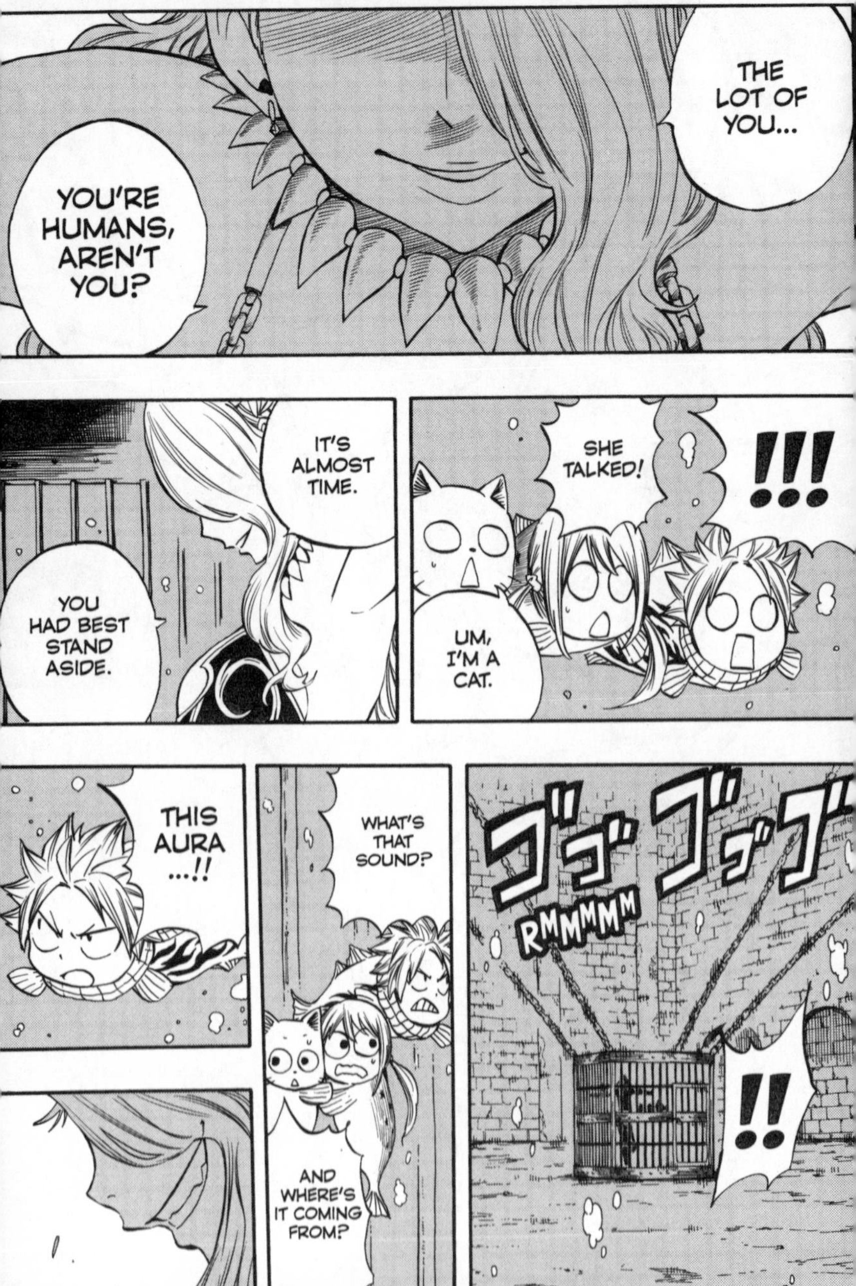
THE LOT OF YOU...
YOU'RE HUMANS, AREN'T YOU?
SHE TALKED!
!!!
UM, I'M A CAT.
IT'S ALMOST TIME.
YOU HAD BEST STAND ASIDE.
ゴゴ ゴゴゴ
RMMMMM
!!
WHAT'S THAT SOUND?
AND WHERE'S IT COMING FROM?
THIS AURA ...!!

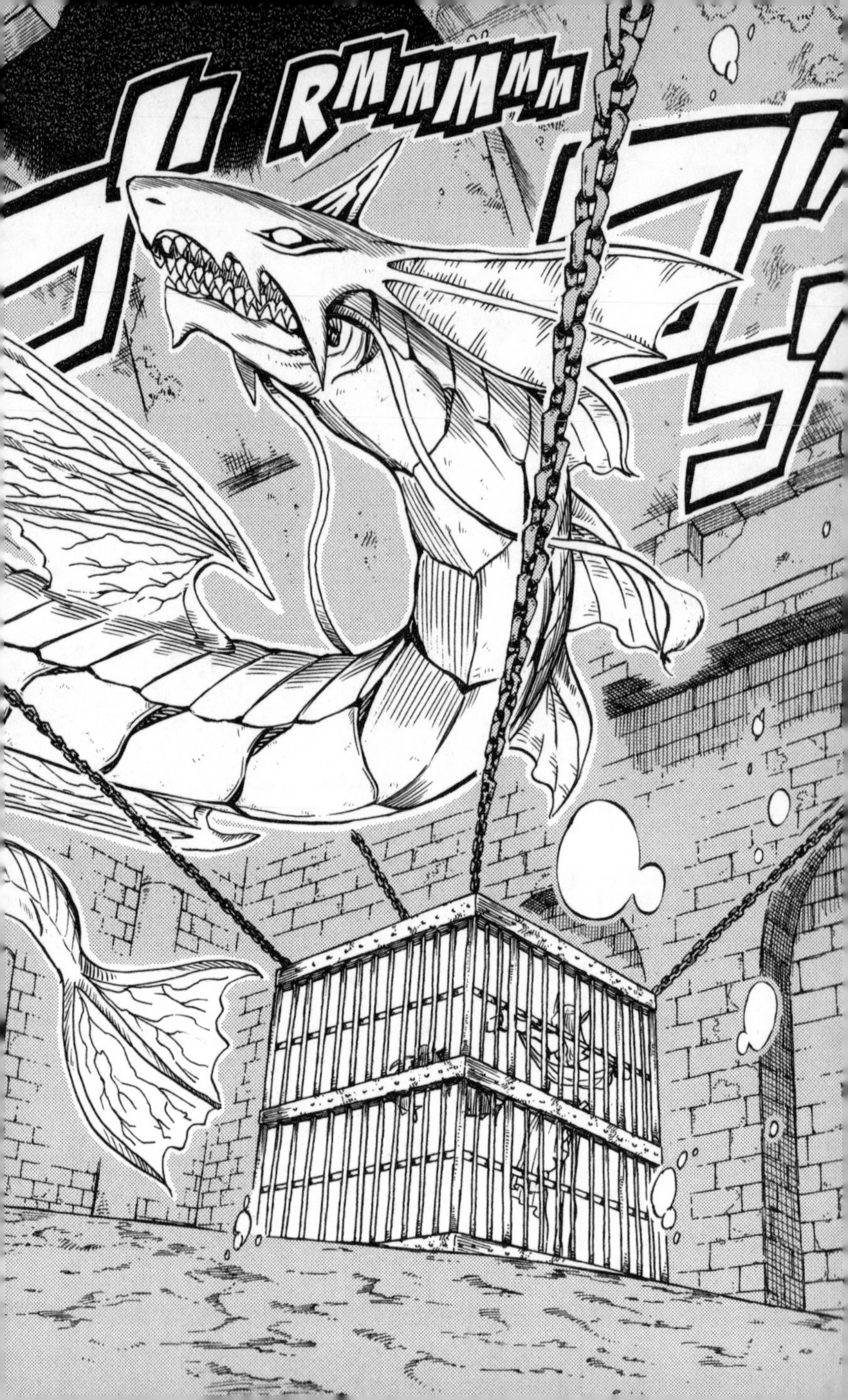
RMMMMMM

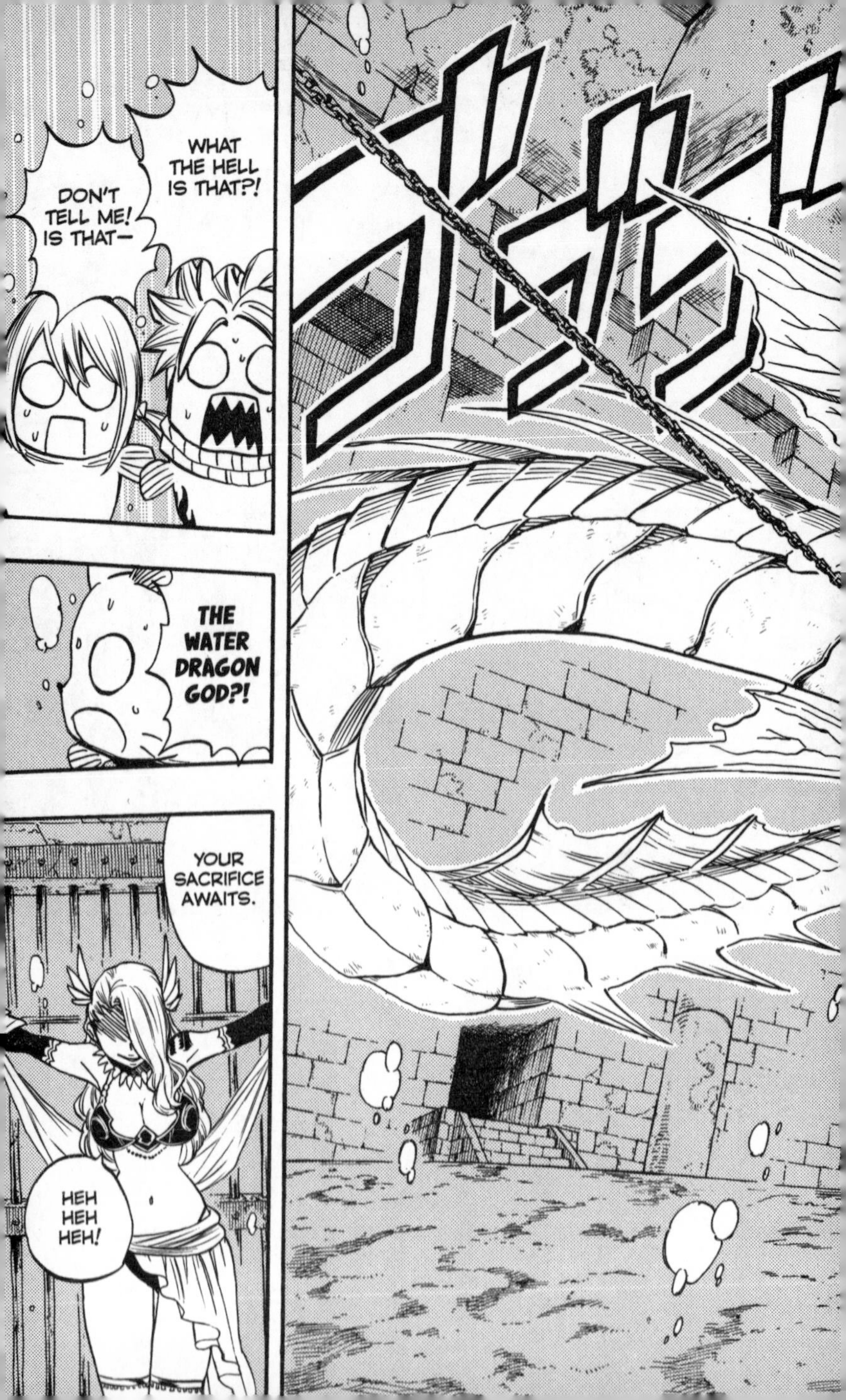
WHAT THE HELL IS THAT?!
DON'T TELL ME! IS THAT—
THE WATER DRAGON GOD?!
YOUR SACRIFICE AWAITS.
HEH HEH HEH!

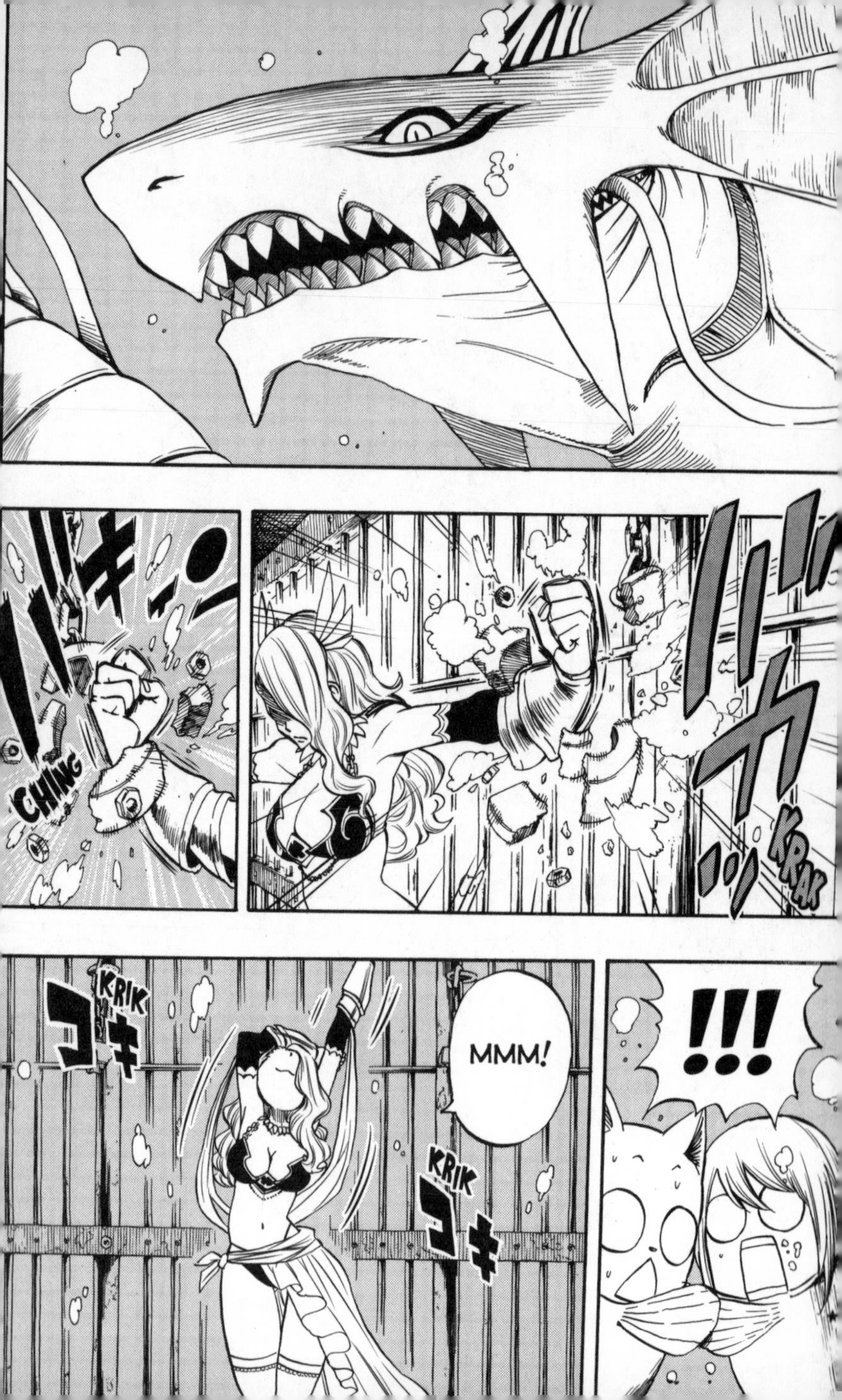
KRAK
CHING
!!!
KRIK
MMM!
KRIK

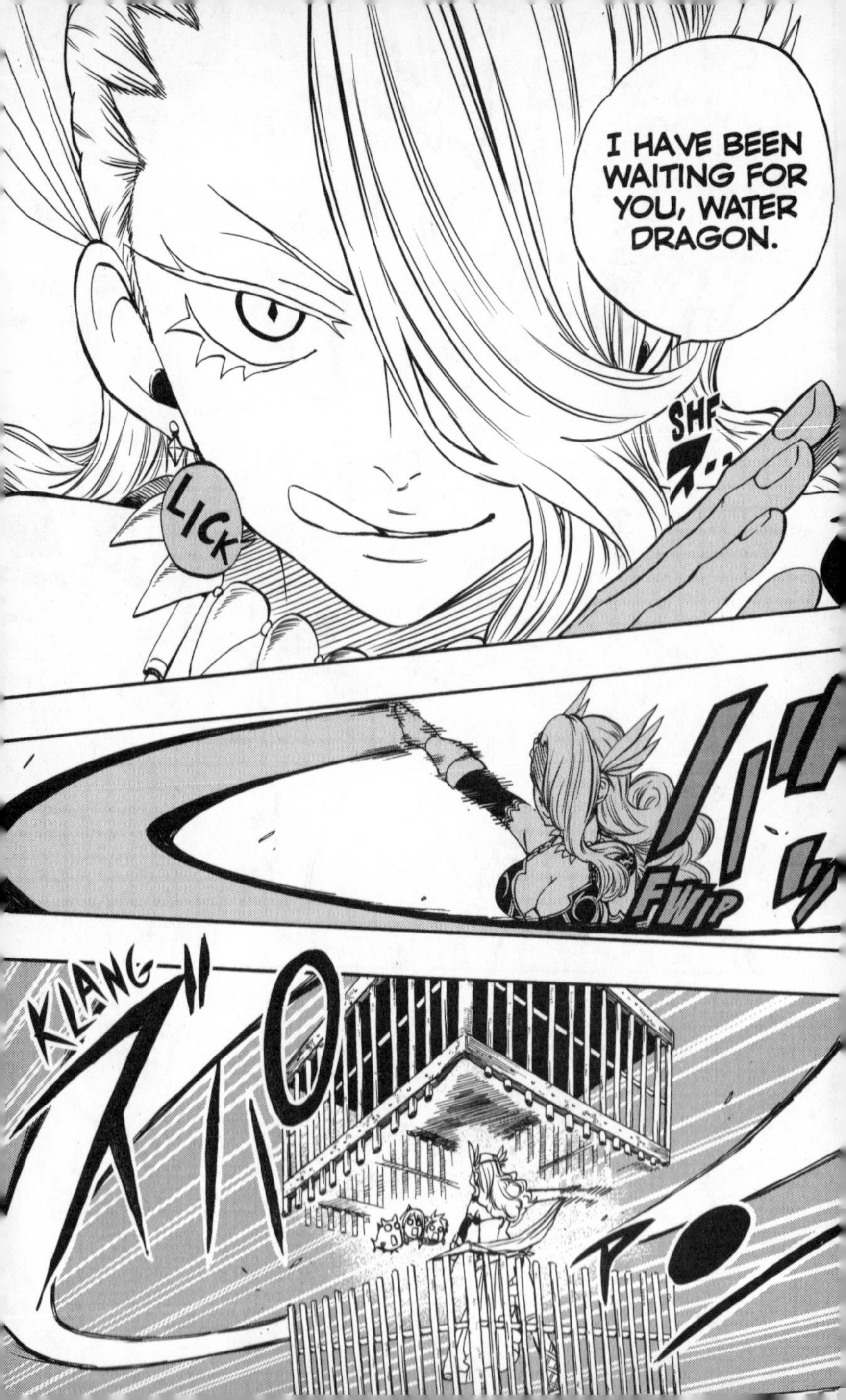
I HAVE BEEN WAITING FOR YOU, WATER DRAGON.
SHF
LICK
FWIP
KLANG

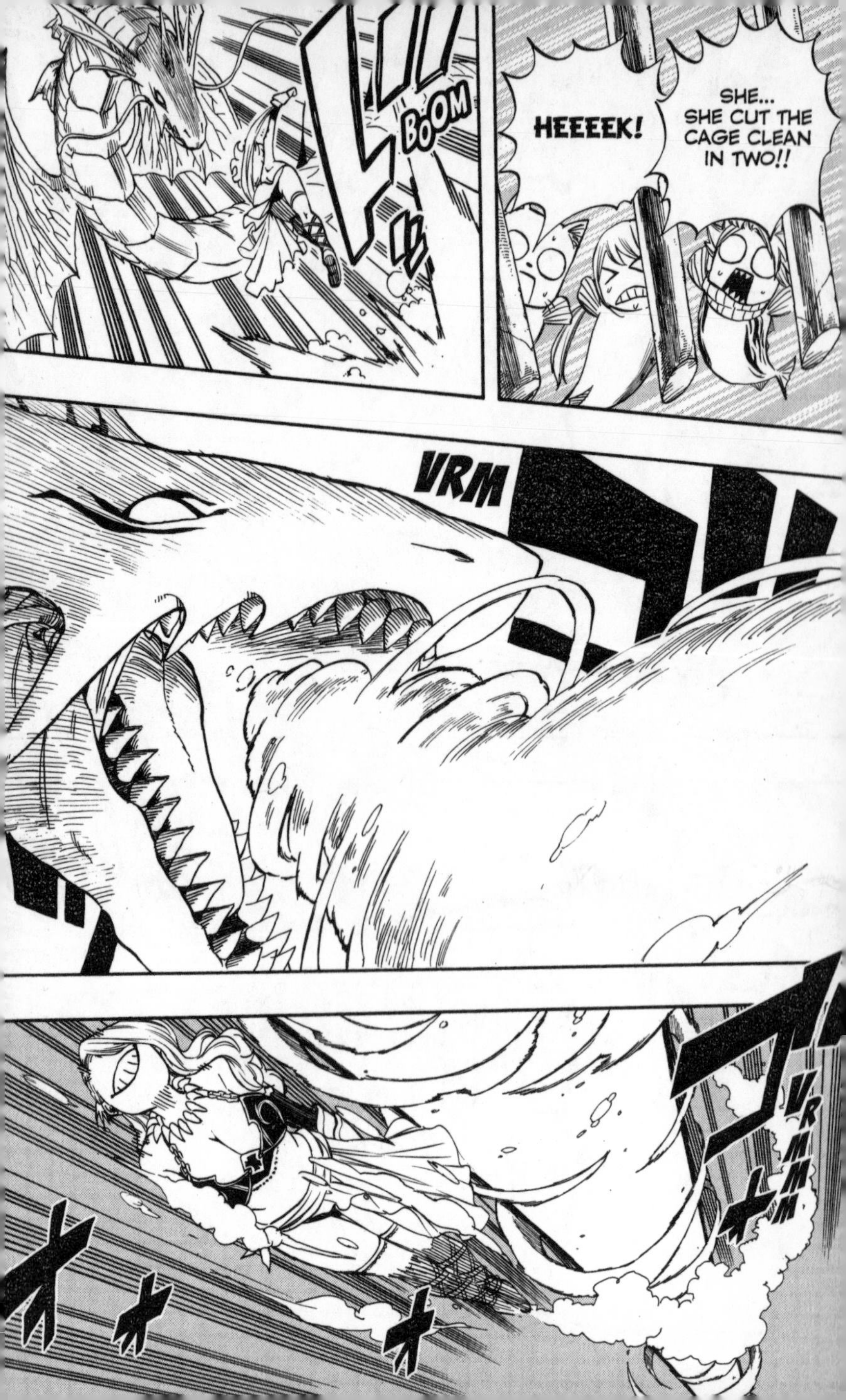
SHE... SHE CUT THE CAGE CLEAN IN TWO!!
HEEEEK!
BOOM
VRM
VRMMMM

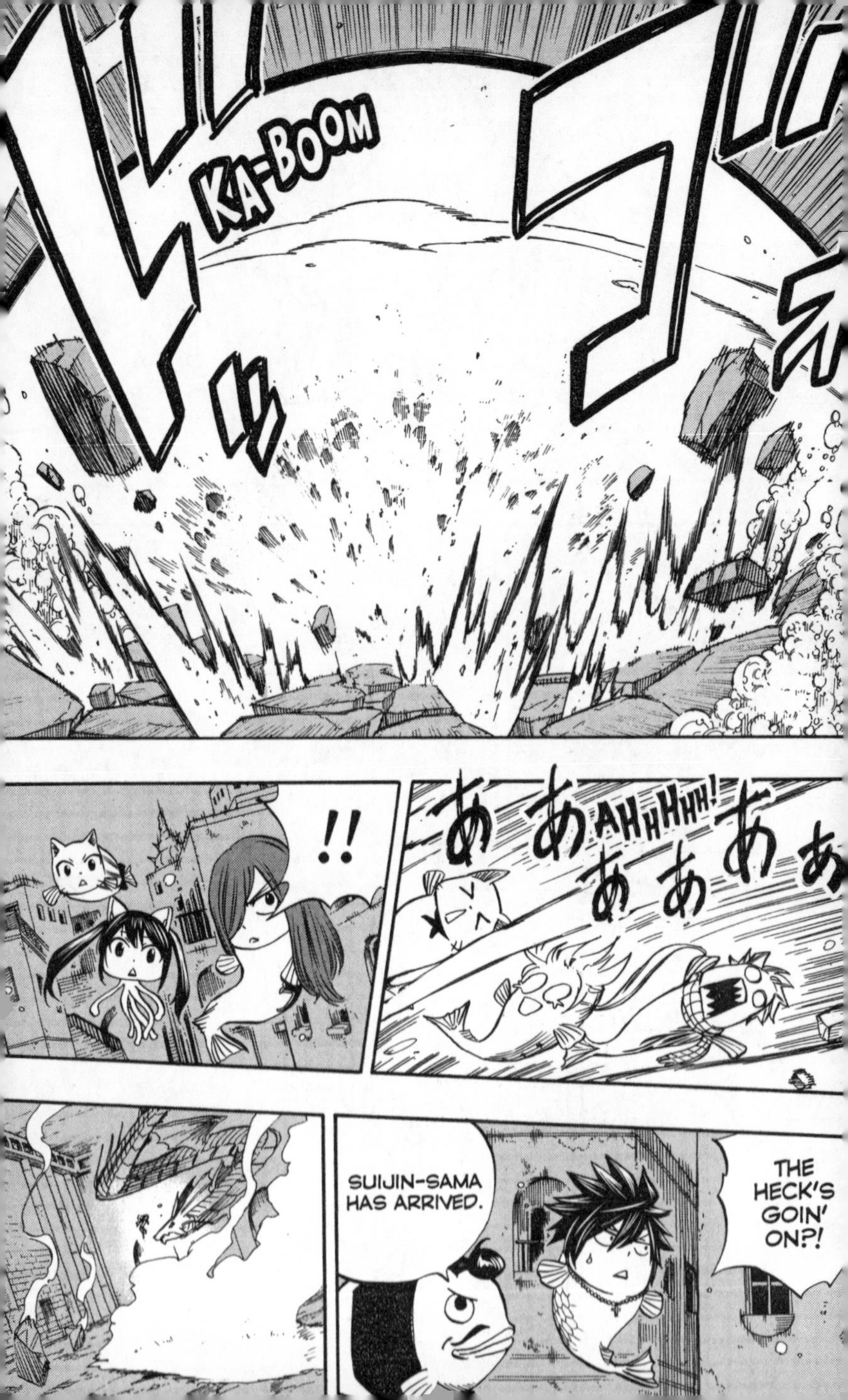
KA-BOOM
ああAHHHHH!
ああああ
!!
THE HECK'S GOIN' ON?!
SUIJIN-SAMA HAS ARRIVED.

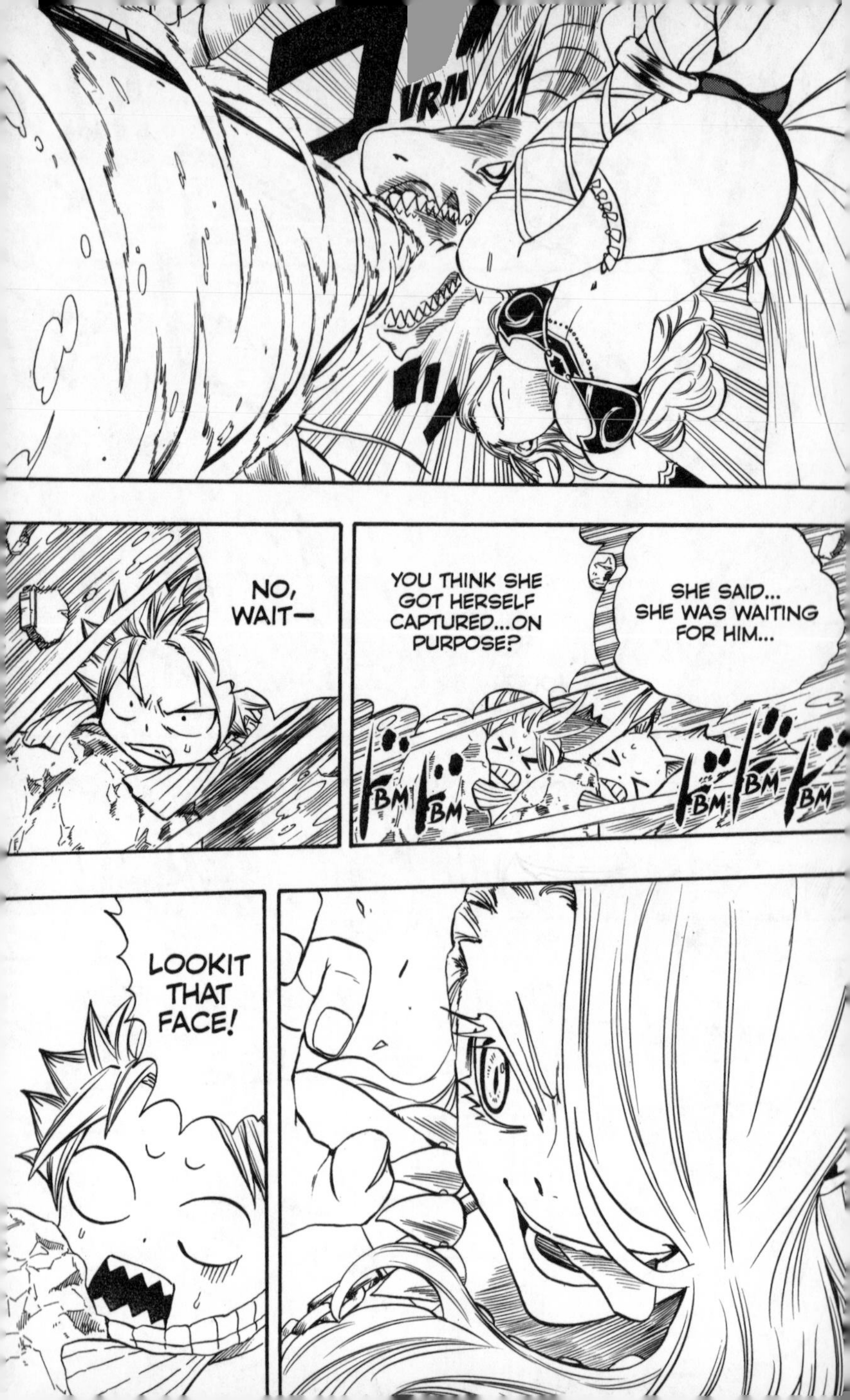
VRM
SHE SAID... SHE WAS WAITING FOR HIM...
YOU THINK SHE GOT HERSELF CAPTURED...ON PURPOSE?
BM
BM
BM
BM
BM
NO, WAIT—
LOOKIT THAT FACE!

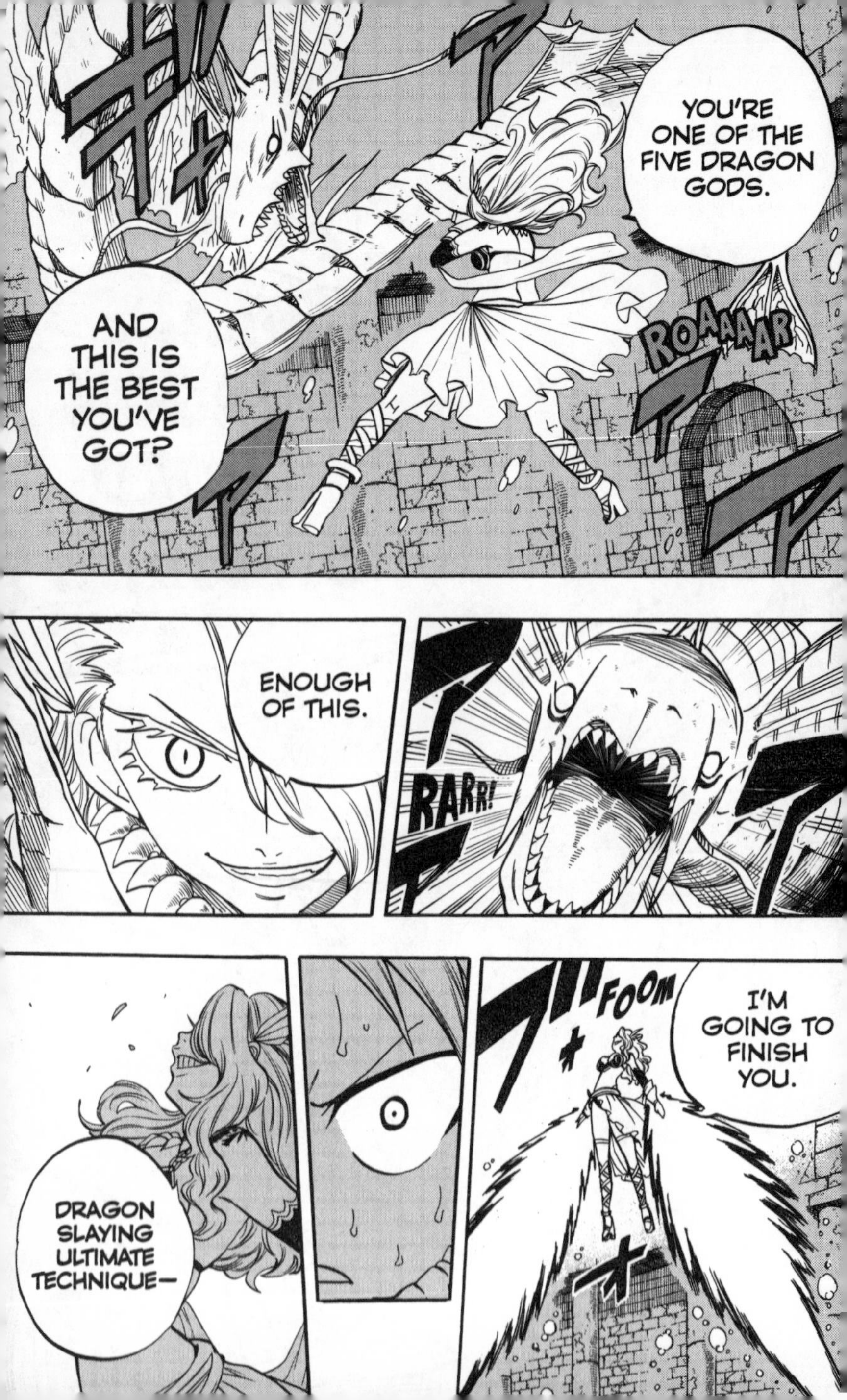
YOU'RE ONE OF THE FIVE DRAGON GODS.
ROAAAAR
AND THIS IS THE BEST YOU'VE GOT?
RARR!
ENOUGH OF THIS.
I'M GOING TO FINISH YOU.
FOOM
DRAGON SLAYING ULTIMATE TECHNIQUE—

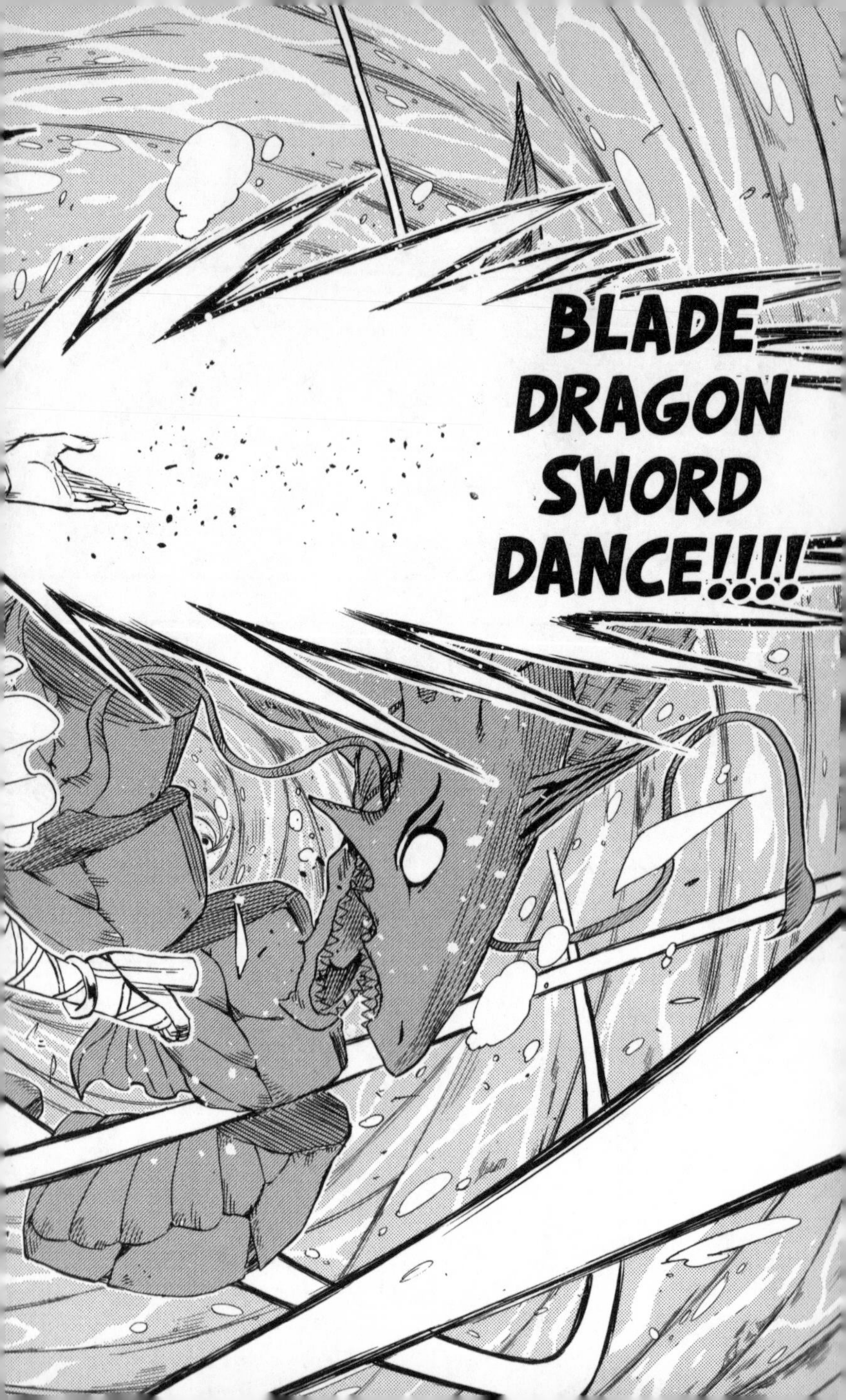
BLADE DRAGON SWORD DANCE!!!!

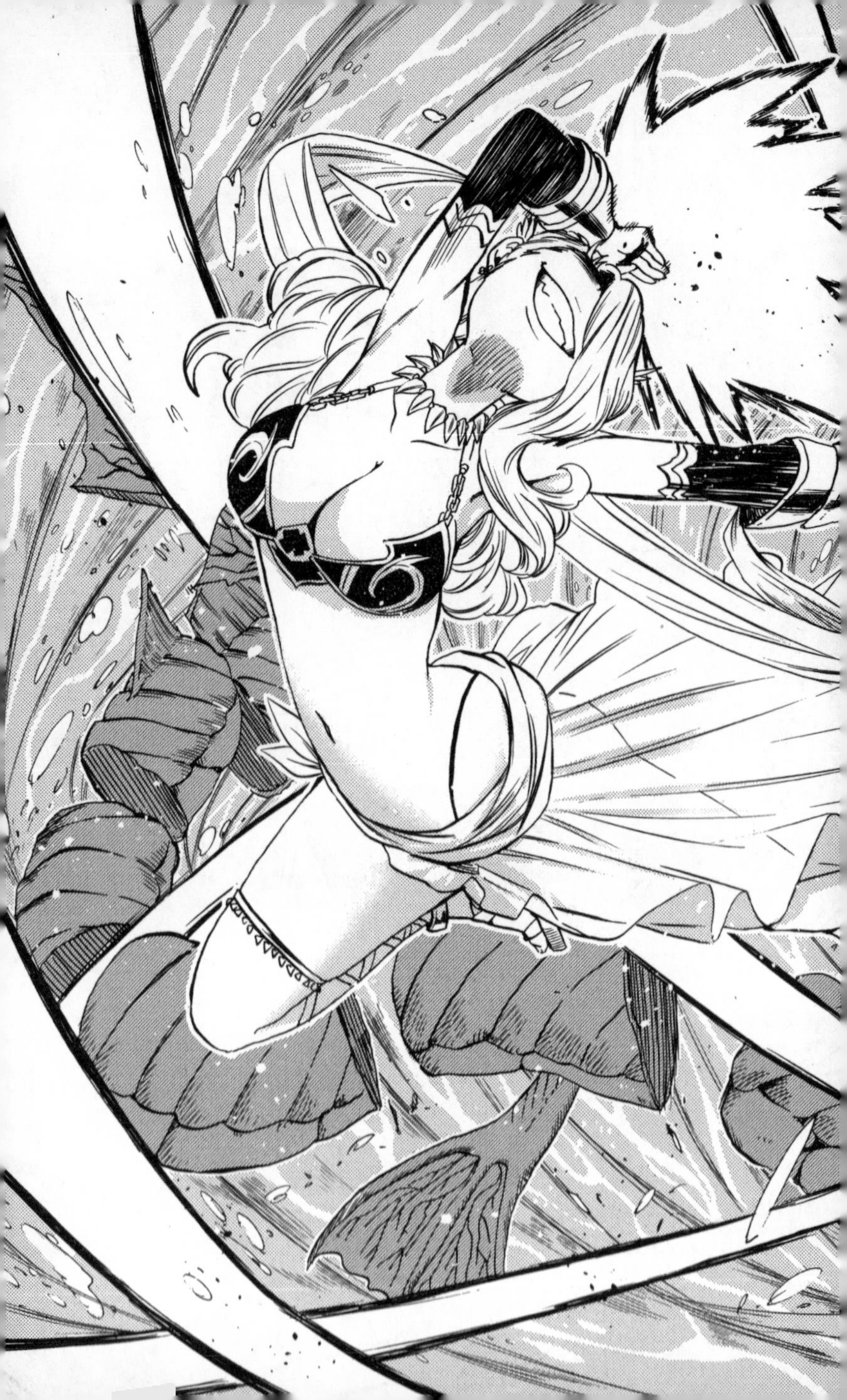

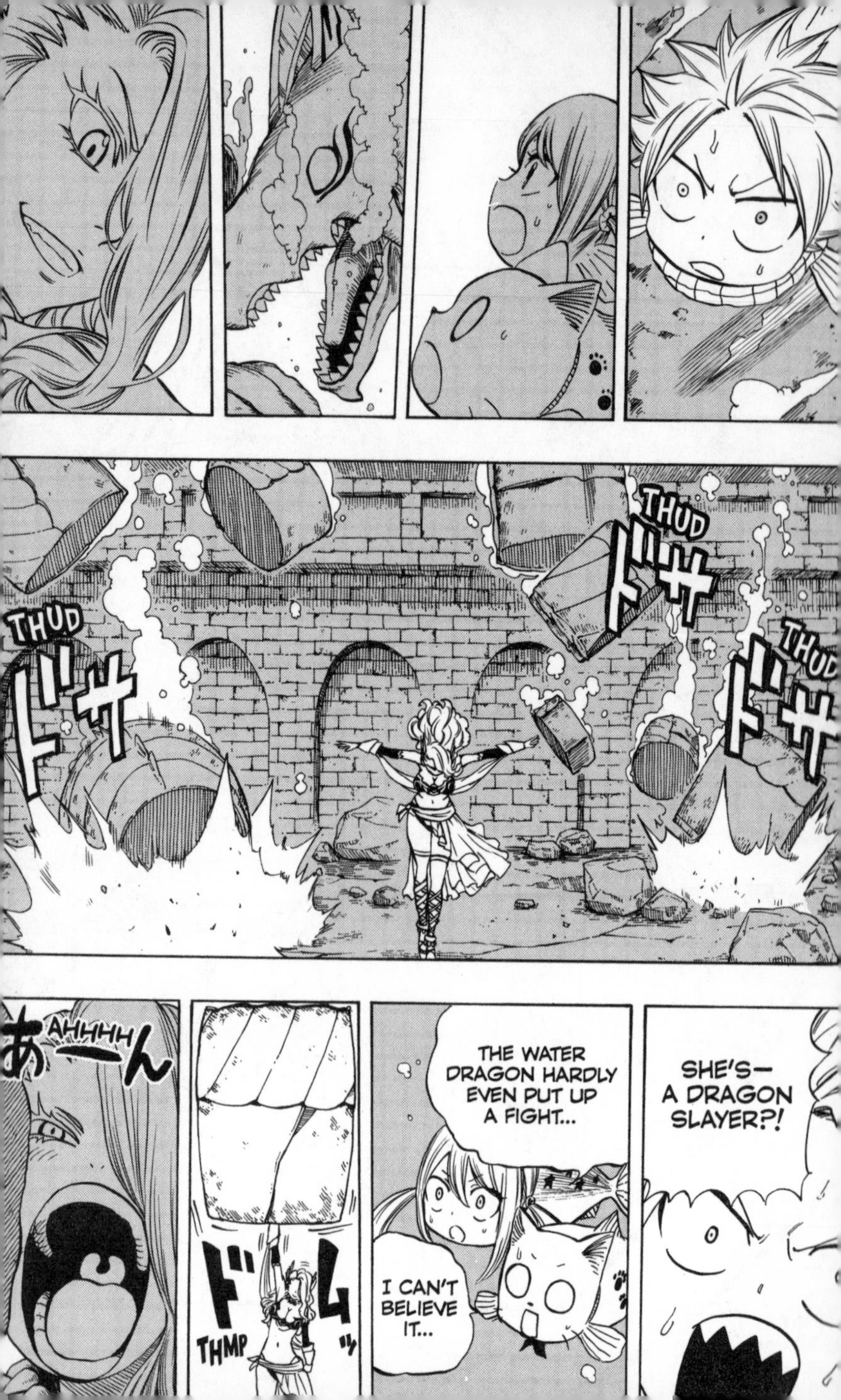
THUD
ドサ
THUD
ドサ
THUD
ドサ
SHE'S— A DRAGON SLAYER?!
THE WATER DRAGON HARDLY EVEN PUT UP A FIGHT...
I CAN'T BELIEVE IT...
ドム
THMP
あーん
AHHHH

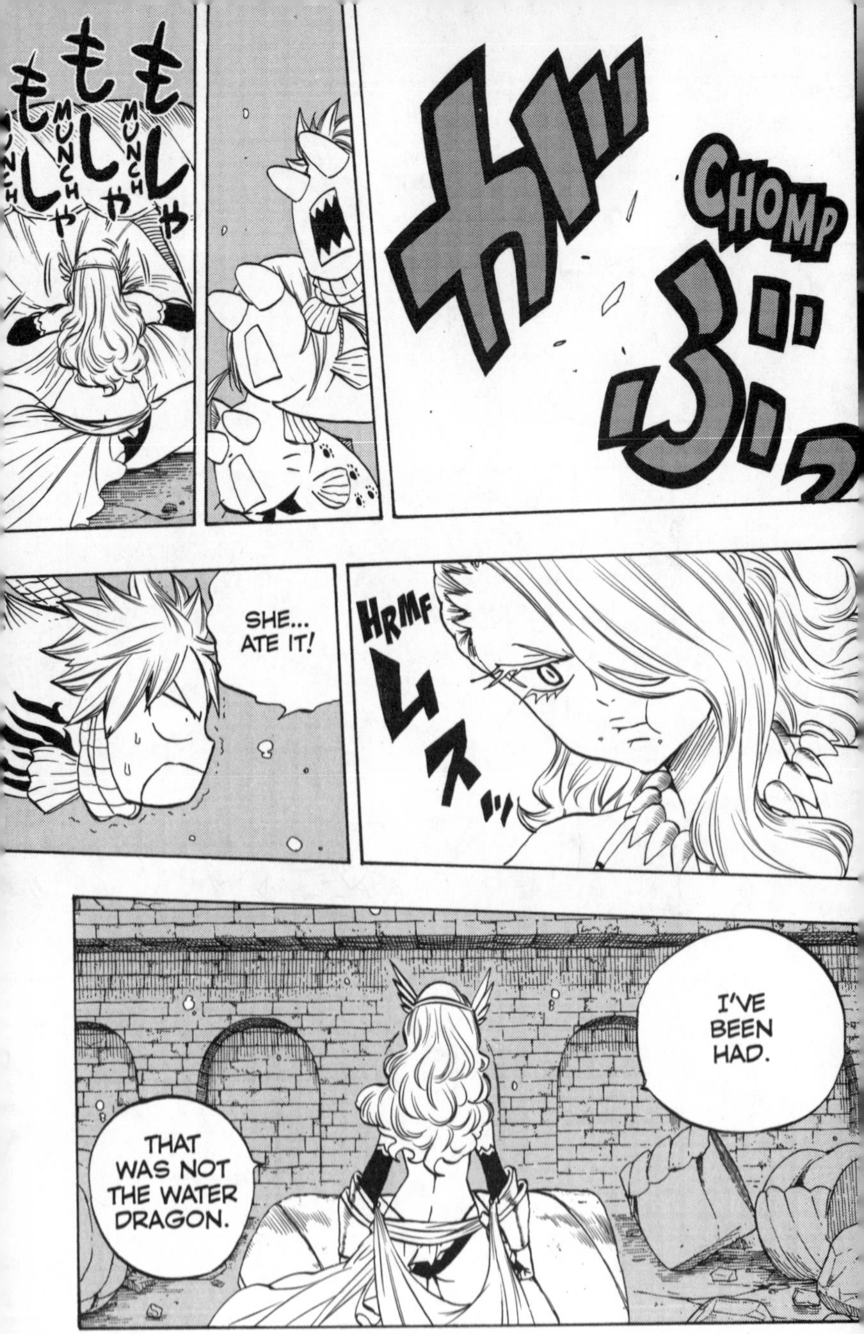
CHOMP
もしゃ MUNCH
もしゃ MUNCH
もしゃ MUNCH
HRMF ムスッ
SHE... ATE IT!
I'VE BEEN HAD.
THAT WAS NOT THE WATER DRAGON.

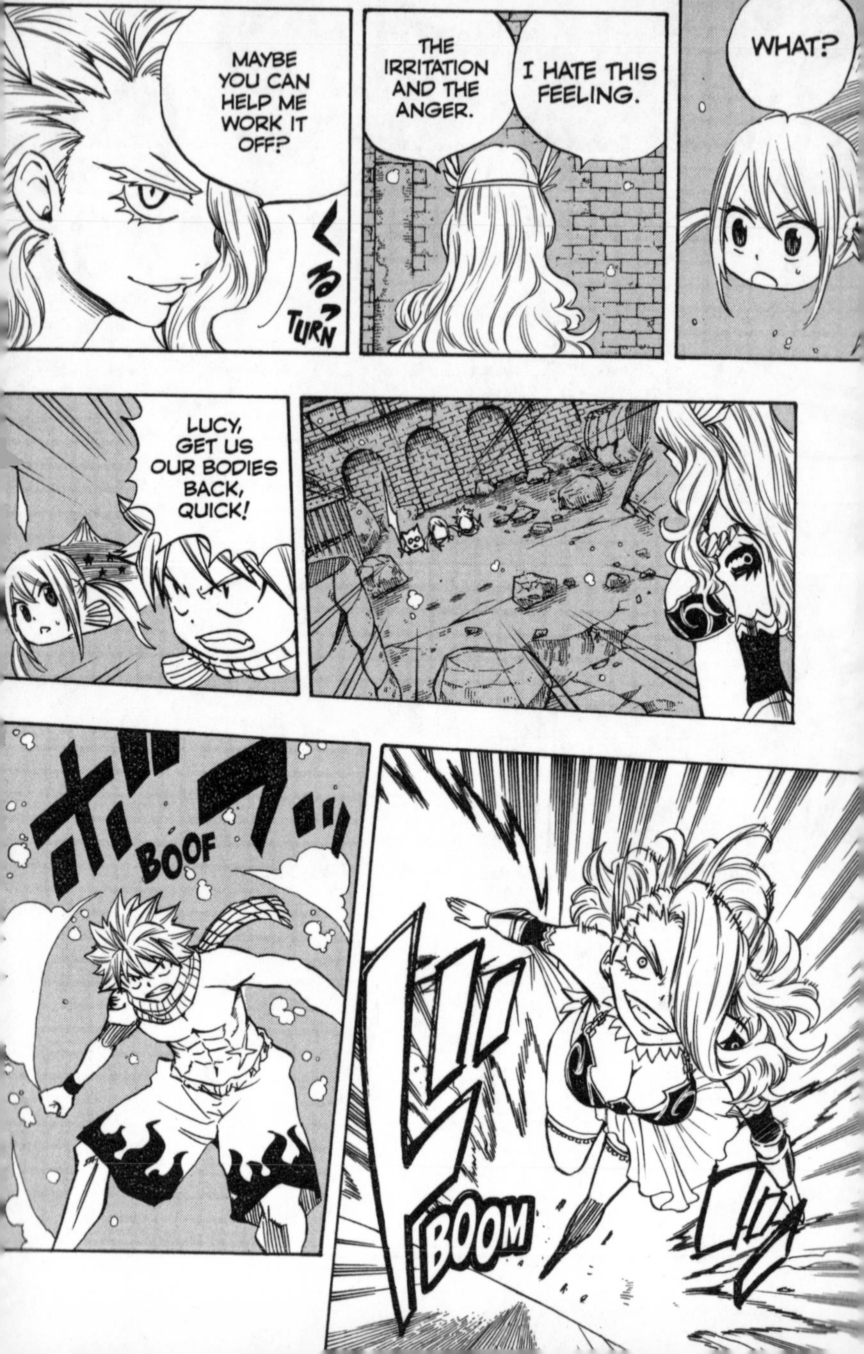
WHAT?
I HATE THIS FEELING.
THE IRRITATION AND THE ANGER.
MAYBE YOU CAN HELP ME WORK IT OFF?
くるっ
TURN
LUCY, GET US OUR BODIES BACK, QUICK!
BOOM
ボウッ
BOOF

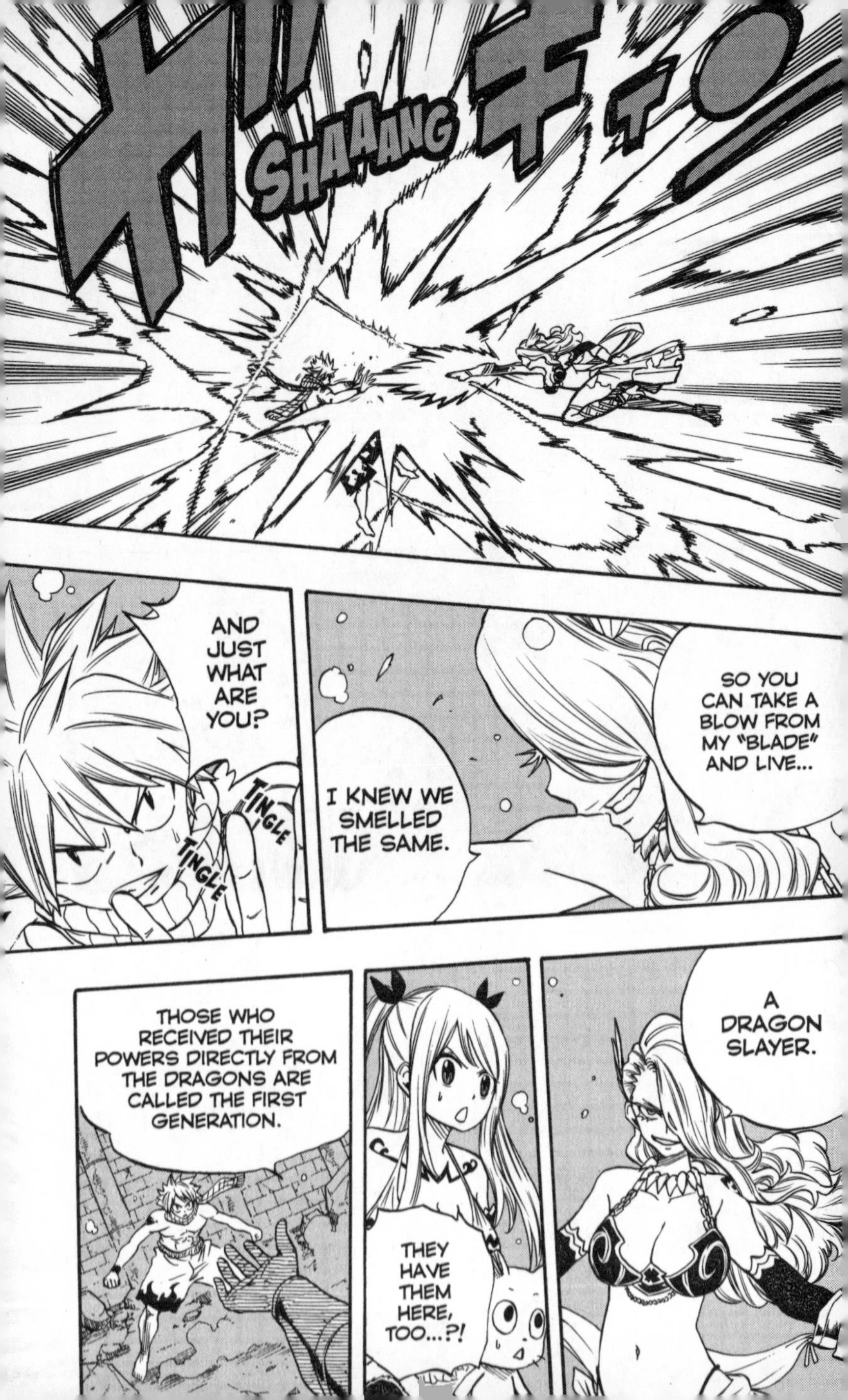
SHAAANG
SO YOU CAN TAKE A BLOW FROM MY "BLADE" AND LIVE...
I KNEW WE SMELLED THE SAME.
TINGLE
TINGLE
AND JUST WHAT ARE YOU?
A DRAGON SLAYER.
THEY HAVE THEM HERE, TOO...?!
THOSE WHO RECEIVED THEIR POWERS DIRECTLY FROM THE DRAGONS ARE CALLED THE FIRST GENERATION.

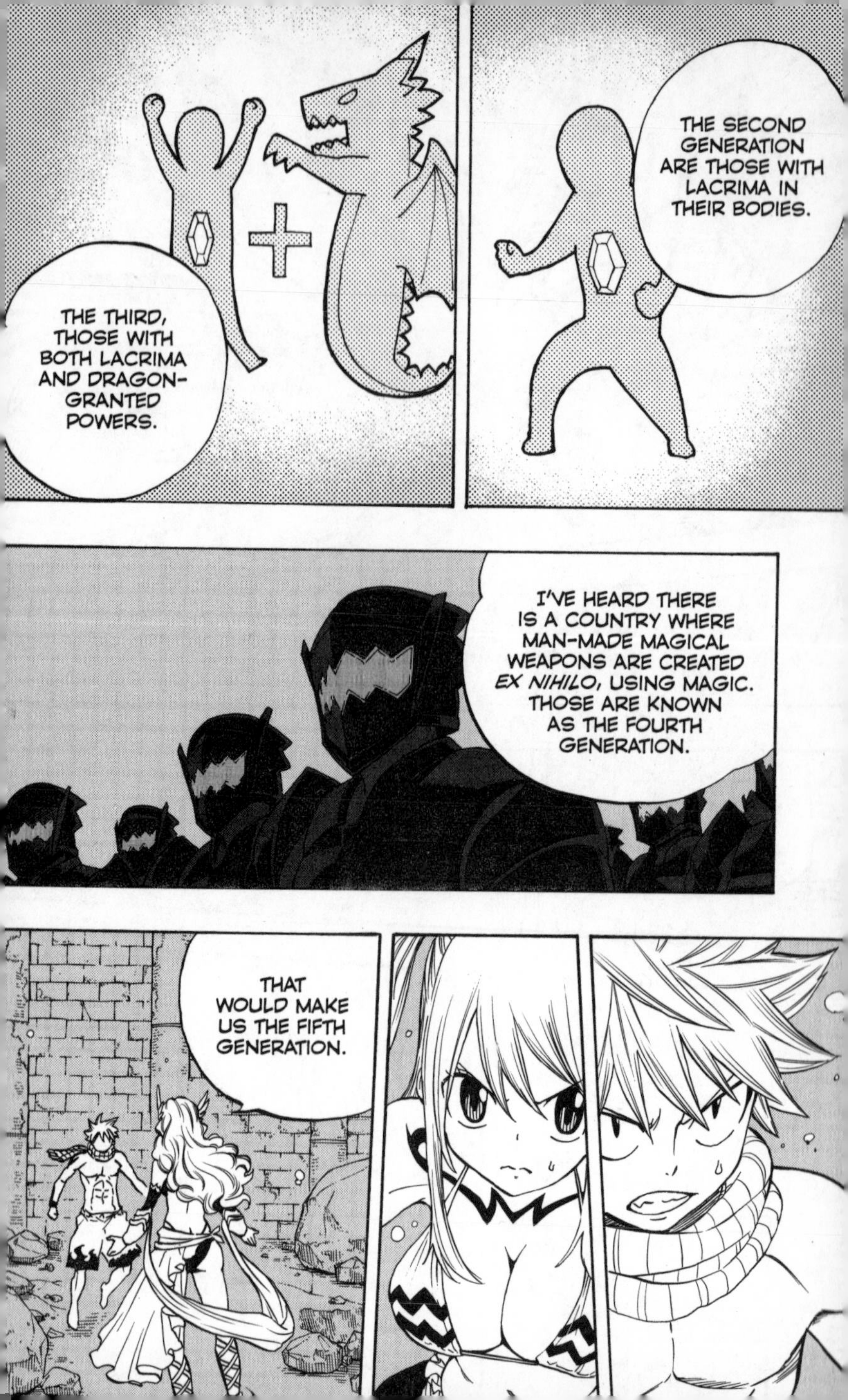
THE SECOND GENERATION ARE THOSE WITH LACRIMA IN THEIR BODIES.
THE THIRD, THOSE WITH BOTH LACRIMA AND DRAGON-GRANTED POWERS.
I'VE HEARD THERE IS A COUNTRY WHERE MAN-MADE MAGICAL WEAPONS ARE CREATED *EX NIHILO*, USING MAGIC. THOSE ARE KNOWN AS THE FOURTH GENERATION.
THAT WOULD MAKE US THE FIFTH GENERATION.

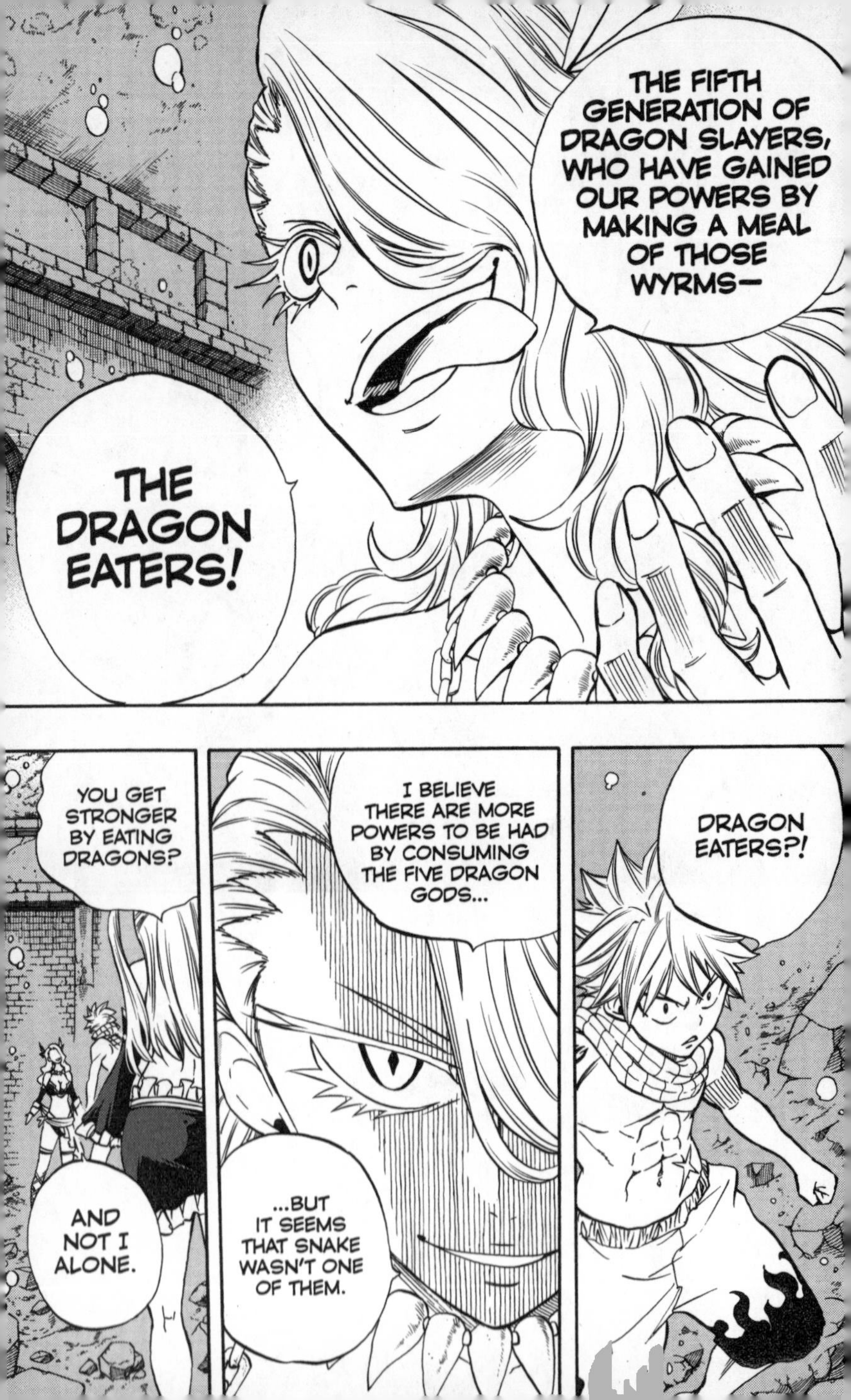
THE FIFTH GENERATION OF DRAGON SLAYERS, WHO HAVE GAINED OUR POWERS BY MAKING A MEAL OF THOSE WYRMS—
THE DRAGON EATERS!
DRAGON EATERS?!
I BELIEVE THERE ARE MORE POWERS TO BE HAD BY CONSUMING THE FIVE DRAGON GODS...
...BUT IT SEEMS THAT SNAKE WASN'T ONE OF THEM.
YOU GET STRONGER BY EATING DRAGONS?
AND NOT I ALONE.

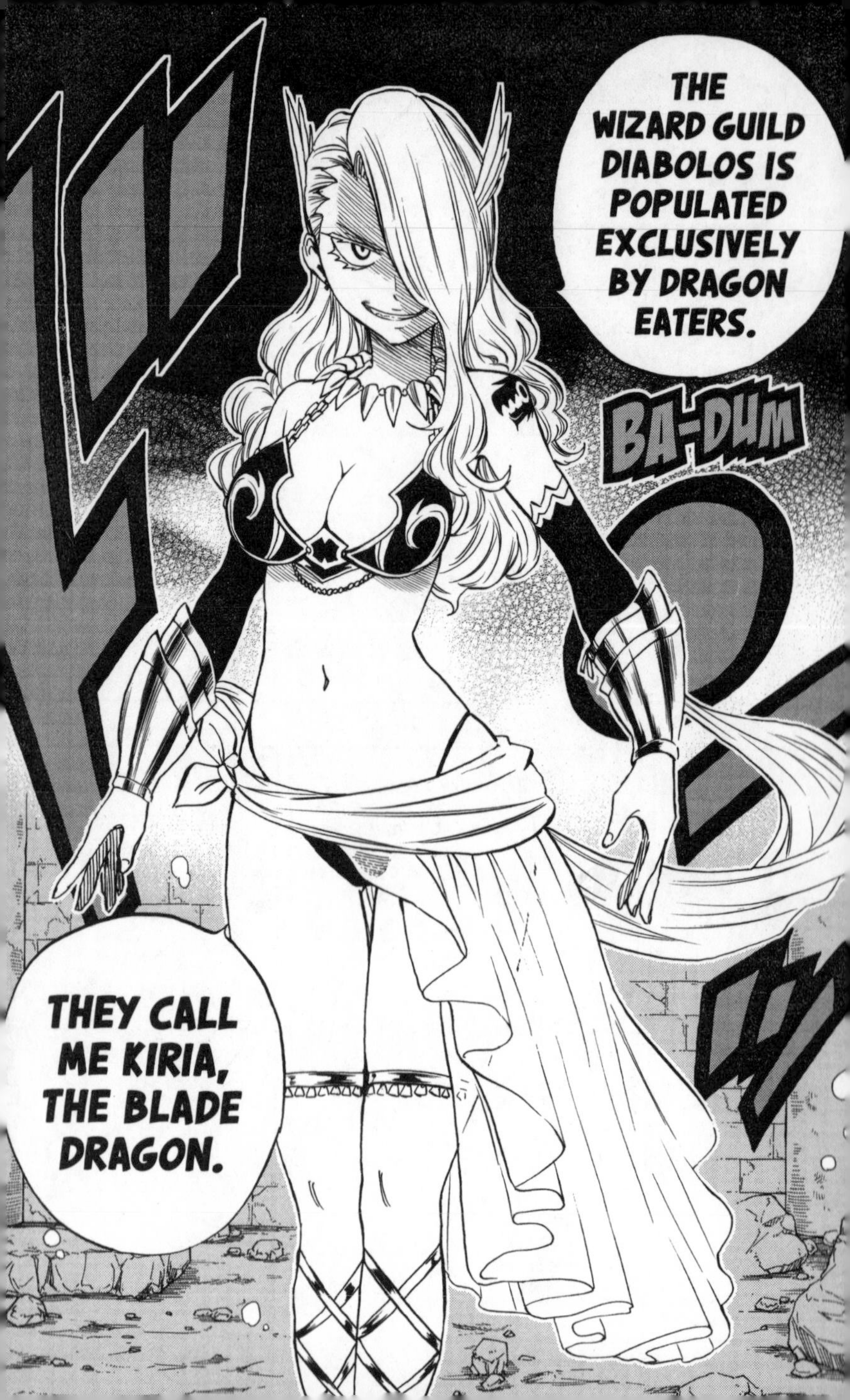
THE WIZARD GUILD DIABOLOS IS POPULATED EXCLUSIVELY BY DRAGON EATERS.
BA-DUM
THEY CALL ME KIRIA, THE BLADE DRAGON.

FAIRY TAIL 100 YEARS QUEST

Chapter 7: The Sea of Dragons

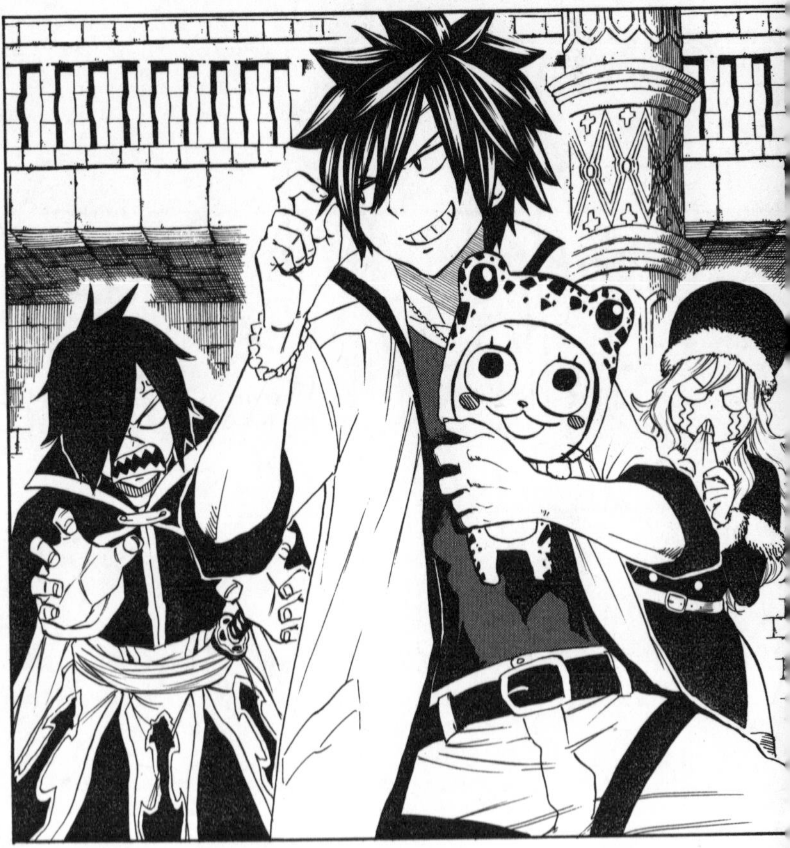

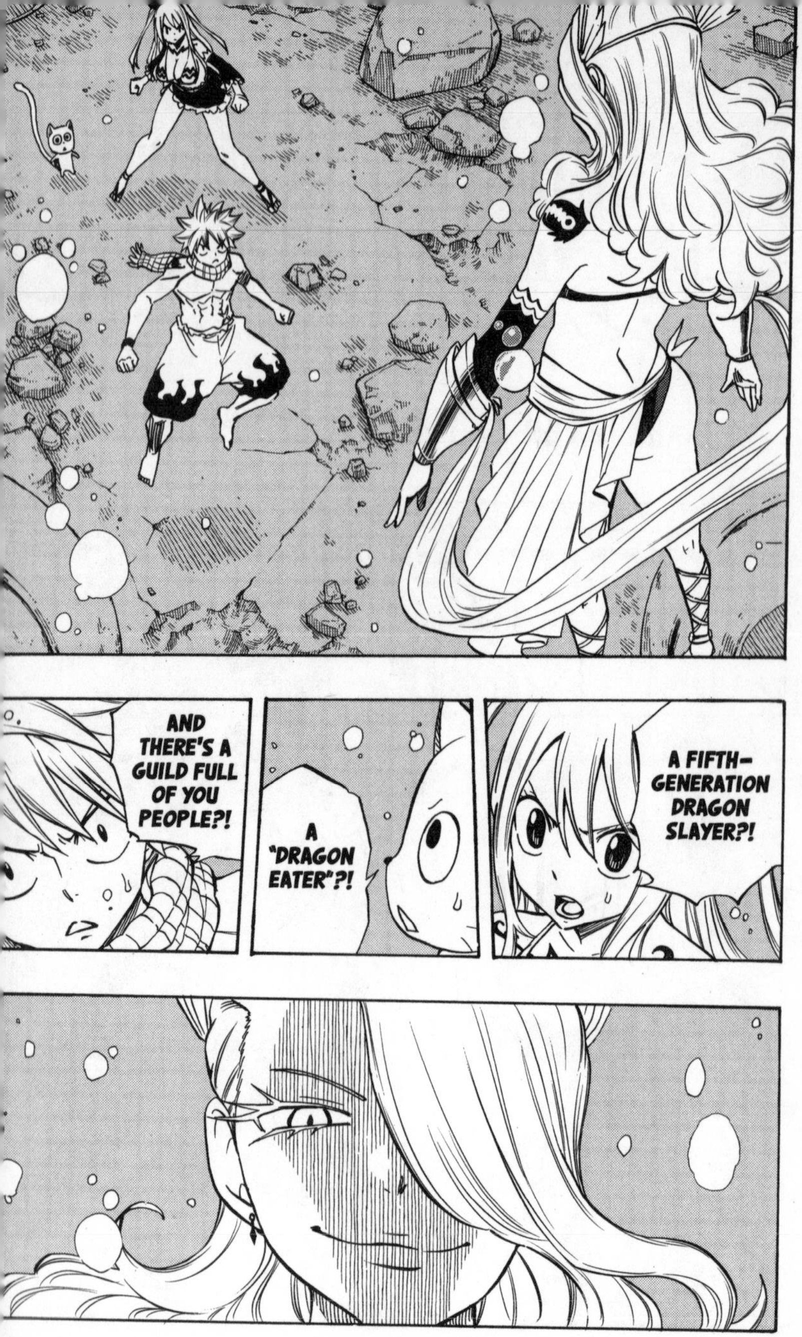
A FIFTH-GENERATION DRAGON SLAYER?!
A "DRAGON EATER"?!
AND THERE'S A GUILD FULL OF YOU PEOPLE?!

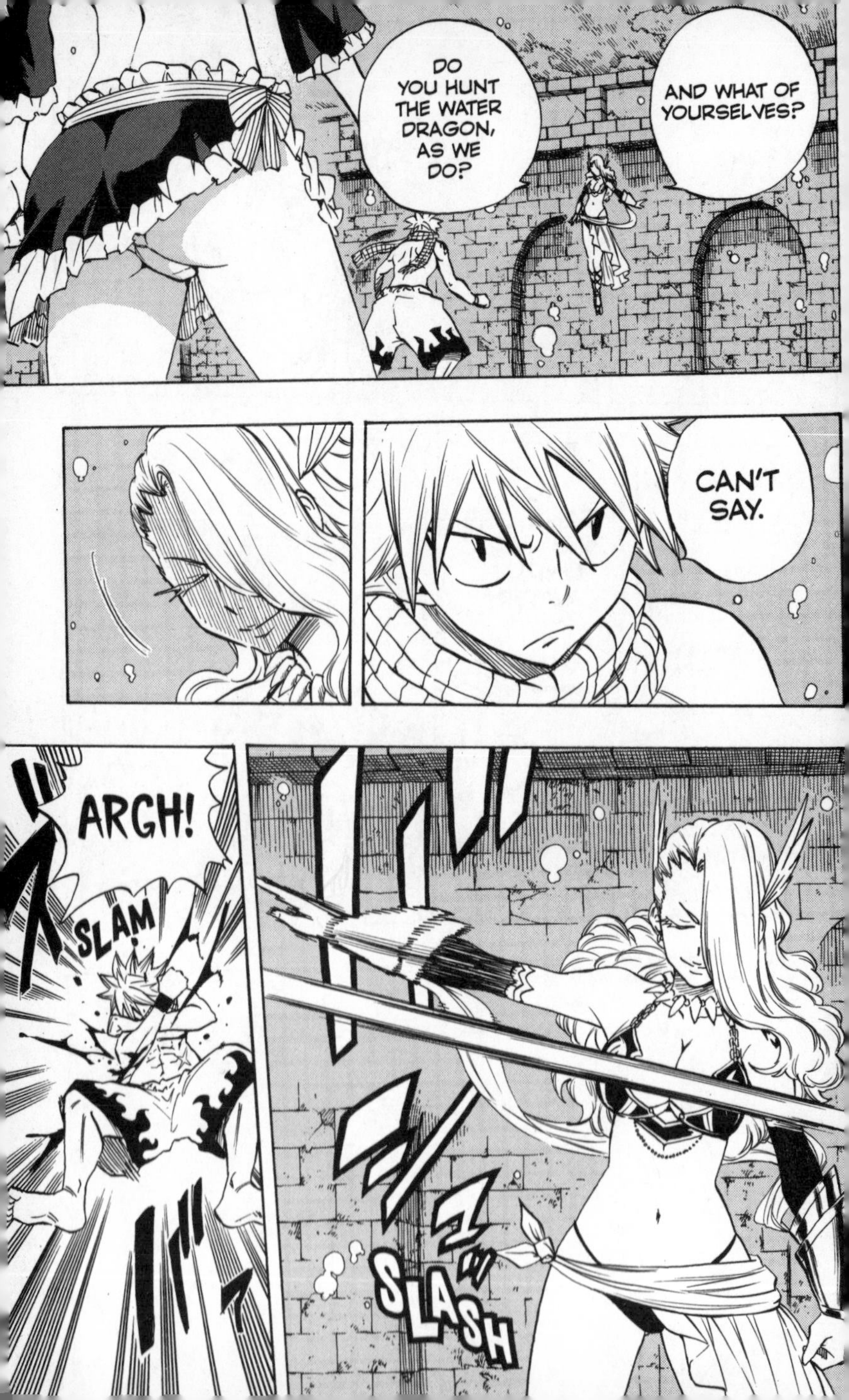
AND WHAT OF YOURSELVES?
DO YOU HUNT THE WATER DRAGON, AS WE DO?
CAN'T SAY.
SLASH
ARGH!
SLAM

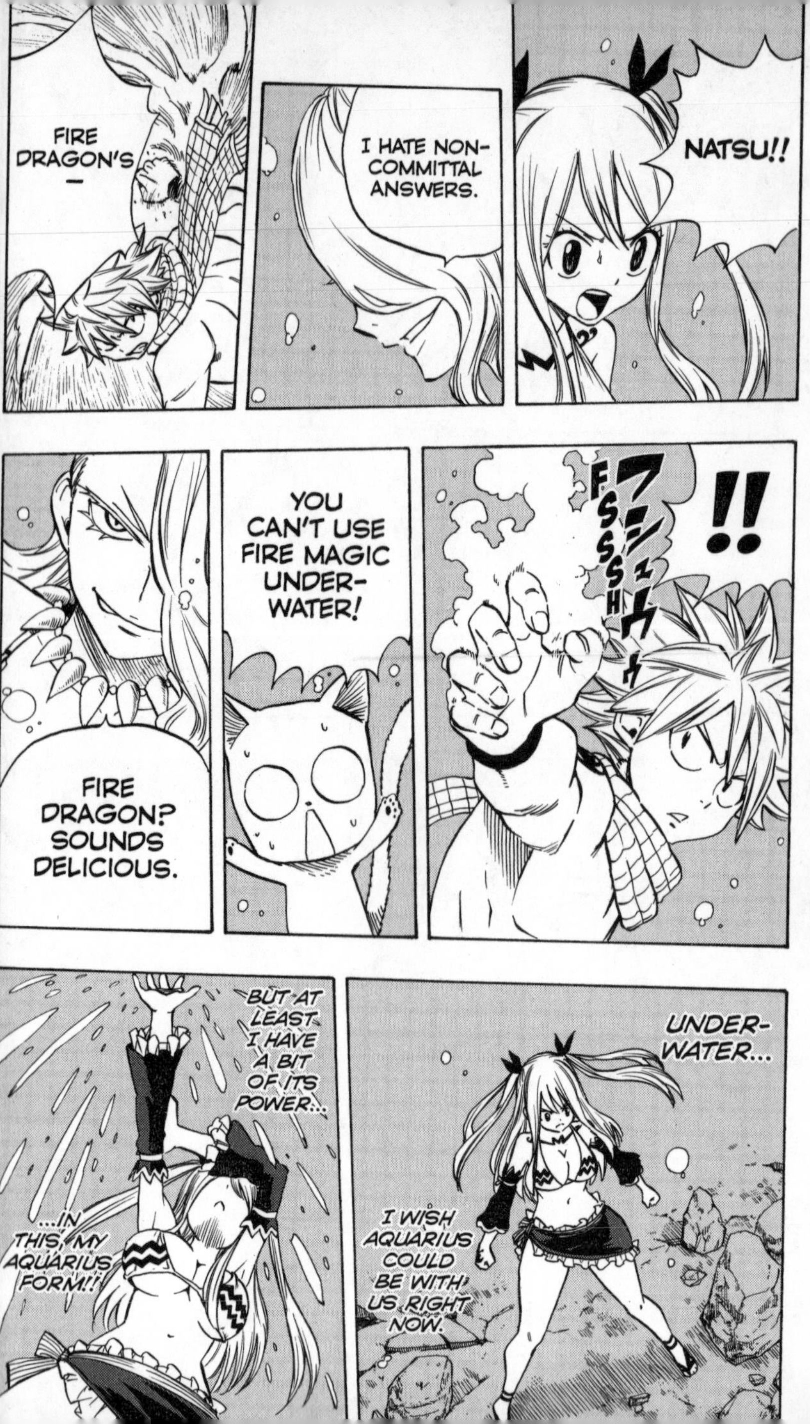
NATSU!!
I HATE NON-COMMITTAL ANSWERS.
FIRE DRAGON'S —
FSSSH
!!
YOU CAN'T USE FIRE MAGIC UNDER-WATER!
FIRE DRAGON? SOUNDS DELICIOUS.
UNDER-WATER...
I WISH AQUARIUS COULD BE WITH US RIGHT NOW.
BUT AT LEAST I HAVE A BIT OF ITS POWER...
...IN THIS, MY AQUARIUS FORM!!

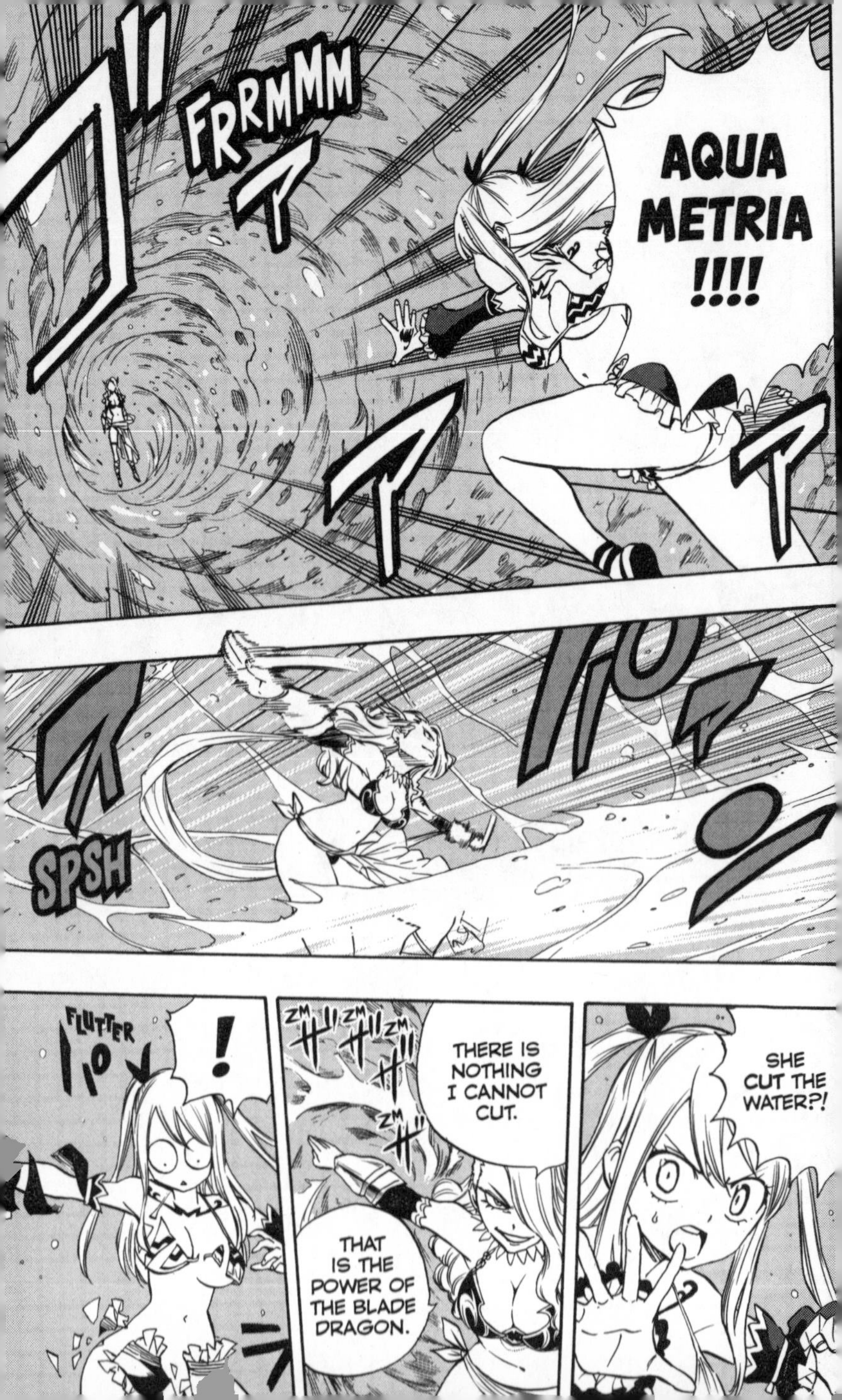
AQUA METRIA !!!!
FRRMMM
SPSH
SHE CUT THE WATER?!
THERE IS NOTHING I CANNOT CUT.
THAT IS THE POWER OF THE BLADE DRAGON.
!
FLUTTER

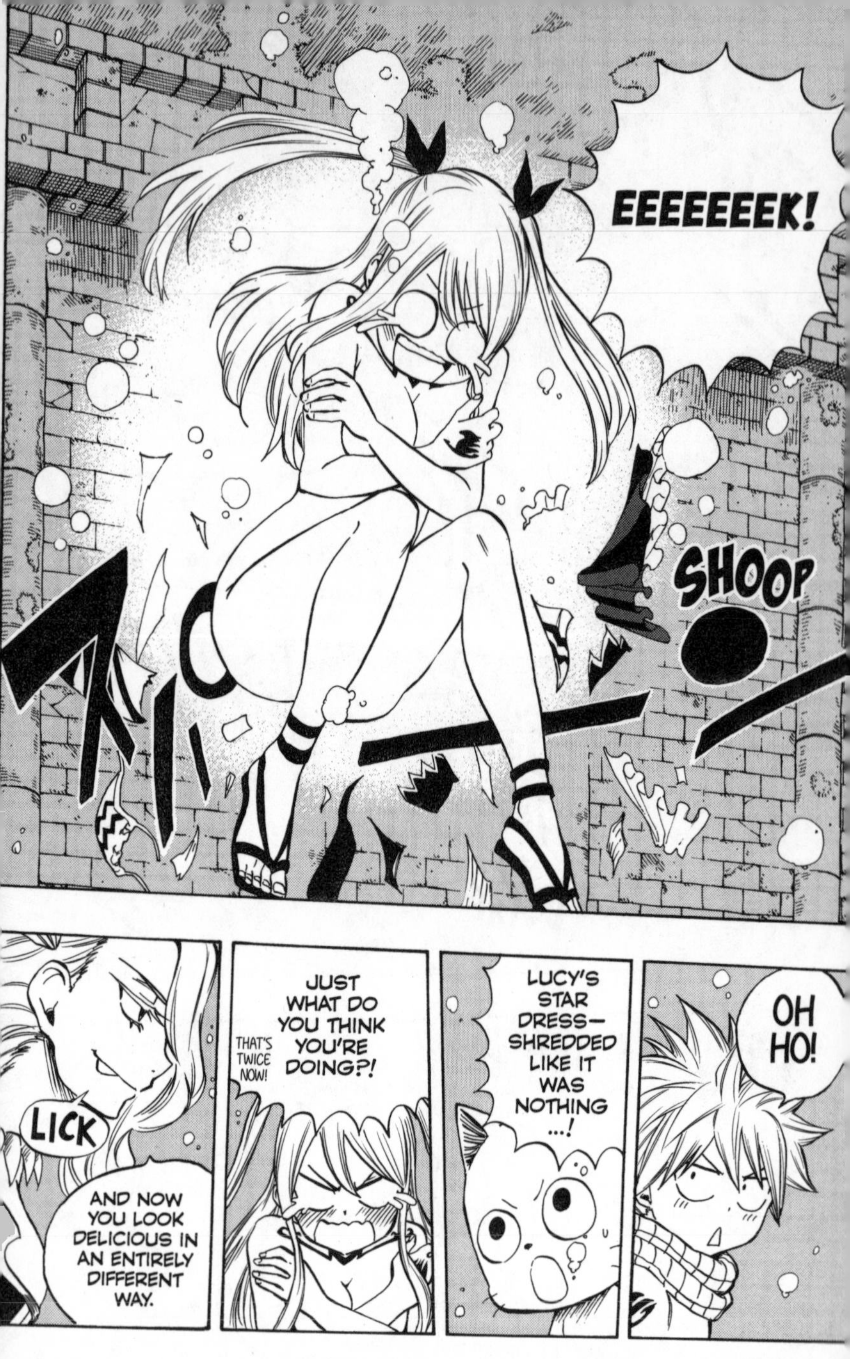
EEEEEEEK!
SHOOP
OH HO!
LUCY'S STAR DRESS— SHREDDED LIKE IT WAS NOTHING ...!
JUST WHAT DO YOU THINK YOU'RE DOING?!
THAT'S TWICE NOW!
LICK
AND NOW YOU LOOK DELICIOUS IN AN ENTIRELY DIFFERENT WAY.

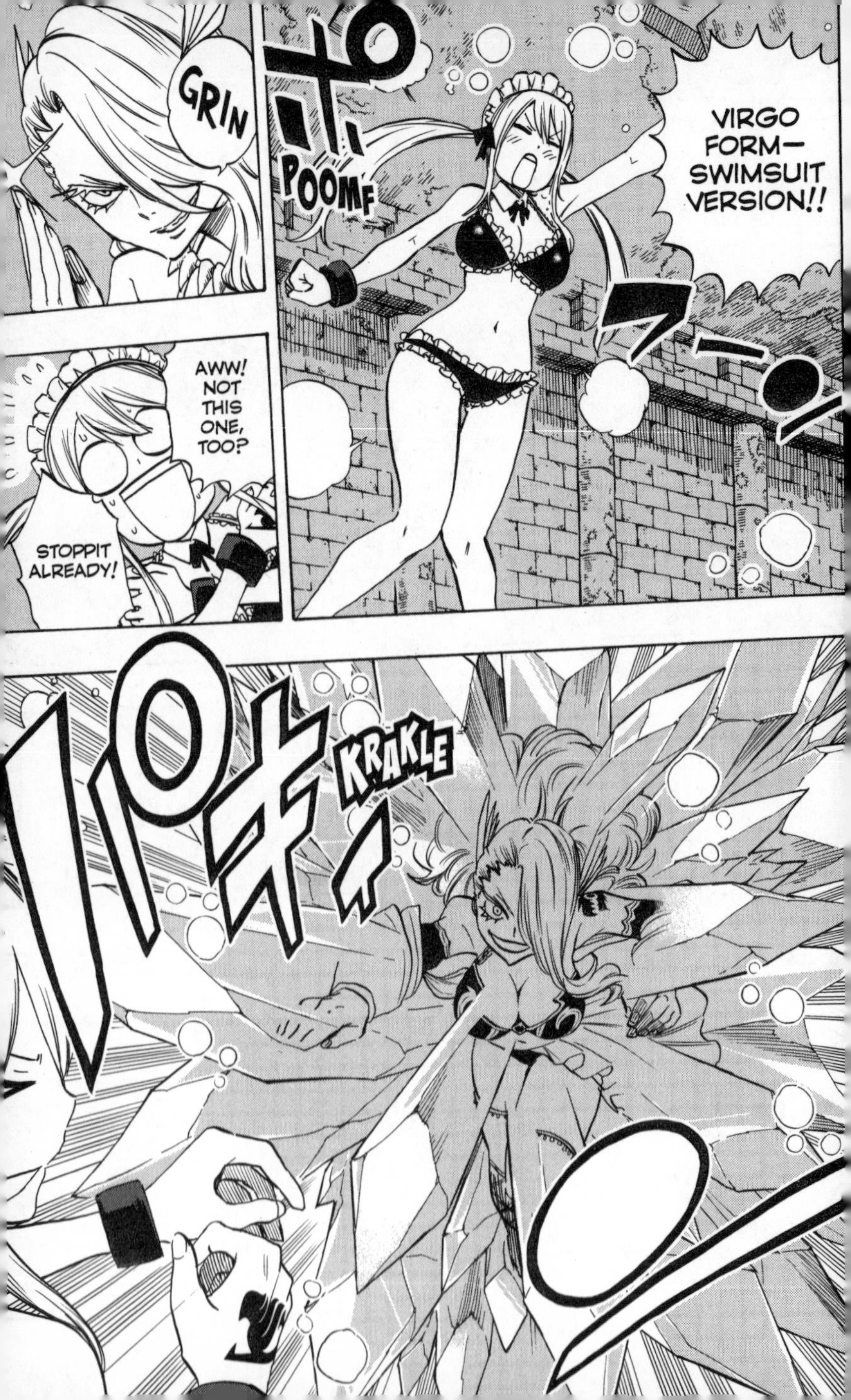
VIRGO FORM— SWIMSUIT VERSION!!
POOMF
GRIN
AWW! NOT THIS ONE, TOO?
STOPPIT ALREADY!
KRAKLE

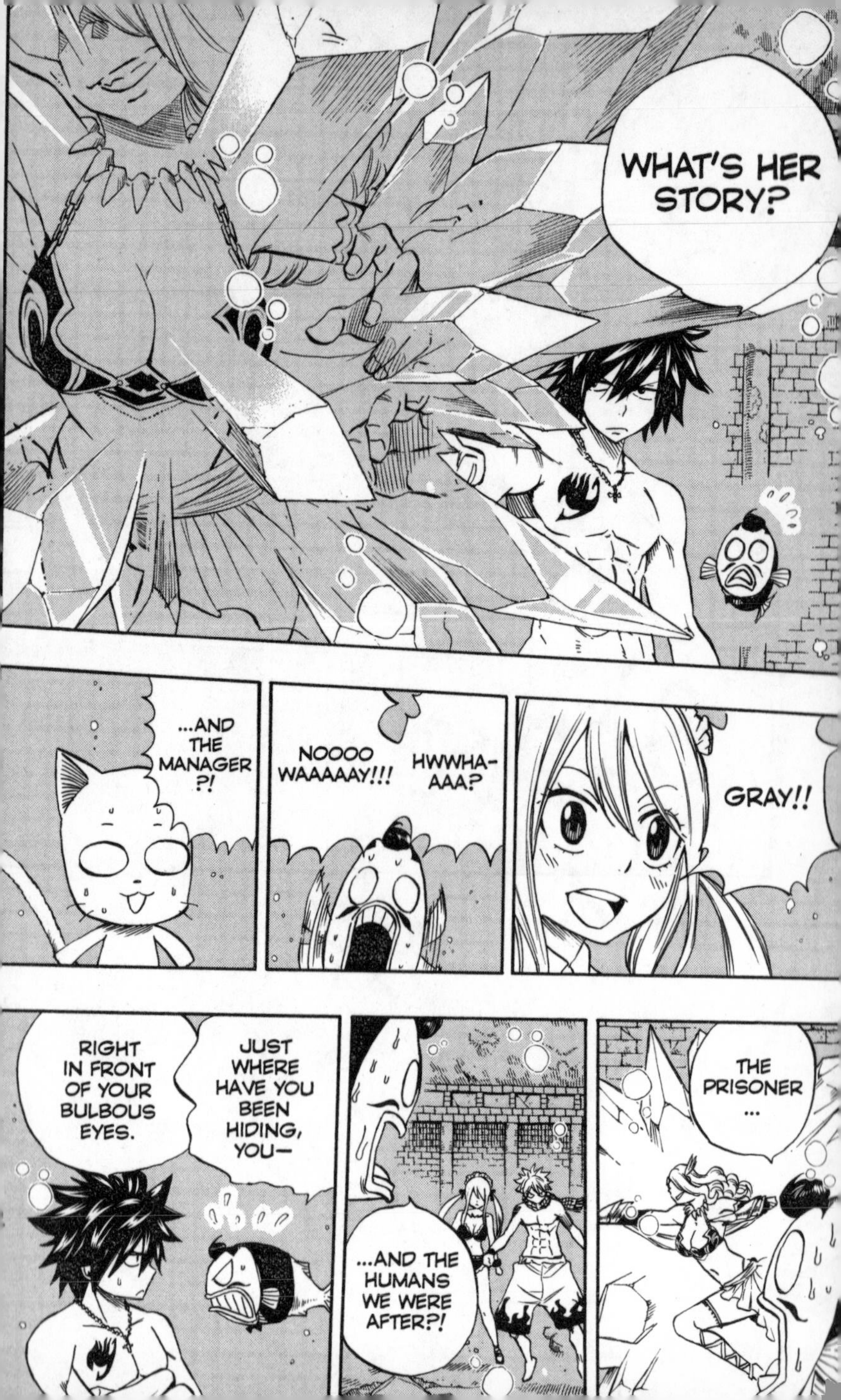
WHAT'S HER STORY?
GRAY!!
HWWHA-AAA?
NOOOO WAAAAAY!!!
...AND THE MANAGER ?!
THE PRISONER ...
...AND THE HUMANS WE WERE AFTER?!
JUST WHERE HAVE YOU BEEN HIDING, YOU—
RIGHT IN FRONT OF YOUR BULBOUS EYES.

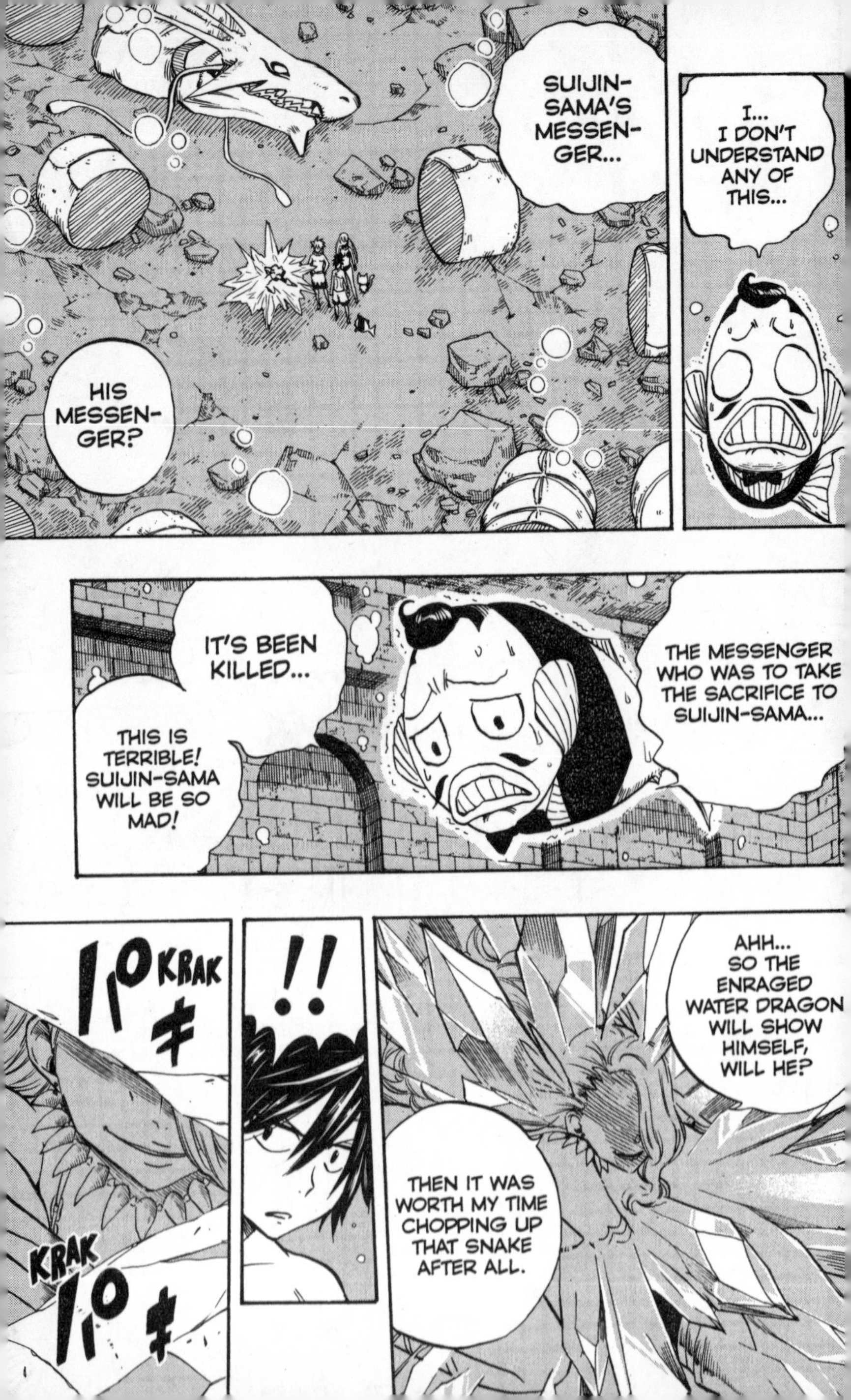
I... I DON'T UNDERSTAND ANY OF THIS...
SUIJIN-SAMA'S MESSENGER...
HIS MESSENGER?
THE MESSENGER WHO WAS TO TAKE THE SACRIFICE TO SUIJIN-SAMA...
IT'S BEEN KILLED...
THIS IS TERRIBLE! SUIJIN-SAMA WILL BE SO MAD!
AHH... SO THE ENRAGED WATER DRAGON WILL SHOW HIMSELF, WILL HE?
THEN IT WAS WORTH MY TIME CHOPPING UP THAT SNAKE AFTER ALL.
!!
KRAK
KRAK

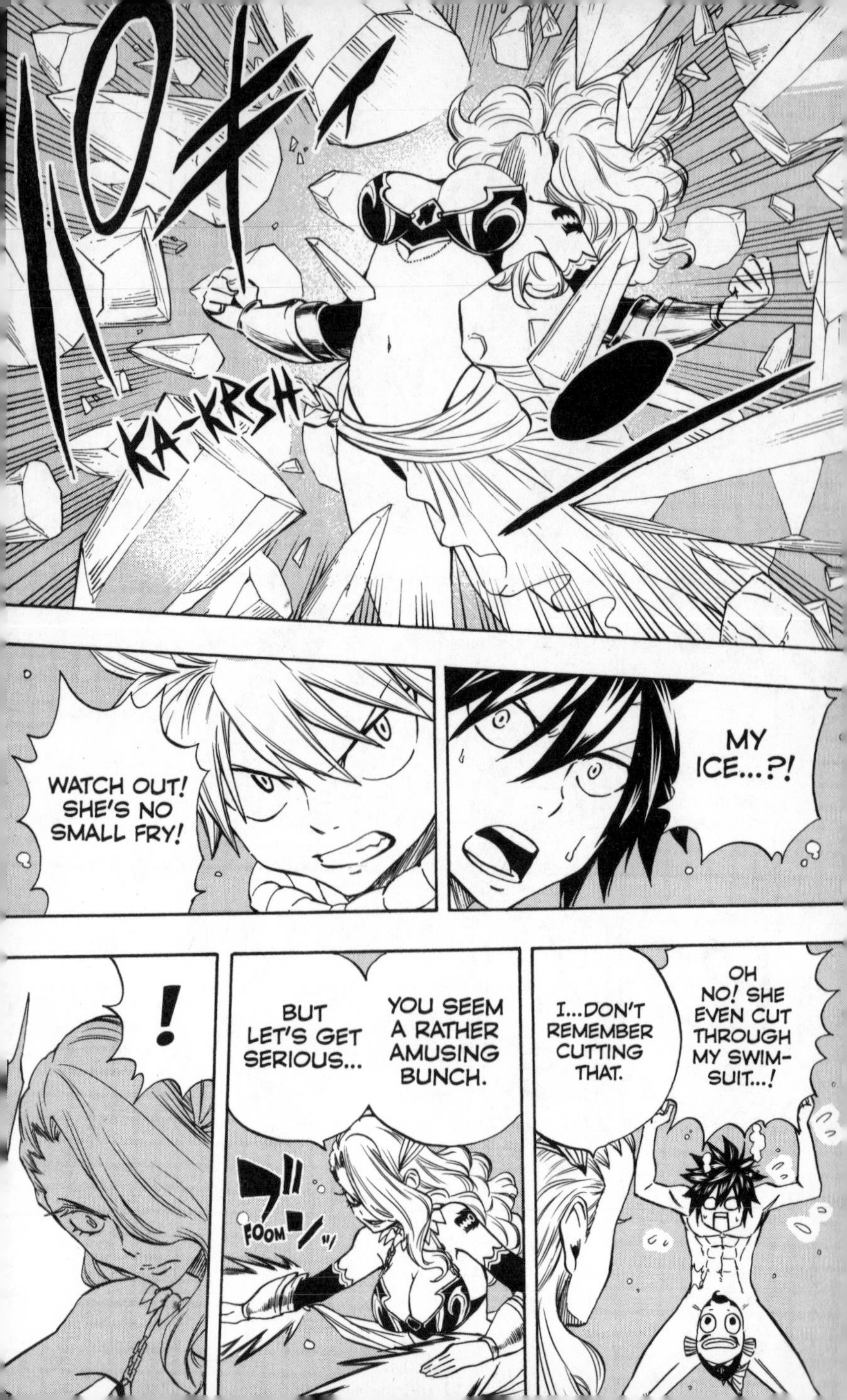
KA-KRSH
MY ICE...?!
WATCH OUT! SHE'S NO SMALL FRY!
OH NO! SHE EVEN CUT THROUGH MY SWIM-SUIT...!
I...DON'T REMEMBER CUTTING THAT.
YOU SEEM A RATHER AMUSING BUNCH.
BUT LET'S GET SERIOUS...
FOOM
!

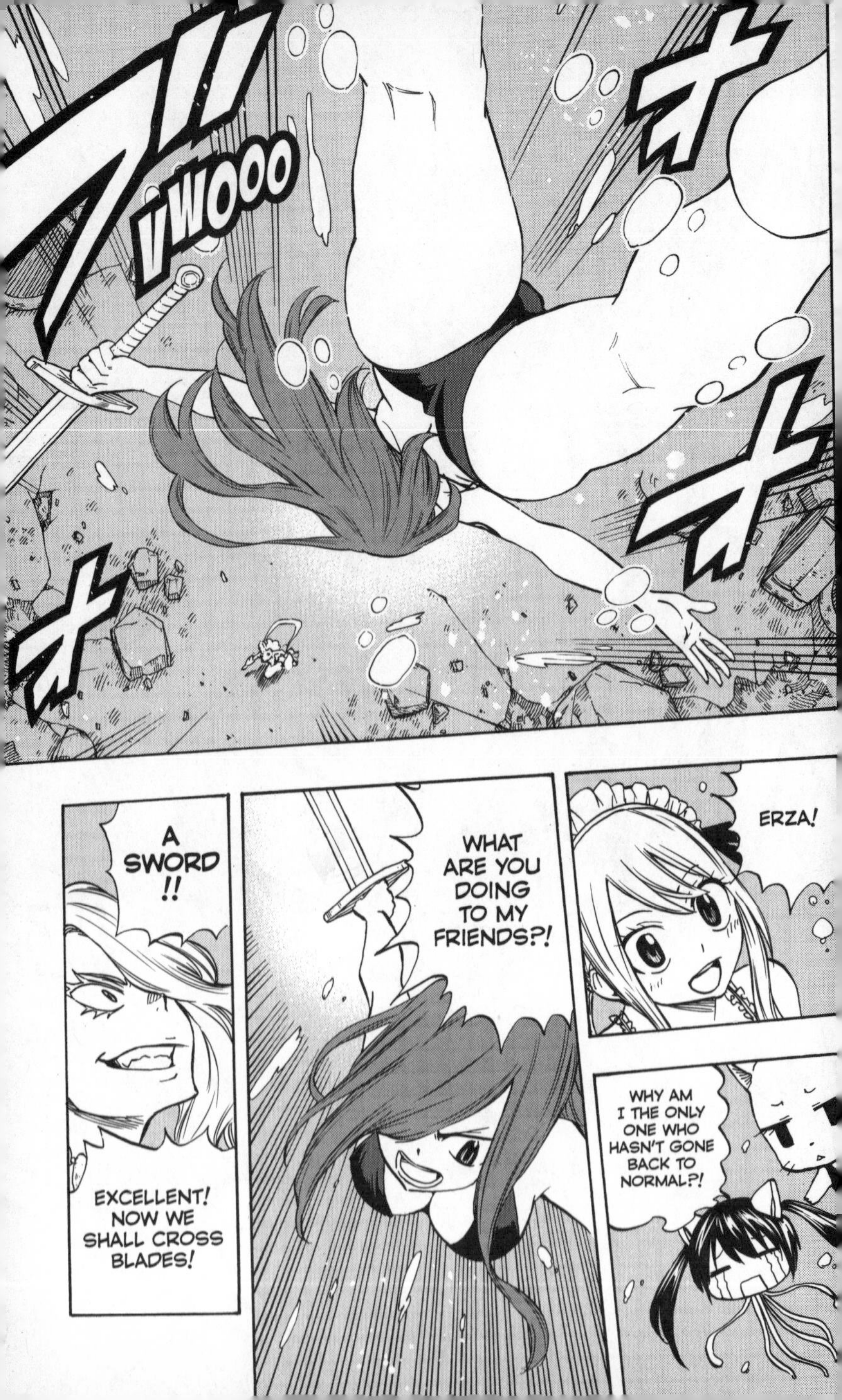
VWOOO
ERZA!
WHY AM I THE ONLY ONE WHO HASN'T GONE BACK TO NORMAL?!
WHAT ARE YOU DOING TO MY FRIENDS?!
A SWORD !!
EXCELLENT! NOW WE SHALL CROSS BLADES!

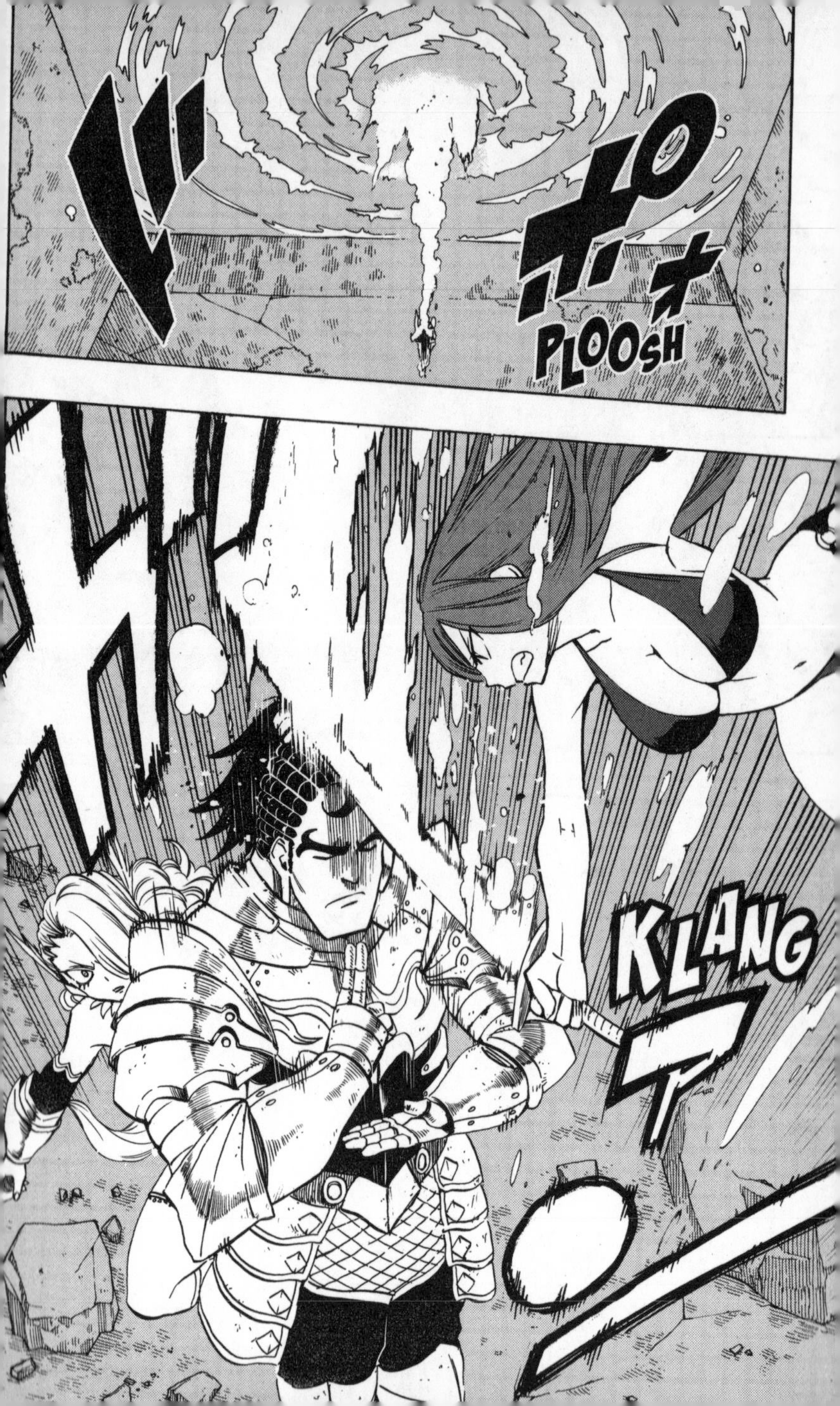
PLOOSH
KLANG

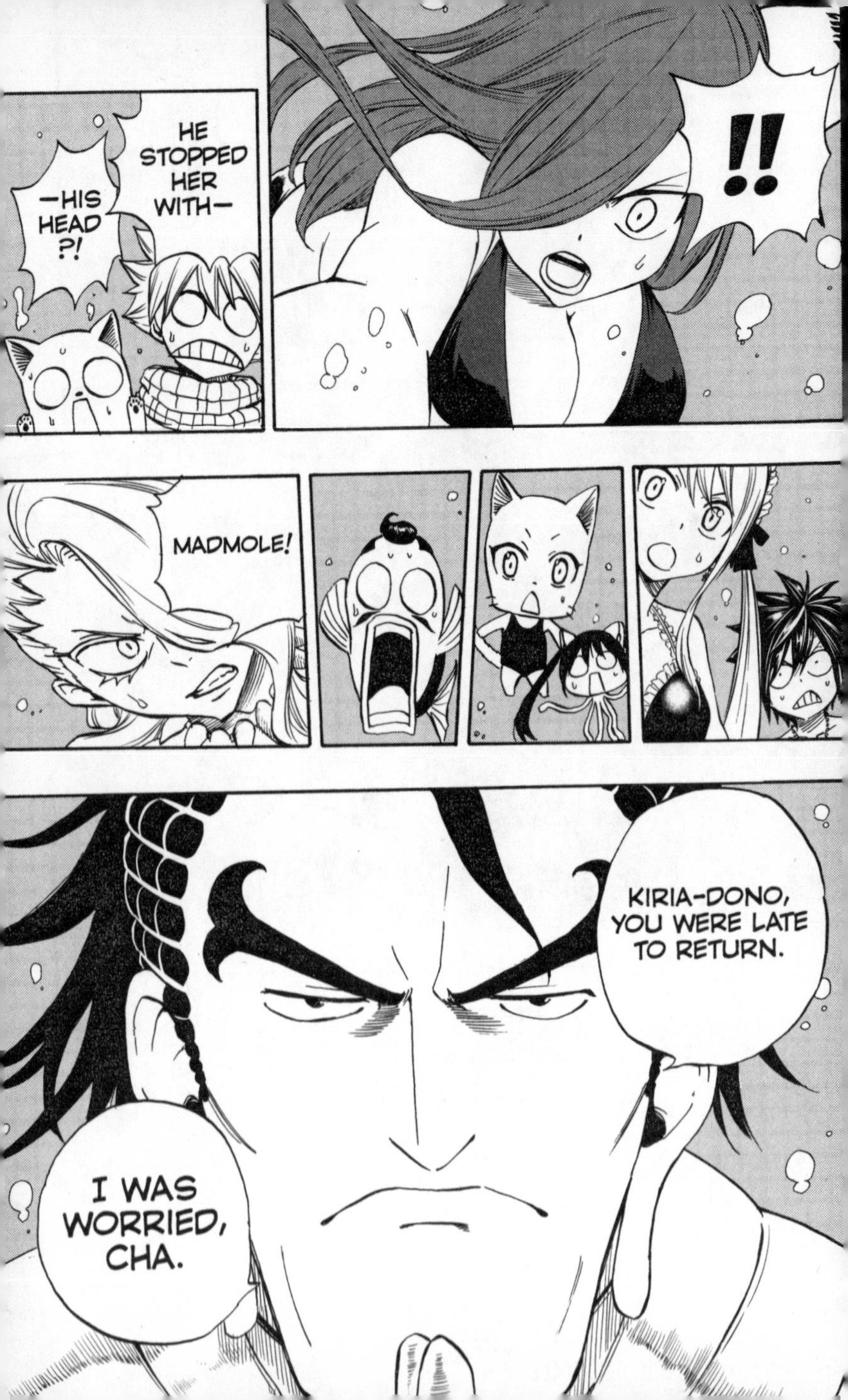
!!
HE STOPPED HER WITH—
—HIS HEAD ?!
MADMOLE!
KIRIA-DONO, YOU WERE LATE TO RETURN.
I WAS WORRIED, CHA.

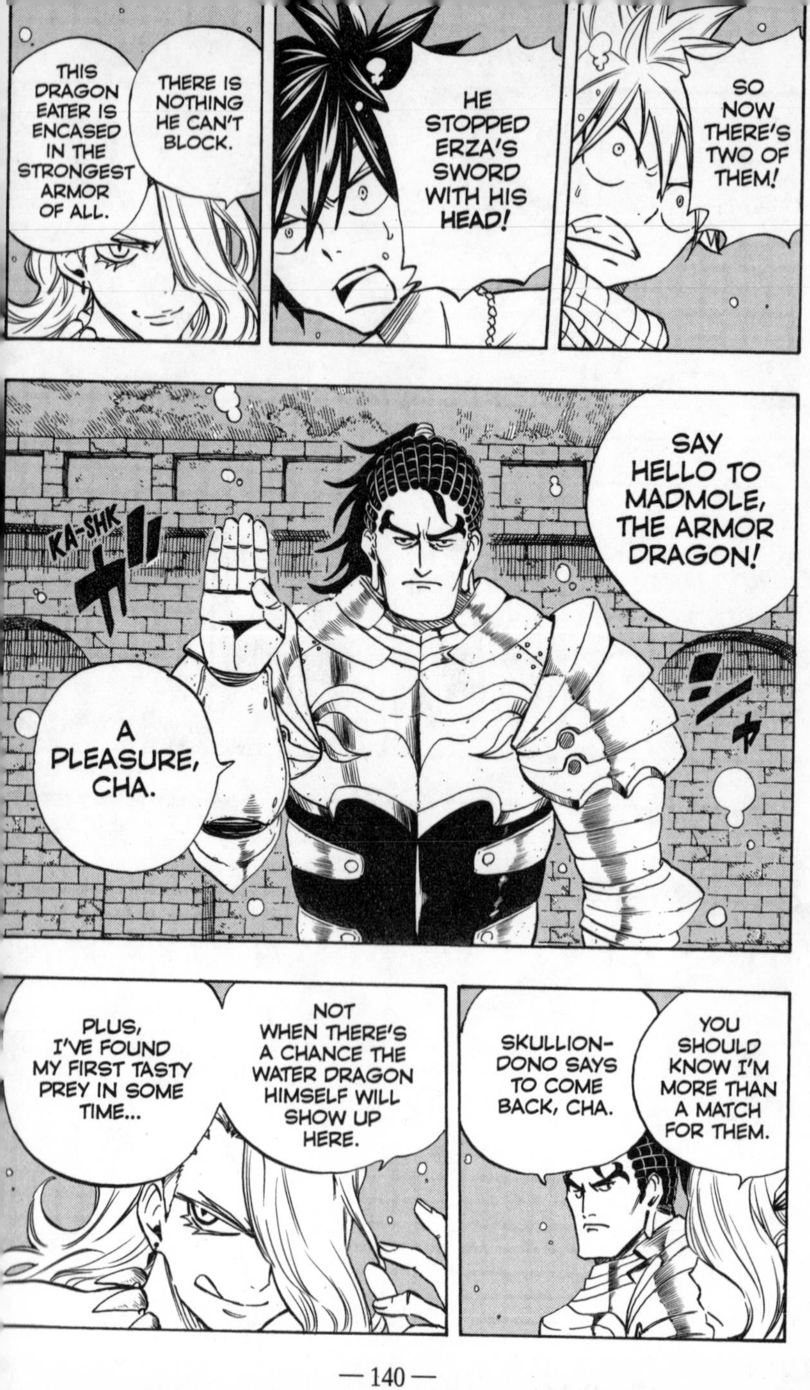
SO NOW THERE'S TWO OF THEM!
HE STOPPED ERZA'S SWORD WITH HIS HEAD!
THERE IS NOTHING HE CAN'T BLOCK.
THIS DRAGON EATER IS ENCASED IN THE STRONGEST ARMOR OF ALL.
SAY HELLO TO MADMOLE, THE ARMOR DRAGON!
KA-SHK
A PLEASURE, CHA.
YOU SHOULD KNOW I'M MORE THAN A MATCH FOR THEM.
SKULLION-DONO SAYS TO COME BACK, CHA.
NOT WHEN THERE'S A CHANCE THE WATER DRAGON HIMSELF WILL SHOW UP HERE.
PLUS, I'VE FOUND MY FIRST TASTY PREY IN SOME TIME...

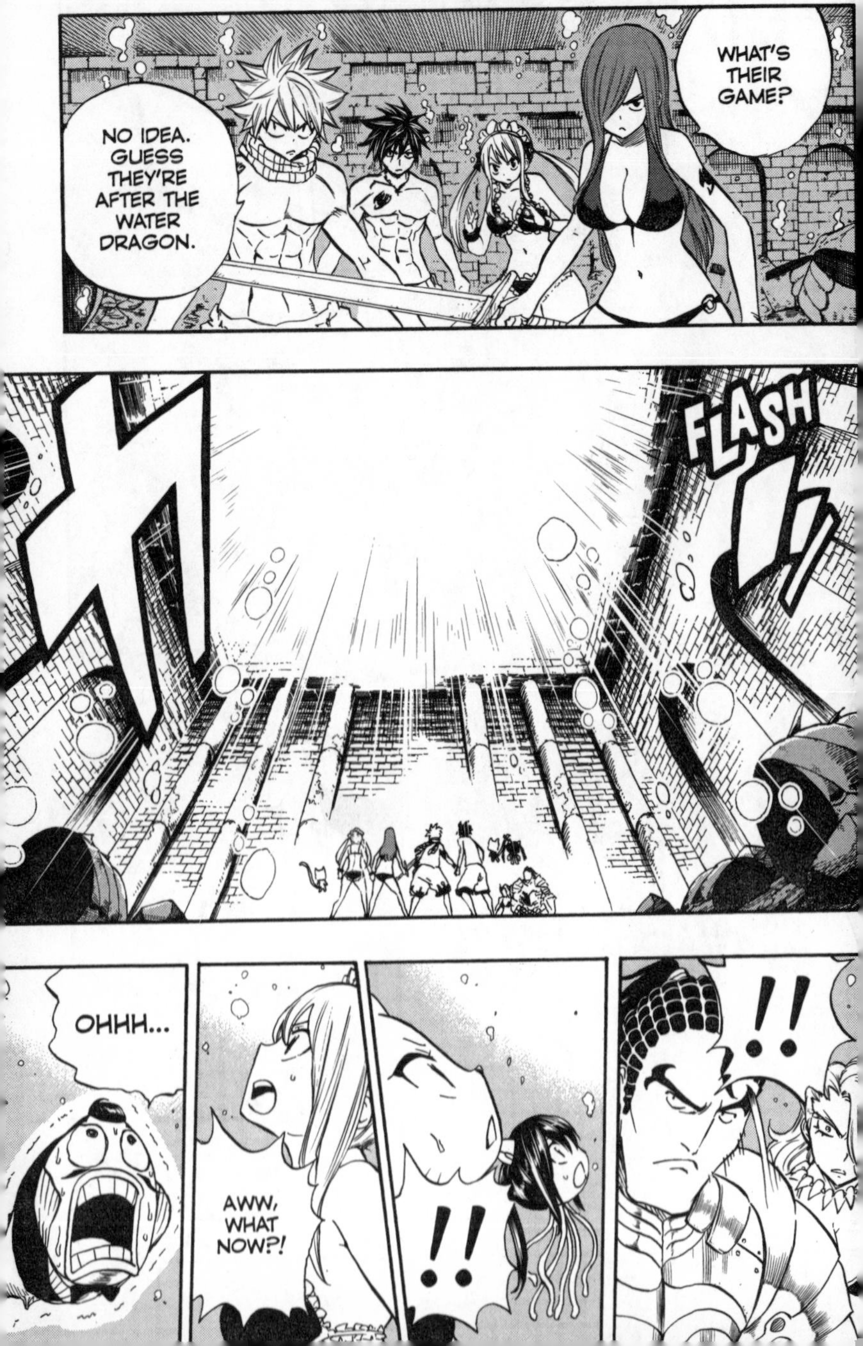

WHAT'S THEIR GAME?
NO IDEA. GUESS THEY'RE AFTER THE WATER DRAGON.
FLASH
!!
!!
AWW, WHAT NOW?!
OHHH...

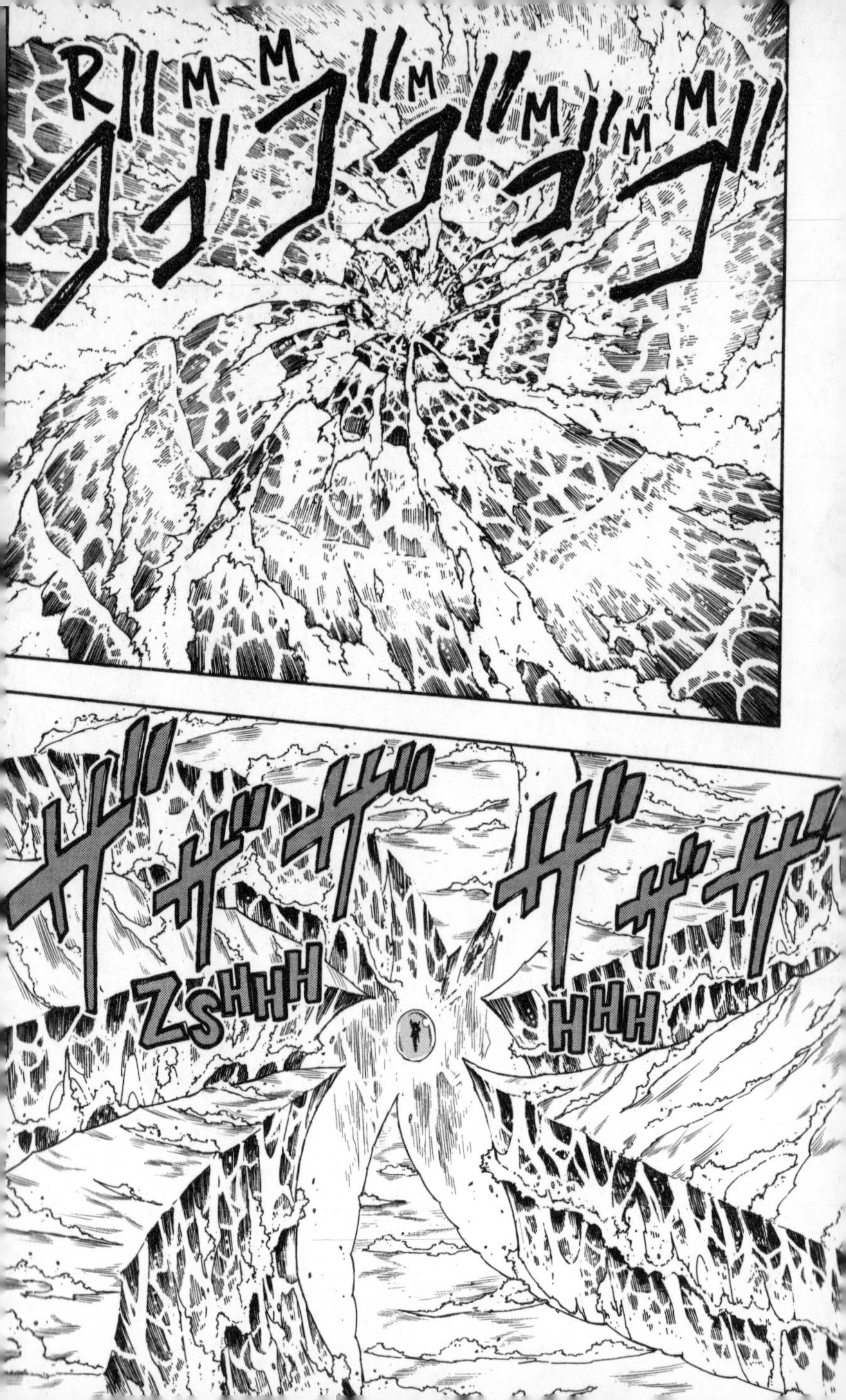
RMMMMMM
ゴゴゴゴ
ザザザ
ZSHHH
ザザザ
HHH

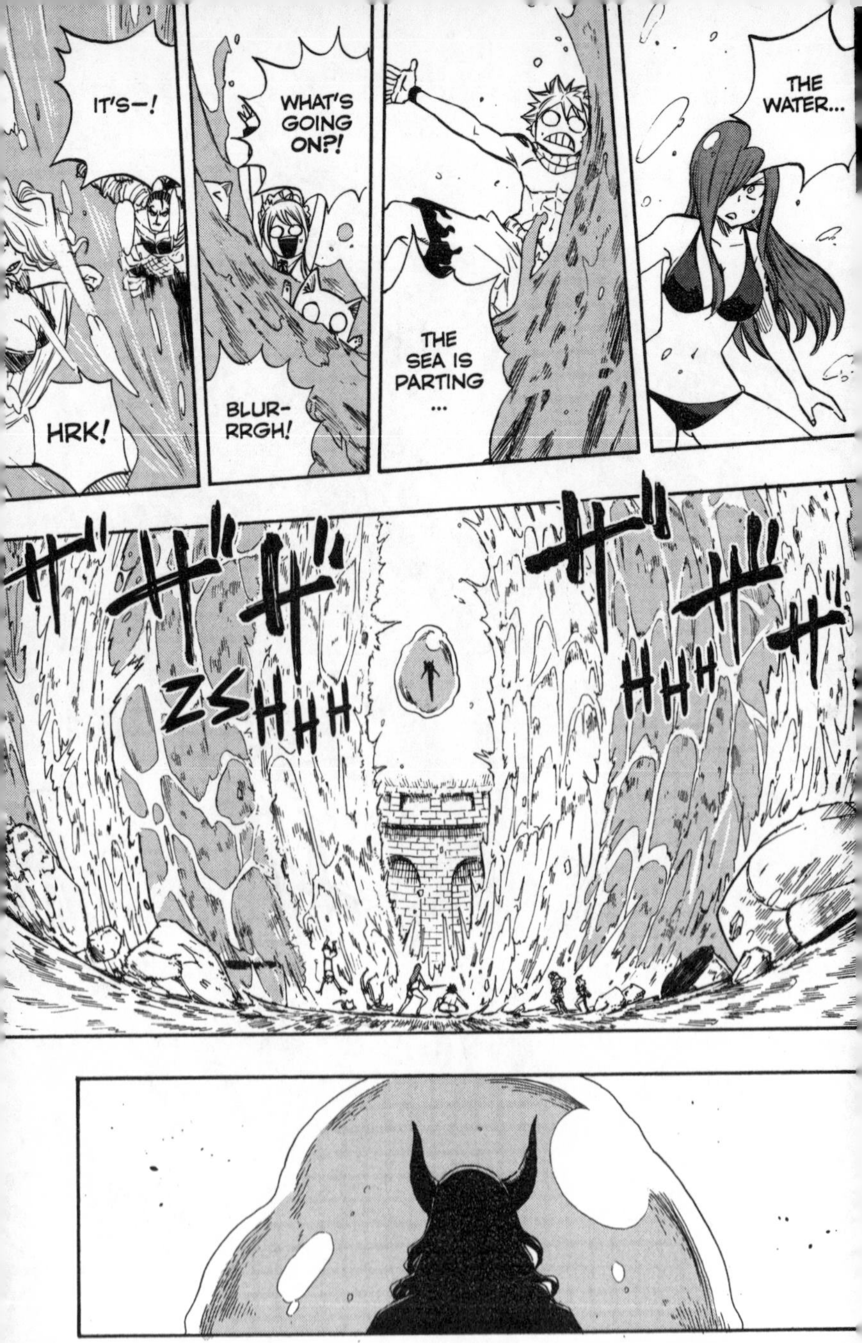
THE WATER...
THE SEA IS PARTING ...
WHAT'S GOING ON?!
BLUR-RRGH!
IT'S—!
HRK!
HHH
ZSHHH

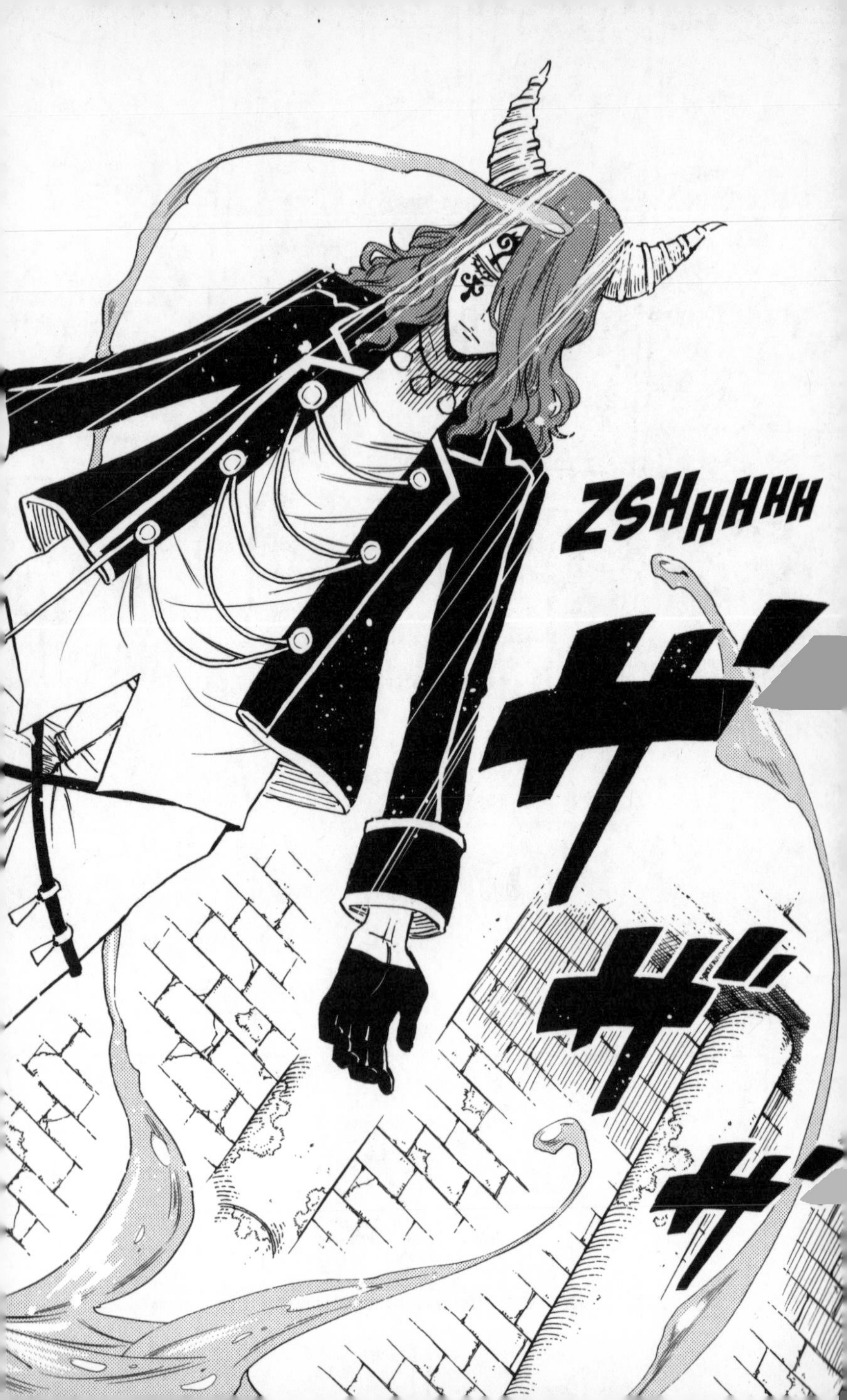
ZSHHHHH
ザザザ

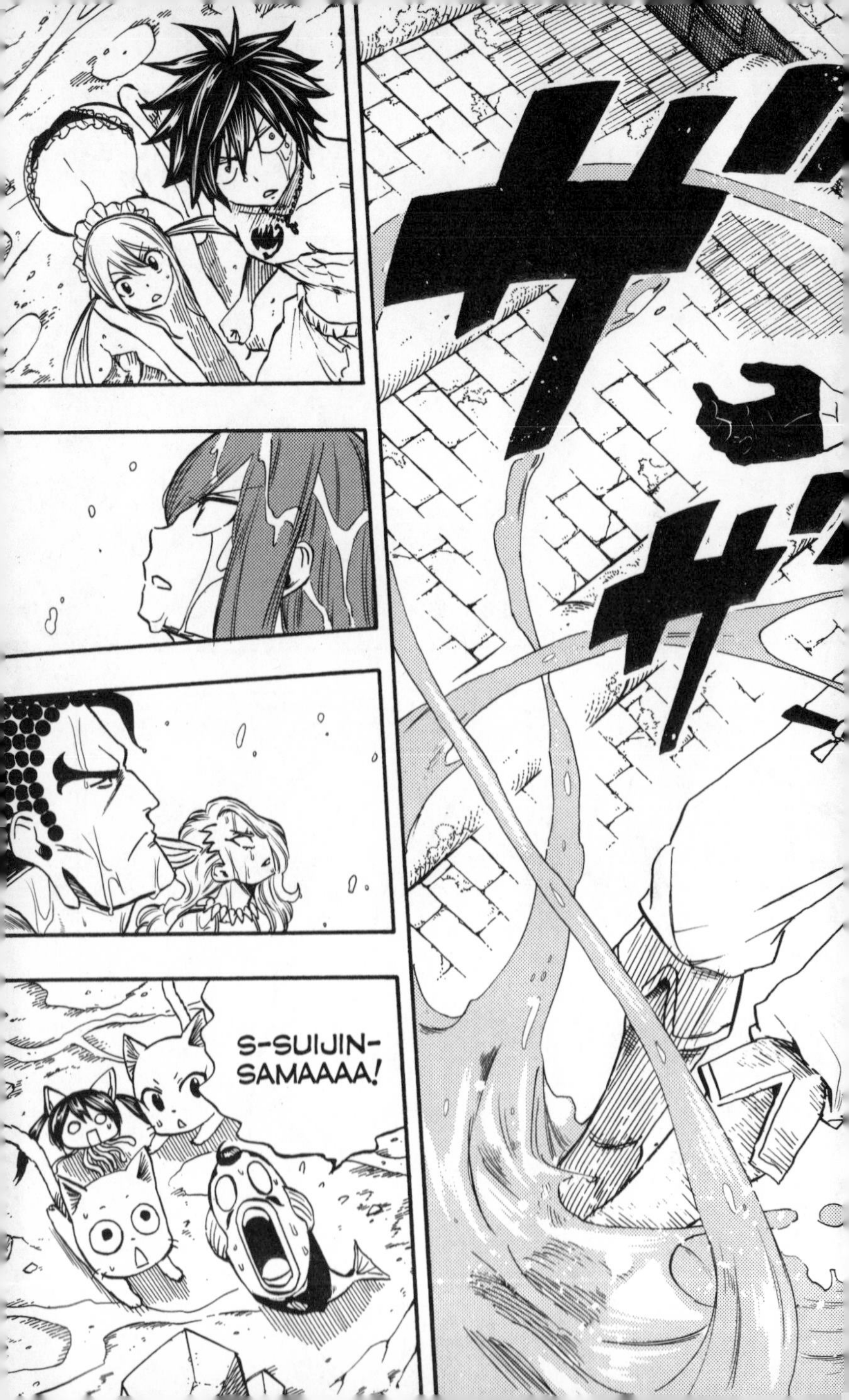
S-SUIJIN-SAMAAAA!

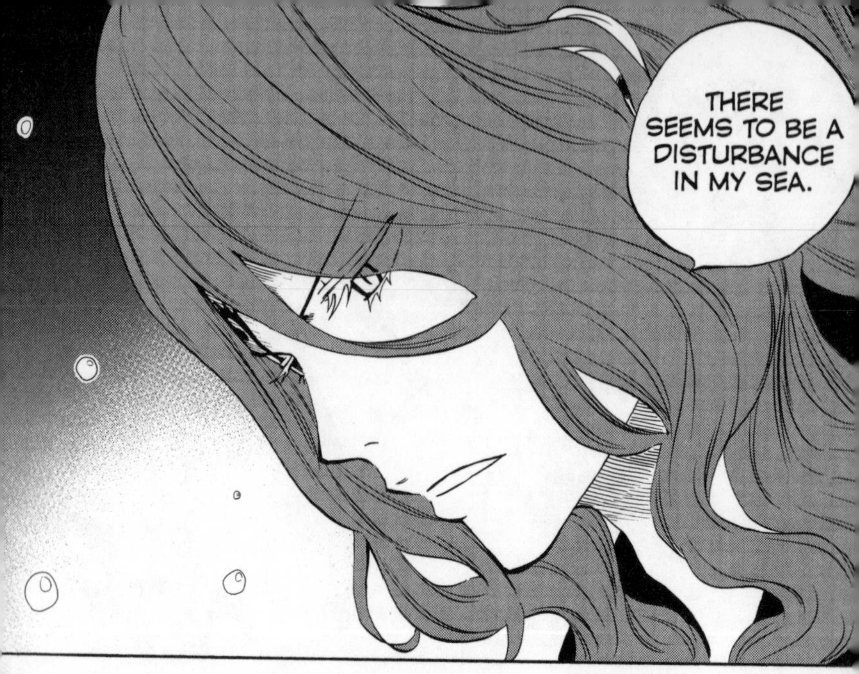
THERE SEEMS TO BE A DISTURBANCE IN MY SEA.

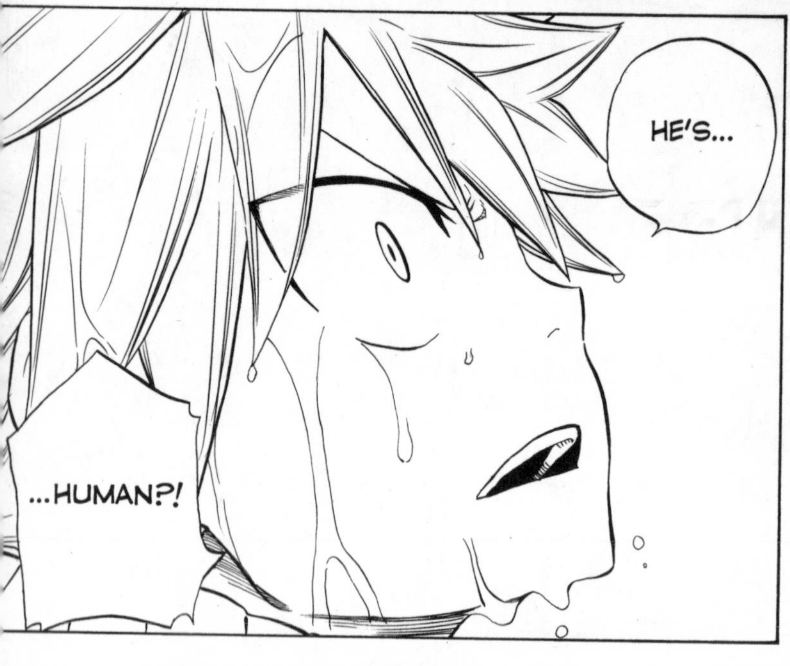
HE'S...
...HUMAN?!

FAIRY TAIL 100 YEARS QUEST

Chapter 8: A Dragon God's Melancholy

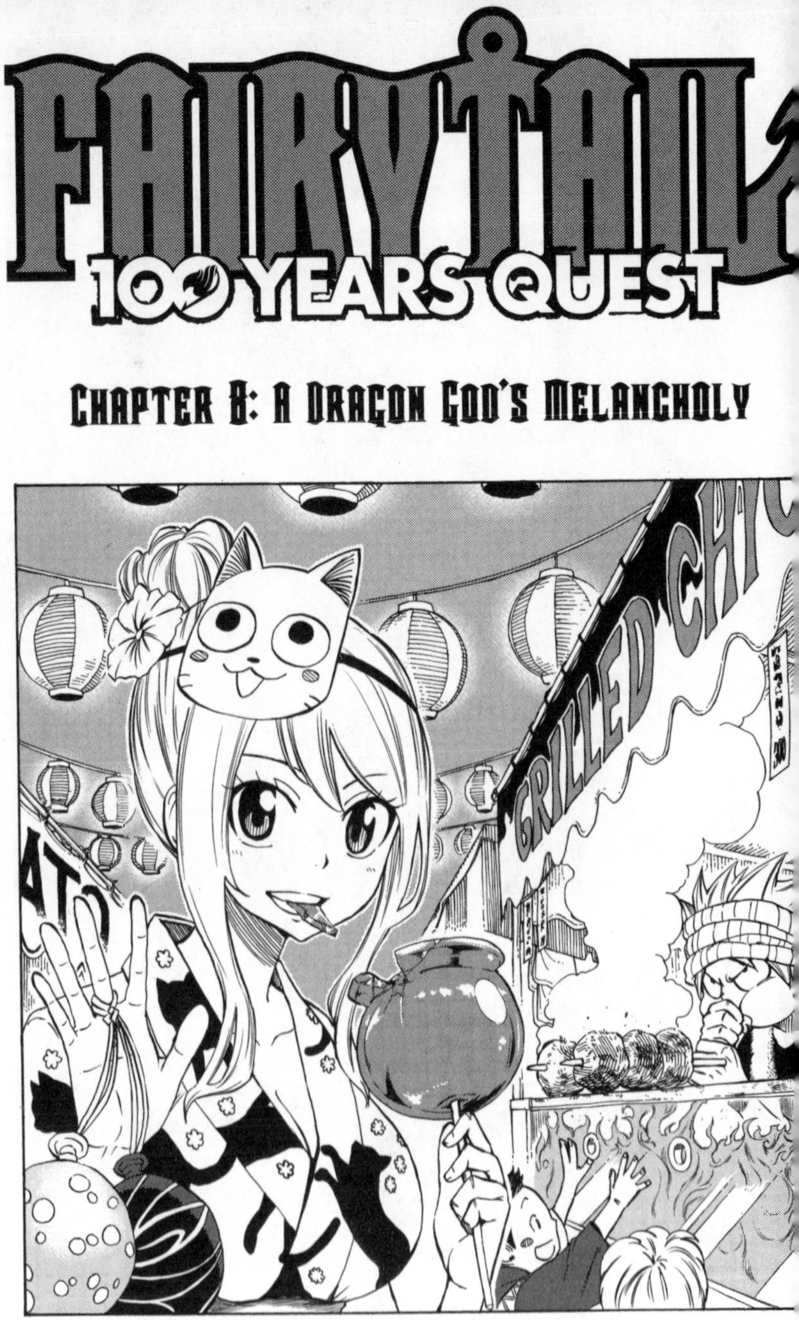
GRILLED CHI

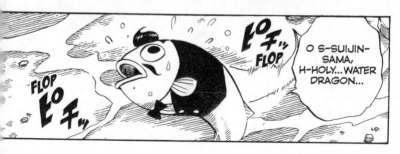

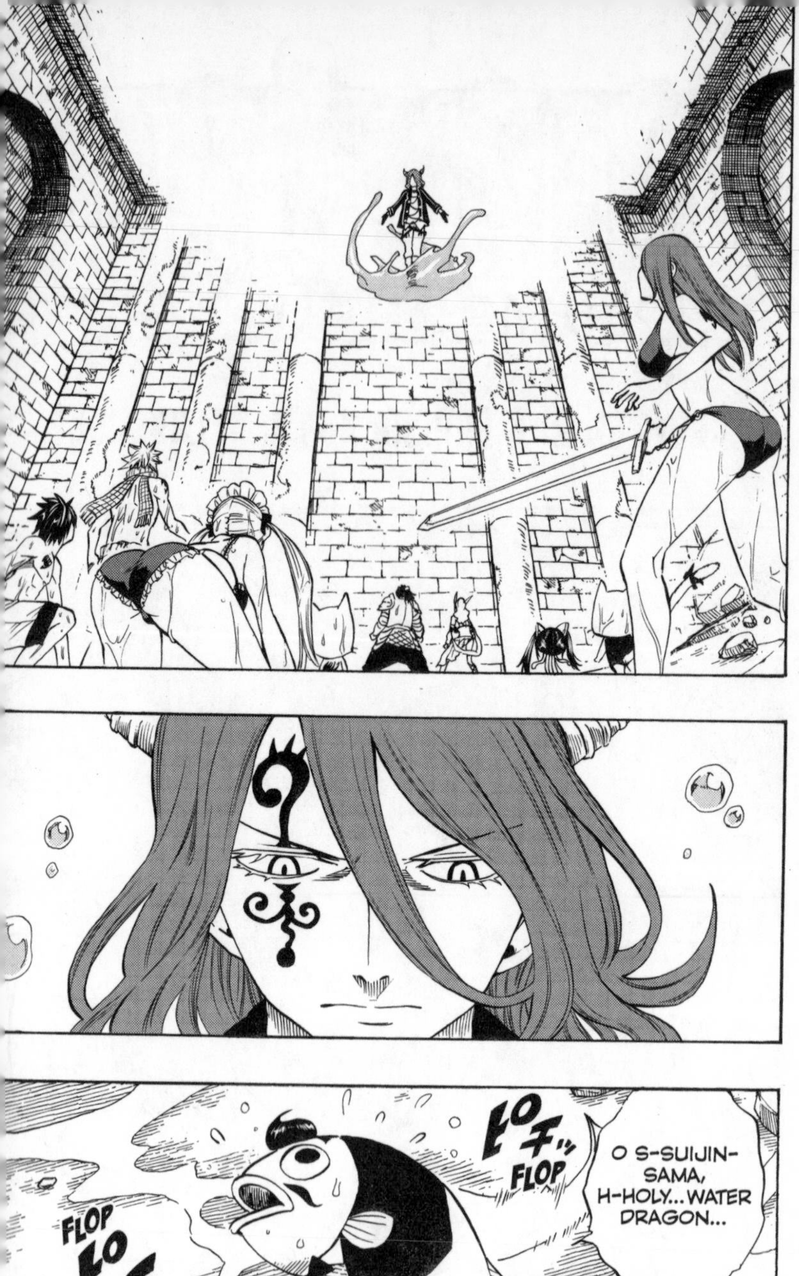
O S-SUIJIN-SAMA, H-HOLY...WATER DRAGON...
ピチッ
FLOP
FLOP
ピチッ

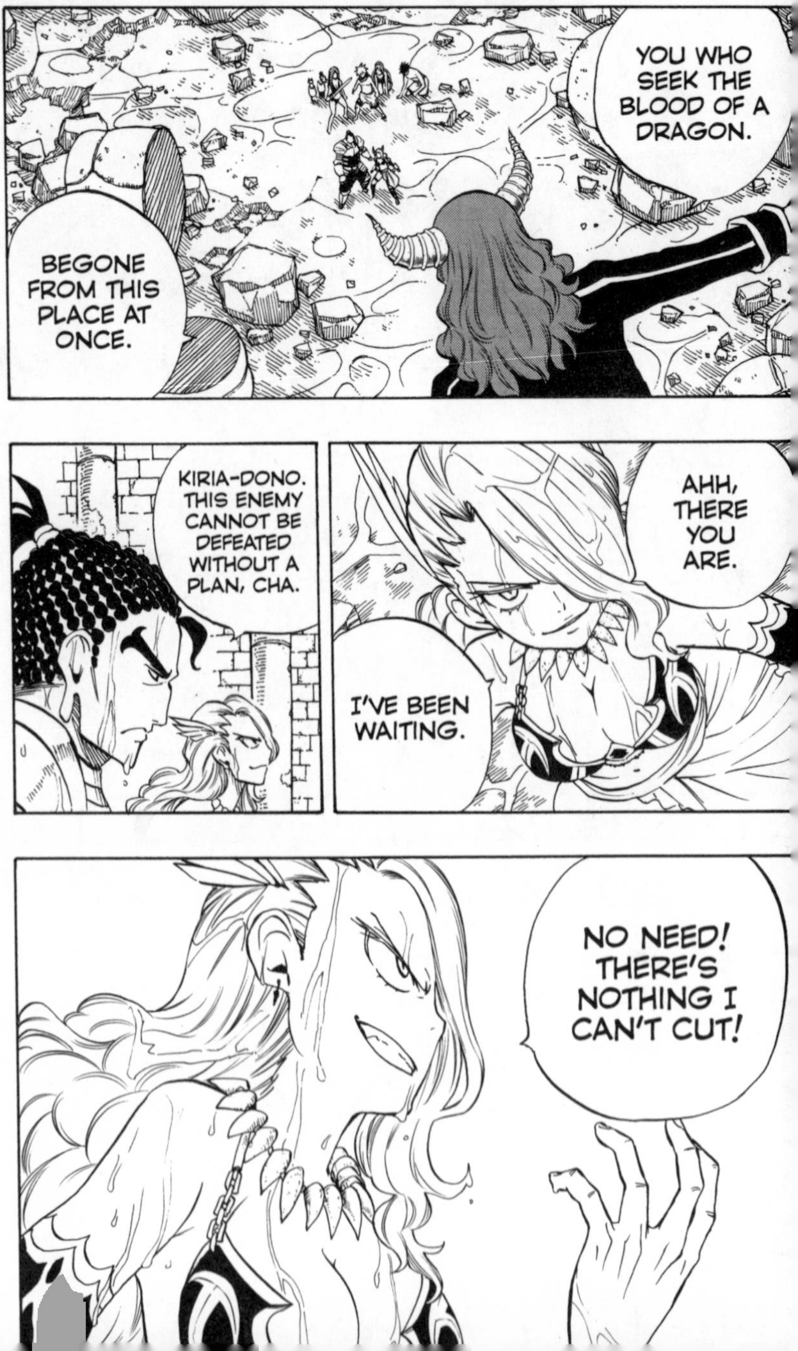
YOU WHO SEEK THE BLOOD OF A DRAGON.
BEGONE FROM THIS PLACE AT ONCE.
AHH, THERE YOU ARE.
I'VE BEEN WAITING.
KIRIA-DONO. THIS ENEMY CANNOT BE DEFEATED WITHOUT A PLAN, CHA.
NO NEED! THERE'S NOTHING I CAN'T CUT!

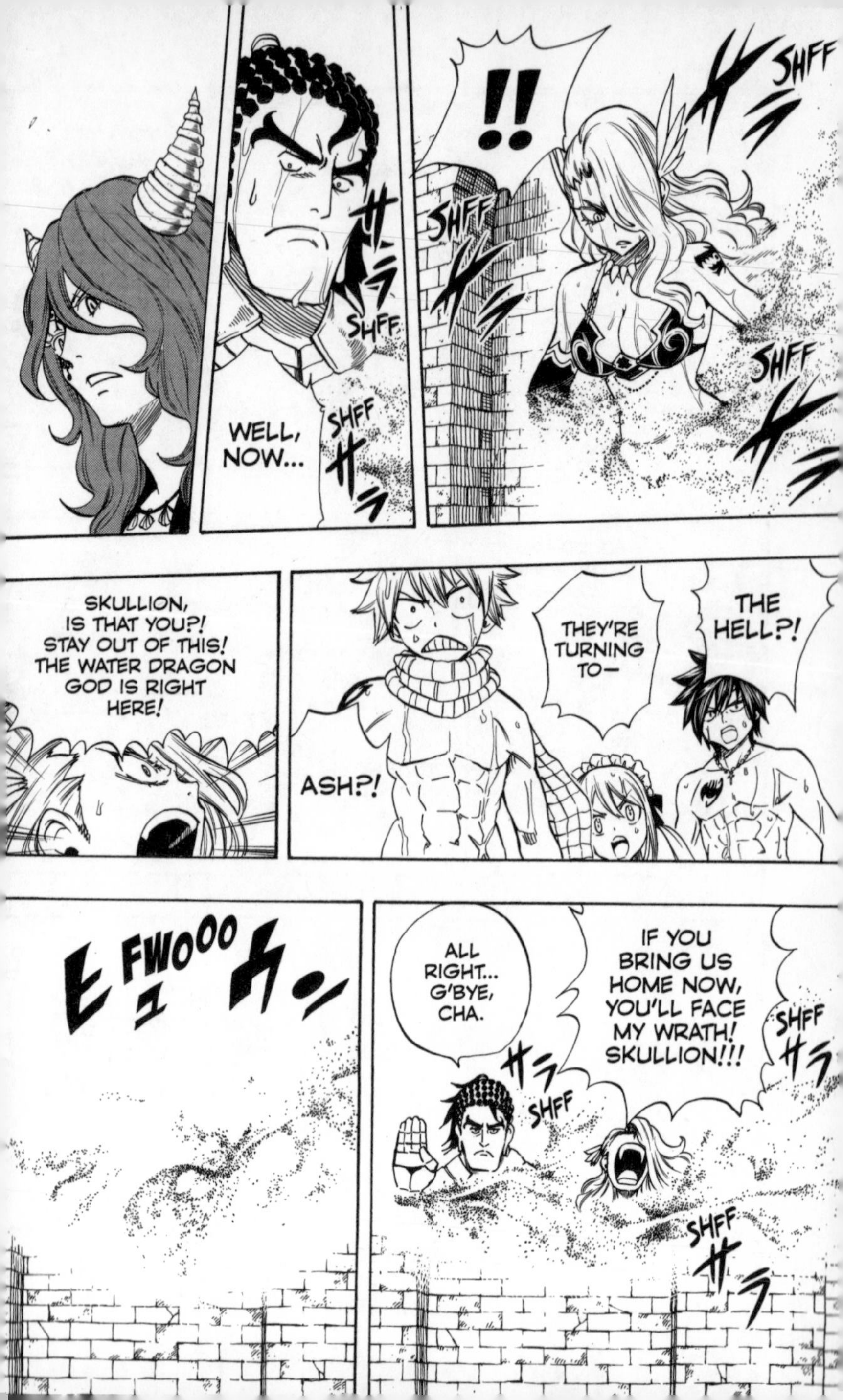
SHFF
!!
SHFF
SHFF
SHFF
SHFF
WELL, NOW...
THE HELL?!
THEY'RE TURNING TO—
ASH?!
SKULLION, IS THAT YOU?! STAY OUT OF THIS! THE WATER DRAGON GOD IS RIGHT HERE!
SHFF
IF YOU BRING US HOME NOW, YOU'LL FACE MY WRATH! SKULLION!!!
ALL RIGHT... G'BYE, CHA.
SHFF
SHFF
FWOOO

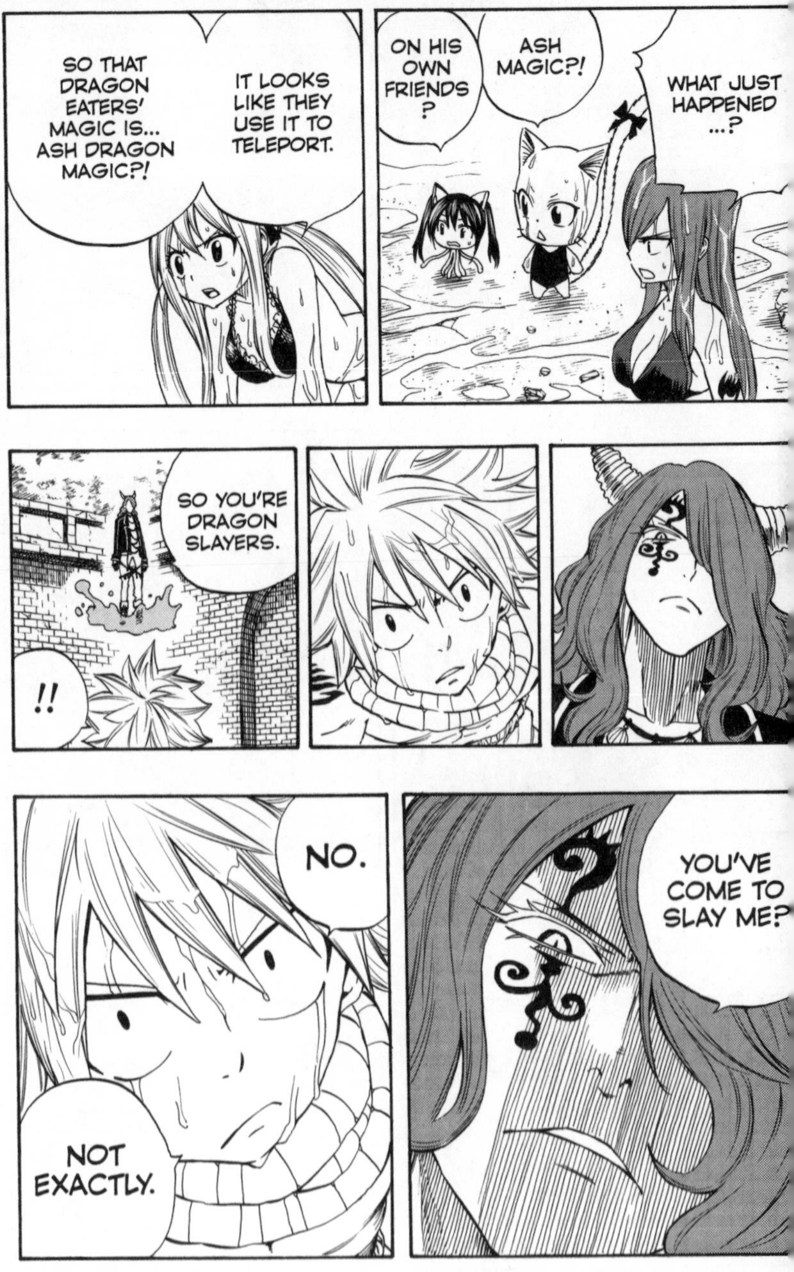
WHAT JUST HAPPENED ...?
ASH MAGIC?!
ON HIS OWN FRIENDS ?
IT LOOKS LIKE THEY USE IT TO TELEPORT.
SO THAT DRAGON EATERS' MAGIC IS... ASH DRAGON MAGIC?!
SO YOU'RE DRAGON SLAYERS.
!!
YOU'VE COME TO SLAY ME?
NO.
NOT EXACTLY.

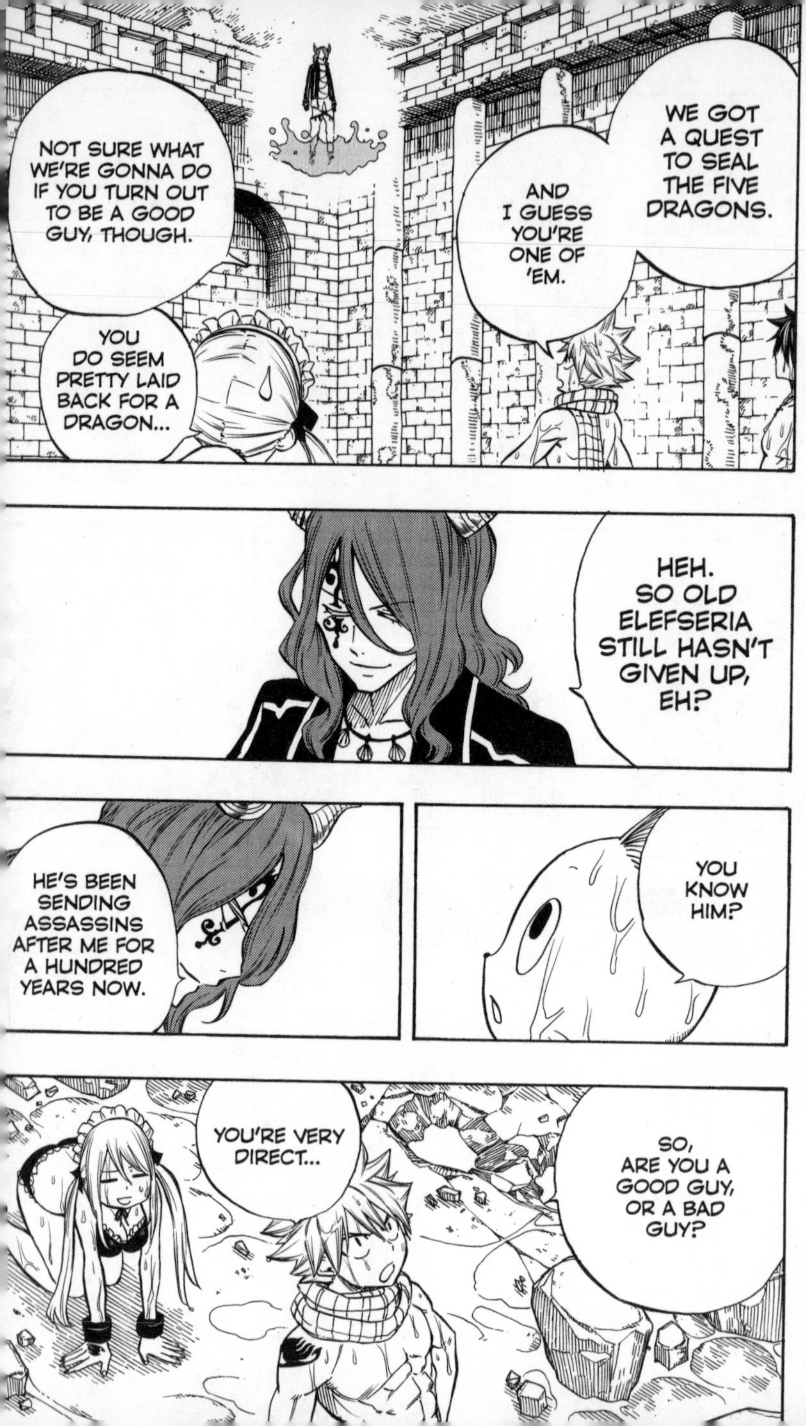
WE GOT A QUEST TO SEAL THE FIVE DRAGONS.
AND I GUESS YOU'RE ONE OF 'EM.
NOT SURE WHAT WE'RE GONNA DO IF YOU TURN OUT TO BE A GOOD GUY, THOUGH.
YOU DO SEEM PRETTY LAID BACK FOR A DRAGON...
HEH. SO OLD ELEFSERIA STILL HASN'T GIVEN UP, EH?
YOU KNOW HIM?
HE'S BEEN SENDING ASSASSINS AFTER ME FOR A HUNDRED YEARS NOW.
SO, ARE YOU A GOOD GUY, OR A BAD GUY?
YOU'RE VERY DIRECT...

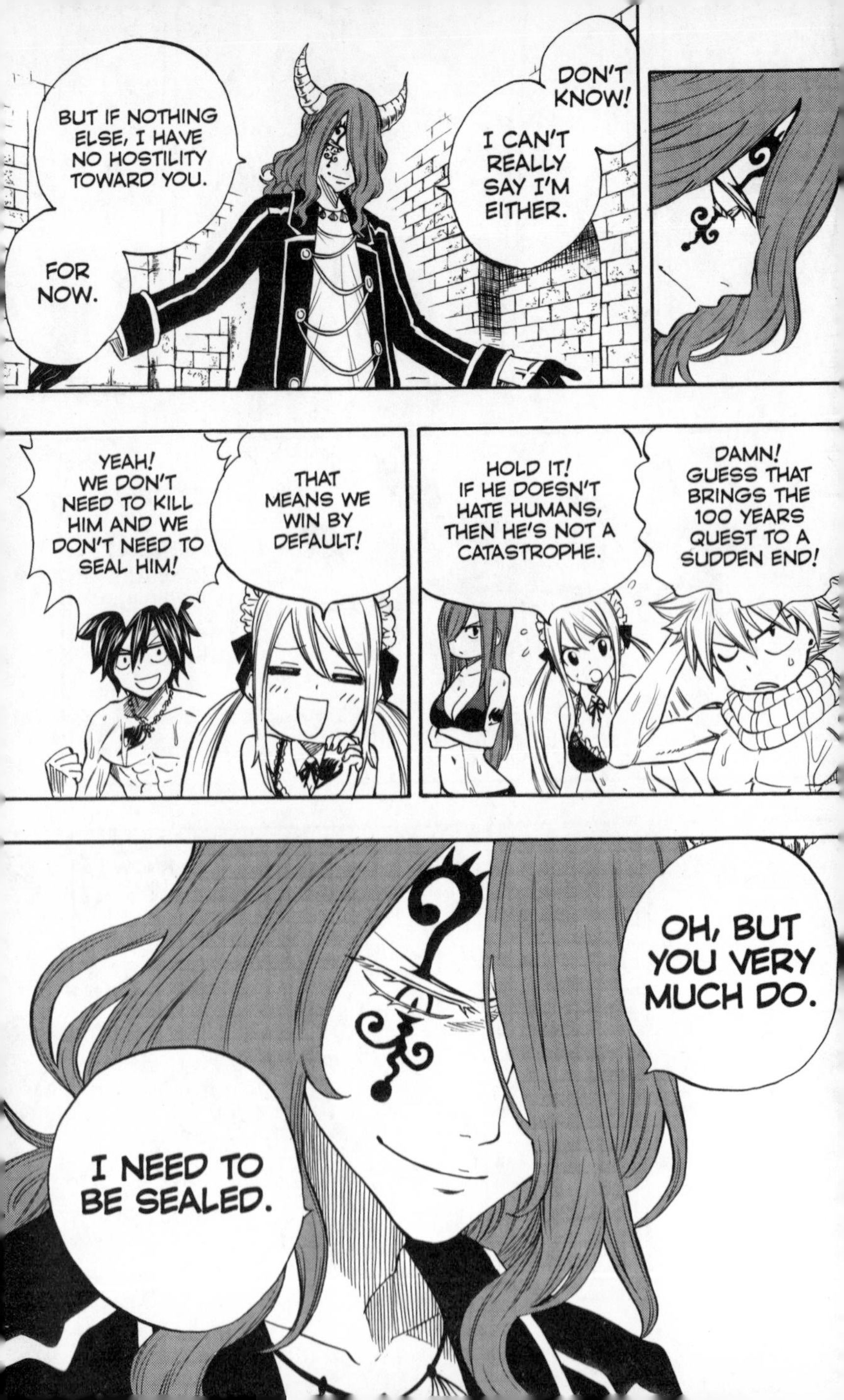
DON'T KNOW!
I CAN'T REALLY SAY I'M EITHER.
BUT IF NOTHING ELSE, I HAVE NO HOSTILITY TOWARD YOU.
FOR NOW.
DAMN! GUESS THAT BRINGS THE 100 YEARS QUEST TO A SUDDEN END!
HOLD IT! IF HE DOESN'T HATE HUMANS, THEN HE'S NOT A CATASTROPHE.
THAT MEANS WE WIN BY DEFAULT!
YEAH! WE DON'T NEED TO KILL HIM AND WE DON'T NEED TO SEAL HIM!
OH, BUT YOU VERY MUCH DO.
I NEED TO BE SEALED.

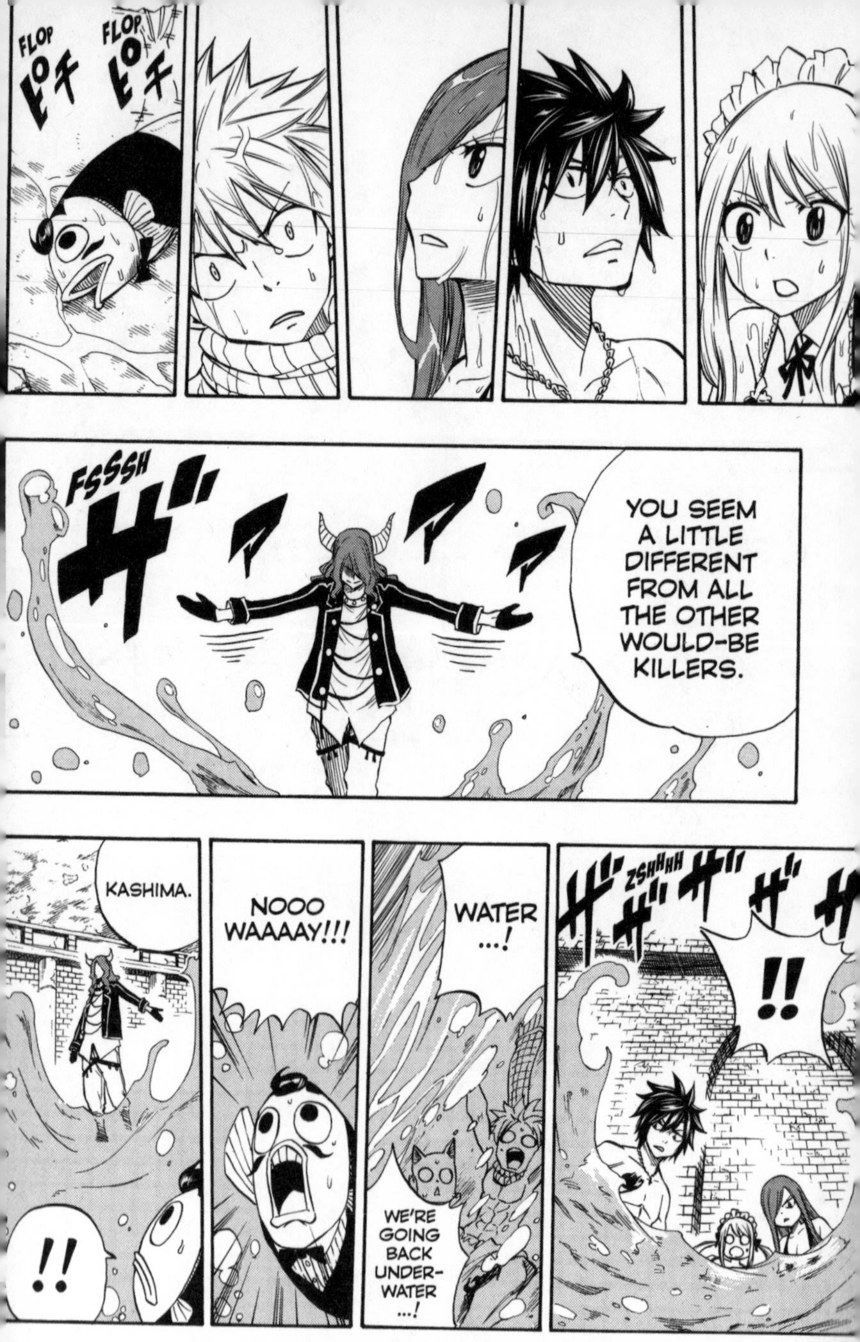
FLOP
FLOP
YOU SEEM A LITTLE DIFFERENT FROM ALL THE OTHER WOULD-BE KILLERS.
FSSSH
ZSHHHH
!!
WATER ...!
WE'RE GOING BACK UNDER-WATER ...!
NOOO WAAAAY!!!
KASHIMA.
!!

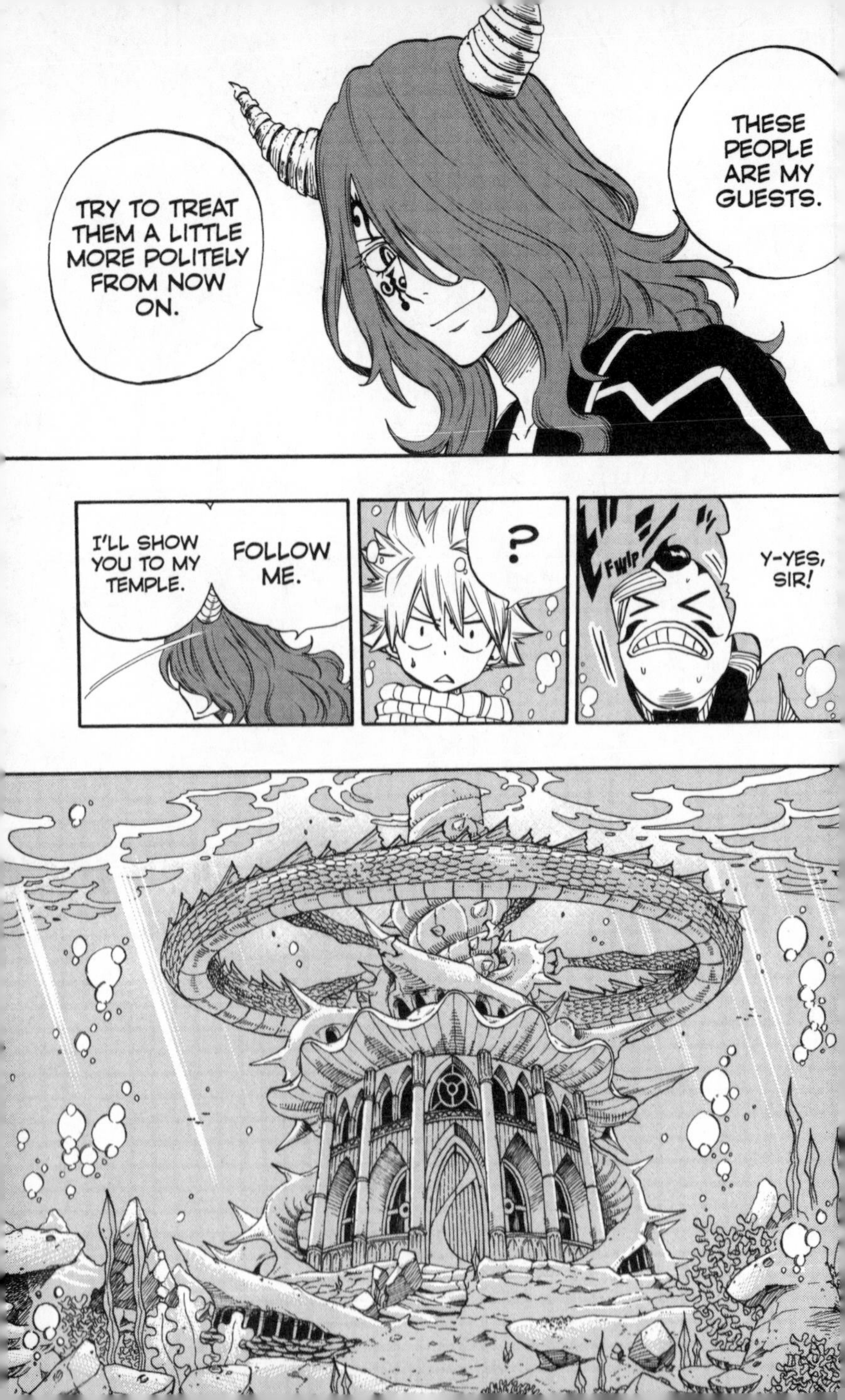
THESE PEOPLE ARE MY GUESTS.
TRY TO TREAT THEM A LITTLE MORE POLITELY FROM NOW ON.
Y-YES, SIR!
FWIP
?
FOLLOW ME.
I'LL SHOW YOU TO MY TEMPLE.

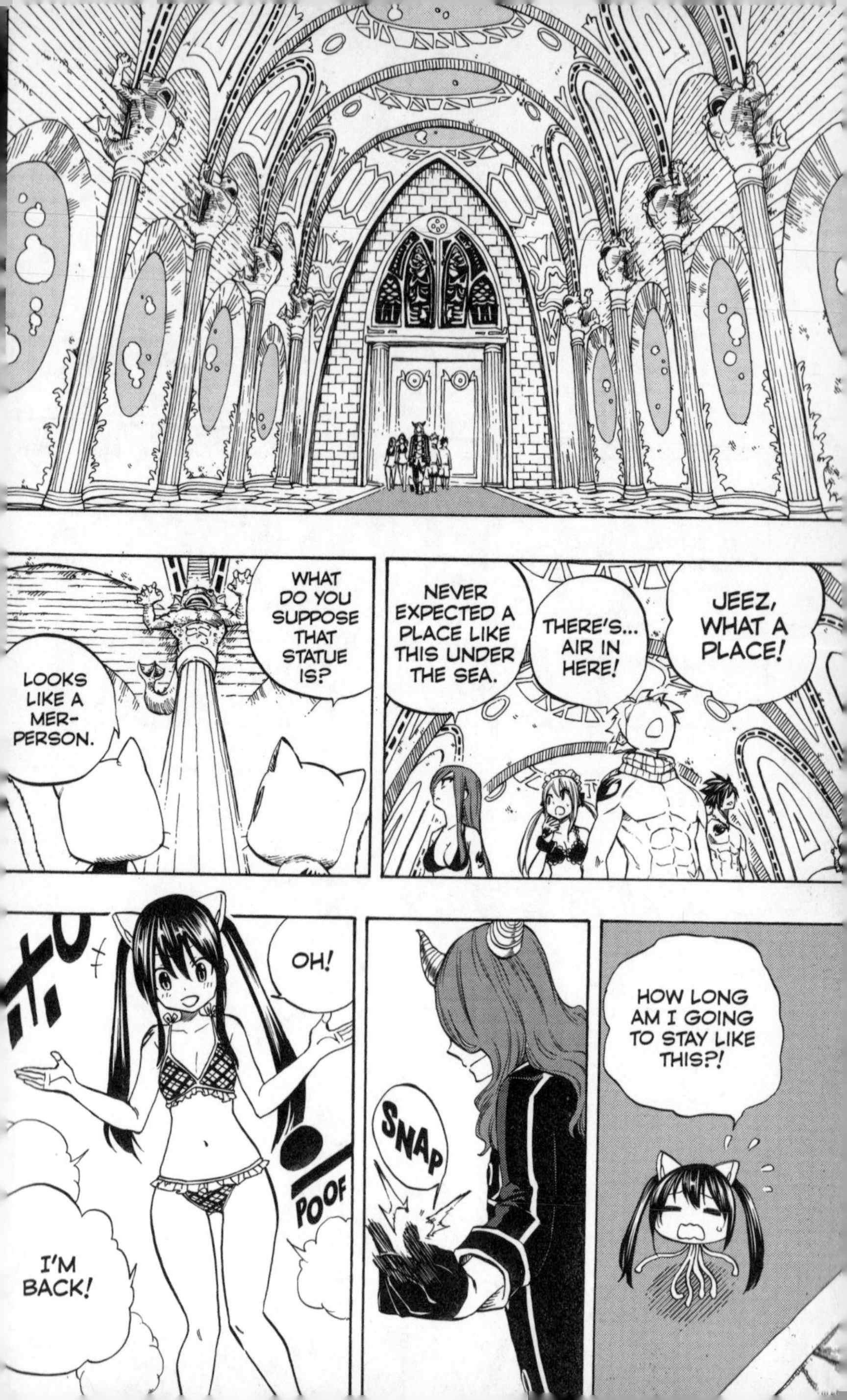
JEEZ, WHAT A PLACE!
THERE'S... AIR IN HERE!
NEVER EXPECTED A PLACE LIKE THIS UNDER THE SEA.
WHAT DO YOU SUPPOSE THAT STATUE IS?
LOOKS LIKE A MER-PERSON.
HOW LONG AM I GOING TO STAY LIKE THIS?!
SNAP
OH!
POOF
I'M BACK!

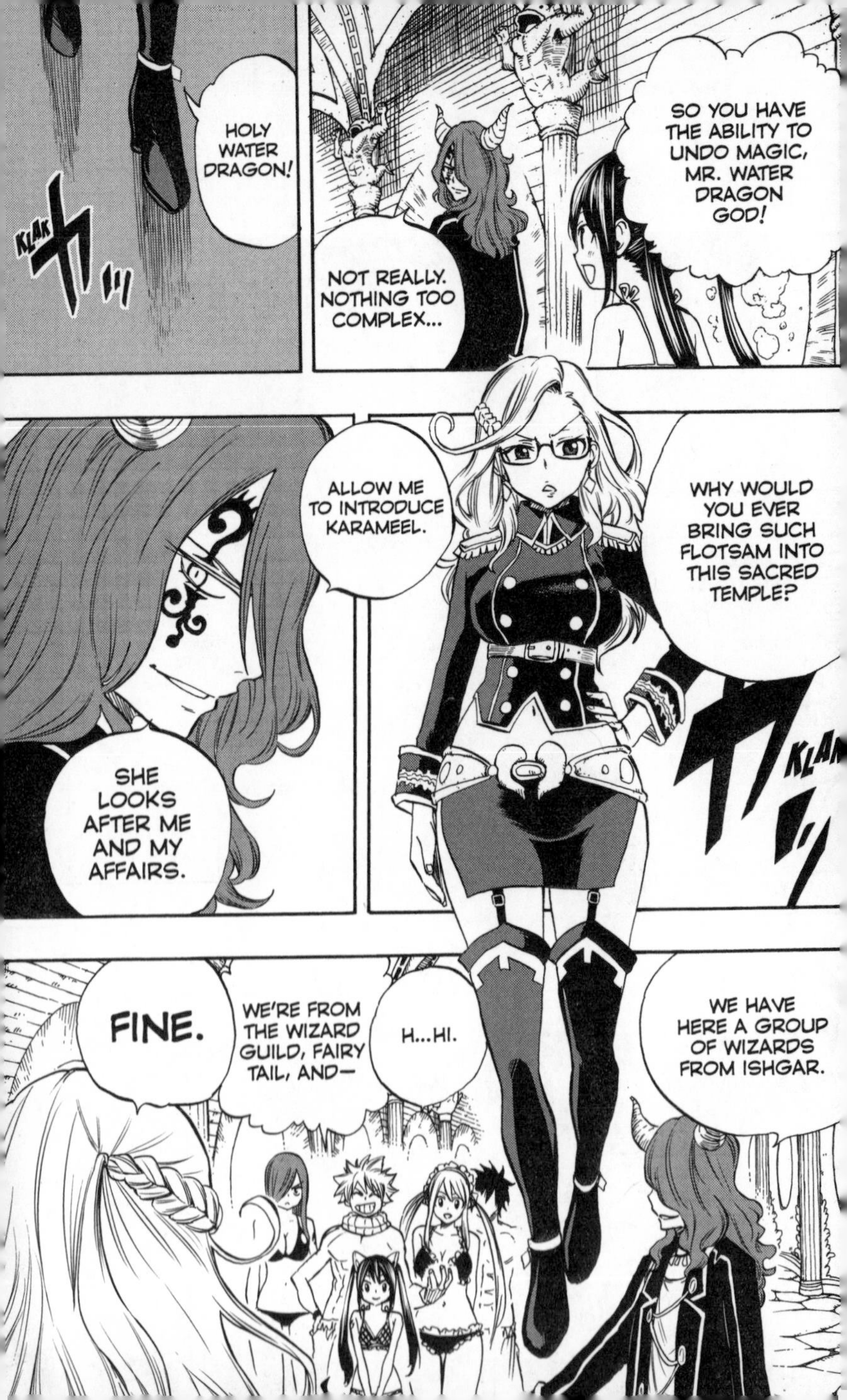
SO YOU HAVE THE ABILITY TO UNDO MAGIC, MR. WATER DRAGON GOD!
NOT REALLY. NOTHING TOO COMPLEX...
HOLY WATER DRAGON!
KLAK
WHY WOULD YOU EVER BRING SUCH FLOTSAM INTO THIS SACRED TEMPLE?
KLAN
ALLOW ME TO INTRODUCE KARAMEEL.
SHE LOOKS AFTER ME AND MY AFFAIRS.
WE HAVE HERE A GROUP OF WIZARDS FROM ISHGAR.
H...HI.
WE'RE FROM THE WIZARD GUILD, FAIRY TAIL, AND—
FINE.

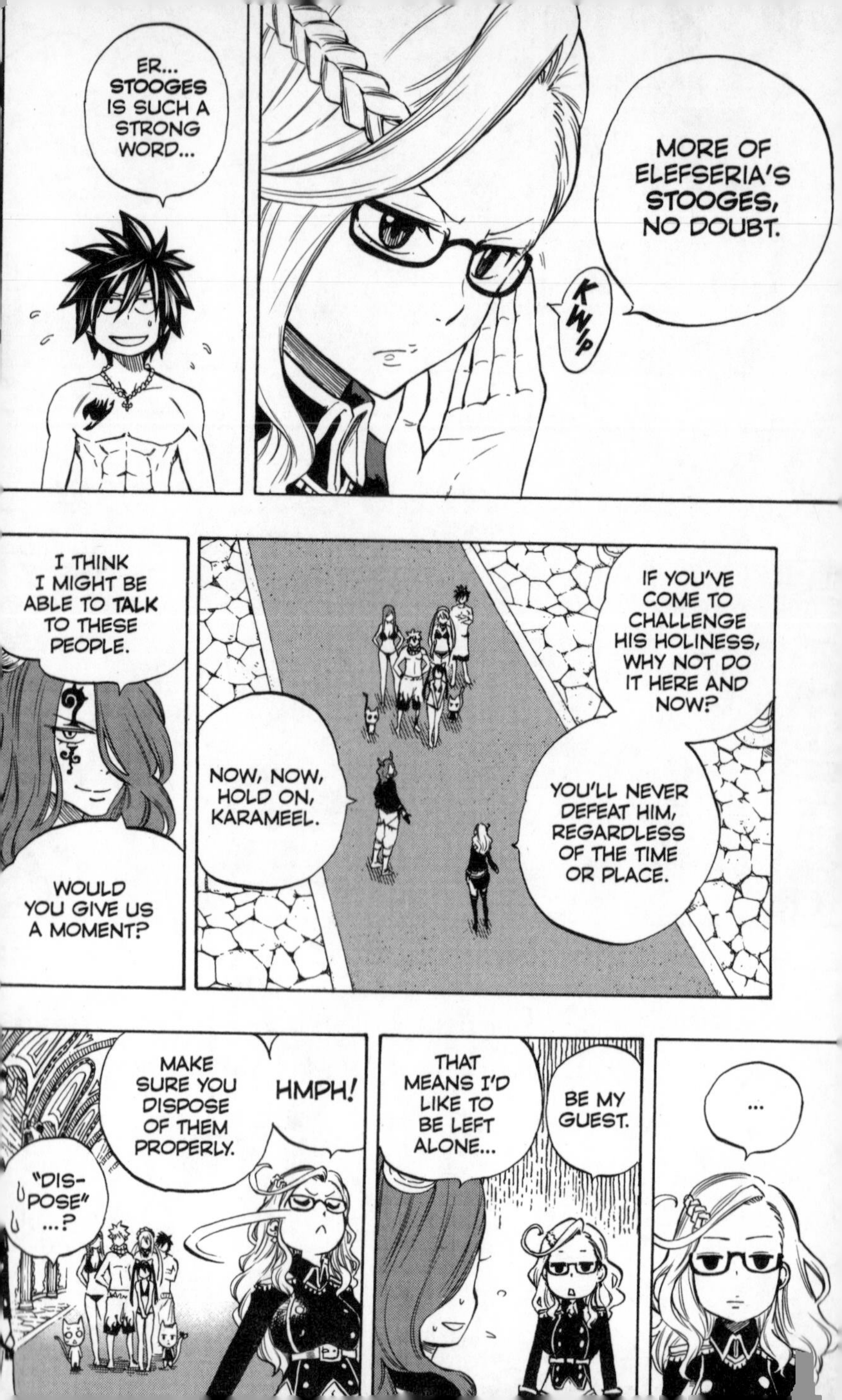
MORE OF ELEFSERIA'S STOOGES, NO DOUBT.
KWIP
ER... STOOGES IS SUCH A STRONG WORD...
IF YOU'VE COME TO CHALLENGE HIS HOLINESS, WHY NOT DO IT HERE AND NOW?
YOU'LL NEVER DEFEAT HIM, REGARDLESS OF THE TIME OR PLACE.
NOW, NOW, HOLD ON, KARAMEEL.
I THINK I MIGHT BE ABLE TO TALK TO THESE PEOPLE.
WOULD YOU GIVE US A MOMENT?
...
BE MY GUEST.
THAT MEANS I'D LIKE TO BE LEFT ALONE...
HMPH!
MAKE SURE YOU DISPOSE OF THEM PROPERLY.
"DIS-POSE" ...?

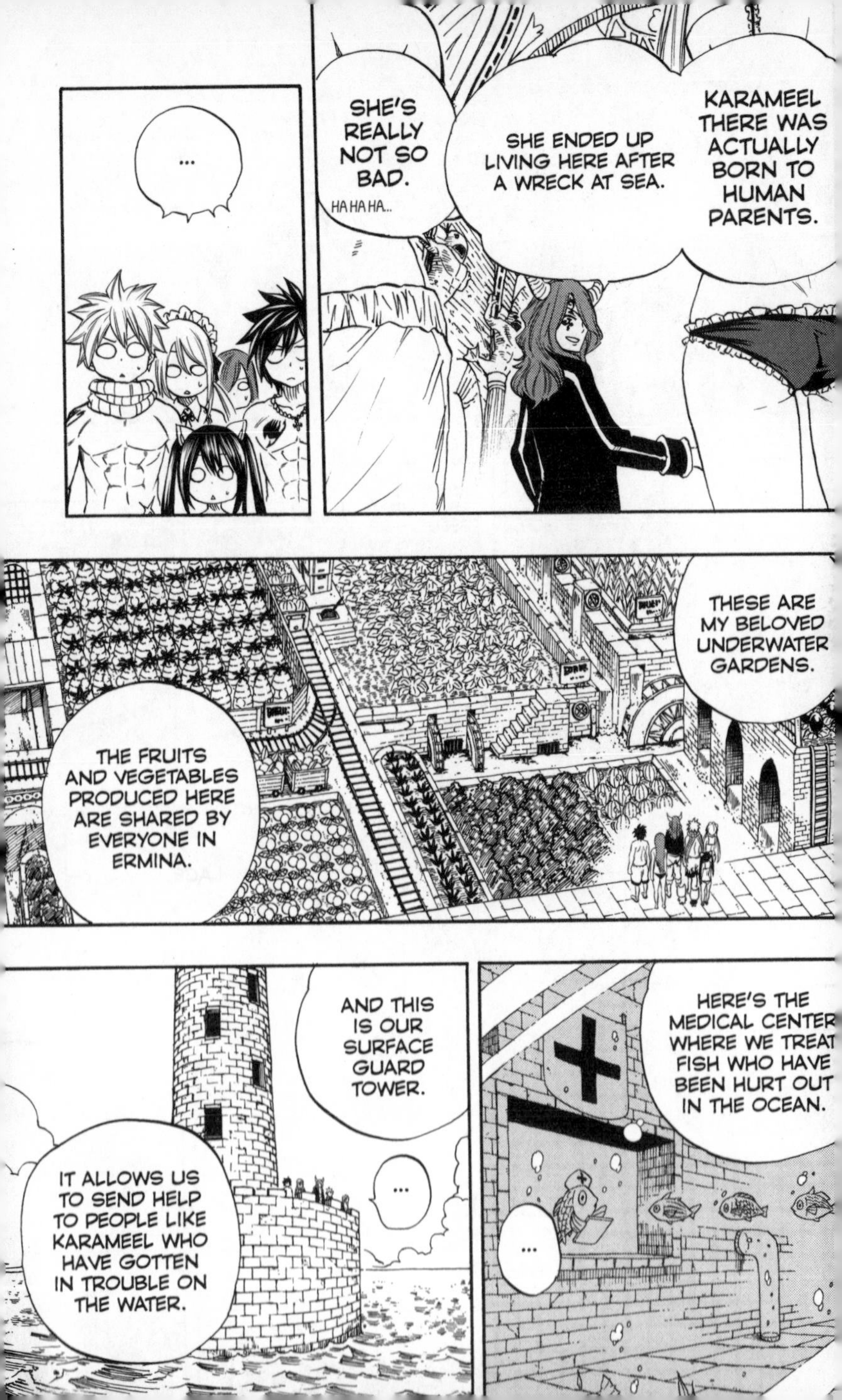
KARAMEEL THERE WAS ACTUALLY BORN TO HUMAN PARENTS.
SHE ENDED UP LIVING HERE AFTER A WRECK AT SEA.
SHE'S REALLY NOT SO BAD.
HA HA HA..
...
THESE ARE MY BELOVED UNDERWATER GARDENS.
THE FRUITS AND VEGETABLES PRODUCED HERE ARE SHARED BY EVERYONE IN ERMINA.
HERE'S THE MEDICAL CENTER WHERE WE TREAT FISH WHO HAVE BEEN HURT OUT IN THE OCEAN.
...
AND THIS IS OUR SURFACE GUARD TOWER.
IT ALLOWS US TO SEND HELP TO PEOPLE LIKE KARAMEEL WHO HAVE GOTTEN IN TROUBLE ON THE WATER.
...

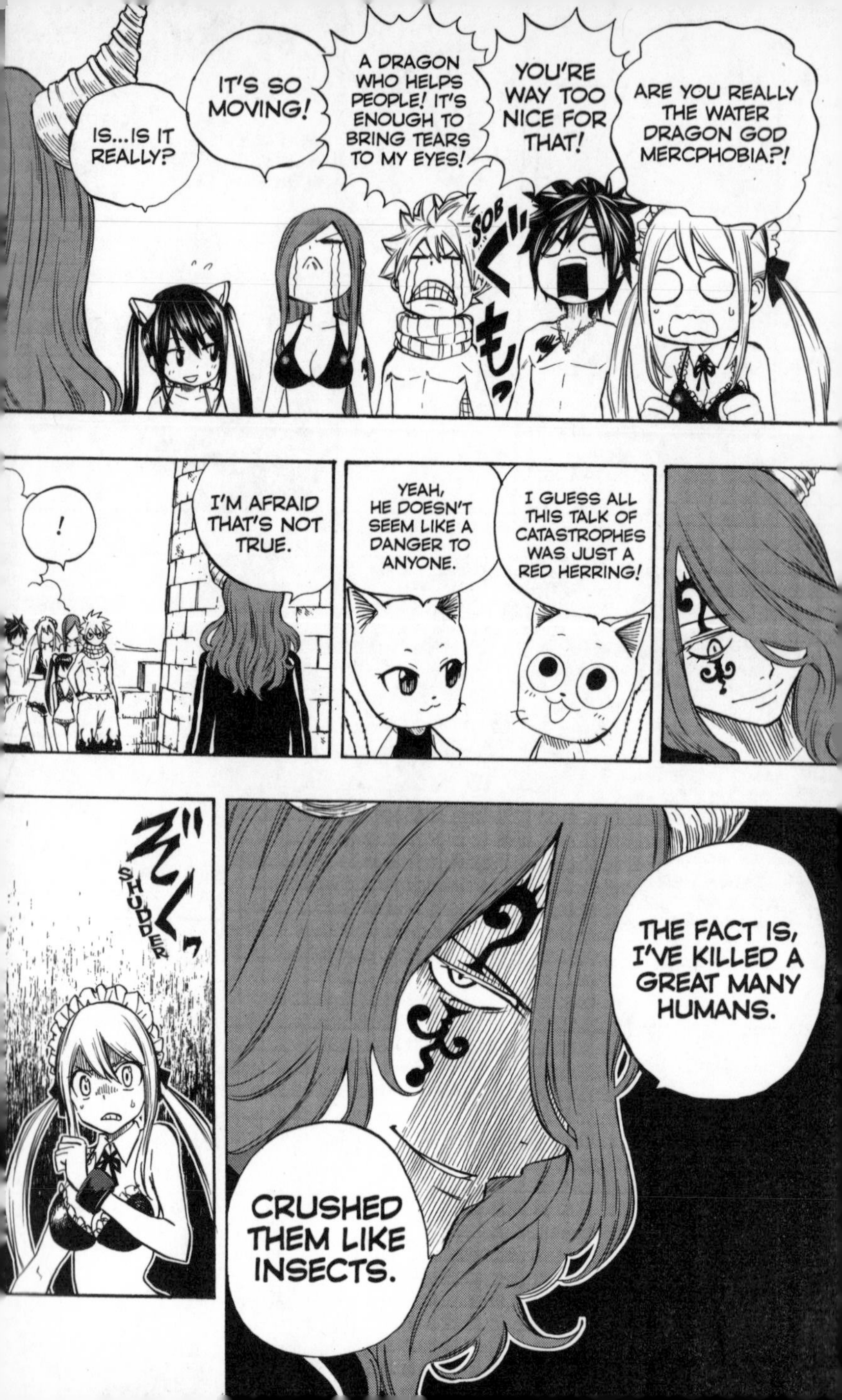
ARE YOU REALLY THE WATER DRAGON GOD MERCPHOBIA?!
YOU'RE WAY TOO NICE FOR THAT!
SOB
A DRAGON WHO HELPS PEOPLE! IT'S ENOUGH TO BRING TEARS TO MY EYES!
IT'S SO MOVING!
IS...IS IT REALLY?
I GUESS ALL THIS TALK OF CATASTROPHES WAS JUST A RED HERRING!
YEAH, HE DOESN'T SEEM LIKE A DANGER TO ANYONE.
I'M AFRAID THAT'S NOT TRUE.
!
THE FACT IS, I'VE KILLED A GREAT MANY HUMANS.
CRUSHED THEM LIKE INSECTS.
SHUDDER

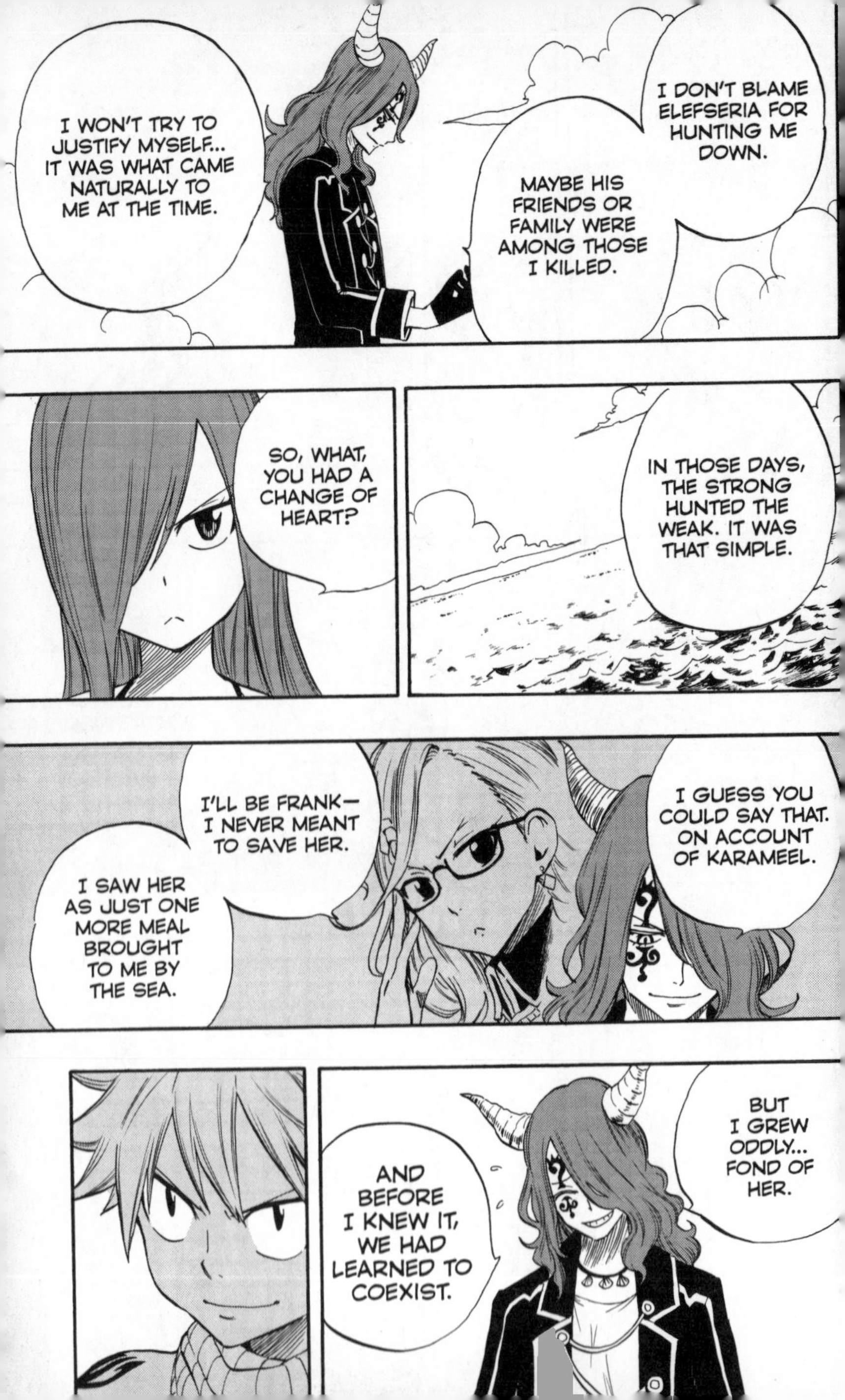
I DON'T BLAME ELEFSERIA FOR HUNTING ME DOWN.
MAYBE HIS FRIENDS OR FAMILY WERE AMONG THOSE I KILLED.
I WON'T TRY TO JUSTIFY MYSELF... IT WAS WHAT CAME NATURALLY TO ME AT THE TIME.
IN THOSE DAYS, THE STRONG HUNTED THE WEAK. IT WAS THAT SIMPLE.
SO, WHAT, YOU HAD A CHANGE OF HEART?
I GUESS YOU COULD SAY THAT. ON ACCOUNT OF KARAMEEL.
I'LL BE FRANK— I NEVER MEANT TO SAVE HER.
I SAW HER AS JUST ONE MORE MEAL BROUGHT TO ME BY THE SEA.
BUT I GREW ODDLY... FOND OF HER.
AND BEFORE I KNEW IT, WE HAD LEARNED TO COEXIST.

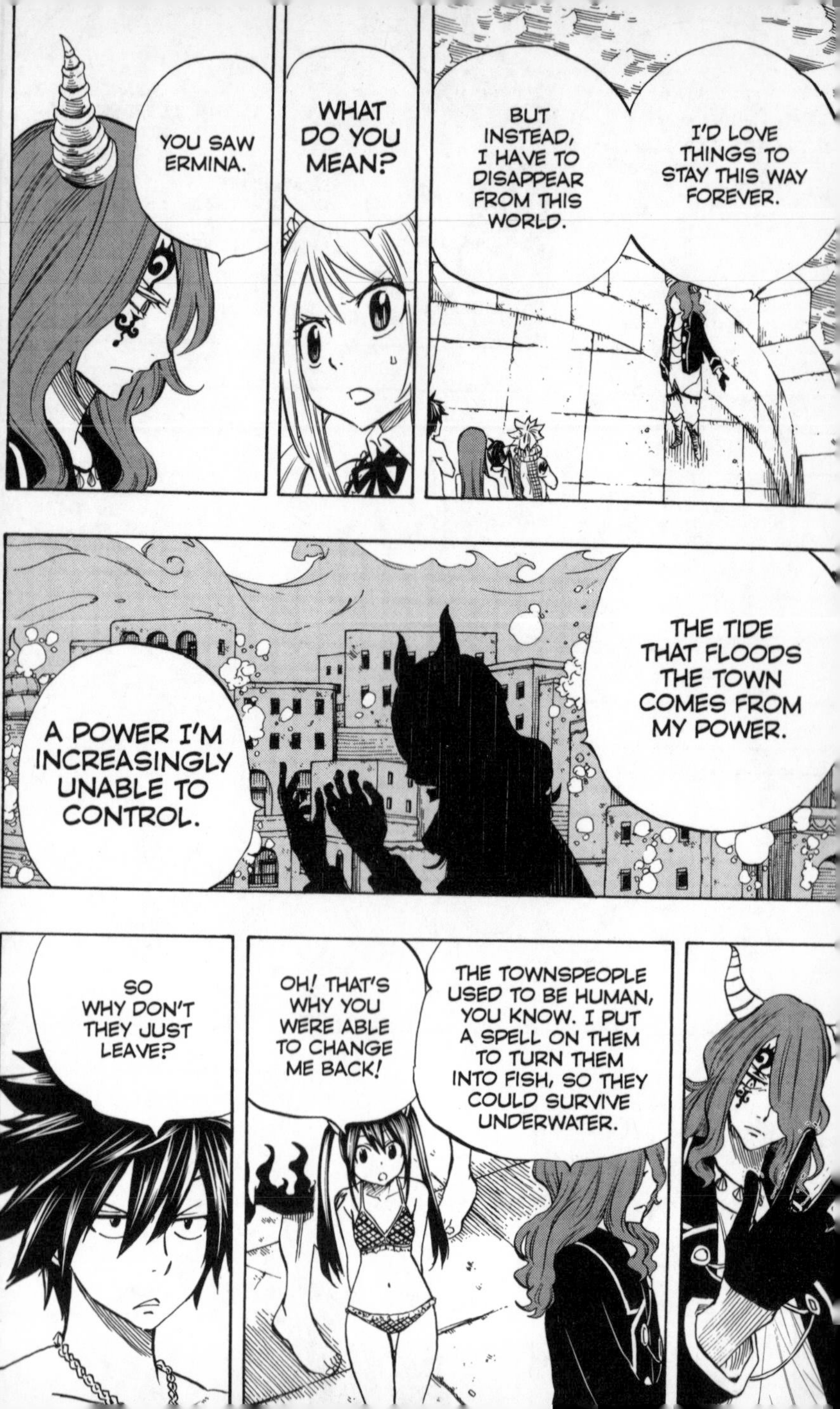
I'D LOVE THINGS TO STAY THIS WAY FOREVER.
BUT INSTEAD, I HAVE TO DISAPPEAR FROM THIS WORLD.
WHAT DO YOU MEAN?
YOU SAW ERMINA.
THE TIDE THAT FLOODS THE TOWN COMES FROM MY POWER.
A POWER I'M INCREASINGLY UNABLE TO CONTROL.
THE TOWNSPEOPLE USED TO BE HUMAN, YOU KNOW. I PUT A SPELL ON THEM TO TURN THEM INTO FISH, SO THEY COULD SURVIVE UNDERWATER.
OH! THAT'S WHY YOU WERE ABLE TO CHANGE ME BACK!
SO WHY DON'T THEY JUST LEAVE?

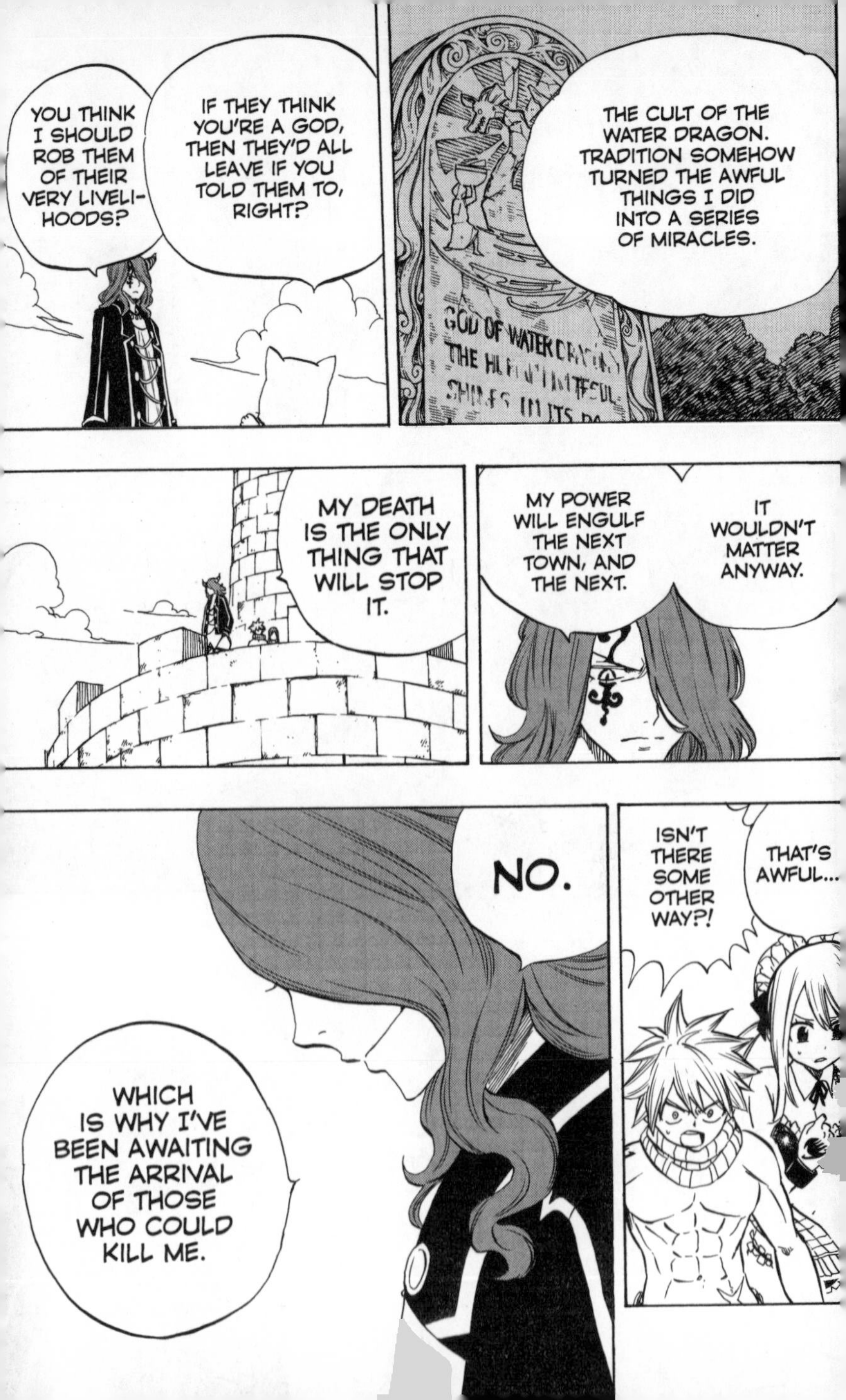
THE CULT OF THE WATER DRAGON. TRADITION SOMEHOW TURNED THE AWFUL THINGS I DID INTO A SERIES OF MIRACLES.
IF THEY THINK YOU'RE A GOD, THEN THEY'D ALL LEAVE IF YOU TOLD THEM TO, RIGHT?
YOU THINK I SHOULD ROB THEM OF THEIR VERY LIVELI-HOODS?
IT WOULDN'T MATTER ANYWAY.
MY POWER WILL ENGULF THE NEXT TOWN, AND THE NEXT.
MY DEATH IS THE ONLY THING THAT WILL STOP IT.
THAT'S AWFUL...
ISN'T THERE SOME OTHER WAY?!
NO.
WHICH IS WHY I'VE BEEN AWAITING THE ARRIVAL OF THOSE WHO COULD KILL ME.

BEFORE THAT, THOUGH... THERE'S ONE THING I HAVE TO DO.

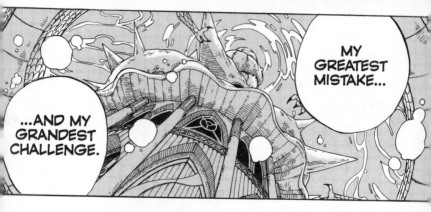

MY GREATEST MISTAKE...

...AND MY GRANDEST CHALLENGE.

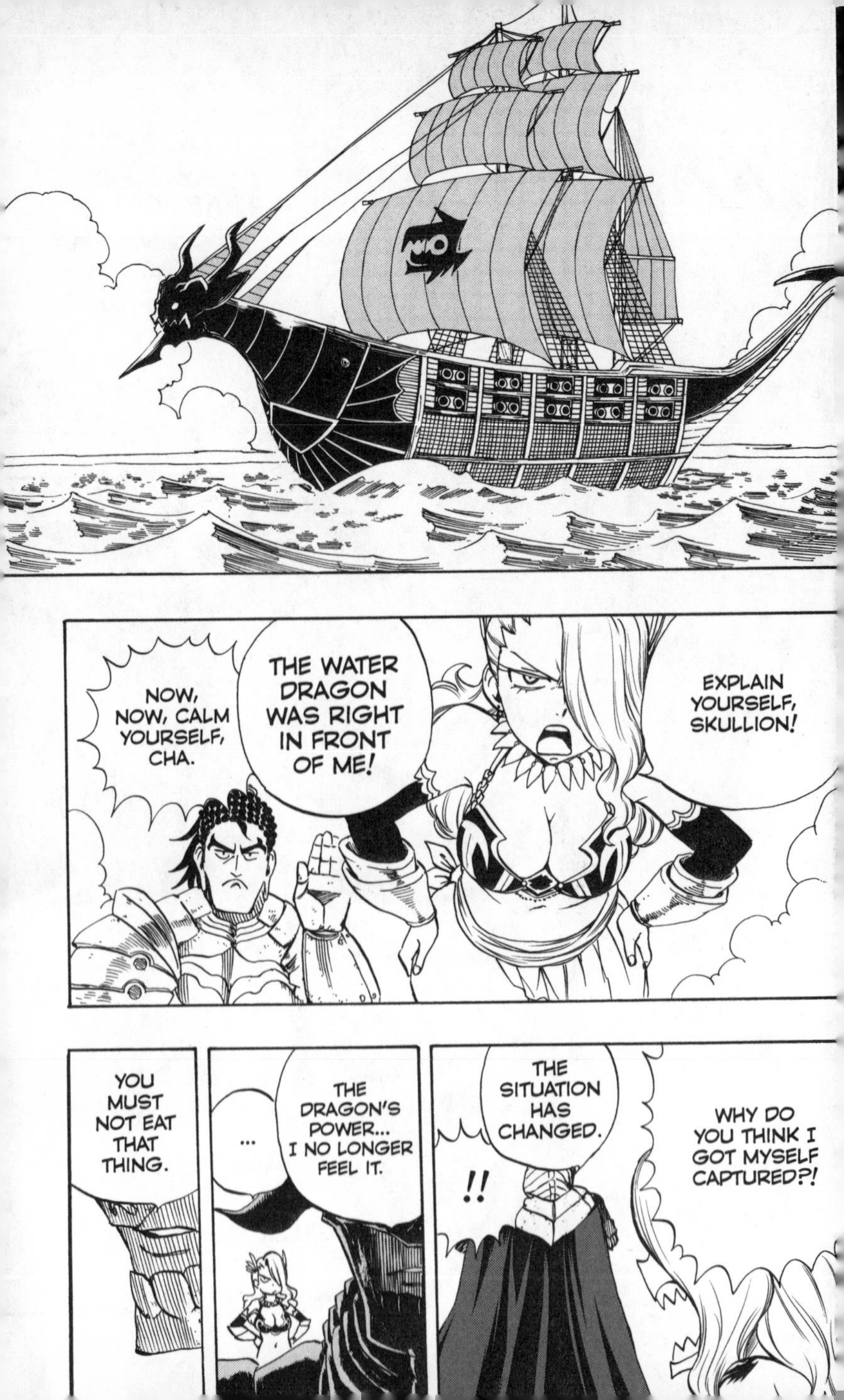
EXPLAIN YOURSELF, SKULLION!
THE WATER DRAGON WAS RIGHT IN FRONT OF ME!
NOW, NOW, CALM YOURSELF, CHA.
WHY DO YOU THINK I GOT MYSELF CAPTURED?!
THE SITUATION HAS CHANGED.
!!
THE DRAGON'S POWER... I NO LONGER FEEL IT.
...
YOU MUST NOT EAT THAT THING.

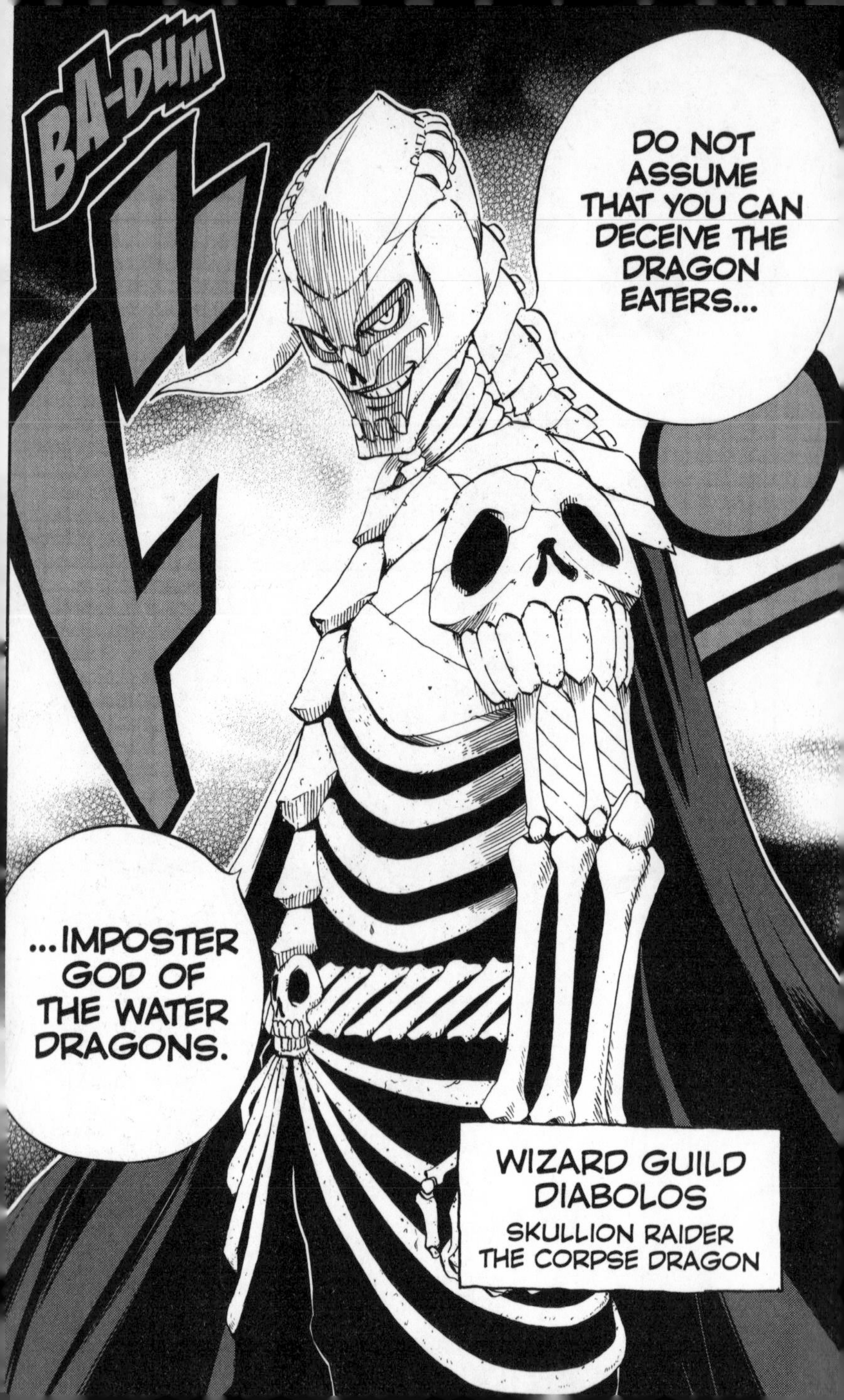
BA-DUM
DO NOT ASSUME THAT YOU CAN DECEIVE THE DRAGON EATERS...
...IMPOSTER GOD OF THE WATER DRAGONS.
WIZARD GUILD DIABOLOS
SKULLION RAIDER THE CORPSE DRAGON

FAIRY TAIL 100 YEARS QUEST

Chapter 9: Black or White?

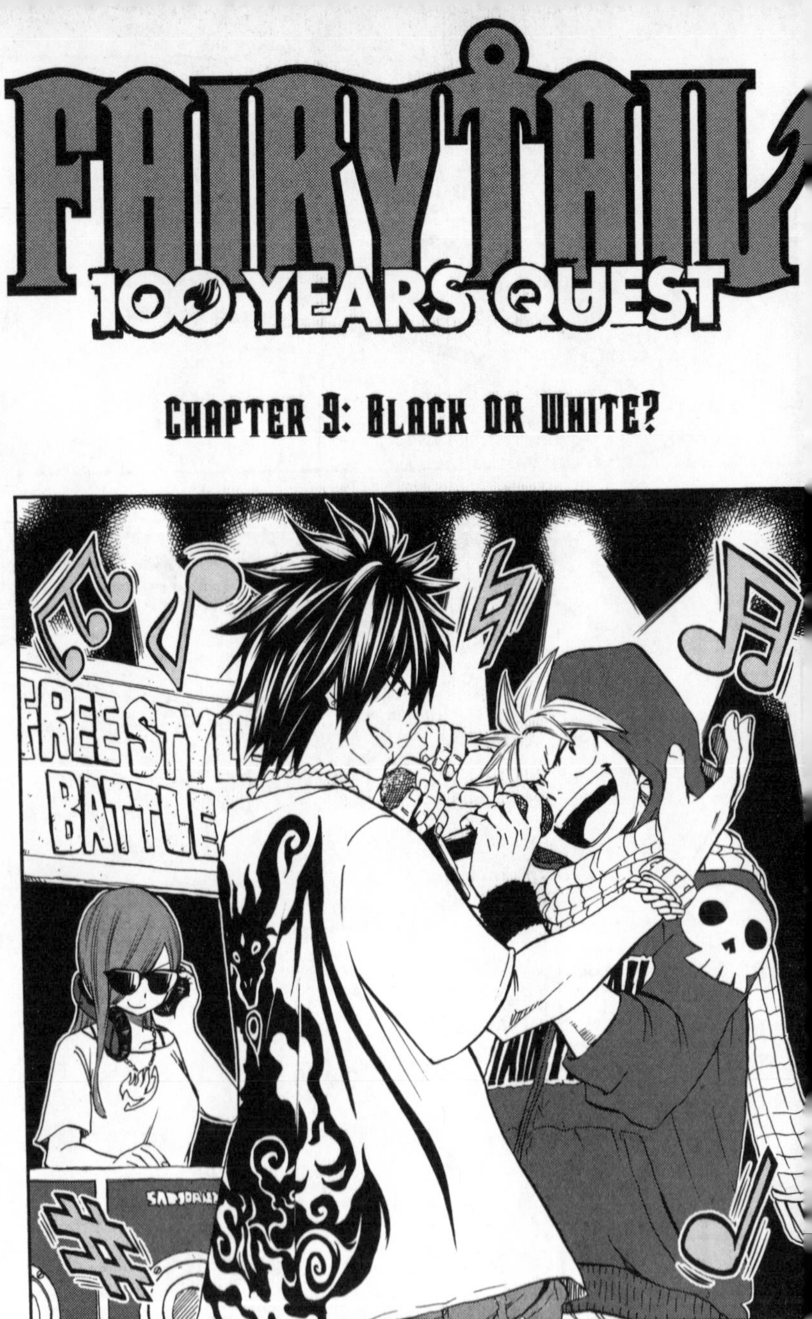
FREESTYLE BATTLE

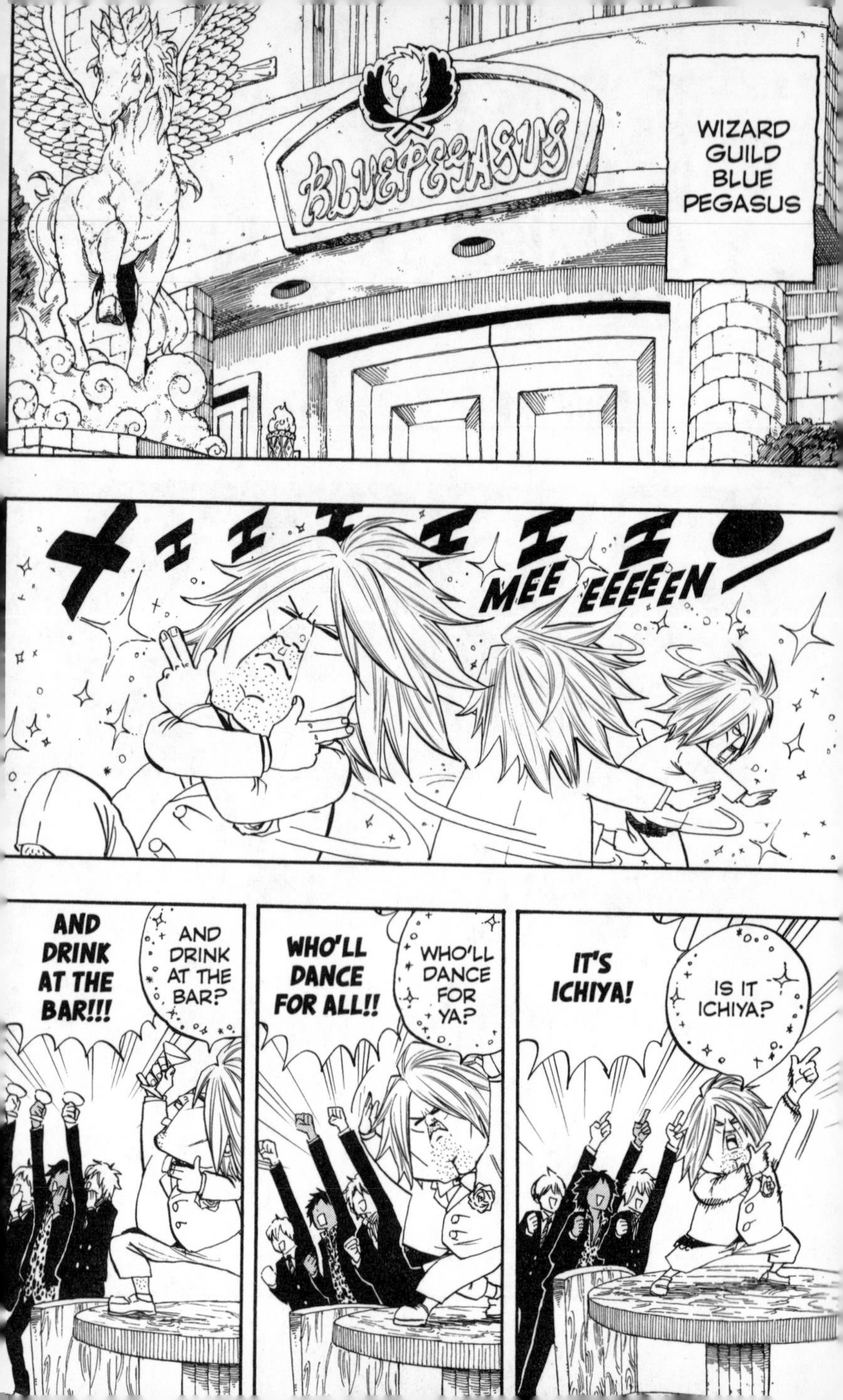
WIZARD GUILD BLUE PEGASUS
BLUE PEGASUS
MEE EEEEEN
IS IT ICHIYA?
IT'S ICHIYA!
WHO'LL DANCE FOR YA?
WHO'LL DANCE FOR ALL!!
AND DRINK AT THE BAR?
AND DRINK AT THE BAR!!!

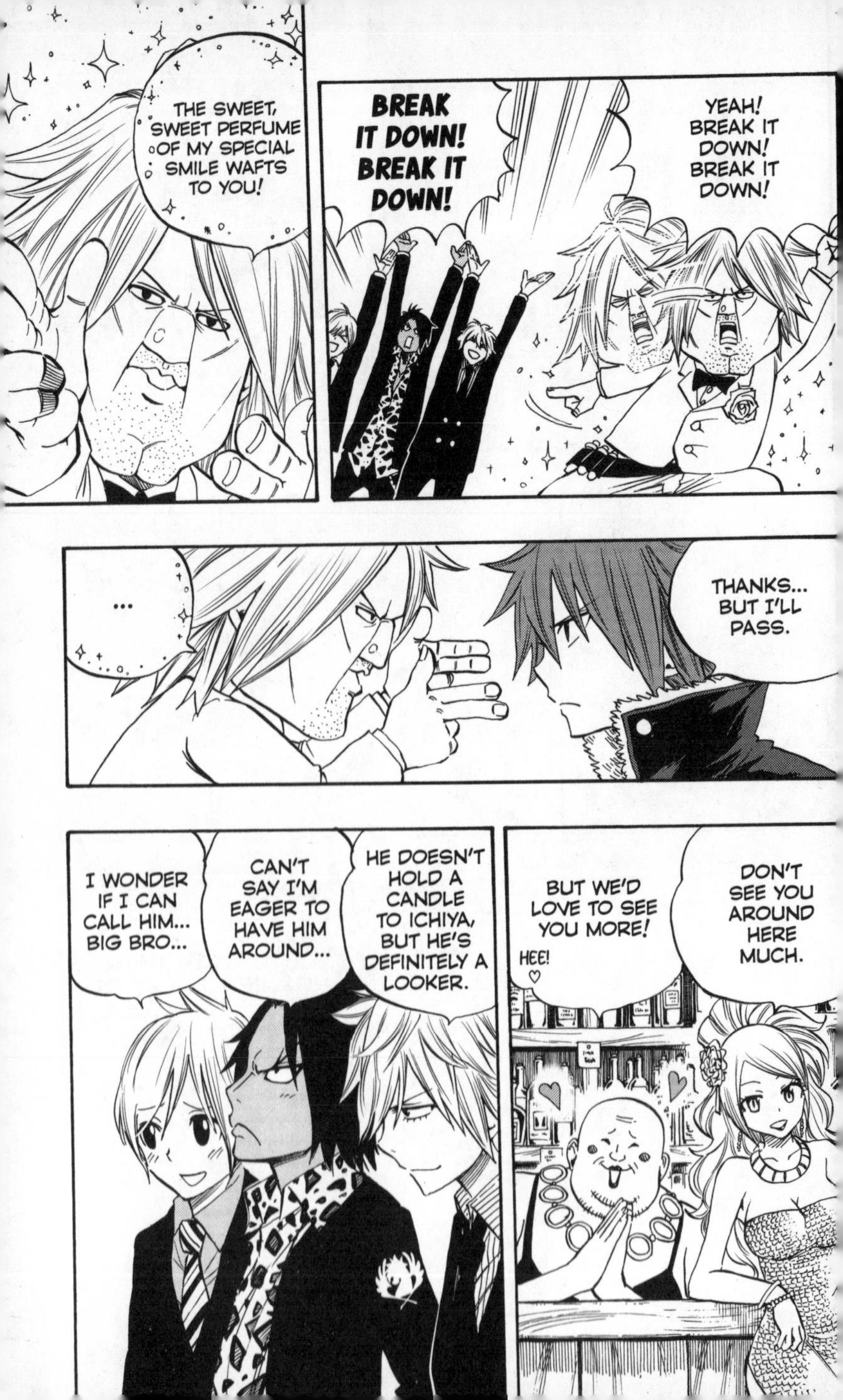
YEAH! BREAK IT DOWN! BREAK IT DOWN!
BREAK IT DOWN! BREAK IT DOWN!
THE SWEET, SWEET PERFUME OF MY SPECIAL SMILE WAFTS TO YOU!
THANKS... BUT I'LL PASS.
...
DON'T SEE YOU AROUND HERE MUCH.
BUT WE'D LOVE TO SEE YOU MORE!
HEE! ♡
HE DOESN'T HOLD A CANDLE TO ICHIYA, BUT HE'S DEFINITELY A LOOKER.
CAN'T SAY I'M EAGER TO HAVE HIM AROUND...
I WONDER IF I CAN CALL HIM... BIG BRO...

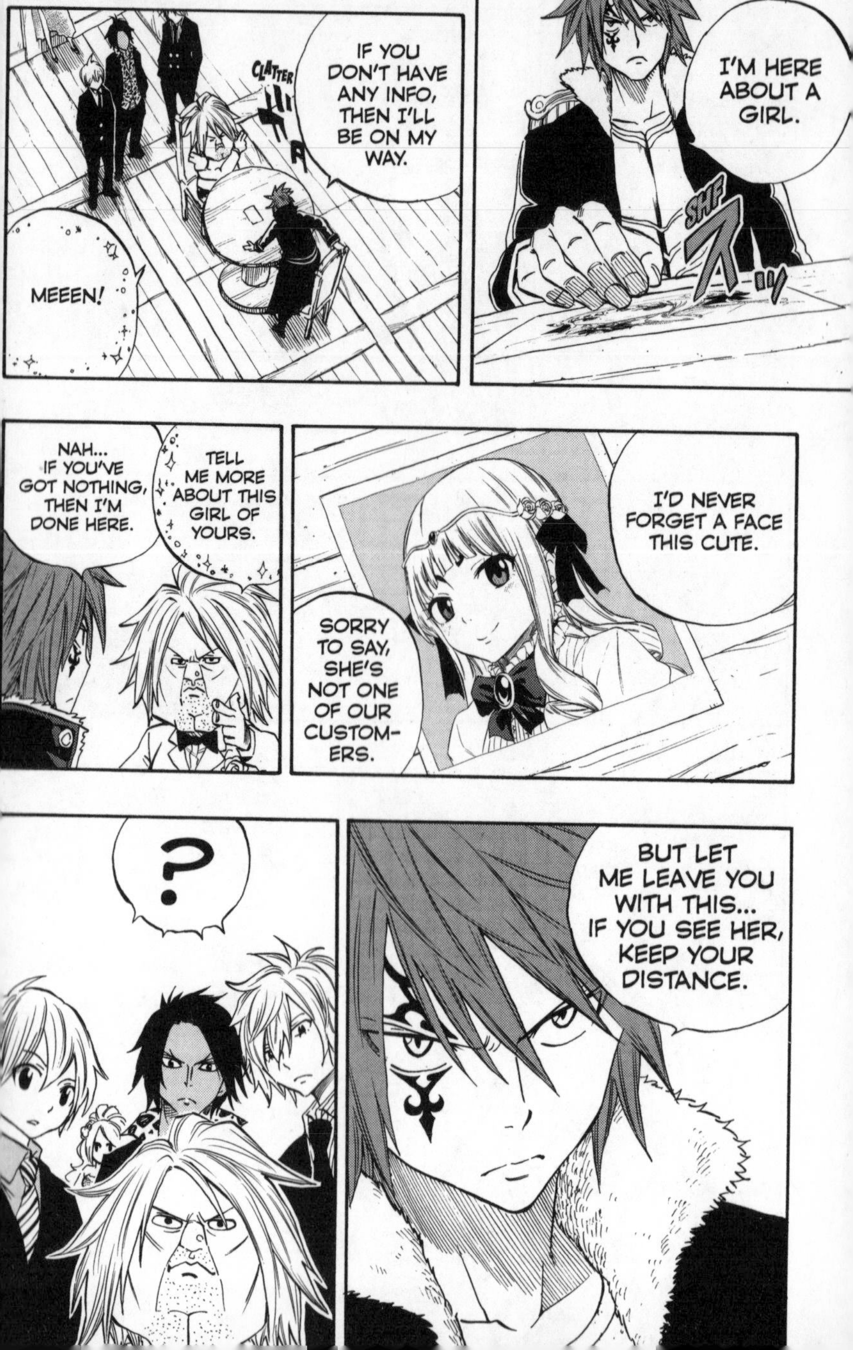
I'M HERE ABOUT A GIRL.
SHF
IF YOU DON'T HAVE ANY INFO, THEN I'LL BE ON MY WAY.
CLATTER
MEEEN!
I'D NEVER FORGET A FACE THIS CUTE.
SORRY TO SAY, SHE'S NOT ONE OF OUR CUSTOM-ERS.
TELL ME MORE ABOUT THIS GIRL OF YOURS.
NAH... IF YOU'VE GOT NOTHING, THEN I'M DONE HERE.
BUT LET ME LEAVE YOU WITH THIS... IF YOU SEE HER, KEEP YOUR DISTANCE.
?

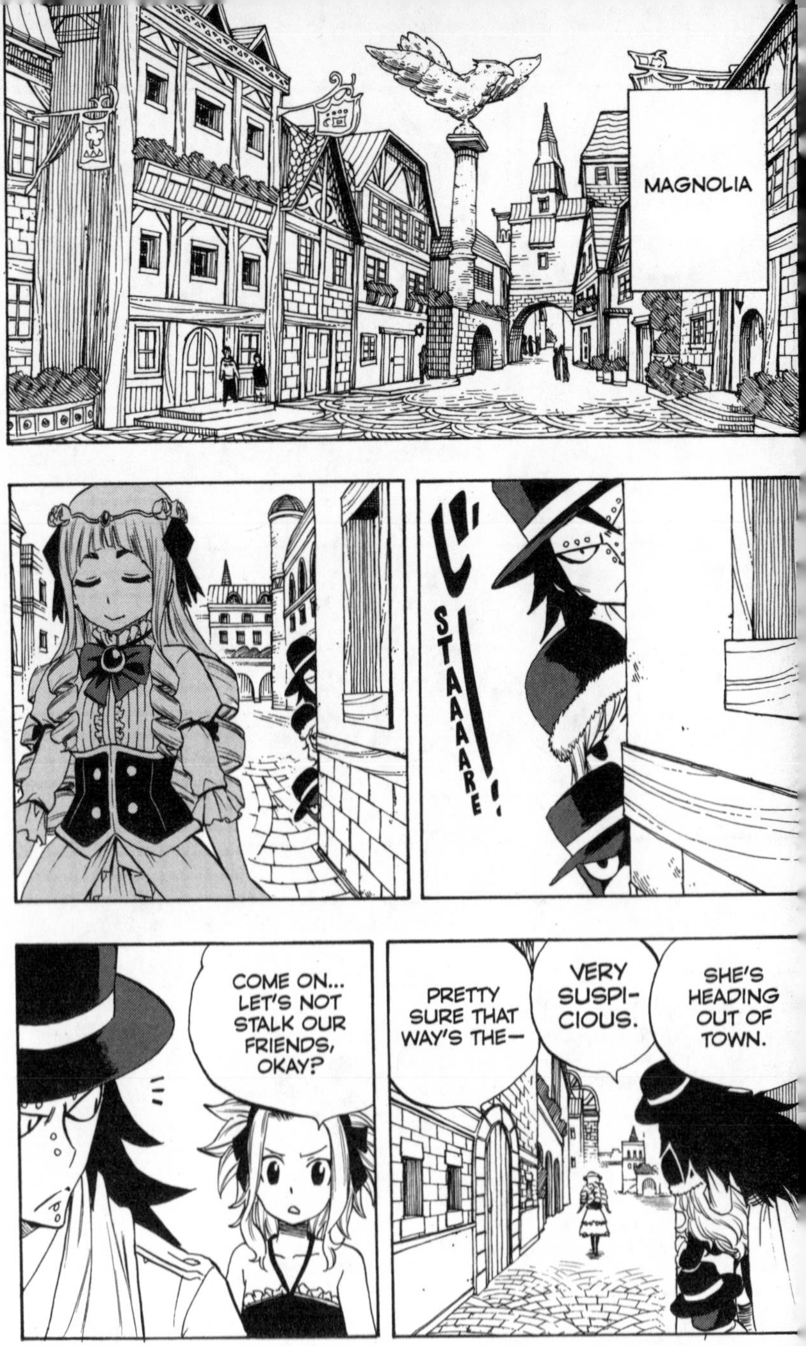
MAGNOLIA
じ STAAAARE
SHE'S HEADING OUT OF TOWN.
VERY SUSPI-CIOUS.
PRETTY SURE THAT WAY'S THE—
COME ON... LET'S NOT STALK OUR FRIENDS, OKAY?

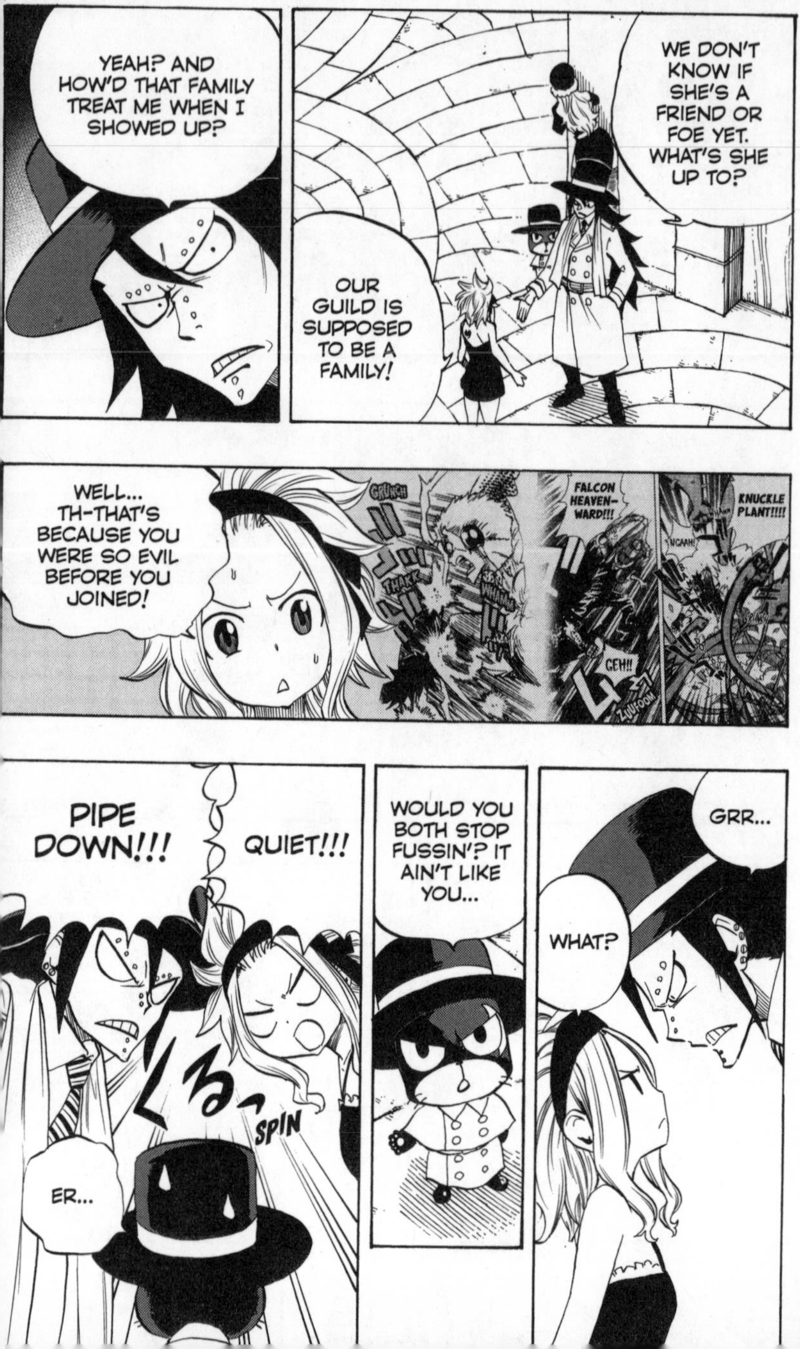
WE DON'T KNOW IF SHE'S A FRIEND OR FOE YET. WHAT'S SHE UP TO?
OUR GUILD IS SUPPOSED TO BE A FAMILY!
YEAH? AND HOW'D THAT FAMILY TREAT ME WHEN I SHOWED UP?
KNUCKLE PLANT!!!!
FALCON HEAVEN-WARD!!!
GEH!!
CRUNCH
THAKK
WHAMM
WELL... TH-THAT'S BECAUSE YOU WERE SO EVIL BEFORE YOU JOINED!
GRR...
WHAT?
WOULD YOU BOTH STOP FUSSIN'? IT AIN'T LIKE YOU...
QUIET!!!
PIPE DOWN!!!
SPIN
ER...

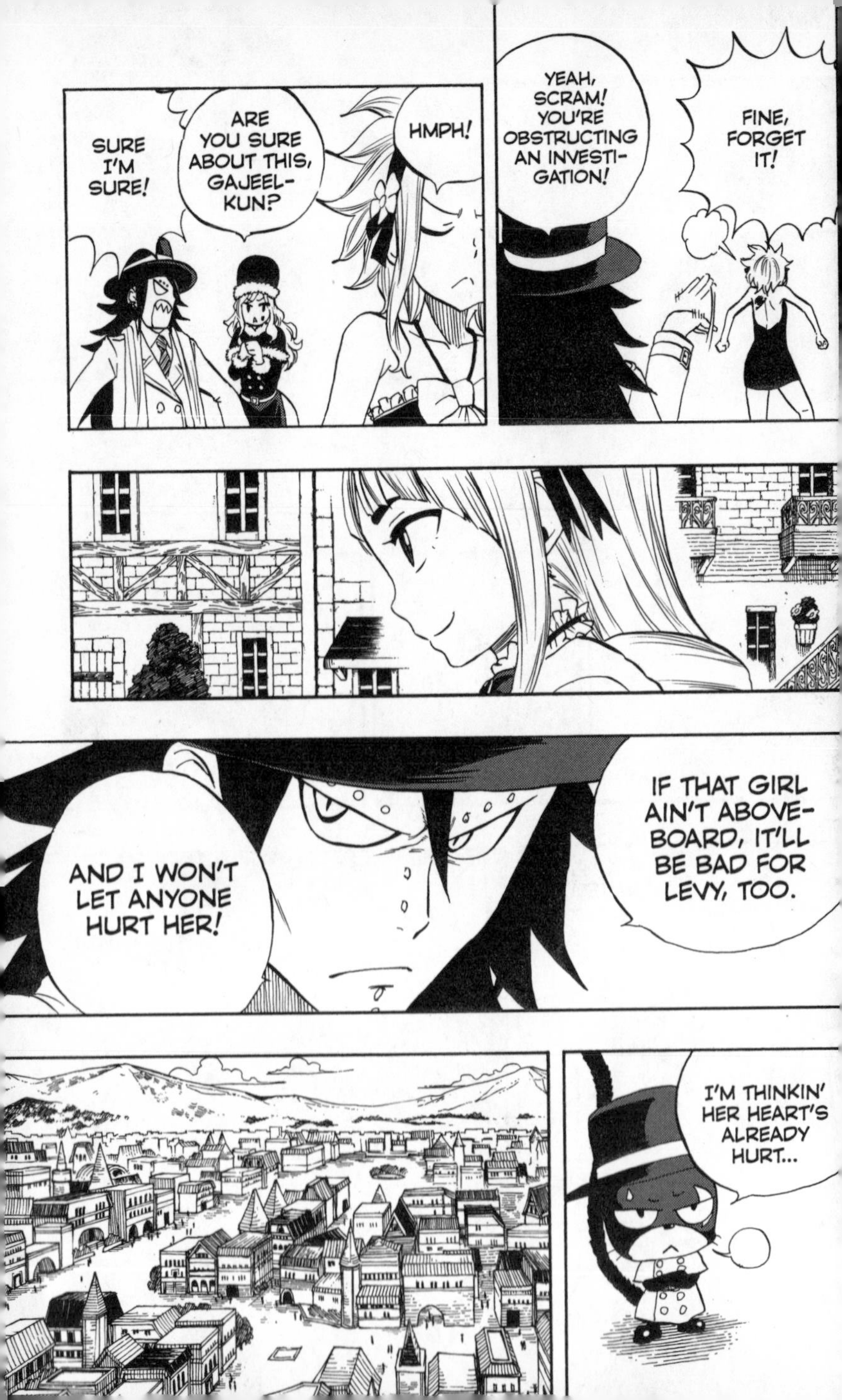
FINE, FORGET IT!
YEAH, SCRAM! YOU'RE OBSTRUCTING AN INVESTI-GATION!
HMPH!
ARE YOU SURE ABOUT THIS, GAJEEL-KUN?
SURE I'M SURE!
IF THAT GIRL AIN'T ABOVE-BOARD, IT'LL BE BAD FOR LEVY, TOO.
AND I WON'T LET ANYONE HURT HER!
I'M THINKIN' HER HEART'S ALREADY HURT...

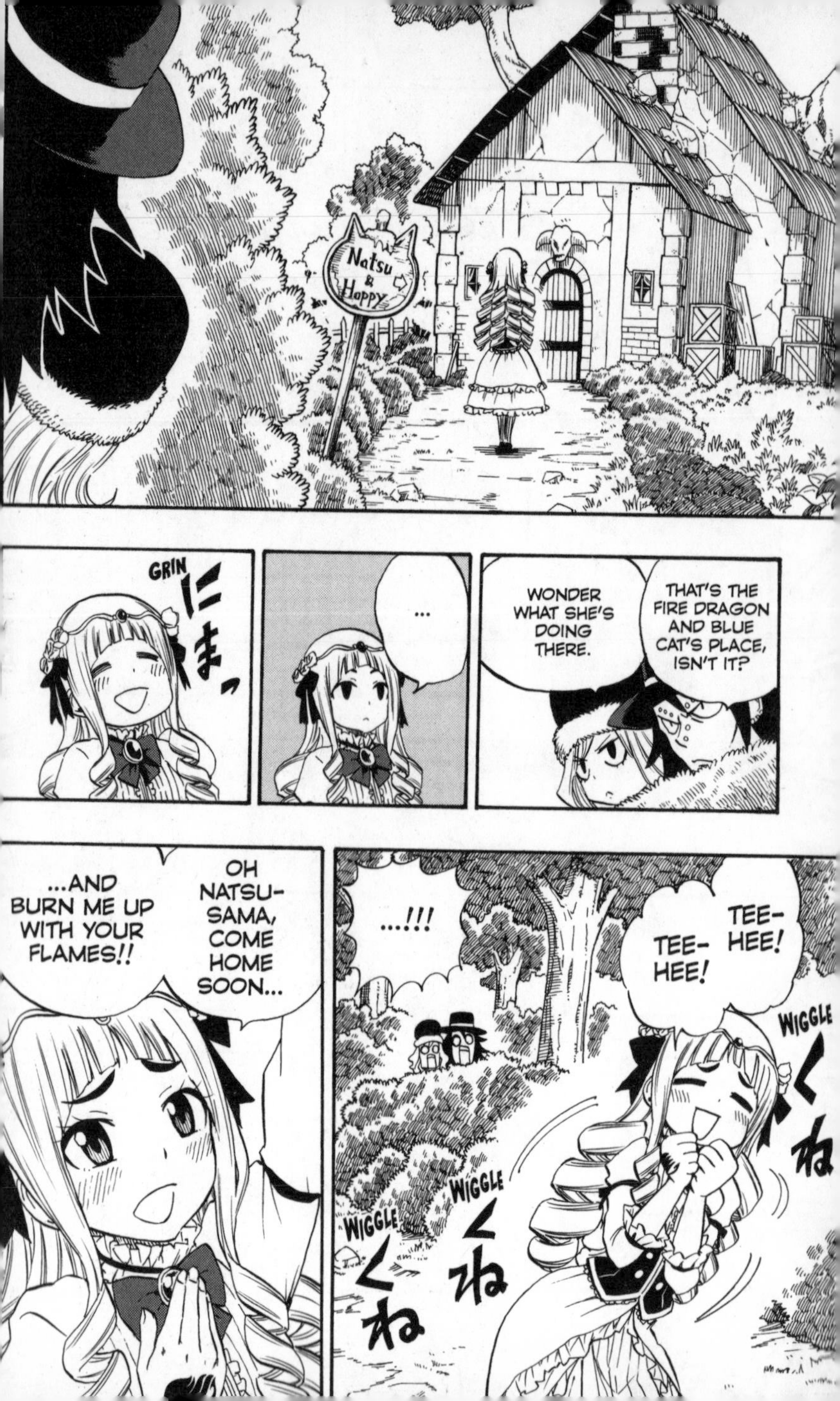
Natsu & Happy
THAT'S THE FIRE DRAGON AND BLUE CAT'S PLACE, ISN'T IT?
WONDER WHAT SHE'S DOING THERE.
...
GRIN
にまっ
TEE-HEE!
TEE-HEE!
...!!!
WIGGLE
くね
WIGGLE
くね
WIGGLE
くね
OH NATSU-SAMA, COME HOME SOON...
...AND BURN ME UP WITH YOUR FLAMES!!

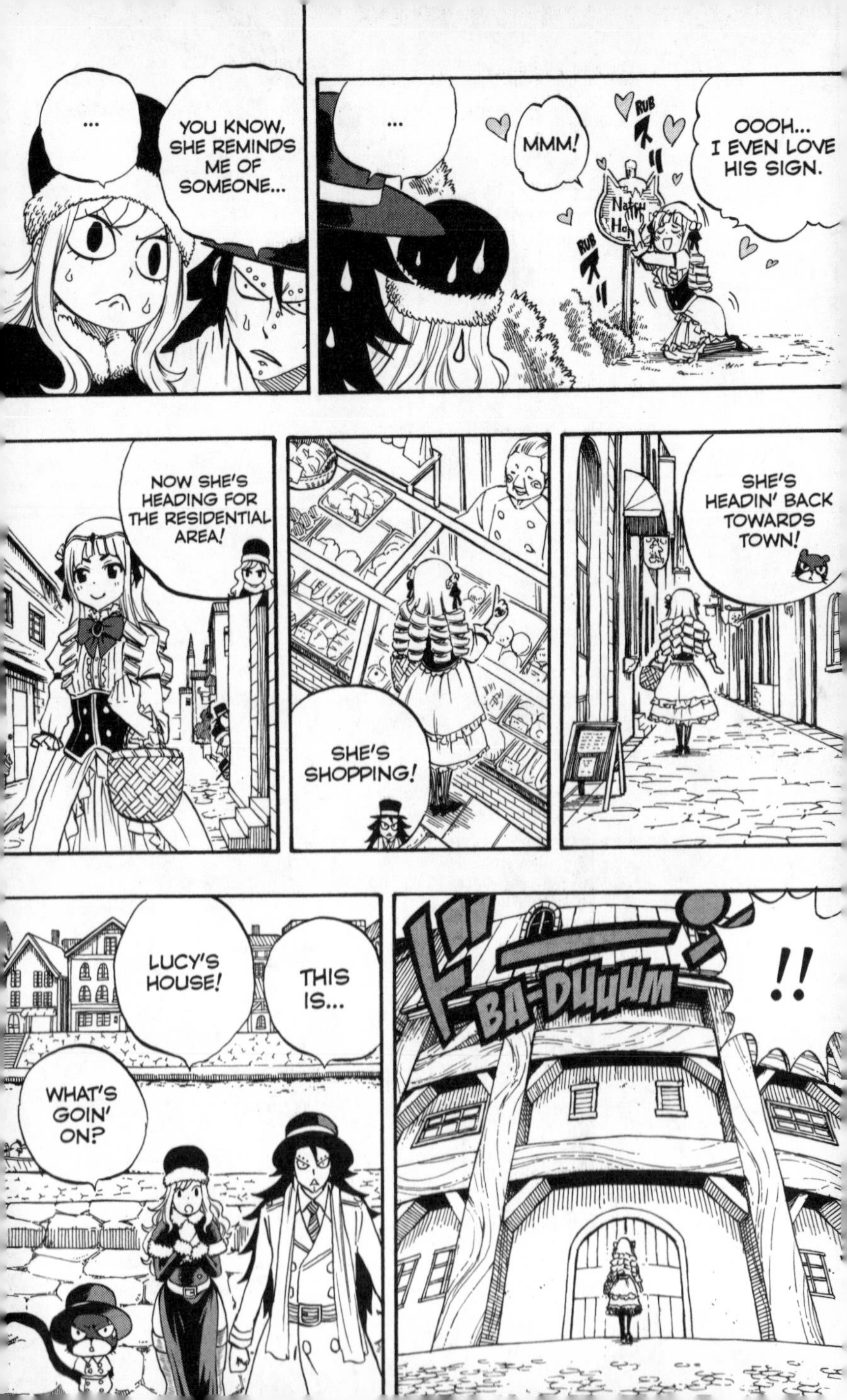
OOOH... I EVEN LOVE HIS SIGN.
RUB
MMM!
RUB
...
YOU KNOW, SHE REMINDS ME OF SOMEONE...
...
SHE'S HEADIN' BACK TOWARDS TOWN!
SHE'S SHOPPING!
NOW SHE'S HEADING FOR THE RESIDENTIAL AREA!
!!
BA-DUUUM
THIS IS...
LUCY'S HOUSE!
WHAT'S GOIN' ON?

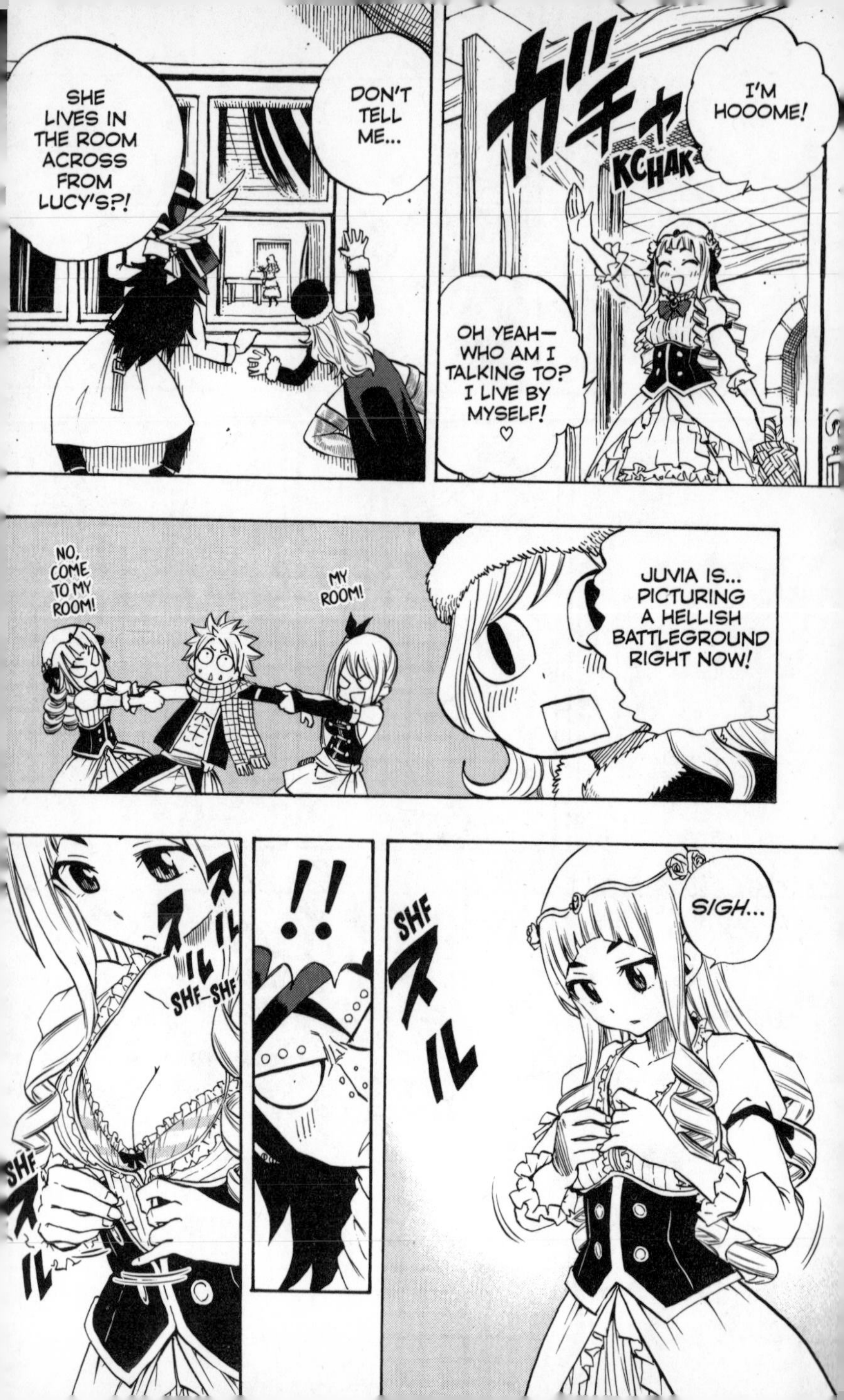
ガチャ
KCHAK
I'M HOOOME!
OH YEAH— WHO AM I TALKING TO? I LIVE BY MYSELF! ♡
DON'T TELL ME...
SHE LIVES IN THE ROOM ACROSS FROM LUCY'S?!
JUVIA IS... PICTURING A HELLISH BATTLEGROUND RIGHT NOW!
MY ROOM!
NO, COME TO MY ROOM!
SIGH...
SHF
スル
!!
スルスル
SHF-SHF
SHF
スル

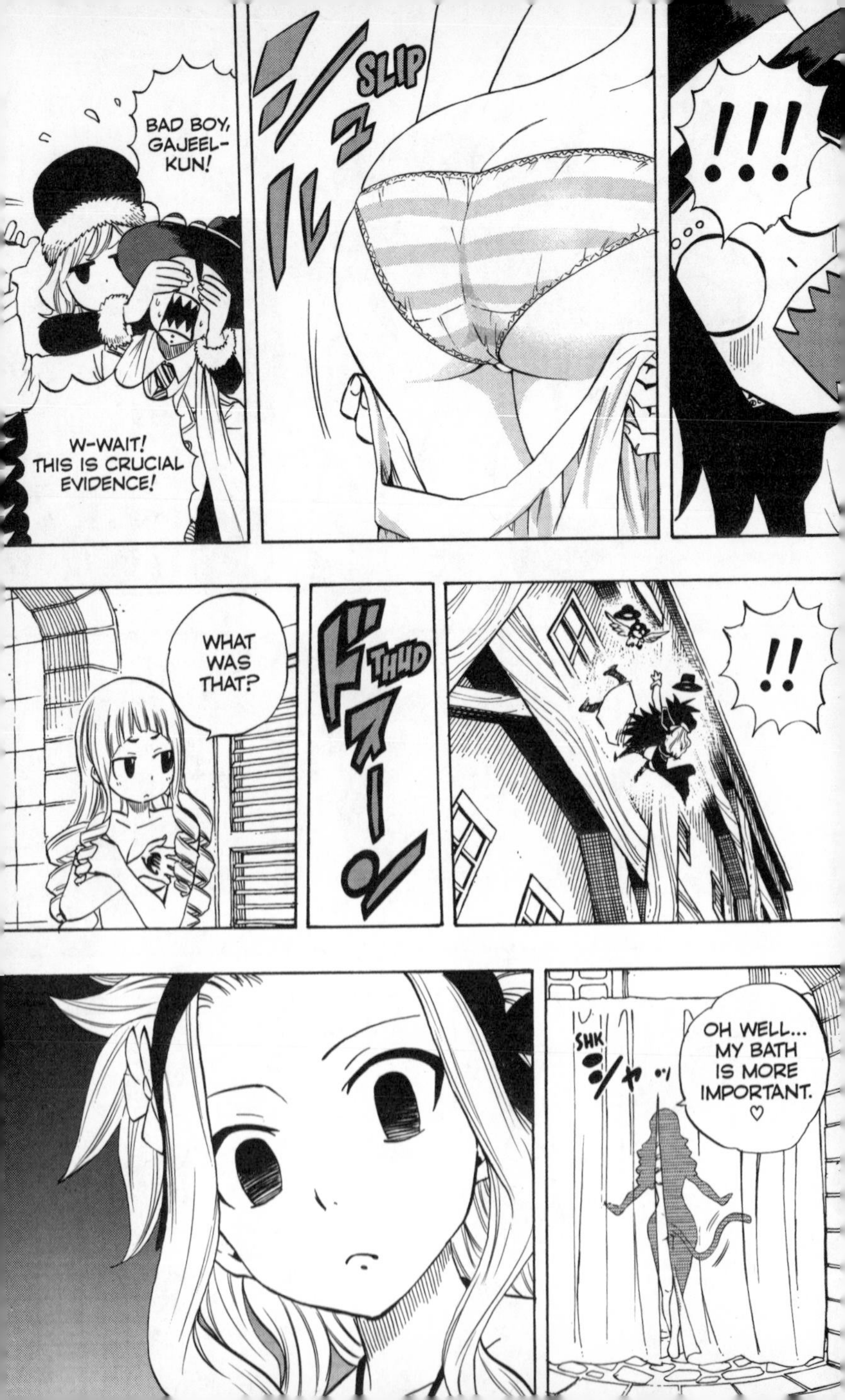
!!!
SLIP
BAD BOY, GAJEEL-KUN!
W-WAIT! THIS IS CRUCIAL EVIDENCE!
!!
THUD
WHAT WAS THAT?
OH WELL... MY BATH IS MORE IMPORTANT. ♡
SHK

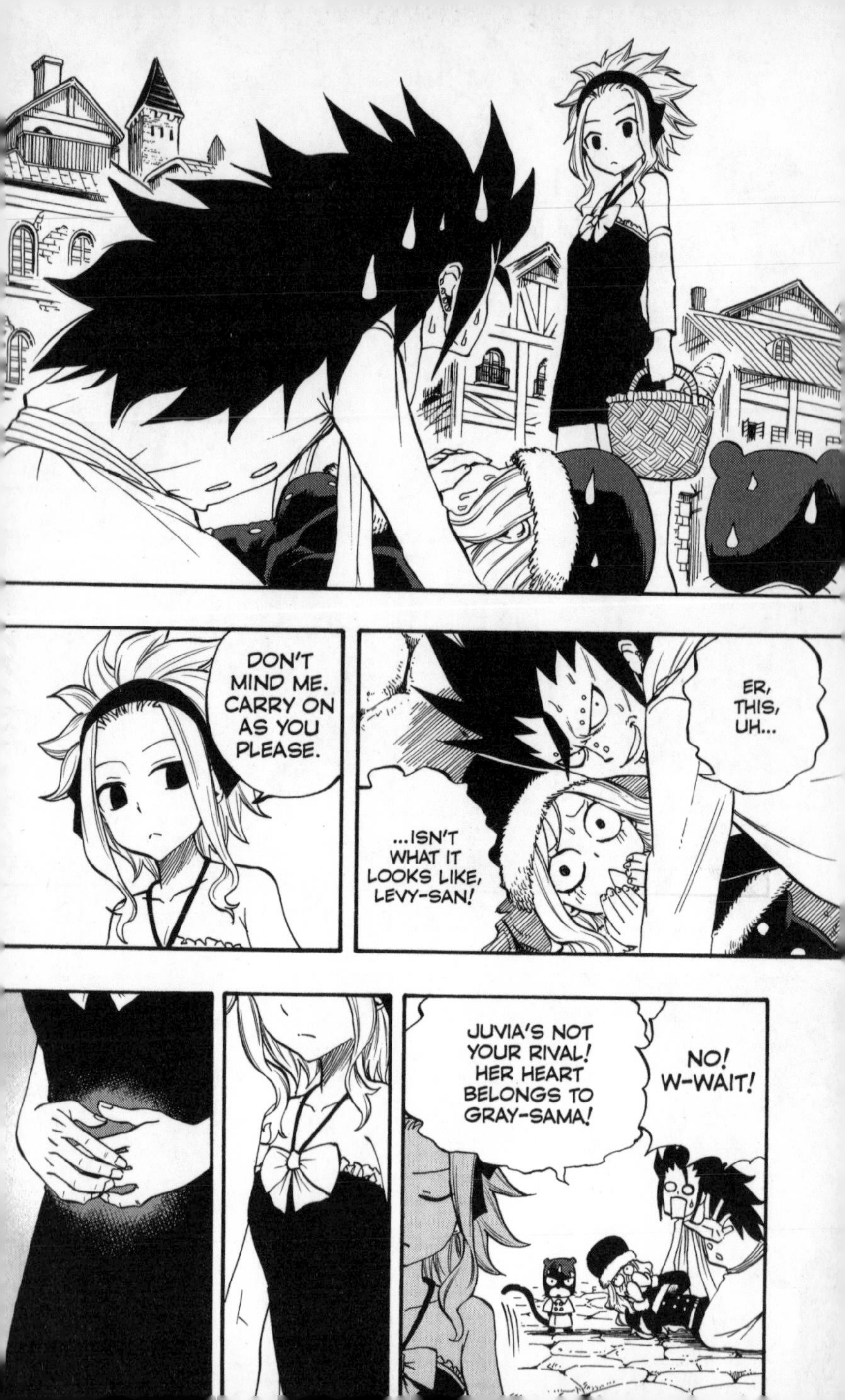
ER, THIS, UH...
...ISN'T WHAT IT LOOKS LIKE, LEVY-SAN!
DON'T MIND ME. CARRY ON AS YOU PLEASE.
NO! W-WAIT!
JUVIA'S NOT YOUR RIVAL! HER HEART BELONGS TO GRAY-SAMA!

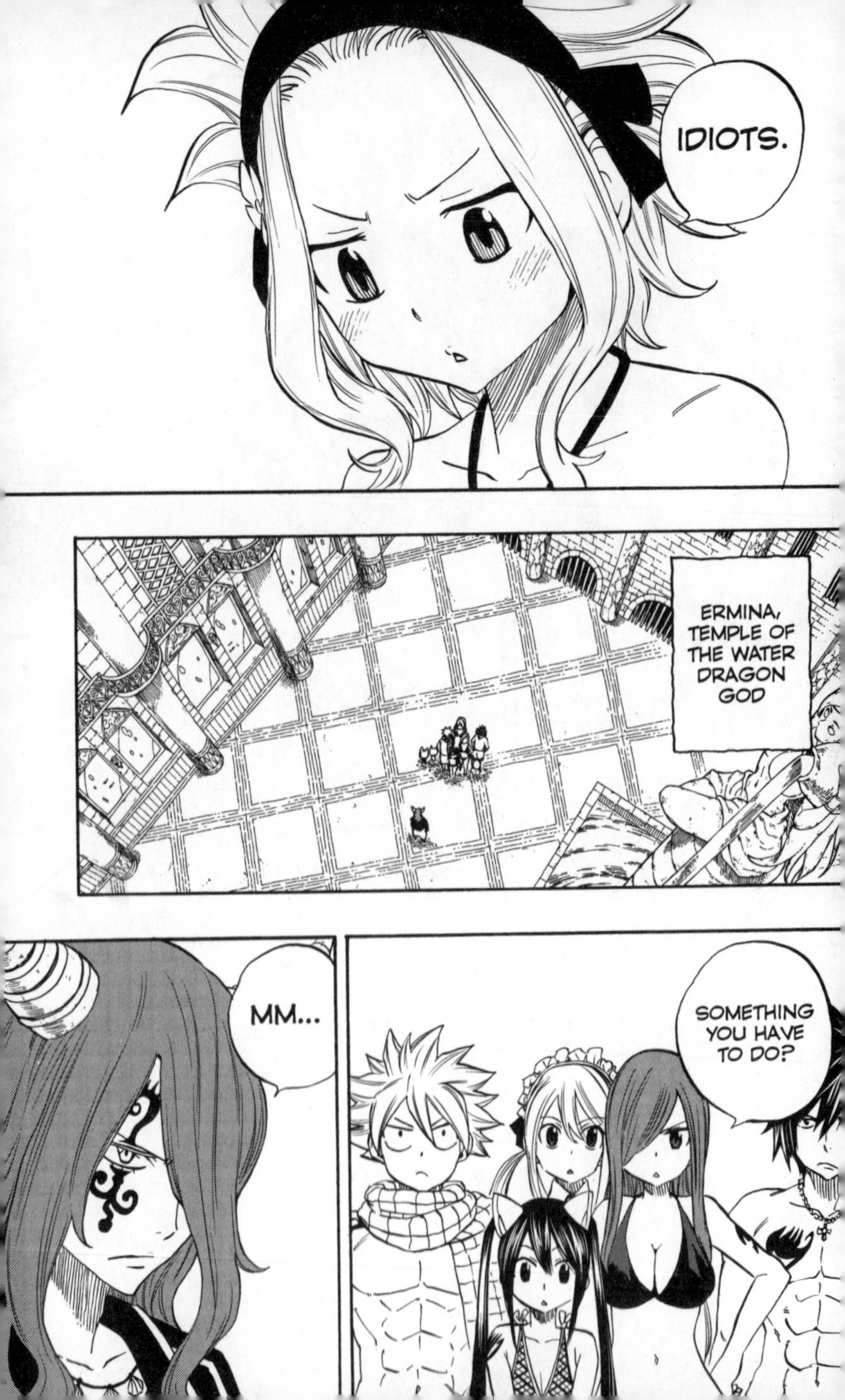
IDIOTS.
ERMINA, TEMPLE OF THE WATER DRAGON GOD
SOMETHING YOU HAVE TO DO?
MM...

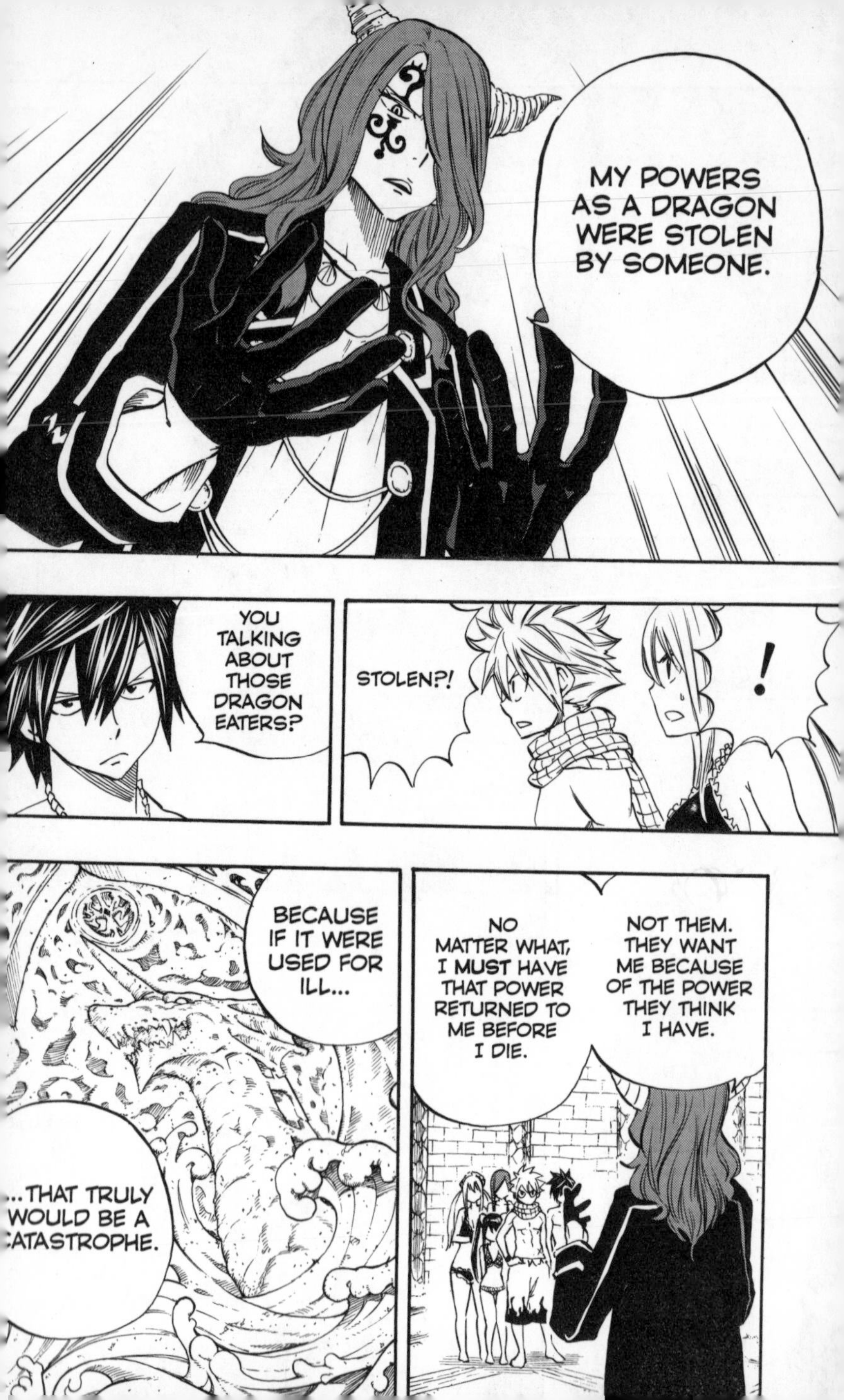
MY POWERS AS A DRAGON WERE STOLEN BY SOMEONE.
!
STOLEN?!
YOU TALKING ABOUT THOSE DRAGON EATERS?
NOT THEM. THEY WANT ME BECAUSE OF THE POWER THEY THINK I HAVE.
NO MATTER WHAT, I MUST HAVE THAT POWER RETURNED TO ME BEFORE I DIE.
BECAUSE IF IT WERE USED FOR ILL...
...THAT TRULY WOULD BE A CATASTROPHE.

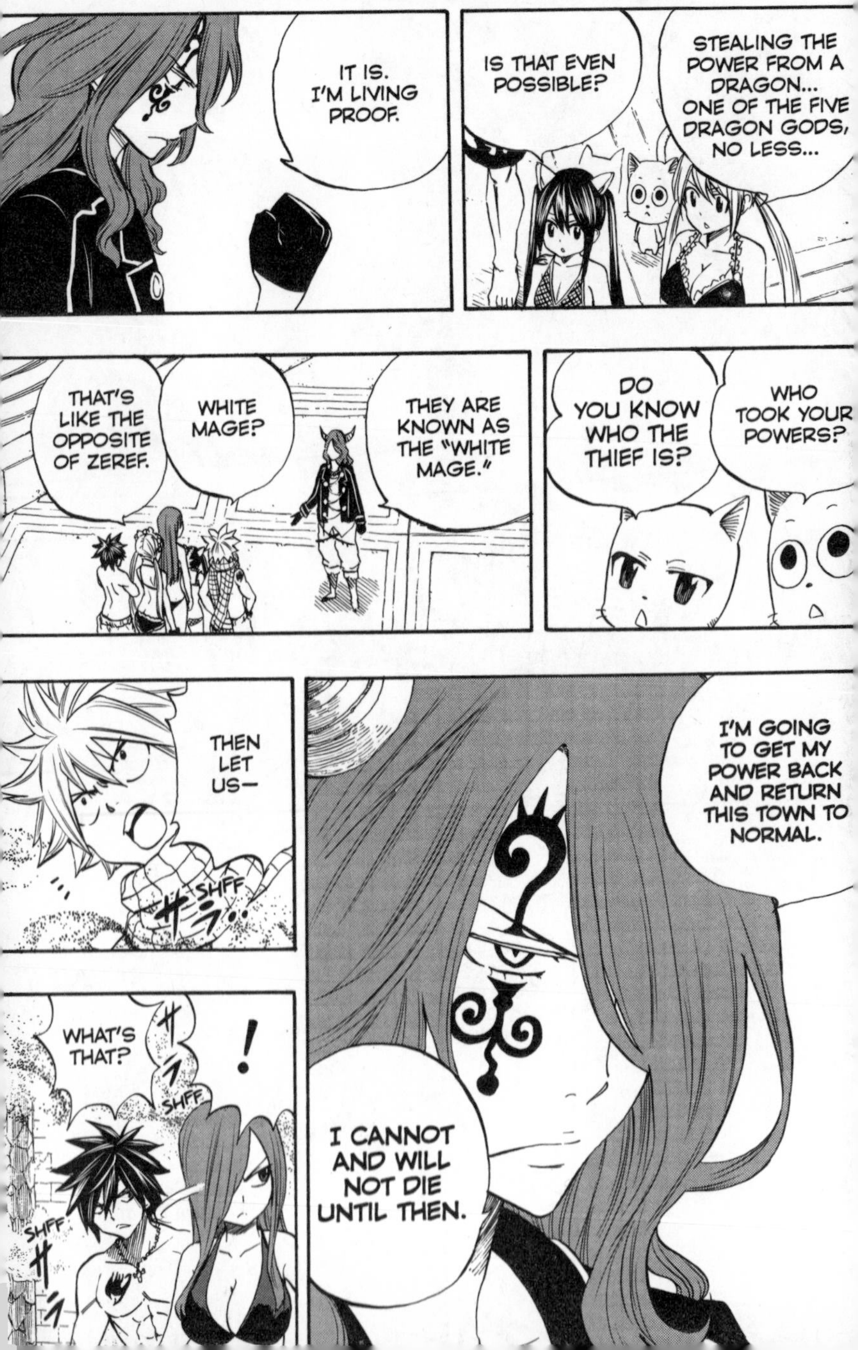
STEALING THE POWER FROM A DRAGON... ONE OF THE FIVE DRAGON GODS, NO LESS...
IS THAT EVEN POSSIBLE?
IT IS. I'M LIVING PROOF.
WHO TOOK YOUR POWERS?
DO YOU KNOW WHO THE THIEF IS?
THEY ARE KNOWN AS THE "WHITE MAGE."
WHITE MAGE?
THAT'S LIKE THE OPPOSITE OF ZEREF.
I'M GOING TO GET MY POWER BACK AND RETURN THIS TOWN TO NORMAL.
I CANNOT AND WILL NOT DIE UNTIL THEN.
THEN LET US—
SHFF
!
WHAT'S THAT?
SHFF
SHFF

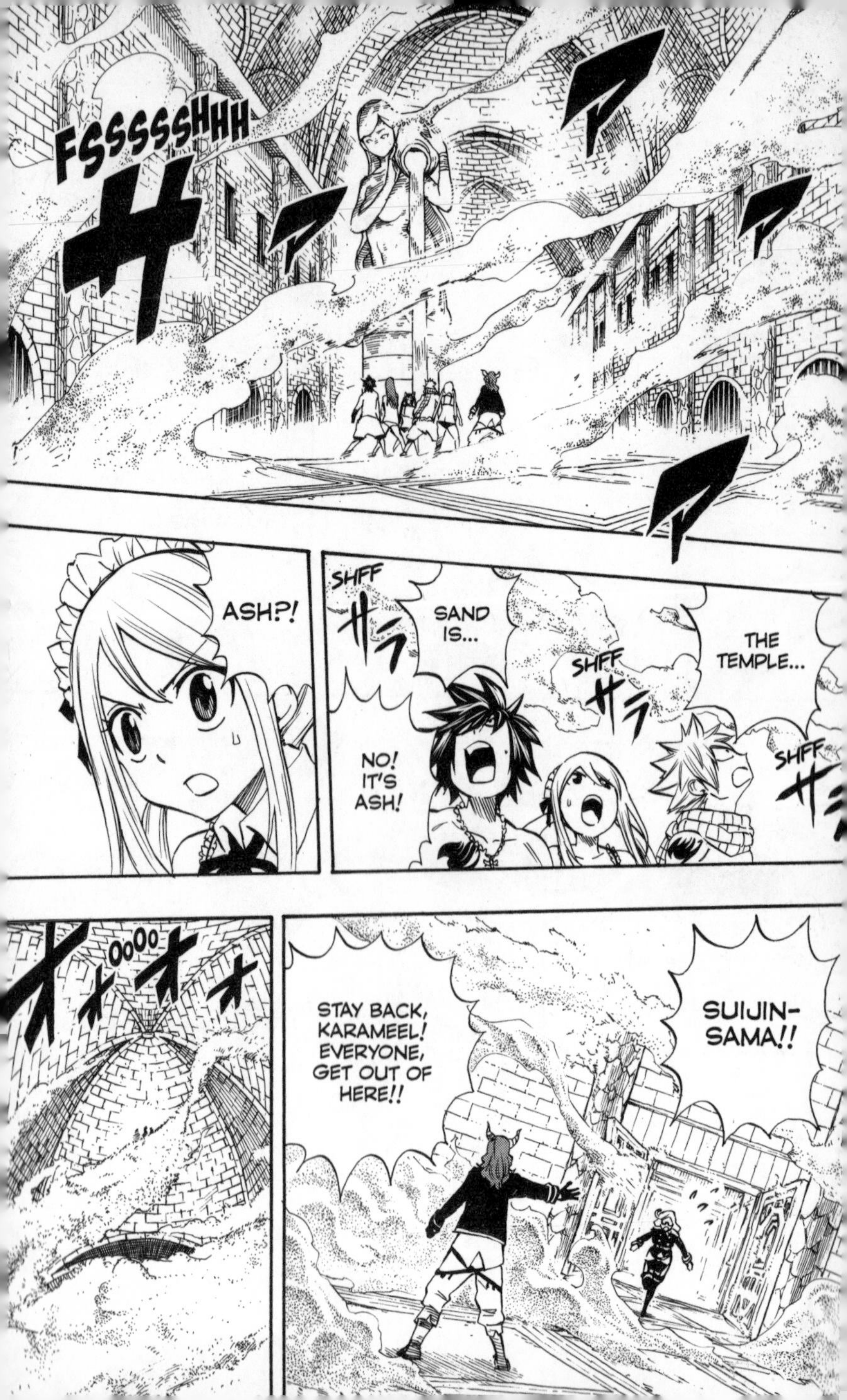
FSSSSSHHH
THE TEMPLE...
SHFF
SHFF
SAND IS...
SHFF
NO! IT'S ASH!
ASH?!
SUIJIN-SAMA!!
STAY BACK, KARAMEEL! EVERYONE, GET OUT OF HERE!!
OOOO

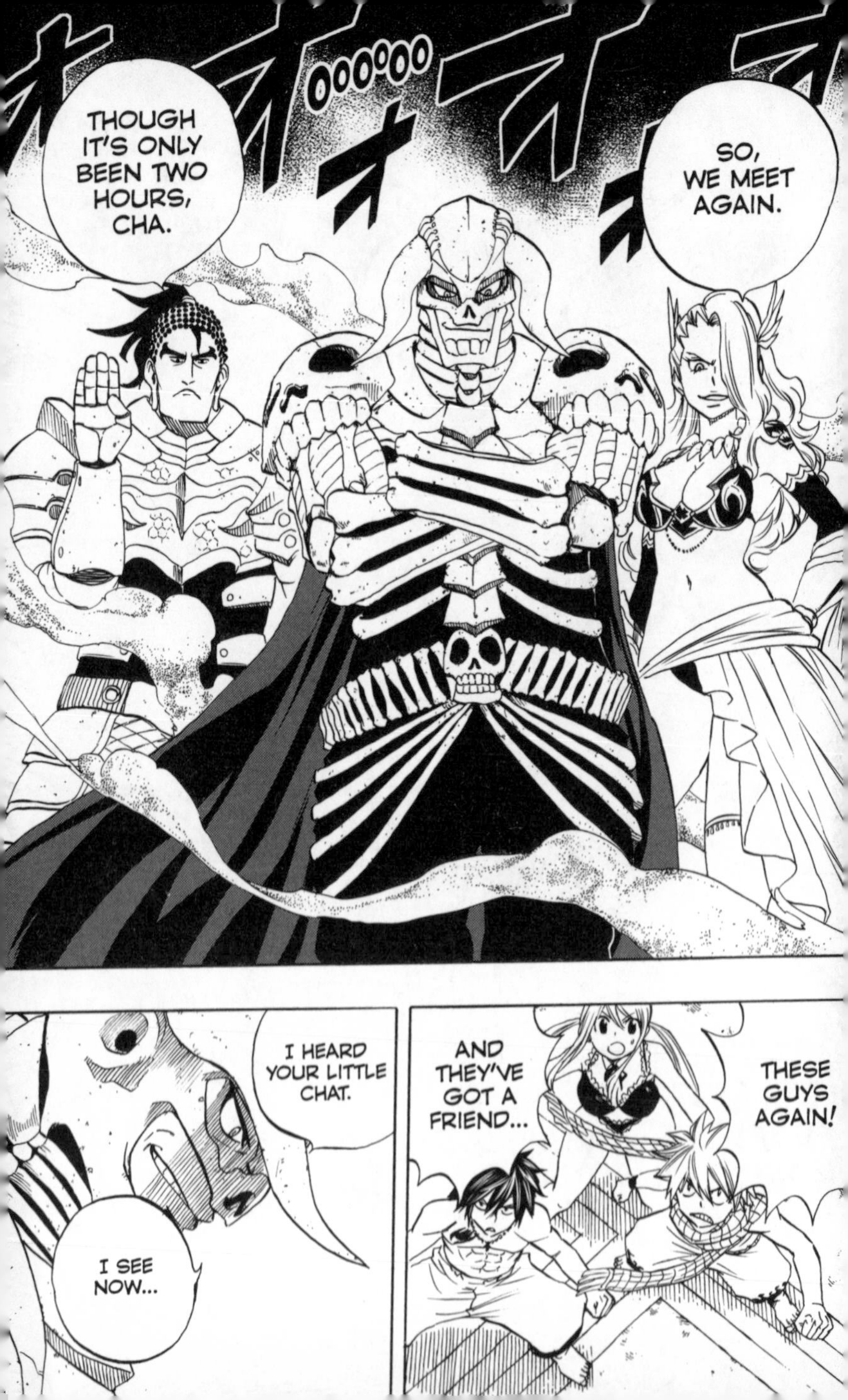
SO, WE MEET AGAIN.
OOOOOO
THOUGH IT'S ONLY BEEN TWO HOURS, CHA.
THESE GUYS AGAIN!
AND THEY'VE GOT A FRIEND...
I HEARD YOUR LITTLE CHAT.
I SEE NOW...

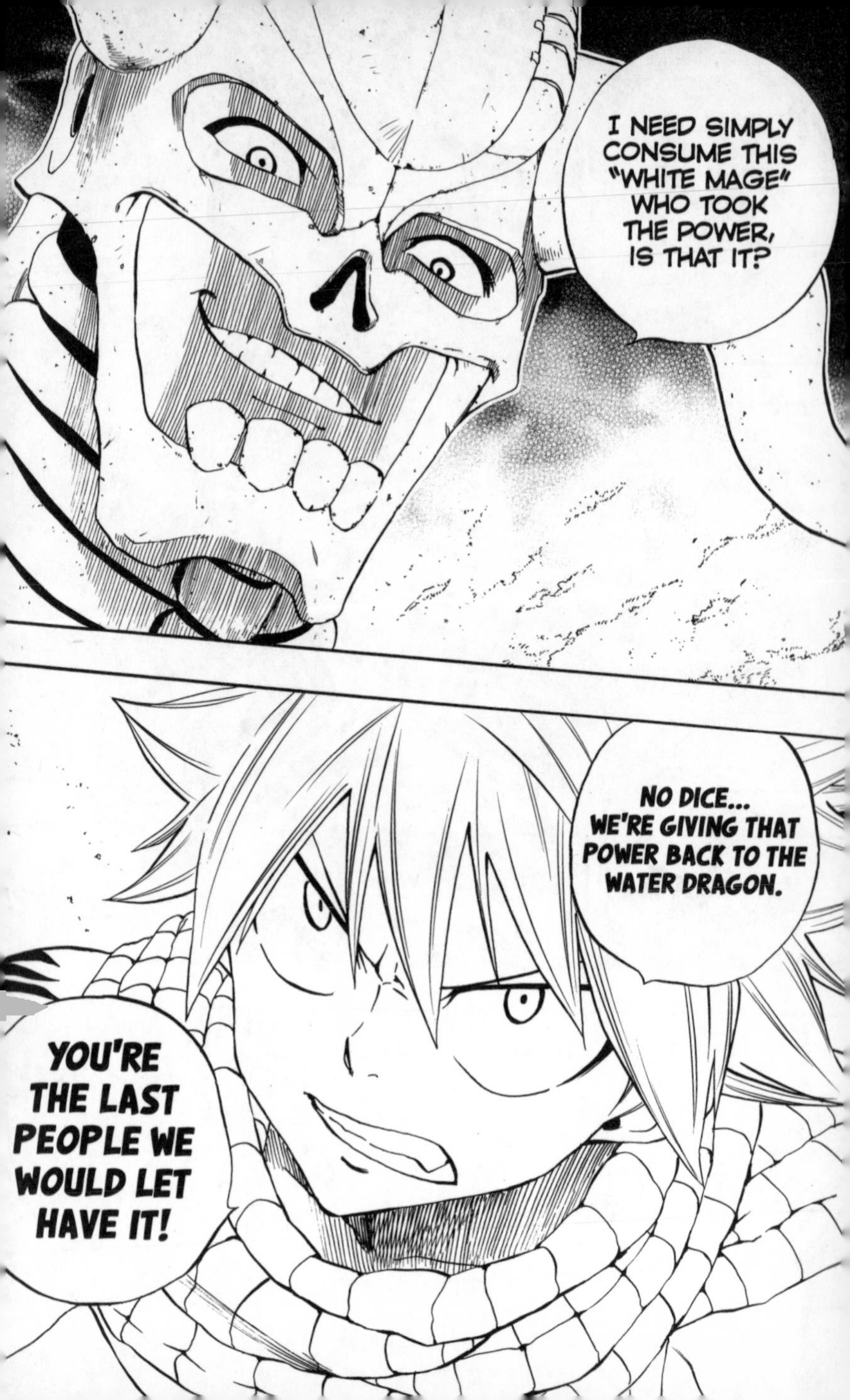
I NEED SIMPLY CONSUME THIS "WHITE MAGE" WHO TOOK THE POWER, IS THAT IT?
NO DICE... WE'RE GIVING THAT POWER BACK TO THE WATER DRAGON.
YOU'RE THE LAST PEOPLE WE WOULD LET HAVE IT!

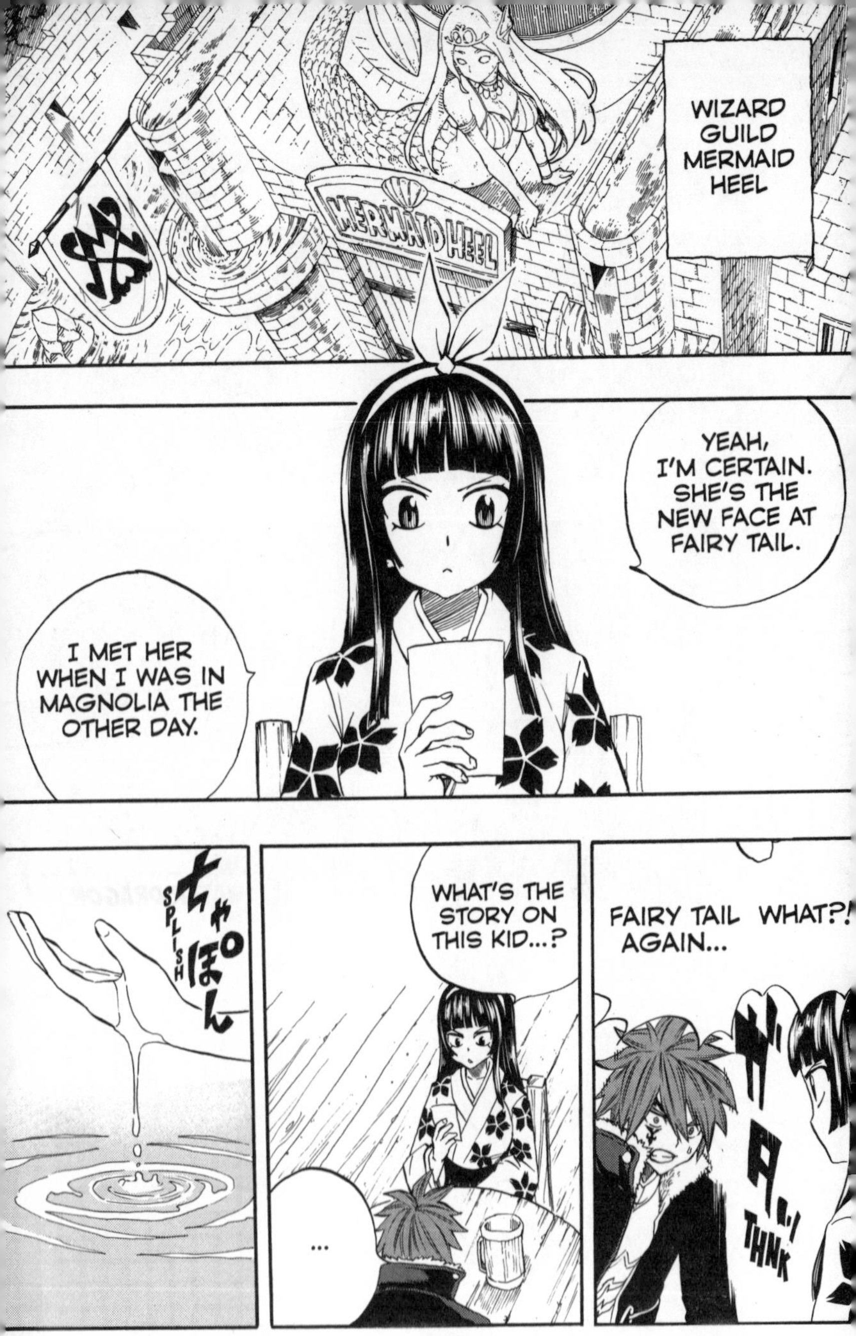
WIZARD GUILD MERMAID HEEL
MERMAID HEEL
YEAH, I'M CERTAIN. SHE'S THE NEW FACE AT FAIRY TAIL.
I MET HER WHEN I WAS IN MAGNOLIA THE OTHER DAY.
WHAT?!
FAIRY TAIL AGAIN...
THNK
WHAT'S THE STORY ON THIS KID...?
...
SPLISH
ちゃぽん

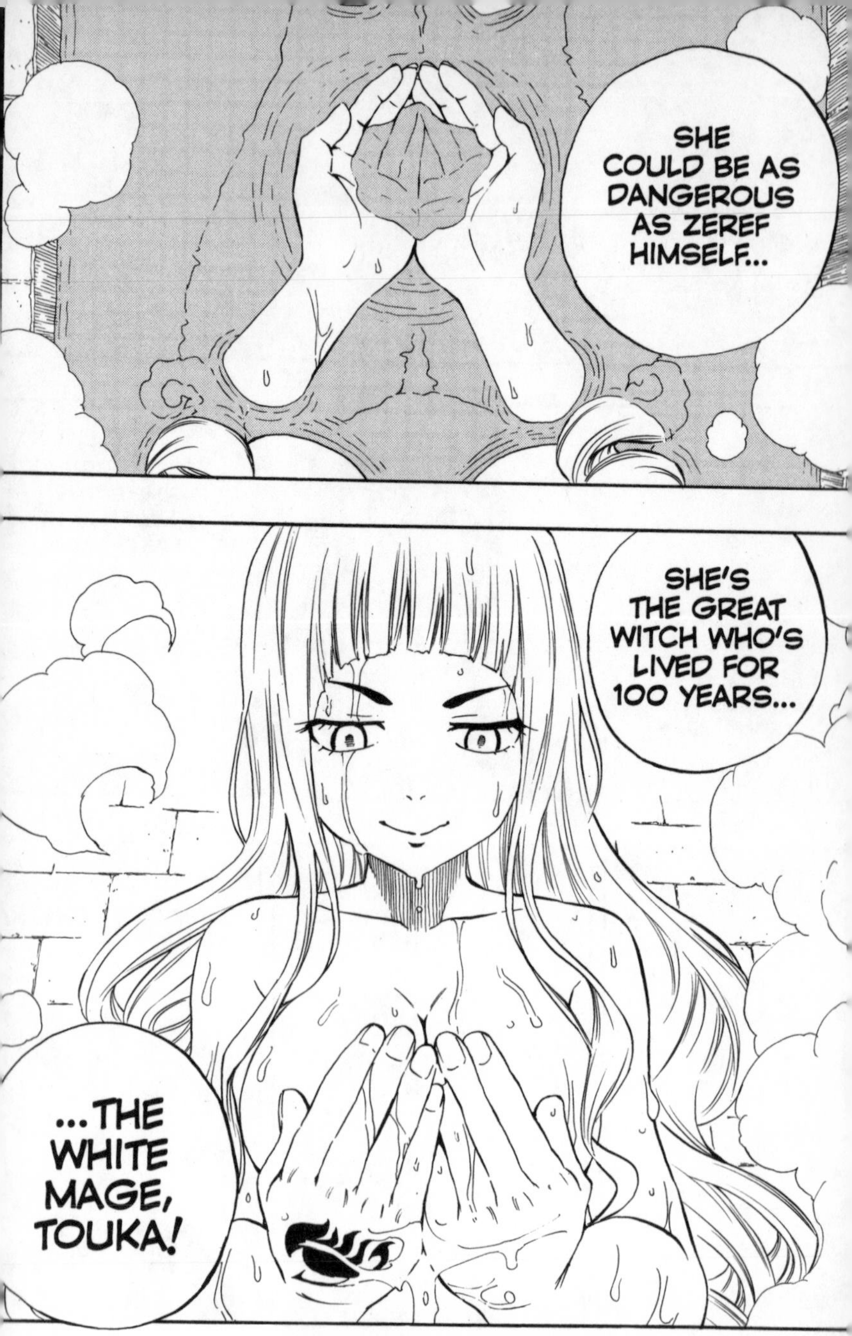
SHE COULD BE AS DANGEROUS AS ZEREF HIMSELF...
SHE'S THE GREAT WITCH WHO'S LIVED FOR 100 YEARS...
...THE WHITE MAGE, TOUKA!

TO BE CONTINUED

FAIRY TAIL
100 YEARS QUEST

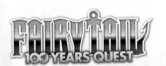

It's hardly been a year since I declared in the final volume of *FAIRY TAIL* that I had no intention of doing a sequel and, well...here's the sequel.

As a matter of fact, when that final volume came out, the storyboarding for 100 Years Quest was already underway, and we had already decided that the artist would be someone other than me. Initially, I was going to leave everything, from the storyboards to the final art, to Ueda-sensei, and that's why I said I wasn't going to continue with FT. But then the editor asked me if I could at least handle the story, so that's how I ended up doing the storyboards! So here we are... I hope this new story won't seem extraneous but will help add new layers to *FAIRY TAIL*'s appeal.

Hiro Mashima

AFTERWORD

Hi! Ueda, your friendly artist, here!

Thank you for picking up Volume 1!

How did you like it? I hope you felt "at home" again in *FAIRY TAIL*…even with me doing the art. I'm honestly a little worried.

Mashima-sensei himself kindly did the storyboards for *100 Years Quest*.

I was blown away by his storyboards every single time and tried really hard to breathe life into the characters. This was my first time drawing fantasy, so I really appreciate the help of my assistants, too. All while doing the weekly release of *EDENS ZERO!* It's a miracle…

A lot of people helped get this book into print. I'm so grateful to all of them. I'll keep giving it everything I've got in hopes of pleasing fans of both *FAIRY TAIL* and of Mashima-sensei!

See you in the next volume!

STAFF

Okuda-kun
Matsuoka-kun
Kabaya-san
Kida-san
Watanabe-san
Suehiro-kun
Katayama-san
Kanzaki-san
Furumoto-kun

RIGHT…

UHH… I NEED AN INTERESTING BACKGROUND THAT'S LIKE BAM!

SORRY ABOUT MY VAGUE DIRECTIONS…

*Shirt: Yu

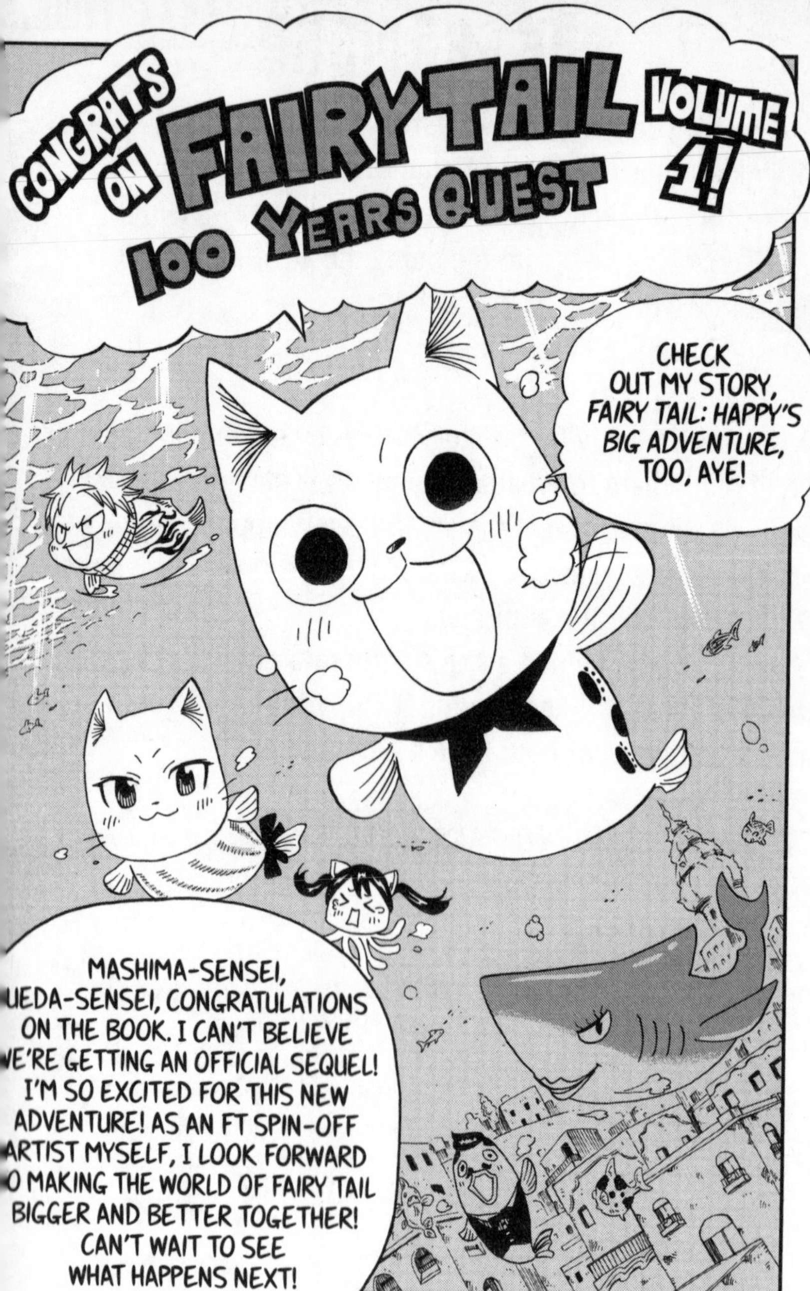
CONGRATS ON FAIRY TAIL 100 YEARS QUEST VOLUME 1!
CHECK OUT MY STORY, FAIRY TAIL: HAPPY'S BIG ADVENTURE, TOO, AYE!
MASHIMA-SENSEI, UEDA-SENSEI, CONGRATULATIONS ON THE BOOK. I CAN'T BELIEVE E'RE GETTING AN OFFICIAL SEQUEL! I'M SO EXCITED FOR THIS NEW ADVENTURE! AS AN FT SPIN-OFF ARTIST MYSELF, I LOOK FORWARD O MAKING THE WORLD OF FAIRY TAIL BIGGER AND BETTER TOGETHER! CAN'T WAIT TO SEE WHAT HAPPENS NEXT!

KENSHIRO SAKAMOTO

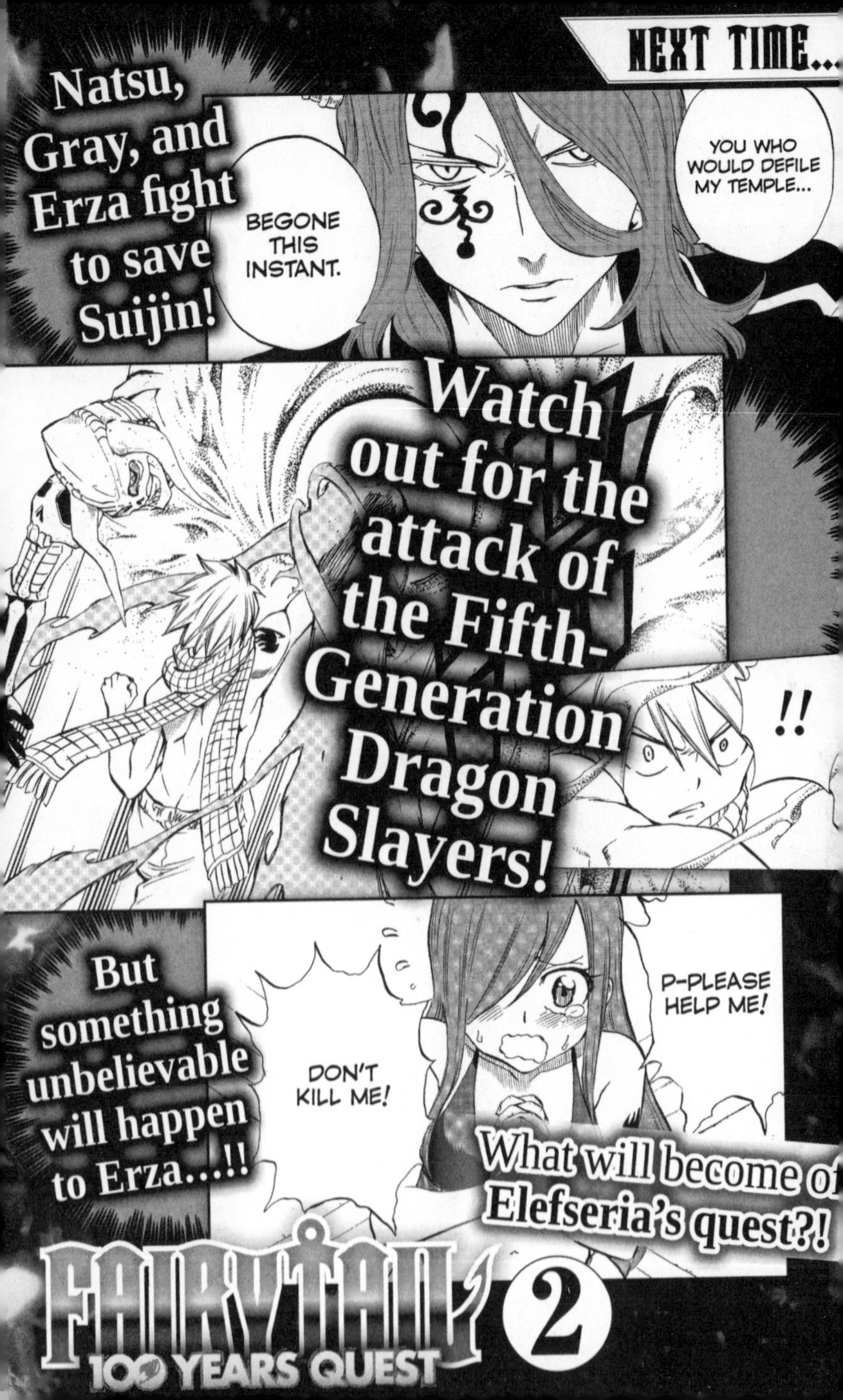
NEXT TIME...
YOU WHO WOULD DEFILE MY TEMPLE...
BEGONE THIS INSTANT.
Natsu, Gray, and Erza fight to save Suijin!
!!
Watch out for the attack of the Fifth-Generation Dragon Slayers!
P-PLEASE HELP ME!
DON'T KILL ME!
But something unbelievable will happen to Erza...!!
What will become of Elefseria's quest?!
FAIRY TAIL 100 YEARS QUEST 2

FAIRY TAIL 100 YEARS QUEST

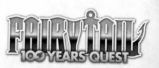

TRANSLATION NOTES

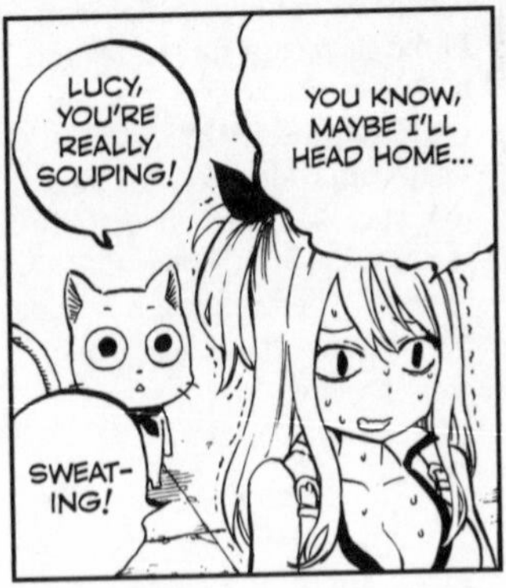
YOU KNOW, MAYBE I'LL HEAD HOME...
LUCY, YOU'RE REALLY SOUPING!
SWEAT-ING!

Souping, page 41

Happy describes the fluid Lucy is exuding as *shiru* (soup), and she corrects him that it's *ase* (sweat). The two characters only differ by a single stroke in Japanese.

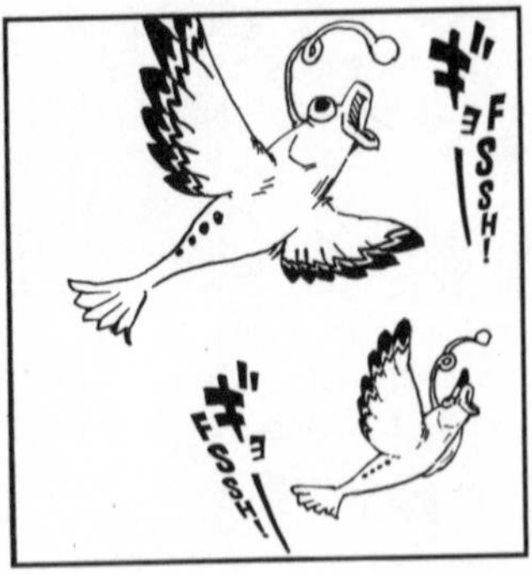
FSSH!
FSSSH!

FSSH, page 52

These fish/bird hybrids emit a cry of *gyoo* in the Japanese. One of the readings for the kanji for "fish" is *gyo*.

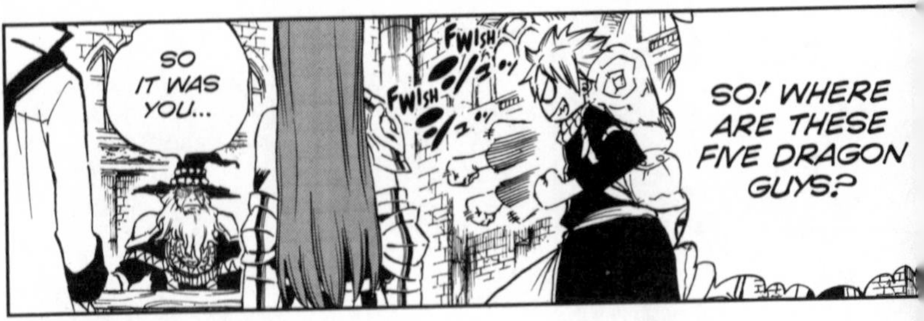
SO! WHERE ARE THESE FIVE DRAGON GUYS?
FWISH
FWISH
SO IT WAS YOU...

Five Dragon Guys, page 54

Natsu pointedly refers to the dragons as *go-nin*, using the counter for people, rather than as *go-tou* ("five head"), using the counter for livestock and other large animals as everyone else has done.

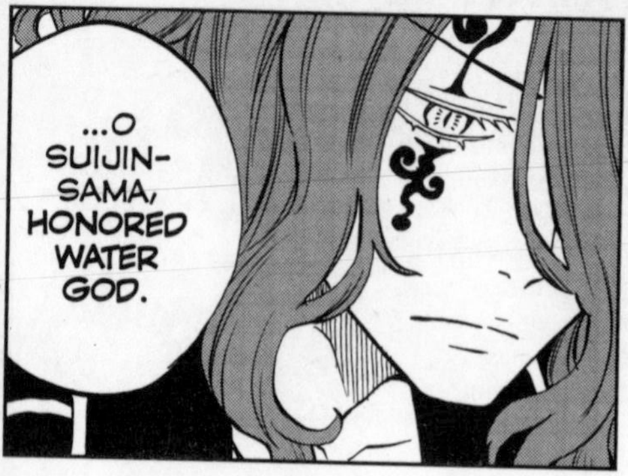
...O
SUIJIN-
SAMA,
HONORED
WATER
GOD.

Suijin-sama, page 66

The name Suijin is composed of the characters for “water god,” and those characters are especially emphasized in Karameel’s final word balloon on this page, to hint to the reader about Suijin’s identity. Later on, however, “Suijin” will straddle a fine line between title and proper name.

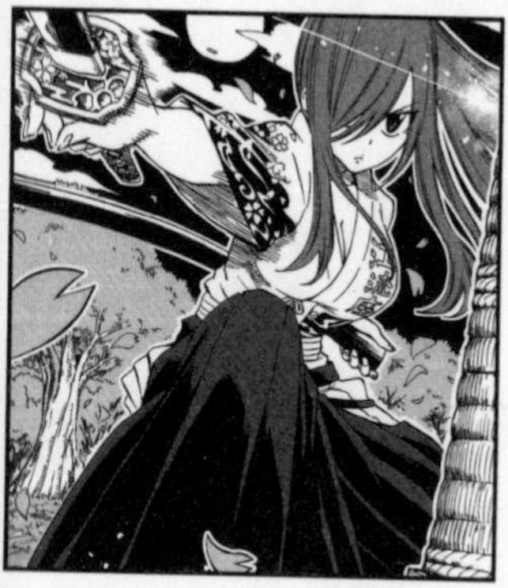

Erza’s Coat, page 67

The kanji characters on Erza’s traditional Japanese top here can be read as *“e-ryuu-za”* or *“e-ru-za.* They literally mean “river-flow seat,” but the point is that they spell out her name phonetically. This practice of using *kanji* (Chinese characters) phonetically is known as *“ateji”* and it can make Japanese readers think of something as old and traditional (like a samurai) or a Japanese motorcycle gang, who often wear jackets with phrases that use *ateji* sayings.

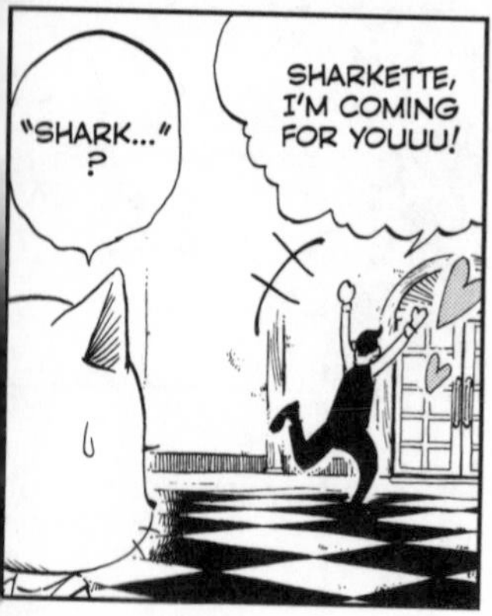
SHARKETTE,
I'M COMING
FOR YOUUU!
"SHARK..."
?

Sharkette, page 71

In Japanese, this character is called Sameko, a name that consists of the word *same* (shark) plus the common feminine name ending *-ko*.

"A young man rescued a turtle...," page 80

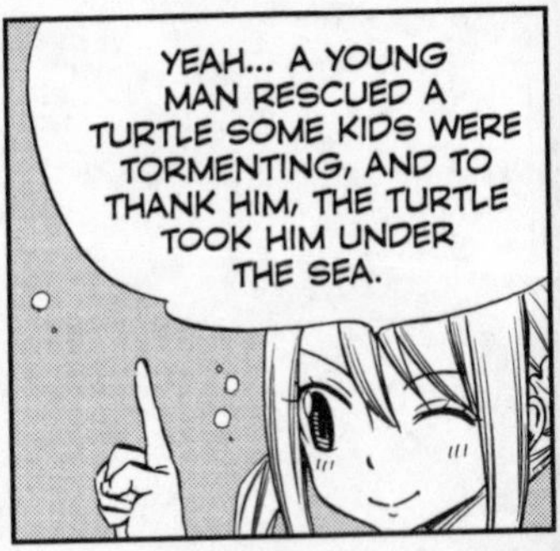
YEAH... A YOUNG MAN RESCUED A TURTLE SOME KIDS WERE TORMENTING, AND TO THANK HIM, THE TURTLE TOOK HIM UNDER THE SEA.

Some of what Lucy refers to in this scene is based on the Japanese fairy tale of *Urashima Taro*. The basic story involves a fisherman who rescues a sea turtle from being tormented by a group of kids. As thanks for being saved, the turtle takes Urashima Taro to an underwater palace called *Ryūgū-jō* (the Dragon Palace), where he is entertained by the princess of the castle. After several days at the palace, Urashima Taro is given a special box as a parting gift and told never to open it. He then returns to land and finds that several years have passed. In the end, he ignores the warning the princess gave him, and opens the box, which turns him into an old man.

It's unclear where the ending that Lucy mentioned came from, but she may be thinking of another fairy tale known as the *The Jellyfish's Errand*, a story that explains how the jellyfish came to be an invertebrate. The story has a common connection with *Urashima Taro* in that they both feature *Ryūgū-jō* as a location and at least one version of the jellyfish story also involves a turtle character, so perhaps that's why Lucy mentions being turned into a jellyfish.

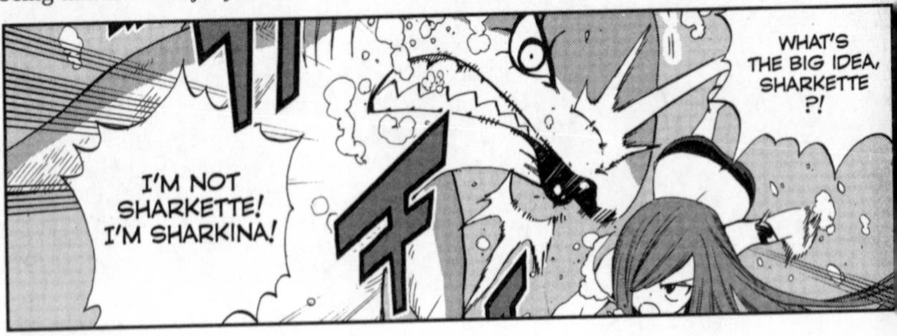
WHAT'S THE BIG IDEA, SHARKETTE ?!
I'M NOT SHARKETTE! I'M SHARKINA!

Sharkina, page 83

This shark identifies herself as Samemi, which also uses the word for "shark" paired with a feminine name ending.

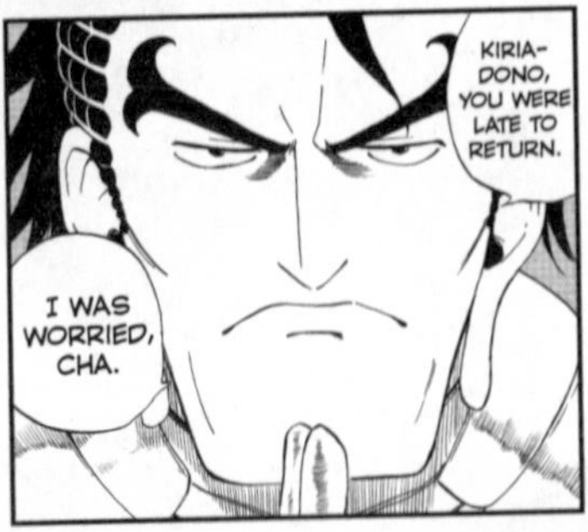
KIRIA-DONO, YOU WERE LATE TO RETURN.
I WAS WORRIED, CHA.

Cha, page 139

Madmole ends many of his sentences with the syllable cha or tcha. It has no specific meaning, but simply gives his dialogue a unique flavor (it's not standard Japanese).

EDENS ZERO
エデンズゼロ

HIRO MASHIMA IS BACK! JOIN THE CREATOR OF **FAIRY TAIL** AS HE TAKES TO THE STARS FOR ANOTHER THRILLING SAGA!

A high-flying space adventure! All the steadfast friendship and wild fighting you've been waiting for...IN SPACE!

At Granbell Kingdom, an abandoned amusement park, Shiki has lived his entire life among machines. But one day, Rebecca and her cat companion Happy appear at the park's front gates. Little do these newcomers know that this is the first human contact Granbell has had in a hundred years! As Shiki stumbles his way into making new friends, his former neighbors stir at an opportunity for a robo-rebellion... And when his old homeland becomes too dangerous, Shiki must join Rebecca and Happy on their spaceship and escape into the boundless cosmos.

Magus of the Library

Mitsu Izumi

MITSU IZUMI'S STUNNING ARTWORK BRINGS A FANTASTICAL LITERARY ADVENTURE TO LUSH, THRILLING LIFE!

Young Theo adores books, but the prejudice and hatred of his village keeps them ever out of his reach. Then one day, he chances to meet Sedona, a traveling librarian who works for the great library of Aftzaak, City of Books, and his life changes forever...

‹ KAMOME ›
SHIRAHAMA

Witch Hat Atelier

A magical manga
adventure for
fans of Disney
and Studio
Ghibli!

Witch Hat Atelier © Kamome Shirahama/Kodansha Lt.

**The magical adventure that took
Japan by storm is finally here,
from acclaimed DC and Marvel
cover artist Kamome Shirahama!**

In a world where everyone takes wonders like magic spells
and dragons for granted, Coco is a girl with a simple dream:
She wants to be a witch. But everybody knows magicians
are born, not made, and Coco was not born with a gift for
magic. Resigned to her un-magical life, Coco is about to
give up on her dream to become a witch…until the day
she meets Qifrey, a mysterious, traveling magician. After
secretly seeing Qifrey perform magic in a way she's never
seen before, Coco soon learns what everybody "knows"
might not be the truth, and discovers that her magical
dream may not be as far away as it may seem…

BATTLE ANGEL ALITA

After more than a decade out of print, the original cyberpunk action classic returns in glorious 400-page hardcover deluxe editions, featuring an all-new translation, color pages, and new cover designs!

KC
KODANSHA COMICS

Far beneath the shimmering space-city of Zalem lie the trash-heaps of The Scrapyard... Here, cyber-doctor and bounty hunter Daisuke Ido finds the head and torso of an amnesiac cyborg girl. He names her Alita and vows to fill her life with beauty, but in a moment of desperation, a fragment of Alita's mysterious past awakens in her. She discovers that she possesses uncanny prowess in the legendary martial art known as panzerkunst. With her newfound skills, Alita decides to become a hunter-warrior - tracking down and taking out those who prey on the weak. But can she hold onto her humanity in the dark and gritty world of The Scrapyard?

The award-winning manga about what happens inside you!

"Far more entertaining than it ought to be... what kid doesn't want to think that every time they sneeze a torpedo shoots out their nose?"
—Anime News Network

Strep throat! Hay fever! Influenza! The world is a dangerous place for a red blood cell just trying to get her deliveries finished. Fortunately, she's not alone…she's got a whole human body's worth of cells ready to help out! The mysterious white blood cells, the buff and brash killer T cells, even the cute little platelets—everyone's got to come together if they want to keep you healthy!

Cells at Work!

はたらく細胞

By Akane Shimizu

Having lost his wife, high school teacher Kōhei Inuzuka is doing his best to raise his young daughter Tsumugi as a single father. He's pretty bad at cooking and doesn't have a huge appetite to begin with, but chance brings his little family together with one of his students, the lonely Kotori. The three of them are anything but comfortable in the kitchen, but the healing power of home cooking might just work on their grieving hearts.

"This season's number-one feel-good anime!" —Anime News Network

"A beautifully-drawn story about comfort food and family and grief. Recommended." —Otaku USA Magazine

sweetness & lightning

By Gido Amagakure

THE MAGICAL GIRL CLASSIC THAT BROUGHT A GENERATION OF READERS TO MANGA, NOW BACK IN A DEFINITIVE, HARDCOVER COLLECTOR'S EDITION!

CARDCAPTOR SAKURA
COLLECTOR'S EDITION
C L A M P

Ten-year-old Sakura Kinomoto lives a pretty normal life with her older brother, Tōya, and widowed father, Fujitaka—until the day she discovers a strange book in her father's library, and her life takes a magical turn...

- A deluxe large-format hardcover edition of CLAMP's shojo manga classic
- All-new foil-stamped cover art on each volume
- Comes with exclusive collectible art card

Cardcaptor Sakura Collector's Edition © CLAMP · Shigatsu Tsuitachi Co., Ltd. / Kodansha Ltd.

A picture-perfect shojo series from Yoko Nogiri, creator of the hit *That Wolf-Boy is Mine!*

Mako's always had a passion for photography. When she loses someone dear to her, she clings onto her art as a relic of the close relationship she once had... Luckily, her childhood best friend Kei encourages her to come to his high school and join their prestigious photo club. With nothing to lose, Mako grabs her camera and moves into the dorm where Kei and his classmates live. Soon, a fresh take on life, along with a mysterious new muse, begin to come into focus!

LOVE IN FOCUS

Praise for Yoko Nogiri's *That Wolf-Boy is Mine!*

"Emotional squees...will-they-won't-they plot...[and a] pleasantly quick pace."
—Otaku USA Magazine

"A series that is pure shojo sugar—a cute love story about two nice people looking for their places in the world, and finding them with each other." —Anime News Network

Futaro Uesugi is a second-year in high school, scraping to get by and pay off his family's debt. The only thing he can do is study, so when Futaro receives a part-time job offer to tutor the five daughters of a wealthy businessman, he can't pass it up. Little does he know, these five beautiful sisters are quintuplets, but the only thing they have in common...is that they're all terrible at studying!

THE QUINTESSENTIAL QUINTUPLETS

negi haruba

FAIRY TAIL: 100 Years Quest volume 1 is a work of fiction. Names, characters, places, and incidents are the products of the author's imagination or are used fictitiously. Any resemblance to actual events, locales, or persons, living or dead, is entirely coincidental.

A Kodansha Comics Trade Paperback Original.

Published in the United States by Kodansha Comics, an imprint of Kodansha USA Publishing, LLC, New York.

Publication rights for this English edition arranged through Kodansha Ltd., Tokyo.

First published in Japan in 2018 by Kodansha Ltd., Tokyo
ISBN 978-1-63236-892-8

Printed in the United States of America.

www.kodanshacomics.com

4th Printing

Translation: Kevin Steinbach
Lettering: Phil Christie
Kodansha Comics edition cover design by Phil Balsman